JOE LOUIS

JOE LOUIS

Hard Times Man

Randy Roberts

Yale UNIVERSITY PRESS

New Haven and London

Published with assistance from the foundation established in memory of
Amasa Stone Mather of the Class of 1907, Yale College.

Yale University Press books may be purchased in quantity for educational, business, or
promotional use. For information, please e-mail sales.press@yale.edu.

Designed by Mary Valencia.
Set in Minion type by Keystone Typesetting, Inc.
Printed in the United States of America.

Library of Congress Cataloging-in-Publication Data
Roberts, Randy.
Joe Louis : hard times man / Randy Roberts.
p. cm.
Includes bibliographical references and index.
ISBN 978-0-300-12222-0 (cloth : alk. paper)
1. Louis, Joe, 1914–1981. 2. African American boxers—Biography.
3. Boxers (Sports)—United States—Biography. I. Title.
GV1132.L6R63 2010
796.83092—dc22
[B]
2010015422

A catalogue record for this book is available from the British Library.

This paper meets the requirements of ANSI/NISO Z39.48–1992 (Permanence of Paper).

10 9 8 7 6 5 4 3 2 1

To Marjie
You make each day better

CONTENTS

PREFACE

> When times get really hard, really tough, He always send you
> somebody. In the Depression it was tough on everybody, but
> twice as hard on the colored, and He sent us Joe.
> Joe Louis was to lift the colored people's heart.
> —*The Autobiography of Miss Jane Pittman*

Thinking back, journalist Robert Lipsyte concluded that it was a "genera-
tional thing."[1] America seemed to be tearing apart at the seams in February
1964. Less than three months before, Lee Harvey Oswald had blown off the
back of President John Kennedy's head. The war in Vietnam had taken a
dangerous, violent turn after the November assassination of President Ngo
Dinh Diem. No longer was the United States supporting even a nominally
democratic regime. Now it was underwriting a war conducted by a corrupt, inefficient military junta headed by a general who had named himself
head of state. At home, Martin Luther King's "dream" had turned into a
nightmare. Medgar Evers gunned down in his driveway, four black girls
killed when a bomb exploded in a Birmingham church, violent protest
marches throughout the South, Malcolm X rejecting integrationists' goals
—the "movement" appeared fractured. Culturally, the look of a new age
was showcased on *The Ed Sullivan Show* on February 12, 1964, when four
mop-topped musicians sang "I Want To Hold Your Hand" to ecstatic and
screaming young girls.

By the last weeks of February, Miami had become the center of the
racial and cultural discontent. The Beatles had arrived for a concert. Malcolm X had come as well, although he was not very forthright with the

reasons. But reporters did not have to dig too deeply for the scoop. Malcolm X had become a fixture in the boxing camp of Cassius Clay, who was scheduled to fight Sonny Liston for the heavyweight championship title. Malcolm stayed in the background, saying little to journalists, but always uncomfortably near the young challenger, smiling at Clay's antics, looking very much like the cat that had caught the canary.

What a story for the sportswriters who had descended on Miami for the fight. It seemed like the birth of a new America, fresh, vibrant, in-your-face. For younger reporters such as Lipsyte, Larry Merchant, and Jerry Izenberg, the story in Miami transcended boxing and even sports—it was about America, about history. Clay was a new America, a brash, confident, outrageous, entertaining spectacle. He was the epicenter of NOW. Just look at the pictures going out from Miami to the world—Clay knocking down the four Beatles, Clay in a serious conversation with Malcolm X, Clay with his mouth wide open proclaiming that he is the chosen one. He was an irresistible story, and the young reporters felt more alive, more hip, just being part of the scene.

A few days before the title match, Joe Louis appeared in Clay's camp. Just a few months short of his fiftieth birthday and still deep in debt to the Internal Revenue Service, the former champion was in town for "walking-around money." The promoters paid him to show up for media events, talk to reporters, and generally lend his considerable prestige to a fight that was regarded as a gross mismatch in Liston's favor. The contrasts between Clay and Louis were stark—Clay was young, articulate, and controversial; Louis was old, quiet, and bland. Clay seemed to dance on air like a pugilistic Astaire; Louis plodded dead-legged and heavy-footed. For Lipsyte, Louis was a "black Dwight D. Eisenhower," a relic from his father's generation, as much a memento of another time as a Roosevelt-Wallace campaign button. Yet the older sportswriters—such legendary scribes as Jimmy Cannon, Red Smith, Arthur Daley, and Barney Nagler—moved from Clay to Louis like a pack of paparazzi deserting a D-lister for a superstar.

Lipsyte did not understand. Later he cornered Nagler and asked why he and the others had wanted to talk to Joe. "How can you hang around that mumbling old has-been, when here's this young beautiful hope of the future?" he asked. Cassius was the story. He was dynamic and interesting, and, something more, he was fun. Nagler looked at Lipsyte almost sadly, because he knew that he could never explain. "You should have seen him then," he offered.

***

Joe Louis: Hard Times Man is about Nagler's "then"—the roughly decade and a half between 1935, when Louis captured the attention of America, and 1951, when his career ended. For just short of twelve of those years Louis was the heavyweight champion of the world, defending his title an astonishing twenty-five times. No heavyweight champion has ever approached those figures. None have ever combined Louis' power, longevity, and grace. It was as if Babe Ruth, Lou Gehrig, and Joe DiMaggio had been a single player, a single black player. Louis was like Franklin D. Roosevelt, a moral compass during a turbulent era. Along with Charles Lindbergh, Roosevelt and Louis were the most written-about men in America. From the middle of the Great Depression to the end of World War II, FDR and Louis were two of the most important physical presences and symbolic forces in America.

Joe Louis is the story of a man, and also of a sport. Boxing is no longer relevant to most Americans. It does not even rate its own tab on *USA Today*'s sports website. Instead, it is grouped with cycling, horse racing, sailing, soccer, the WNBA, and several other activities in the "More Sports" category. No newspaper or sports magazine has a full-time boxing writer. This had not always been the case. In the nineteenth century, the most recognized and important athlete in America was boxer John L. Sullivan. In the twentieth century, that distinction would be a toss-up between boxers Joe Louis and Muhammad Ali. It is doubtful that any boxer will compete for the title in the twenty-first century. For many Americans today, it is difficult to remember a time when boxing was vitally important, when the heavyweight champion was, in the words of Eldridge Cleaver, "as a symbol . . . the real Mr. America."[2] During Joe Louis' years in the ring there were only two professional sports that consumed the interests of Americans: baseball and boxing. Winning a World Series ring was the pinnacle of team competition. Winning a heavyweight championship belt was the greatest individual honor. For this reason, I provide a detailed consideration of the meaning of that title for Americans. From the late nineteenth century until the Great Depression, John L. Sullivan, Jack Johnson, and Jack Dempsey helped define what it meant to be a man in America.

Although the mythology holds that baseball is the National Pastime, boxing has been a more global and democratic sport. Winning the World Series has nothing to do with the world. But winning a world boxing championship does. Louis defended his belt against Americans, South Americans, and Europeans; people from around the world listened to radio broadcasts of his most important fights. In fact, somewhere close to one hundred million people heard the 1938 Louis-Schmeling broadcast. Furthermore, during the vast majority of Louis' ring career, major league baseball was closed to black Americans. From the mid-1880s until 1946 "organized baseball" forced black players to perform on segregated teams in segregated leagues. When, finally, Jackie Robinson did integrate baseball, black and white sportswriters counseled him to be like Joe Louis. As Robinson said at the beginning of "baseball's great experiment," "I'll try to do as good a job as Joe Louis has done. . . . He has done a great job for us and I will try to carry on."[3] The color line was never a mandated policy decision in boxing, so only in the ring could black and white athletes compete on anything close to an equal footing. And in the first half of the twentieth century, this made all the difference for millions of black and white Americans.

Although I am interested in the life and career of Joe Louis, in this book I focus in large part on the meaning of that life and career. What did it mean to be Joe Louis? What did Joe Louis mean to black Americans? How was the image of Joe Louis manipulated and presented to millions of people around the world? Why did Hans J. Massaquoi, the child of an African father and a German mother whose formative years were spent in Nazi Germany, decide in a true act of "double consciousness" to switch his allegiance from a fighter who shared his nationality to one who shared his race?[4] From the beginning of Louis' life, through his marvelous career, to his death, the twin themes of race and nationalism, issues that have vexed black Americans for more than one hundred and fifty years, had coiled around the champion like a snake.

1

A Land Without Dreams

How in hell did you happen?
—*Chicago sociologist Robert E. Park to Richard Wright*

If he lasts long enough, every fighter has the moment. Some experience it early—and it ends their careers. For others it comes later—and it ends their careers. And the rest? Well, they're the real fighters.

Accounts differ on when the moment happened in Joe Louis' career. Maybe it was his first amateur fight. More likely it was his second. It doesn't really matter. All that's important is that Louis was a raw-boned youth, unschooled in the craft of boxing and badly mismatched. It was spring 1932, a hard time to be black in America. Black unemployment rates in northern cities ran two to four times higher than the rates for white workers, and in the South hard times drove black tenant farmers and sharecroppers off their land. In Detroit, where Louis lived, unemployment for blacks hovered at 60 percent. Many critics believed that the federal government was powerless to solve the nation's economic troubles; others felt that no one in the Capitol cared what happened to black men.

Louis was one of several million out-of-work blacks. His stepfather, Pat Brooks, was unemployed, and so were his brothers. Although Brooks was dubious about Louis' decision to fight, he knew that even amateurs got merchandise checks for ten or twenty dollars that could be redeemed in food. That certainly carried some weight, and he gave his unenthusiastic consent. Fighting was not much of a career, but by then Louis had dropped out of school, spent too much time on the streets, and displayed no aptitude for anything else.

1

He was thrown into the ring against Johnny Miler, a tough light-heavyweight whose real name was John Miletich. Miler had potential. He was ambitious, scrappy, experienced, and four years older than Louis. Detroit fight people said that he was going places. Even before fighting Louis, Miler almost certainly engaged in a few professional bouts—the line between top amateurs and novice professionals was at best fuzzy, honored more in the breach than the observance. Shortly after fighting Louis he won the Detroit Golden Gloves light-heavyweight title and earned a place on the U.S. Olympic team. After the Olympics he fought professionally as a heavyweight, amassing a respectable record against some of the finest fighters of the mid-1930s. He sparred with Primo Carnera when the Italian was heavyweight champion of the world. He fought an exhibition against Max Baer after the California fighter had knocked out Carnera for the crown. In short, Louis entered the ring almost criminally mismatched.

Miler knew how to fight, Louis did not. But Joe had seen a photograph of the white boxer and was convinced he could beat him. He thought that it would be the beginning of a successful career. When the bell rang, Miler closed the distance, feinted, and lashed out with punches that Louis was not in a position to defend. Then he moved out of reach, making Louis' wild counters look foolish. Within seconds another exchange ended with Louis on the canvas. He struggled to his feet without a plan or a hope. His head felt numbed, his rhythm skipping beats. Miler knocked him down again and again and again. Seven times in the first two rounds. "Joe's face was all skinned up. He took a bad whipping," recalled his friend Walter Smith.[1] "He was a bewildered young kid," *Ring* editor Nat Fleischer commented.[2] "He really didn't know what he was doing—and after taking the first shot only dimly knew where he was."[3] Smith said the locals used to kid Joe: "He was just like an elevator going up and down." But he kept getting to his feet, knowing with a dead certainty that there was more pain waiting for him.

Boxing is a brutal, unforgiving sport. People play baseball and basketball, football, tennis, and golf. No one *plays* boxing. Fighting is not a game. Getting hit in the face, having your eyes cut, swallowing your own blood, trying to move away from your opponent in a dull, mental fog—it is not like bogeying a hole in golf or striking out in baseball. It takes a certain aptitude, both physical and mental, to endure a painful one-sided fight. In his contest against Miler, Louis discovered no hidden recess of talent. He did not display any remarkable skills. But he did get up. He did finish the fight on his feet. He lost, but he did not quit. He showed, as Smith recalled, the "heart of a champion."

***

"I couldn't dream that big," said Joe Louis in 1948.[4] He could not have imagined as a child in Alabama that one day he would earn millions of dollars, dress in custom-tailored clothes, and drive luxury automobiles. "I never dreamed such things when I was a kid. That never come across my mind. No, I don't dream back, hardly at all, on when I was a kid in Alabama. It seems like people expect you to dream that way, but I'm not cut out like that."

In January 1944, after ringing in the New Year with the soldiers at the Tuskegee Army Air Field, he took a publicity junket to his birthplace. The modest dwelling looked "like a good wind would have blown it down," he said. "No paint, loose boards, and it sagged all over."[5] It slumped like an old man, surrounded by overgrown bushes and weeds. Just another sharecropper's shack in a red-clay, farmed-out, all-but-forgotten cotton field not too far from the Georgia state line. It was not a place that inspired dreams—not for a son of a mentally ill black sharecropper.

Joe Louis' life is peculiarly American. It was part of the bond that he would form with millions of other Americans. It was the American success story—up from poverty to the heights of a chosen profession, the leap from nothing to everything in the blink of an eye. From Benjamin Franklin and Horatio Alger to Jay Gatsby and Jack Dempsey to Johnny B. Goode and Elvis Presley—it is the original American creation myth. The context of lives, the historical forces that shaped them, can be explained, but not the individual, unique qualities. "This is the mystery of Democracy," President Woodrow Wilson said in a speech at the dedication of the log cabin where Abraham Lincoln was born, "that the richest fruits spring up out of soils which no man has prepared and in circumstances where they are least expected."[6]

Joe Louis Barrow was born in that sharecropper's shack on May 13, 1914, while his father and older siblings worked outside in a cotton field. In every conceivable physical and metaphorical sense, he was literally born at the dead end of a dirt road. In Joe's case, the road was a dusty stretch a little less than three miles southeast of LaFayette, Alabama, a tiny artery off of Chambers County Road 1083. The dirt road, County Road 488, meanders east toward the Buckelew Mountains, through a hilly terrain.

There was nothing exceptional about his birth, no predictions of fame and fortune, no thoughts beyond just another mouth to feed. He was the seventh of eight children born to Munroe "Mun" Barrow and Lillie Reese Barrow. Mun, by most accounts, was a big man, 6 foot 3 inches and 200 or so pounds, who could work from sunup to sundown and then into the night. But he was mentally unstable, and by 1914 he had begun to drift away, sometimes moody, occasionally angry, but more often just eerily quiet and withdrawn. Before long he would disappear from the Barrows' family life, committed to the Searcy Hospital for the Colored Criminally Insane in Mount Vernon, Alabama. After Mun was gone, Lillie became close to Pat Brooks, a widower with a number of children of his own—accounts vary between six and nine. They soon married, and Pat became the only father Joe ever knew.

After Joe Louis became famous, there were people who knew him in Alabama who said that they sensed something special about him. Arthur Shealey, his cousin, said that as a youth when Joe helped pick cotton he would fill the first bag, tie it to the branch of a tree, and then every time he reached the end of a row, he would drop his bag and punch away at the hanging sack. Lillie, Shealey said, had to take a switch to Joe to get him back to work. In the 1930s and 1940s, other locals told somewhat less vivid stories that emphasized the size of Joe's hands or his unnatural strength. He was a good lad, his aunt Cora Barrow told a reporter, "but he was de very devil when he got mad; and he'd try to beat the tar out-a anybody what crossed him, then."[7]

Probably none of the stories were true. The hard fact was that Joe was an easy child not to remember. In the brood of children, Joe stood out the least. To begin with, he was a slow developer. He was late to walk and talk, and when he did talk, he badly mispronounced words and stuttered. His language problems made him self-conscious, so he kept his mouth shut as much as possible. He was a loner. He seldom went to what passed for a school and instead rambled through the backcountry catching snakes and fishing. He worked when he was told, went to the Baptist church on Sundays, and played mostly with the other children in his family. He rarely got into fights, showed no real signs of aggressiveness, and was best known for his quiet, good nature.

***

Louis' Alabama childhood took place in the Indian summer of southern white supremacy, not many years before the entire edifice began to crack around the foundation and slowly crumble. It was a time when cotton was still king in the South, when it was planted to the front door and virtually every fertile field turned white at harvest time. Cotton boomed during World War I. To keep the product out of German hands, England bought large amounts of American cotton at artificially inflated prices. Reacting to the sudden boon, farmers scrambled to buy more land to plant more cotton. Times were good—for a while. But the high prices encouraged other nations to get into the cotton business, cutting into the American market share, and the end of the war pricked the price bubble. In the spring of 1920 a pound of cotton sold for $0.42 on the New Orleans market; by the fall it had plummeted to $0.20 and by year's end had slid to $0.13. And it continued to fall in the early 1920s. Cotton farmers were left with mortgages on land they had bought at inflated prices and little income to meet their debts.

Adding to their woes, the boll weevil arrived in Alabama the year Louis was born. In some years the hungry weevils destroyed as much as 75 percent of the cotton crop, driving farmers off their land and forcing millions of tenant farmers and sharecroppers to migrate out of the South. Altogether, the boom and the bust, the war and the weevil, created an atmosphere of anxiety and fear. In Atlanta and Montgomery people talked about the New South, about diversification of the economy and better times ahead, but outside the cites, in the festering cotton fields and the decaying small towns, southerners knew better. A way of life was dying—and, as in the past, someone had to pay the price.

In the South that meant blacks. Race was the soul of southern culture, and the Jim Crow laws that institutionalized the separation of blacks and whites were the constant, daily, humiliating reminders of the white belief that blacks were inferior. Jim Crow ruled virtually every area of life. As late as 1898 an editorial in the Charleston *News and Courier*, the oldest newspaper in the South, attempted a reductio ad absurdum argument against the establishment of Jim Crow cars on trains.

If there must be Jim Crow cars on the railroads, there should be Jim Crow cars on the street railways. Also on all passenger boats. . . . If there are to be Jim Crow cars, moreover, there should be Jim Crow waiting saloons at all stations, and Jim Crow eating houses. . . . There should be Jim Crow sections of the jury box, and a separate Jim Crow dock and witness stand in every court—and a Jim Crow Bible for colored witnesses to kiss. It would be advisable also to have a Jim Crow section in county auditors' and treasurers' offices for the accommodations of colored taxpayers. The two races are dreadfully mixed in these offices for weeks every year, especially about Christmas. . . . There should be a Jim Crow department for making returns and paying for the privileges and blessings of citizenship. Perhaps, the best plan would be, after all, to take the short cut to the general end . . . by establishing two or three Jim Crow counties at once, and turning them over to our colored citizens for their special and exclusive accommodation.[8]

The absurdity of this exposition, of course, was lost in the coming decade as white southerners raced to segregate the races in every walk of life. The distinguished historian C. Vann Woodward noted, "Apart from the Jim Crow counties and Jim Crow witness stand, all the improbable applications of the principle suggested by the editor in derision had been put into practice—down to and including the Jim Crow Bible."[9]

And so it went in the region where Louis was born. Signs reading "White" and "Colored" salt-and-peppered the landscape. For travelers, Jim Crow laws separated the races on railroad cars, railway station waiting rooms, streetcars, and steamboats. Jim Crow laws separated the races when they ate in restaurants, slept in hotels, drank at water fountains, and relieved themselves in public washrooms. There were Jim Crow sections in movie houses and theaters, Jim Crow entrances and exits, Jim Crow stairways and windows, Jim Crow hospitals and prisons, Jim Crow orphanages and mental facilities, and Jim Crow parks and circuses. It almost goes without saying that there were Jim Crow schools. Southern whites went to the respectably funded schools, southern blacks to the miserably funded ones. Black and white students did not mix. Nor did their textbooks mix during the long hot southern summers, when school authorities stored the textbooks used by the different races in separate closets. Even in such matters literary, the idea of miscegenation was repellant to southern whites.

Unwritten codes filled in the spaces not covered by the law. Although blacks and whites worked alongside one another, passed one another on the streets, and daily exchanged greetings, they all knew the rules. Blacks, regardless of their age, addressed whites, regardless of their age, as "mister" or "miss." Whites, regardless of age, addressed blacks, regardless of their age, by their first names, except when they called a male of any age "boy." Blacks who entered a home of a white person always used the back door. In fact, unless a black was entering the home as a domestic, whatever business needed tending was best tended on the back porch, or, in cases of particularly nasty weather, in the kitchen. If a black stepped into the living room or dining room of a white person's home, she had better have a cleaning rag in her hands or he had better be wearing butler's garb.

The street also had its codes. Blacks gave way to whites on sidewalks and crosswalks. If a black and white approached a doorway to a store at the same time, the black stepped aside or politely held the door. Whether in a home or on a street, in a cotton field or at a drinking fountain, the message of the codes was the same: blacks might live in close proximity to whites, but they should have no doubts about the "natural order of things." Recalling his childhood in the South, Melton A. McLaurin defined that order: "Like many such families in a small town, we assumed that blacks of the village were in residence primarily to serve us, and we used their labor to support our comfortable lifestyle."[10]

The legal fiats of the legislators and the unwritten codes of a closed society were strictly enforced by legal and, increasingly, extralegal efforts. As one of the leading students of southern history and culture observed, the litmus test of a true southerner was belief that the South should "remain a white man's country." Jim Crow laws provided the framework for the notion. The Ku Klux Klan and other similar white supremacist organizations contributed additional, direct muscle for enforcement. Founded in 1866, the original Klan had battled northern attempts to reconstruct the racial order of the South. That Klan expired along with northern plans for a new racial configuration. The Klan was reborn on Thanksgiving night 1915 at Stone Mountain, Georgia, near where the immense bas relief of Jefferson Davis, Robert E. Lee, and Stonewall Jackson would one day be carved. Shaken by the pulse of modern America, the heartbeat movements of immigration, urbanization, and modernism, Klansmen drew a line in the red dirt, saying, in effect, "Enough!" They reached into their pockets for their dues, mumbled their oaths, and hooded their heads, paying homage to the doomed gods of their region's racial past.

To be sure, the Klan that grew and thrived after 1915 was not a single-issue organization. It was as much anti-Catholic, anti-Semitic, anti-immigrant, anti-evolution, and anti-alcohol as it was anti-black. And it blossomed in northern cities as well as southern villages. But its burning crosses and midnight rides struck terror in the hearts of southern blacks. Particularly in the South, Klansmen regarded blacks as symbols of America's lost Eden and fall from grace. In a very real sense, the sweet scent of magnolias and the swinging bodies in the Billie Holiday song "Strange Fruit" recall the primal fear engendered by the reign of the Klan.

An American—and not just southern—popular culture reinforced the racial order. The outrageous stereotypes of the late nineteenth- and early twentieth-century "coon songs" gave way to the dangerously racist plays and films of the second decade of the century. The year after Joe Louis was born, African Americans suffered several theatrical and pugilistic indignities. In theaters across the country the vilest, most distorted racism played to packed, cheering houses. That year, the Fox Film Corporation adapted Edward Sheldon's play *The Nigger* for the silver screen. The Harvard-educated Sheldon tells the story of a virtuous southern governor who discovers that he is a "quadroon," and this small amount of black blood, he reasons, renders him unfit for the rights and duties of white society. In quick order he resigns from office, forfeits his plantation, and breaks off his engagement to his white fiancée. Although a barrage of protests convinced Fox to change the title of the film to *The Mystery of Morrow's Past,* the production left no doubt that there was a "color line" in America, a division that not only separated the races but also governed the order of civilized life.

The controversy raised by the Fox film, however, seemed like a lighted match compared to the firestorm surrounding another of the year's racist productions. *The Birth of a Nation,* director D. W. Griffith's film about the emergence of the Ku Klux Klan, premiered in Los Angeles on February 8, 1915, in defiance of a court injunction obtained by the city's branch of the National Association for the Advancement of Colored People (NAACP). During the next year it would spur other injunctions, face waves of protests, and achieve the distinction of becoming the most controversial film in the industry's history. "If this had been a third-rate film, a tenth-rate film," remarked one critic of *The Birth of a Nation* during a roundtable discussion, "we wouldn't be sitting here now talking about it."[11] Sadly, it is a great, terrible film, like Leni Riefenstahl's *Triumph of the Will,* a motion picture that adroitly employs all the arts of the most gifted filmmaker to promote a flawed, twisted ideology. Griffith's film glorifies the Ku Klux Klan, portraying the hooded night riders as nobly responding to aggressive, licentious black libertines. Ultimately, in the minds of many white Americans, Griffith's scurrilously provocative production justified every aspect of Jim Crow existence.

From East Coast to West, the film played to packed houses and rousing cheers. It became America's first blockbuster, eventually seen by some 200 million people; it is, adjusting for inflation, perhaps the biggest grossing film of all time. The film's success and popularity muffled the roars of protest from the NAACP. Giving *The Birth of a Nation* an imprimatur of legitimacy was its status as the first film shown in the White House—the White House of Virginia-born and Georgia-raised Woodrow Wilson. During the showing Wilson seemed lost in thought, and afterward he supposedly said, "It is like writing history with lightning. And my only regret is that it is all so terribly true."[12]

Some northern blacks used the realities of the prize ring to counter Griffith's outlandish fictions. Near the Stroll, in the African American section of Chicago, as well as in black quarters of Baltimore, New York, and several other cities, theater owners screened bootleg copies of the 1910 interracial heavyweight title fight between Jack Johnson and Jim Jeffries for their patrons. Johnson's punches, his obvious superiority and undeniable dominance, were real, not the vile fictions of an unbalanced and teetering racial order. "How great is the difference between [the Johnson-Jeffries] picture and *The Birth of a Nation*?" a Chicago *Defender* writer asked the city censors. "In the former, we see the camp life of trained athletes, and subsequently their wonderful skill. In the latter, terrible pictures of white men raping colored girls and women and burning of colored men at the stake."[13]

But in 1915 even Johnson's victory over Jeffries had been partially erased. On April 5 in Havana, Cuba, Jess Willard, the "Great White Hope," had knocked out the aging and badly conditioned champion. After the fight Willard asserted his Jim Crow convictions, telling the press that before the Johnson match he had never fought a black fighter and he intended not to fight another.

***

This, then, was the world Joe Louis Barrow was born into, a world whose economic, political, social, and cultural dictates pressed down upon black Americans. President Wilson had segregated all the departments of the federal government. White southerners had segregated virtually every institution in Dixie. The leaders of organized baseball had drawn a rigid color line in their sport. Jess Willard had done the same in the heavyweight division. Even Booker T. Washington, the most prominent black leader in the country, argued that equality in most things was an unrealistic notion. In his Atlanta Exposition speech (1895) he counseled blacks to work for concrete economic gains and reconciliation with white southerners. For the time being, at least, there was no need to stretch for civil rights, political power, or higher education. Those stars were out of reach. Instead, he said, "In all things that are purely social we can be as separate as the fingers, yet one as the hand in all things essential to mutual progress."[14] At no point in his most important address did Washington challenge, or even question, the reign of Jim Crow.

In the 1940s Louis vividly recalled the poverty of his Alabama years but claimed that he "never knew anything about race." "No one talked about it. . . . If there was lynch talk, it never got to me or my folks. . . . I never got to know about such things until we got to Detroit."[15] And perhaps it did not enter into his thinking in Alabama. But decades later Louis shared another memory. "I remember black people getting together and talking about how much white blood they had, how much Indian blood they had, but hardly . . . anybody would talk about how much black blood they had."[16] Floyd Tillery, a journalist who visited Chambers County in 1935, confirmed such racial discussions. He claimed that Mun had more white and Indian blood than black, and that some members of the Barrow clan looked like "Indian braves and princesses" and others "are as fair as any Anglo-Saxon." "Our forebears were born in slavery time and you know how it was then with good-looking mulatto women," one of the oldest of the Barrows told Tillery. "There was no marryin', of course, but us is got the best white blood in the whole county in our veins—and the best Indian blood, too." Tillery observed that few of the Barrows were dark-skinned, "though many are the typical freaky-looking zambos. Others are pleasantly pigmented like the 'Brown Bomber'—very light yellow, with wavy hair and brown or blue eyes."[17]

The splitting of racial hairs, the preference for white and Indian blood, illuminated the emotional impact of the culture of Jim Crow. In the South, blacks occupied the bottom of the racial hierarchy. Color was everything— the lighter the better. "You see the Barrows have alluz wanted to stay as white as dey could," said one of Joe's boyhood friends.[18] Race did matter. It was capable of twisting minds and torturing thoughts. As writers like Richard Wright have shown, Jim Crow thinking could easily, almost inevitably, turn to self-hatred for many blacks. Born in rural Mississippi in 1908, Wright experienced the same environment as Louis, the same grinding poverty, educational disadvantages, and racial thinking. No wonder University of Chicago sociologist Robert E. Park asked, when meeting Wright for the first time, "How the hell did you happen?" How could any black escape the nightmarish landscape of the Jim Crow South? The same question could be asked of Joe Louis.

A combination of poverty and race drove the Brooks-Barrow family out of Alabama. Tumbling cotton prices and ravenous boll weevils made it all but impossible for Pat Brooks to support his family. Then one night in 1925 several hooded Klansmen stopped Brooks and Lillie when they were returning home. Before they were hauled out of their car one of the Klansmen recognized Brooks. "That's Pat Brooks," he told the others. "He's a good nigger."[19] Brooks drove on, but in his mind he was already leaving Dixie.

***

In 1925, Pat Brooks was just one of tens of thousands of African Americans departing the South. Most boarded Jim Crow railway cars and watched as the cotton fields, tobacco farms, and rice plantations of home gave way to land planted with corn and wheat. In the Midwest they stopped at stations without the familiar "White" and "Colored" signs. Most continued to ride the train until it reached one of the booming midwestern cities— Detroit, Chicago, Gary, and Cleveland—or one of the northern cities with established black communities. No longer was the landscape planted with crops. Instead of corn and wheat they saw factories, some larger than cities, breathing fire and belching smoke. They had arrived in a place that looked like hell but promised heavenly opportunities.

Brooks and, less than a year later, the rest of his family were part of the Great Migration. Between 1915 and 1940 more than 1.5 million blacks moved from the South to the Northeast, Midwest, and West. Most left for the same reasons Brooks did—to escape economic privation and racism, and to gain a chance at prosperity and the dream of a better life. Brooks headed for one of the most popular destinations, Henry Ford's massive automobile plants on the Rouge River in Detroit. Word had reached Brooks in Alabama that Ford paid more for a day's work than could be earned honestly anywhere else.

At the turn of the century, about the time that Ford arrived in the city, Detroit's population was 285,000. A quarter-century later it had grown to 1.25 million people, ranking behind only New York, Chicago, and Philadelphia. During that time Ford's empire, a vast complex for building affordable automobiles, burgeoned into a national treasure and a symbol of the country's greatness. In 1908 Ford introduced the Model T, a people's car, relatively inexpensive, easy to fix, and simple to operate. In the next two decades his company sold more than 15 million Model T's. If, as a journalist wrote, Detroit had become "Eldorado," Ford himself had become Midas. Everything he touched seemed transmuted into gold, and instead of hoarding it, he passed out some of it to his workers. In 1914 he began to pay his workers five dollars a day, a fabulous amount that more than doubled the going rate in other industries.

"Five dollars a day!" That was what every tenant farmer and sharecropper working a worn-out patch of dead dirt in the South heard. "Five dollars a day!" The news shot across Dixie like a bullet. The four words became a mantra and a magnet. For southern blacks the phrase was a new Emancipation Proclamation, the promise of a better life in a better place. Bluesman Blind Arthur Blake captured the central place of the city in "Detroit Bound Blues."

> I'm goin' to Detroit, get myself a good job
> I'm goin' to Detroit, get myself a good job
> Tried to stay around here with the starvation mob
>
> I'm goin' to get a job, up there in Mr. Ford's place
> I'm goin' to get a job, up there in Mr. Ford's place
> Stop these eatless days from starin' me in the face
>
> When I start to makin' money, she don't need to come around
> When I start to makin' money, she don't need to come around
> 'Cause I don't want her now, Lord. I'm Detroit bound.[20]

The lure of five dollars a day made Detroit the destination of choice for thousands of African Americans. Between 1910 and 1920 the city's black population swelled from 5,700 to 41,000; by 1930 it had leapt to 120,000.

Not even New York or Chicago ever experienced such an influx of African Americans. The news of the fabulous pay and liberal laws in Detroit spread like wildfire through black newspapers, recruitment broadsheets, and word-of-mouth. There was no Jim Crow, no strange fruit hanging from trees, no "obstacles for a colored man"—or so it was said.

The truth . . . well, it always takes a different shape. The truth was that jobs for a black man were seldom as good or as well paying as those for a white man. Most blacks did not get one of those five-dollar-a-day jobs, and if they did, they got the worst, most dangerous ones. At Ford or Dodge Brothers or Cadillac Motors, for example, blacks breathed the toxic fumes in spray-paint rooms or wet-sanding departments. Or they earned every cent of their wage in the foundries, sweating from the heat of giant furnaces and praying that some accident did not dump molten steel onto them. Whites considered working in foundries, like collecting garbage and cleaning homes, "Negro work."

And the truth was that white real estate agents channeled African Americans into the Black Bottom section of Detroit, on the east side of the city between the Detroit River and the Grand Trunk railroad tracts. There, centered along Hastings and St. Antoine streets, white landlords charged outrageous rents for squalid housing. Black Bottom housing gave new meaning to the word "substandard"—as likely as not, roofs leaked, plaster cracked, wallpaper peeled, and windows didn't open or didn't shut. Most houses lacked running water, outhouses emitted fetid odors, and public services were few and poor. The Black Bottom was the most neglected section of Detroit—ignored by streetcar magnates, city water officials, and police chiefs. It was a place almost too cold to survive in during winter and too hot to live in during summer, a part of the expanding industrial city where crime went virtually unchecked and disease found a welcoming environment. The Black Bottom was pretty much what Great Migration blacks found in every major city north of Dixie.

The Brooks/Barrow odyssey in the North was fairly typical. Pat got a job in the Ford plant, and the older children got what jobs they could, but there never seemed to be enough money to pay the high rents and put food on the table. The family moved regularly—from a place they shared with a family on Macomb Street to one on Catherine Street to another on Mullett Street. After the onset of the Great Depression, times became even more difficult. Family members did what they could, but a job in the auto plants was almost impossible to come by for blacks, and all other jobs paid poorly. "My mother had to go down to the relief place and wait in line to get a few bucks a week," Joe Louis recalled.²¹ It helped a little. But not enough. Not nearly.

✳✳✳

Joe was twelve years old in 1926, when he arrived with his family in Detroit. He went to Duffield Elementary School, but, he said, he "couldn't take to learning" any better than he had in Alabama. "I couldn't hardly get past the sixth grade," he admitted.²² He stood out as the biggest kid in his class, and he watched his younger sister catch and pass him in school. School officials soon assigned him to the Bronson Trade School, an institution that taught woodworking and other trades to "slow" students. John Roxborough, who later became his manager, said Bronson was for the "scholastically retarded."²³ Joe liked the trade curriculum better than the academic one. "I did cabinetmaker's work at Bronson; made nice things. I made little tables and shelves and knickknack closets. I was pretty good at it."²⁴ But in 1929, when Pat Brooks lost his job at Ford, Joe left Bronson and took what paying work he could find. He swept factory floors, delivered ice in the summer and coal in the winter, and took various other odd jobs that required only a strong back and arms.

He also spent more nights on the street corner with the Catherine Street gang. "We had fights, but nothing much; just gang fights the way kids do. You got into a fight and you just punched the best you could."²⁵ Perhaps to get her son away from the gang activities, his mother arranged for him to take violin lessons. It sounds like a scenario out of a Depression-era boxing film—perhaps Anatole Litvak's *City for Conquest* or Clifford Odets' *Golden Boy*—but there is unimpeachable corroboration for Louis' account of his brief, unsuccessful affair with the violin. Joe took five or six lessons, never mastered the scales, and suffered some good-natured verbal abuse from his friends.

During Louis' violin stage, a friend, an amateur boxer named Thurston McKinney, asked Joe to spar with him. Louis felt honored, at least until McKinney landed a few hard punches. Then he felt less flattered. "I got mad," Louis remembered. "I let go my right. It caught him on the chin. His eyes got glassy and his knees buckled, and if I hadn't moved fast to hold him up, I would have knocked him out—and he was the Golden

Gloves Lightweight Champion of Detroit." "Man," McKinney told him later, "throw away that violin."[26] He told Joe that he should take the money he was using for violin lessons to rent a locker at the local gym. Thurston showed him copies of *Ring* magazine, and Joe studied the pictures of the world champions and leading contenders. There was money in boxing, maybe a future, something that Joe could not see in the violin. It all made sense. "A violin felt small in my hands," he later recalled, but those same big hands fit nicely into a pair of boxing gloves.[27]

And there was something else. Sparring with McKinney made him feel different. Nothing in Jim Crow Alabama or Henry Ford's Detroit had prepared him for it. "You can't imagine how I felt," he told a writer. "I don't know how to describe it. It was like a power pumping through me. Maybe it's something like people getting religion. . . . There was something professional about it."[28] This "something professional," this combination of self-worth, accomplishment, and limitless possibilities, was something Louis had never experienced. It was life-changing. In 1932, when he was eighteen years old, he began to train at the Brewster Recreation Center.

A series of good local trainers—such men as Atler Ellis and Holman Williams had fine ring careers—initiated Louis in the basics of boxing. The sport is not one that comes naturally to anyone—there is nothing natural about closing the distance on an opponent so that you can hit him. Because at that distance he can punch you as well. It takes discipline, and overcoming one's all too instinctual fears of getting hit in the face, to even begin boxing. All boxers, even the greatest, get hit repeatedly in training and in fights. It is an unavoidable part of the sport. In addition, most boxers throw more punches with their weaker hand. A right-handed fighter leads with his left, sets up his opponent with his left, and separates himself from less talented fighters by his ability to effectively score with his left. A good boxer is almost like a switch hitter in baseball, and the talent is developed over years of practice.

Louis learned the "Brewster style" of boxing—left jab, right hand, left hook; stick and move; step in, step out, step in. It was a slick style, one developed in countless gyms across the country. In 1932 and 1933, before his body filled out, the jab-jab, hit-and-move style fit him perfectly. He trained with lighter, faster fighters—lightweights, welterweights, middleweights—to develop his foot and hand speed. After losing to Johnny Miler at the beginning of his amateur career, a defeat that made him question his decision to give up the violin, he returned to the gym with a new determination.

Beginning in January 1933 he fought under his new ring name, Joe Louis, often and successfully. Although in 1933 he lost in the finals of the National Amateur Athletic Union (AAU) tournament, he returned in 1934 to win both the AAU and the national Golden Gloves light-heavyweight titles.

As an amateur Louis attracted attention. Other amateurs in his weight division were faster and boxed more skillfully, and a few of them out-pointed him. But none had his power. He could hit with either hand. Eddie Futch, another Brewster product who would later become a legendary trainer, felt the power. Although he was only a lightweight, he occasionally sparred with Joe. Futch was smart. Before he sparred with Louis he studied his technique. "I told myself, if he wants me to work with him, I've got to know when those punches are coming. I've got to know the moves he makes before he punches, because he never telegraphs anything. The left hook came out of nowhere. Bang. If he hit you with a shot, you never saw the punch coming. You just saw a light in your head. Like a camera flash going off. Bang."[29]

Futch also noticed that Louis was hungry to learn every aspect of the craft. Raw when he began his amateur career, Joe accumulated new skills with each fight. In November 1933, Stanley Evans, a slick, crafty boxer, outpointed him in a three-round fight. Three months later in a rematch Louis defeated Evans. By mid-1934 Louis no longer fought like an amateur. Unlike a novice, he no longer threw long punches; instead, he moved close to his opponent and threw short shots. Futch recalled, "He had the quickest counter. If you threw a left hook, he'd counter with a left hook."[30] And when he hit you, it hurt for days. "Anywhere he hit you," Futch said of sparring with Louis, "you'd feel it. The next day you were as sore as if you'd been in a real fight. Even if he didn't hit you much, just blocking those shots was like being in an automobile accident. You didn't know how sore you were until you woke up the next morning."[31]

By mid-1934 Louis had won fifty of fifty-four amateur fights, forty-three of those victories by knockout. It was the sort of success that attracted the attention of more people than just fighters. The world of boxing was filled with fringe figures, hustlers, gamblers, and mobsters looking for a quick buck or a long-term meal ticket. They haunted the hundreds of basement gyms that peppered Depression America, trolled the second- and third-rate fight clubs, and came alive in the smoke-filled air of amateur tournaments. They weren't really trainers or managers or promoters, but, if it seemed to give them an edge, they professed that they were trainers, managers, promoters, and more. Boxing insiders called them "sharks" or "barracudas"; they preyed on young talent, spinning tales of glory and riches and picking their bones in the process. Starting in 1934, and continuing for the rest of his life, Joe Louis would be surrounded by these men.

George Slayton—a.k.a. George Moody—was one of this breed. He was an a.k.a. sort of operator. For a short time in 1933 he was Louis' trainer, though he knew very little about the craft of boxing. Richard Bak accurately defined him as a the "prototypical Hasting Street hustler, dabbling in the usual activities—pimping, bootlegging, running numbers—before finally settling into a career as a bail bondsman."[32] He played a bit role in Louis' life: "managing" Joe for one of his few amateur losses, then in the locker room introducing the fighter to John Roxborough, one of the major players in the street life of Black Bottom and Paradise Valley, the home to more scams and hustles than could be found in any other corner of Detroit.

Roxborough was a singular looking man. His face was almost perfectly round. It looked like a balloon on the verge of popping, or, perhaps, something out of the workshop of the Wizard of Oz. He was bald and plump and had a tiny, perfectly trimmed mustache. Poised and well spoken, he dressed as immaculately as a Wall Street banker and smelled like a flower shop. He was unlike anyone Louis had ever met. "This man had real class," Louis recalled. "He was a very light-skinned black man. . . . He didn't seem flashy, but stylish and rich-looking. He had a gray silk suit, the kind you don't buy off the rack. It made me look twice. His attitude was gentle, like a gentleman should be."[33] Roxborough told Louis that he had been impressed with his skills, and when he got the chance he should drop by his real estate office.

Roxborough had his hands in many activities, some of them illegal. His father, a New Orleans lawyer, had moved his family to Detroit in 1899, and his brother, also a lawyer, was one of Michigan's first black legislators. For a time Roxborough also studied law, but he soon concluded that there was not much money to be made from black clients. Instead, he became a bail bondsman, a job that acquainted him with men from some lucrative, if shady, walks of life. Most importantly, he learned the intricacies of the numbers racket. He did dabble, at least on the surface, in real estate and insurance from his office on St. Antoine, but most of his money came from running the Detroit numbers operation. He was in the perfect place at the perfect time. Between World War I and the Great Depression, as blacks streamed endlessly into Detroit and found employment in the automobile and other industries, Roxborough offered them a chance to escape the life of a Ford mule and strike it big. All they had to do was buy a number and then hope that it appeared in the next day's newspaper. Why not? It didn't cost much, and life was pretty much a lottery, anyway. The nickels and dimes and quarters piled up, and Roxborough got his cut.

Like other black numbers operators—men like Gus Greenlee in Pittsburgh and Julian Black in Chicago—Roxborough was also a figure in the black community and the local sports scene. He was active in the Young Negro Progressive Association and the Urban League. In addition, he helped bankroll the Negro League baseball team the Detroit Stars and kept his hand in the city's fight scene, lending money to promising prospects and contributing to local fight clubs. In Joe Louis, Roxborough saw an opportunity, a chance to make some money in a profession with very few rules. When Joe dropped by his office, Roxborough made a few small investments. He took Louis to Long's Drugstore and told the owner to give the fighter any boxing supplies he wanted. Roxborough would pay the bills. He also gave Joe some of his old clothes—expensive ties, shirts, and coats—and made sure the fighter ate properly and got to bed early. For a while Louis lived with Roxborough, who provided him with spending money, real boxing shoes and trunks, and a terrycloth robe. He took care of Joe like a son, asking nothing in return.

But mostly he talked to Louis, man to man, brother to brother. Joe had talent, he said, but lots of fighters have talent. Ability was not enough. He needed management, black management. "He told me about the fate of most black fighters," Louis said, "ones with white managers, who wound up burned-out and broke before they reached their prime. The white managers were not interested in the men they were handling but in the money they could make from them. They didn't take the proper time to see that their fighters had a proper training, that they lived comfortably, or ate well, or had some pocket change"—the things Roxborough provided.[34] It was the same sell, the same "pocketful of mumbles" but with some extra race talk, that had won over countless fighters in the past.

It worked. Joe liked and admired Roxborough, calling him "Roxie" when it was just the two of them and "Mr. Roxborough" when anyone else was around. Roxborough convinced Louis of his good intentions, and then won over Lillie Barrow Brooks, who had to cosign the contract because her son was not yet twenty-one. In truth, it was an easy sell. Roxborough was a respected man in black Detroit, a man who contributed to charities and civic affairs. Furthermore, everything he said about white managers was essentially correct. Most exploited white as well as black fighters, but particularly black fighters. Louis probably had no chance of succeeding with a white manager. Maybe a few good paydays, perhaps a bit more if he went in the tank for a few fights, but not a career that would take him to the top of the profession. Not a championship fight or a title. That might be out of reach with Roxborough as well, but at least the two men had a racial bond.

Roxborough assumed that Louis would spend another year in the amateur ranks, but in June 1934 Joe said that he wanted to turn professional. Why? Roxborough asked. "Mr. Roxborough, I want the money," he answered. It made perfect sense to Roxborough. "That's why I was in the numbers racket—and I've never been ashamed of it—and I said 'Okay, Joe, I'll find you a good manager and a good trainer.' "[35] Roxborough, of course, planned on controlling Louis' career, but he needed a comanager with more money and connections in boxing circles. He turned to Julian Black, the numbers king in Chicago who had large real estate holdings, owned the speakeasy Elite Number 2, and had a stable of fighters. Black had the same polished look as Roxborough. Light-skinned, processed hair slicked back just right, a Beau Brummell appearance—Black was stocky and walked with a limp and looked every inch a success. An associate who knew him well wrote, "He was very, very clever and especially clever with numbers."[36] Black could see through scams like they were glass. He was known as a man you didn't cross. It was said that he paid his debts and, one way or another, got what was owed him. Louis noticed at once that he seemed nice "but was basically a tough guy."[37] Black had once lent Roxborough a pile of money when the Detroit man's numbers business ran into some trouble. So there was a debt to be repaid, and, besides, Roxborough trusted Black and knew he could make things happen. Quieter than Roxborough, preferring to work behind the scenes, he promised that he could help advance Louis' career.

Black's first and most inspired suggestion was to relocate Louis to Chicago and to hire Jack Blackburn as a trainer. It was a risky choice as well. Blackburn had mastered all the requisite skills—and then some. Born in Versailles, Kentucky, in 1883, a son of a peripatetic Baptist preacher, he began boxing professionally in 1899. Although only a tall, thin lightweight and welterweight, he often fought much heavier boxers, including several of the finest black heavyweights of his era. He used to say that he didn't care how much an opponent weighed as long as he had two hands. During his career Blackburn fought evenly against such greats as Sam Langford, Joe Gans, "Philadelphia" Jack O'Brien, and Harry Greb. Although he never won a title—indeed, he was so good a fighter that no champion would even fight him with the title on the line—boxing authorities recognized him as a master craftsman, a brilliant defensive tactician, and an insightful student of the sweet science. After he retired from the ring, those skills made him one of the finest trainers of the century.

On the surface, then, Blackburn appeared a logical choice to teach Louis the finer points of the profession. But Blackburn came with some dangerous baggage. The discrimination he had confronted in the ring, the blatant injustices that had marked his career, and the lack of a championship belt to attest to his abilities had left a bitter taste in his mouth, a taste that he tried to wash down with alcohol. Legendary trainer Ray Arcel knew Blackburn well and liked him immensely. But he was not blind to his fellow trainer's nature. "Blackburn had a rough life," he explained as a preamble to the trainer's strengths and weaknesses. "He was a bad guy. He used to get drunk and have fights. He killed a couple of guys. He was a great trainer. You talk about trainers! *He was a great trainer.*"[38]

One time back in early 1909, at the height of his fighting career, Blackburn got very drunk and extremely angry. He and his common-law white wife Maude Pillion got into a set-to with Alonzo Polk and his wife, Mattie. Blackburn settled the argument with a gun, killing Polk, wounding Mattie, and also shooting Maude. Policemen found him near the bodies, clubbed him unconscious, and locked him away. The fighter was sentenced to fifteen years in prison, and while inside he became a boxing instructor and taught the manly art to prisoners, the warden, and the warden's sons.

He got out of prison in 1913 and resumed his boxing career. He tried to rein in his deadly temper, and mostly he was successful. "I was just another nigger," he told Arcel. "If I walked into a saloon, the wise guys would pop off . . . I had to walk out because there was only one solution, I'da had to kill 'em."[39] So he tried to keep his mouth shut and mind his own business. But it was challenging to keep tight control over his anger, especially when he was drinking, in which case, another one of his friends admitted, "he was wholly unnatural."[40] Sometimes he didn't walk away. Sometimes, as an associate remarked, Blackburn's eyes turned "blood red" and he was "ungovernable, mean, and just plain bad, with his temper just a hair trigger away from violence."[41] A knife fight with his brother Fred left a razor scar running ear to mouth down the left side of his face, and more than once he got himself into violent confrontations. On one occasion in 1935, after a drunken argument, he pulled out a gun and opened fire, killing an elderly bystander and wounding a nine-year-old girl. People who knew Blackburn almost universally agreed that he had the angriest eyes that they had ever seen. Normally quiet, tending to stay on the periphery of the action, Blackburn was not the sort of person reporters engaged in idle conversation. As Eddie Futch, another great trainer who got along well with Blackburn, admitted: "Blackburn was a mean person, as mean as he looked."[42]

As a trainer Blackburn was not a "race man." He was a money man—and the money was in training white fighters. They were the ones who got the shot at the titles and the bigger purses; they were the ones who got the good end of fixed fights and the bad decisions from crooked referees and officials. And since Blackburn received a percentage of their purses, it stood to reason that he wanted to train them. Working out of George Trefton's gym in Chicago, he guided Bud Taylor to the bantamweight title and Sammy Mandell to the lightweight crown. He also was picked to teach the promising white heavyweight Art Lasky how to fight. He showed little interest in working with black fighters, no matter how talented, because he knew the sport would only break their hearts and leave them penniless and hopeless.

In 1934, when Black and Roxborough approached Blackburn about working with Louis, the trainer, who seemed decades older than he really was, told the two numbers men to "bring the white boy around" and he would take a look at him. When Roxborough said Louis was black, Blackburn lost interest. "I won't have no truck with a colored boy," he said. "Colored boys ain't got much chance fighting nowadays—unless they just happen to be a world-beater."[43] But times being hard during the Depression, he did take a look at Louis.

"I gives him the eye, and I'm still not impressed," Blackburn recalled. Louis was a gangling, raw-boned twenty-year-old, a little over six feet and about 175 pounds, "a big, easy-going Negro boy with high water pants and too much arms for his coat sleeves."[44] He showed signs of strength and power but plodded around the ring gracelessly and threw punches off balance. He was not a world-beater or even, to Blackburn's trained eye, particularly gifted. He told Black and Roxborough as much, but he also knew enough about the two men to respect their eye for money if not boxing talent. Neither man had climbed to the top of their cities' numbers rackets by being stupid or losing money. He explained how difficult the world was for black heavyweights, the slim chances of success for even a gifted one. But Louis' managers offered him thirty-five dollars a week for four weeks' effort, after which they could resume the conversation. Blackburn, unemployed and arthritic, needed the money but was brutally honest: "I got to tell you, you'll never make a success of this kid, but I need the job. He ain't going to make no money worth shaking your finger at. Remember he's a colored boy."[45]

Before finally accepting, Blackburn remembered that he told Louis, "So you think you can get somewhere in this fighting game? Well, let me tell you something right off. It's next to impossible for a Negro heavyweight to get anywhere. He's got to be very good outside the ring and very bad inside the ring. Mr. Roxborough, who has known you for quite a while, is convinced that you can be depended on to behave yourself, but you've gotta be a killer, otherwise I'm getting too old to waste any time on you." Louis listened quietly, intently, then answered, "I ain't gonna waste any of your time."[46]

During the next month Blackburn began to reshape Louis' ring technique. He started with proper footwork, working on getting Louis to keep his weight balanced and his feet planted so that he would be in position to throw a power punch at any time. He worked on Louis' left and on getting his weight behind his punches. He taught Joe how to slip punches, roll with punches, and block punches—all the details of being a professional. The central idea of professional boxing is defensive. The fighters who have the longest, most successful careers are the ones who absorb the fewest solid punches. Louis learned quickly. He paid attention, took criticism well, and trained diligently.

A bond developed between the two men, built on love and respect for boxing. They called each other "Chappie," but Louis readily accepted the pupil's role. He wanted so badly to be a boxer. "He was so . . . intense," his friend Eddie Futch recalled. "He was a student of boxing, most people don't realize that. They think he was just a puncher. But he was a student of boxing."[47]

Blackburn's major contribution to Louis' new style was what he took away from his old style. As an amateur Louis bounced and moved. Like other Detroit fighters, he had labored to be a slick boxer. Blackburn limited the movement, getting Louis off his toes. He wanted Joe to fight more flat-footed. Instead of dancing in the ring, Louis became a stalker, aggressively moving forward, cutting off the ring, and closing on his opponent. After spending a few months in Chicago, Louis returned to Detroit. Futch noticed the change: Blackburn "had Louis fighting like a heavyweight." The stick-and-move was gone. "Blackburn took that away from him. He got him sliding in, cutting off the ring, using a good left hand—not bouncing all over the place."[48] Blackburn recognized that Louis' greatest gift was his power, and he developed a style that maximized Joe's chances of landing hard punches. He did not want to leave anything to chance. He had seen too many black fighters robbed of victories by hometown decisions and crooked referees. "You can't get nowhere nowadays trying to outpoint fellows in the ring," Blackburn told Louis. "It's mighty hard for a colored boy to win decisions. The dice is loaded against you. You gotta knock 'em out and keep knocking 'em out to get anywheres. Let your right fist be your referee. Don't ever forget that. Let that right fist be your referee!"[49]

Louis listened, soaking in all the advice. He was beginning to understand the craft of prizefighting. He would soon be introduced to its culture.

2

Emperors of Masculinity

> Boxing is for men, and is about men, and *is* men. A celebration of the lost
> religion of masculinity all the more trenchant for being lost.
> —*Joyce Carol Oates*

William Lyon Phelps, B.A. Yale, M.A. Harvard, and Ph.D. Yale, was the very model of rectitude. In his forty-one years as a literature professor at Yale he was known for his wide-ranging scholarship, astute critical pronouncements, and unimpeachable humanity. He was the quintessence of the gentleman scholar. In fact, it was Phelps who provided a lasting American definition of a gentleman when he pronounced, "This is the first test of a gentleman: his respect for those who can be of no possible value to him."

Phelps, like many of Yale's students and professors, came from a religious family. His father was an orthodox Baptist minister—New England Baptist, not southern Baptist. Daily, as an act of filial love, he would read the news to his elderly father. One day in 1892, as he was working through the newspaper, he read the headline about the outcome of a prizefight— CORBETT DEFEATS SULLIVAN—and then turned the page. Never in his life had he heard his father mention Corbett or Sullivan, or prizefighting, for that matter. Such activities were beneath the scope of the Phelps family. The younger Phelps assumed that his father did not know "anything on that subject, or cared anything about it." But the son was mistaken. As he turned the page his father "leaned forward and said earnestly, 'Read it by rounds!' "[1]

The statement must have given William Lyon Phelps pause. The world in which he had grown to manhood, the one he had inherited from his

father, that clannish White Anglo-Saxon Protestant America, was chang-
ing. The days when the only emotion that a prizefight would elicit from a
New England Baptist minister was disgust were drawing to a close. And
John L. Sullivan stood as a symbol of a new world.

***

Why Louis decided to enter the world of prizefighting is rather simply
answered. Poverty, lack of opportunities, and a talent for hitting people
steered him into the ring. A more difficult question is why professional
boxing, and especially the heavyweight championship, mattered to Americans in the first four decades of the twentieth century. For most of modern
history, the sport of prizefighting was publicly deplored, politically outlawed, and morally condemned. It was considered barbarous and archaic, a
throwback to a time when man walked with his knuckles scraping the
ground. But for various reasons a new construction of the meaning of
boxing was emerging—in the beginning of the nineteenth century in England and at the end of that century in America.

In England bare-knuckle boxing had enjoyed the popularity and patronage of sporting aristocrats. In the mid-eighteenth century, the early
decades of the nineteenth century, and again briefly in the mid-nineteenth
century, the prize ring captured the popular imagination. Ideal for betting,
easily corruptible for gamblers, and diffused with an argot, traditions,
and culture all its own, prizefighting attracted wealthy supporters with a
healthy *nostalgie de la boue.*

It also communicated the basic social and cultural instincts of English
life. As practiced under the London Prize Ring Rules, it was an uncom-
promising, violent activity. Fighters battled with their bare fists. A round
lasted until one of the contestants threw or knocked his opponent to the
ground. The felled fighter then received a thirty-second rest, after which he
had to "come up to scratch," a line drawn in the center of the ring. All
important matches were battled until a fighter was too beaten to "toe the
line." Fights could, and often did, last for hours, with the combatants
sustaining terrible beatings. But particularly in the first two decades of the
nineteenth century, when Britons were battling Frenchmen on the waves of
the Atlantic and the dirt of the Continent, prizefighting symbolized the
bulldog tenacity, the refusal to give an inch, of John Bull. Regency boxers
showed the nation how to confront danger, absorb frightful punishment,

win with grace, and lose with dignity. The very language of the ring—including such phrases as "the manly art of self-defense," "toe the line," "up (or not up) to scratch," and "throwing one's hat into the ring"—connected boxing to the most revered masculine traits of the age. Wellington may have won the Battle of Waterloo on the playing fields of Eton, but his officers and soldiers learned something about being a man from the examples of the English prize ring.

But bare-knuckle boxing generally languished in the United States. Not until the 1840s did it begin to establish roots in American soil, and then only with a certain "unsavory" class of men. American prizefighting was a product of ethnic, working-class culture, and most of the early American boxers were Irish immigrants. It was generally an illegal fringe activity, populated and patronized by Irish politicians, saloon keepers, emigrant runners, shoulder hitters, pickpockets, second-floor men, pimps, prostitutes, and other sorts of "unworthies," along with a small group of sons of privilege out for a good time. But the bloody, violent sport spoke to working-class men whose lives were similarly violent. As the historian Elliott J. Gorn eloquently observed, "The death sounds of livestock slaughtered in public markets, the smell of open sewers, the feverish cries of children during cholera season, the sight of countless men maimed on the job, all were part of day-to-day street life."[2] Bare-knuckle fighting was brutal, brutish, and, occasionally, deadly. But so was immigrant, working-class life.

In the two decades before the Civil War, interest in the prize ring outgrew its ethnic base. Part of the reason was that the sport had found a voice. The "penny press" redefined what news was fit to print. Beginning with Benjamin Day's *New York Sun* and James Gordon Bennett's *New York Herald* in the 1830s, newspaper editors discovered that there was an inexhaustible market for stories about murder, violence, mayhem, crime, and prostitution, along with sordid tales of alcoholism and drug addiction. "News," they concluded, was a malleable commodity, and as the stewards of the "news" they determined what it was and what it was not, altogether an enviable seat to occupy. Sex, violence, and drugs, especially if they were accompanied by eye-popping illustrations—sold newspapers. And prizefighting, surfeit with blood and violence, nicely fit into their updated definition of the news.

During the 1840s and especially the 1850s the penny press gave prizefighters a national audience. "Yankee" Sullivan, Tom Hyer, John Morrissey, and John C. Heenan—three of the four Irish or first-generation Irish American—received significant newspaper coverage during the years when hundreds of thousands of hungry potato-famine Irish were arriving on American shores. Their greatest fights were often against native-born Americans, a dramatic factor that would not be lost on later generations of promoters. A match that pitted a native American butcher against an Irish day laborer underscored undeniable American ethnic and working-class rivalries. The mid-century popularity of bare-knuckle boxing reached its pinnacle on the eve of the Civil War when American champion John C. "Benicia Boy" Heenan traveled to England to battle the British champion Tom Sayers.

The Heenan-Sayers fight occupied the attention of English-speakers on both sides of the Atlantic. Currier and Ives made a lithograph of the fighters, sporting magazines offered sage opinions about the combatants, and newspapers documented virtually every drop of sweat the two fighters shed during training. "If you go to the market," a reporter commented, "the odds are your butcher asks you which man you fancy, and if you want to bet on it. Your newsman smiles as he hands you your daily paper, and informs you that 'there is something new about the great fight in it this morning.' If you drop into Bryant's or Christy's in an evening, you are certain to hear some allusion to the Benicia Boy or Sir Thomas de Sayers that never fails to bring down the house."[3] The fight ended in a forty-two-round draw. Not long after the fight the Civil War began, and Americans no longer needed prizefighting to satisfy their demand for violent action.

Prizefighting fell on hard times after the Heenan-Sayers match, evolving from working-class sport to criminal-class activity. Fixed fights, gang violence, and unruly spectacles were so much the order of the day that even the penny press lost interest. With the likes of Jesse James and Billy the Kid to report on, journalists saw no reason to follow an arcane, dying sport in which the new golden rule was that the person with a Colt revolver makes the rules. When journalists did write about boxing they generally waxed eloquently about the golden age of the ring, a time that was different and infinitely better than their own ragged, corrupt era. For many Americans, prizefighting was a "relic of barbarism," an activity that smacked of bear-baiting and bull-baiting, with no place in a civilized society.

Then, in the 1880s, John L. Sullivan, the Boston Strong Boy, swaggered onto the pugilistic stage, changing suddenly and dramatically the fortunes of the sport. A son of potato-famine immigrants, Sullivan was born in 1856 in the Boston suburb of Roxbury. His father was a day laborer, and John L. appeared set to follow in his father's muddy shoes, scraping a living by performing backbreaking manual labor during the day, then tying one on and getting into fights at night. It soon became apparent that he was a better fighter than worker, though in the late 1870s, when Sullivan began fighting for stakes, there was not much money to be made in either endeavor. Still, as a prizefighter he was showered with the cheers and respect of his peers, rewarded in ways that satisfied his enormous ego and defused his restless, violent energy.

By 1880, the year of Sullivan's first important match, prizefighting was in transition. The bare-knuckle, fight-to-the-finish London Prize Ring Rules were being replaced by the Queensberry Rules, named after their author, Henry Sholto Douglas, the eighth Marquis of Queensberry. Written in 1866, the Queensberry Rules mandated three-minute rounds with a minute rest between rounds, a knockout if a felled fighter could not regain his feet in ten seconds, and gloves for fighters. The rules barred all wrestling, grappling, and throwing maneuvers, and permitted matches to be contested as fights to the finish or for a predetermined number of rounds. Essentially the same rules that are in effect today, the Queensberry Rules appeared, at least on the surface, to promote a sport that would be less violent, and certainly less bloody, than traditional bare-knuckle prizefighting.

Sullivan preferred the new code, but on rare, important occasions he fought under the old London Prize Ring Rules. That was exactly what he did on February 7, 1882, when he battled Paddy Ryan for the heavyweight championship. In a short, brutal nine-round battle, Sullivan pounded Ryan into submission. After the fight, Ryan confessed, "I never faced a man who could hit as hard. I don't believe there is another man like him in the country. . . . Any man that Sullivan can hit, he can whip."[4] Trying to give reporters a sense of Sullivan's hitting power, he claimed, "When Sullivan struck me, I thought that a telegraph pole had been shoved against me endways."[5] The fight was sponsored by Richard Kyle Fox's *National Police Gazette,* the leading prizefighting periodical, and it was billed as the "championship of the world," the first use of that designation in boxing. The title "champion of the world" suited Sullivan just fine, and he immediately proceeded to transform it into a cash cow.

John L. took the title on the road. During his Grand Tour of 1883–84 he visited twenty-six (of thirty-eight) states, five territories, the District of Columbia, and British Columbia. Traveling to major cities and smaller hamlets, his band of boxers staged demonstrations of the "manly art of self-defense." To prove his own superiority, Sullivan offered a handsome reward to anyone who lasted four rounds with him. Few tried, none succeeded. For millions of Americans, Sullivan was Homeric, a cross between Hercules and Paul Bunyan. He was personable and friendly when he was not drunk, and frightful and awe-inspiring when he was. But drunk or sober, he was always the "Great John L."

Sullivan made a small fortune on his Grand Tour, certainly near $90,000 (perhaps as much as several million 2010 dollars). As a point of comparison, the president of the United States made $25,000 a year, a successful New York City lawyer $50,000, and a university professor $2,500. No professional athlete of the era made anywhere near Sullivan's income. As his biographer accurately claimed, "His name, his face, and his deeds were now known throughout the land."[6] Saloon keepers placed his picture above their bars, journalists wrote hundreds of lurid stories about his exploits, and his image regularly appeared on the cover or in the pages of the *National Police Gazette*. He was America's public bad boy—a frequently drunken, brawling spectacle who, nonetheless, captured the hearts of millions of his fellow citizens. Even his standard barroom boast—"My name's John L. Sullivan and I can lick any son-of-a-bitch alive"—seemed more a touching affectation than anything sinister. Such popular songs as "Let Me Shake the Hand That Shook the Hand of Sullivan" attested to his grip on the public's imagination.

In late 1887 Sullivan took his traveling boxing tour to Great Britain, where he was greeted with the same enthusiasm as in the United States. He conformed to British stereotypes of the American—big, boisterous, and as open as the American continent—and was an astonishing success. On one cold, foggy December day he even breakfasted with the elite Scots Guards, followed by an audience with Edward, Prince of Wales. Edward quizzed Sullivan about several of his fights, and the son of Irish immigrants asked the future king of England when was the last time he had had a fistic go. The two exchanged views on one thing or another, and then the American fighter put on an exhibition of his craft. According to some accounts, when the two exchanged goodbyes, Sullivan added, "If you ever come to Boston, be sure to look me up. I'll see that you're treated right."[7] The story might be apocryphal, but given the fighter's casual, democratic nature, it might just be true. King or commoner, Sullivan treated every man as an equal, none as a superior.

By the end of Sullivan's British tour his legend seemed complete. And it would have been for a run-of-the-mill icon, but there was never anything ordinary about John L. Overweight, out of shape, road weary, and drunk much of the time, he was ready to take on another challenge. Fox's *National Police Gazette* considered Sullivan ancient history and had begun touting Jake Kilrain as the new "champion of the world." Sullivan took umbrage. A large panel in the center of his championship belt, given to him by his Boston backers and supporters, bore the legend, "Presented to the Champion of Champions, John L. Sullivan, by the Citizens of the United States," and that was how he regarded himself. He was America's champion, the citizens' champion, something akin to the president of pugilism, the first among equals. Even more exaltedly, he was the Emperor of Masculinity. He had a word for Fox's champion, and it was not suitable for the era of the genteel literary tradition. Even in his condition, he was ready once again to toe the line.

An epic battle followed, one that poet Vachel Lindsay appropriated to frame his poem about fin de siècle America:

> When I was nine years old, in 1889,
> I sent my love a lacy Valentine.
> Suffering boys were dressed like Fauntleroys,
> While Judge and Puck in giant humor vied.
> The Gibson Girl came shining like a bride
> To spoil the cult of Tennyson's Elaine.
> Louisa Alcott was my gentle guide . . .
> Then . . .
> I heard a battle trumpet sound.
> Nigh New Orleans
> Upon an emerald plain
> John L. Sullivan
> The strong boy
> Of Boston
> Fought seventy-five rounds with Jake Kilrain.[8]

And what a seventy-five rounds it was! Because bare-knuckle prize-fighting was illegal in every state in the Union, promoters arranged to hold the contest on a rural patch of turf in Mississippi owned by Charles Rich, a local timber baron. Participants and spectators made the hundred-mile trip from New Orleans to Richburg in trains, and at 10:13, on the morning of July 8, with the sun already hot in the sky, Sullivan and Kilrain toed the line for what would turn out to be the last bare-knuckle heavyweight championship fight in history.[9]

Kilrain ended the first round in fifteen seconds when he threw Sullivan to the turf, landing hard on his opponent. He also scored first blood—always a major betting point—in the sixth with a right to the champion's ear. With blood streaming down his neck, Sullivan "grinned savagely," then quickly responded, dazing and flooring Kilrain with a hard shot. The fight was now barely twenty minutes old, but Kilrain was hurt and in danger of losing. He responded by going on the defensive, circling away from Sullivan's powerful right, often going down without being hit or thrown, trying to prolong the fight. Sullivan had trained hard for the match, and he looked in peak condition, but as the temperature rose to over one hundred degrees and humidity rolled in from the Gulf Coast, no one knew how long he could last under the scorching Mississippi sun.

And so the fight dragged on, round after round. In the stands, freshly built of pinewood from Rich's sawmill, spectators' pants stuck to the bubbling pitch. The backs and chests of both Irish American fighters burned and blistered. Everyone sucked in hot mouthfuls of air that seemed filtered through a blast furnace. Against all odds the combatants continued, two determined athletes locked in a fight to the finish, one hurt but patient, the other pressing the attack but impatient.

Sullivan tried to goad Kilrain into a slugfest. "You're a champion, eh? A champion of what?" he yelled, his dark eyes seeming to some "almost wild." Kilrain said nothing. Spectators grumbled and jeered at the challenger's delaying tactics. Kilrain said nothing. Sullivan's punches cut and bruised Kilrain's face and caused red blotches on his stomach, chest, sides, and arms. And still Kilrain said nothing. He fought to survive, hoping something would alter the course of the match. Ten rounds, fifteen, twenty, twenty-five, thirty. Sullivan began to tire. His trainer asked how long *he* could keep going: "I can stay here until daybreak tomorrow," he promised.

By the fortieth round, Kilrain's seconds had to lift him out of his corner stool and help him to the scratch. He was fighting on guts and hope. Then, in the forty-fourth round, Sullivan began to vomit uncontrollably. Some people in the crowd believed that he had been drinking an elixir of alcohol and tea to bolster his strength, and a wag commented, "Don't worry, John L. is just getting rid of the tea." Seeing an opening, Mike Donovan in Kilrain's corner implored his man to attack, but the fighter refused, saying,

"No, I won't, Mike; no I won't . . . John, I won't hit you while you are vomiting." Instead he asked the champion, "Will you draw the fight?" "No, you loafer," Sullivan yelled back, and rushed his opponent.

Sullivan recovered. Kilrain lingered. Fifty rounds, fifty-five, sixty, sixty-five, seventy. Blood, mud, sweat, and blisters from the sun covered both men. Kilrain could not outfight Sullivan, and it was now clear that he could not outlast him either. In the seventy-fifth round Sullivan punched Kilrain at will, knocking him down, and sending him wandering dazed along the ropes. One of the challenger's corner men asked Sullivan if he would give Jake a thousand dollars to give up. Although the fight was strictly winner-take-all, Sullivan agreed. But his backers overruled his generosity. "That settles it then," the champion said, "we'll fight." Then Mike Donovan, Kilrain's manager, threw in the sponge. "I will not be a party to manslaughter," he said. The fight was over—a fight that set a standard for tenacity and fortitude well into the era of Joe Louis.

Spectators at the match knew with a certainty absolute that they had witnessed an epic moment. Greedily grabbing anything that might by even the most lenient definition be considered a souvenir, they bought what they could and scavenged everything else. The soft hat Sullivan ritualistically threw into the ring at the start of the proceedings went for fifty dollars, the buckets that held ice water twenty-five dollars. Slivers of the pine ring post that had once flown Sullivan's colors sold for five dollars each. They were the fistic equivalent of pieces of the True Cross.

Across the country the press treated the fight like an American version of the set-to between Achilles and Hector outside the walls of Troy. The "rage of Achilles," his mixture of bluster, pride, and boyishness, was not a far stretch from the Great John L.'s. Reporters covering the White House received requests from the inside for news of the fight. Thousands of curious people in cities across the country crowded outside telegraph offices waiting for bulletins of the outcome. Even the *New York Times*, the voice of bourgeoisie sensibility, gave the fight front-page coverage under the headline "THE BIGGER BRUTE WON."[10]

Sullivan was now the unrivaled emperor of American popular culture. In the ring, on tours, and on the stage, he was cheered, admired, and adored. It did not matter that he put on weight or made drunken spectacles of himself. With no worlds left to conquer, he accepted a champion's final act. On September 7, 1892, a decade after defeating Paddy Ryan for the title, he lost the belt in New Orleans to James J. Corbett, a younger, faster, better-conditioned, and immensely talented fighter. It was a legally staged fight, contested under the Marquis of Queensberry rules. Years of steady drinking and overeating had left John L. in no condition to fight at a championship caliber. It was clear from the start that he would lose. The end came in the twenty-first round of the contest. Sullivan, fighting as he always did by pressing forward, was powerless to catch Corbett and defenseless against his opponent's punishing punches. Finally, Corbett trapped Sullivan in a corner, feinted, and landed a perfectly timed right to the jaw. Sullivan dropped to his knees, but slowly pulled himself up to his feet and stood proud, defenseless, and doomed. Corbett moved in, took aim, and ended Sullivan's reign as champion.

Then the unexpected happened. The fight was over, the referee had counted John L. out, and his corner men had revived him as best they could. But instead of staying put in his corner, he stumbled to the ropes and gripped a ring post, holding up his right hand and signaling the spectators to quiet down. "Gentlemen—gentlemen," he began, speaking in exhausted, halting breaths. "I have something to say. All I have to say is that I came into the ring once too often—and if I had to get licked I'm glad I was licked by an American. I remain your warm and personal friend, John L. Sullivan."[11]

To be sure, Sullivan was a reflection of the swaggering, clanging, combative late nineteenth century. He was all of its strengths and contradictions. "He was a hero and a brute," wrote Elliott Gorn, "a bon vivant and a drunk, a lover of life and a reckless barbarian. . . . He cut through all restraints, acted rather than contemplated, and paid little regard to the morality or immorality of his behavior. He was totally self-indulgent, even in acts of generosity, totally a hedonist consuming the good things around him and beckoning others to do the same."[12]

For the sport of boxing, Sullivan was the critical transitional fighter. But his cultural orbit reached well beyond his own sport. For men of his times and later, he was an irresistible icon of strength and masculinity. When Theodore Dreiser was a young journalist he met Sullivan, and the image stuck with him the remainder of his life. "And then John L. Sullivan, raw, red-faced, big-fisted, broad-shouldered, drunken, with gaudy waistcoat and tie, and rings and pins set with enormous diamonds and rubies— what an impression he made! Surrounded by local sports and politicians of the most rubicund and degraded character. . . . Cigar boxes, champagne buckets, decanters, beer bottles, overcoats, collars and shirts littered the floor, and lolling back in the midst of it all in ease and splendor his very great self, a sort of prize-fighting J. P. Morgan." Dreiser's attempt to interview Sullivan about such subjects as his plans and the value of exercise drew only rich, friendly laughs from the former champion. "Write any damned thing yuh please, young fella, and say that John L. Sullivan said so. That's good enough for me. If they don't believe it, bring it back here and I'll sign it for yuh. But I know it'll be all right, and I won't stop to read it neither." That was enough for Dreiser, who said he "would have written anything [Sullivan] asked me to write." "I adored him," he concluded.[13]

Millions of Americans felt the same way. For American popular culture, Sullivan pioneered the landscape of twentieth-century celebrity culture. For men of his time, he was a flag-waver, a champion of the common man, and the very expression of what an American was. He was all that—and more.

Sullivan was always Sullivan, of course, but his overgrown personality still does not explain why he became *the* central male icon of the late nineteenth century. What was it about America that was so receptive to John L.'s charms, such as they were, and was not at all receptive to Paddy Ryan or Joe Goss, the man Ryan knocked out for the title? Americans' notice of Sullivan did not take place in a cultural vacuum. Throughout the country a more spirited and violent popular culture was taking shape. Americans could hear it in the marches of John Philip Sousa, see it in the violent clash of bodies on college gridirons, and read it in the sudden explosion of books about Napoleon. Sullivan fought during a national moment that Theodore Roosevelt labeled the "strenuous age," a period of history that witnessed the swelling of Anglo-Saxon chauvinism, deadly confrontations between labor and management, and, at the end of the 1890s, war between the United States and Spain. The entire mise-en-scène of the age helps to explain the importance of Sullivan.

But most of the outward manifestations of cultural change—and this included John L. Sullivan—originated in a seismic shift in what it meant to be a man. Put simply, notions of masculinity were being reformulated. Although sex is biologically determined, gender is a complex social construction. Ideas of "manliness" and "masculinity" are never fixed absolutes; they are fluid and changing. During the eighteenth century, for example, a man's identity was inseparable from his place in society. He was the head of a household and a part of a community, expected to act with decorum and restraint, interacting with his peers in a mild-mannered, soft-spoken, courteous, and pleasant manner. That behavior, so well enshrined in the char-

acter and actions of George Washington or Thomas Jefferson, was the outward expression of manliness.

In the nineteenth century, as a new construction separated the public
and private spheres of men and women, manliness took a slightly different
shape. A man was more defined by his position in the workplace. To a large
extent, a "man" was defined as the opposite of a "boy." Boys were wild and
careless, "primitive spirits" full of "animal spirits." They were immature,
impulsive, and undependable. Men were different; they controlled their
baser urges and met their responsibilities. The ideal mid-Victorian man
had a certain softness, a willingness to sentimentally express his deepest
feelings, and a firm commitment to his religious faith. He was not a bragger
and a bruiser, a swaggerer and boozer ready to outdrink and outfight the
man standing next to him at the bar of a saloon. Rather, he was the man
who could write to another man confessing his brotherly love, play an
active role in a religiously based reform society, and read to his children
each night as they sat in the parlor.

Toward the end of the century there was a growing sense, dimly felt at
first but gaining strength with each year, that something was dreadfully
wrong with American men. They had grown weak and dispirited. Countless
reports of male "neurasthenia," the weakening or loss of the essential "nerve
force," and nervous collapse appeared in newspapers and magazines. The
weekly attendance at local reform societies' meetings, at gatherings of various charitable groups, and at church services; the constant reading of social-
improvement pamphlets and religious tracts; the talk, talk, talk of a better
world and a better mankind and "What would Jesus do?"—it was all culmi-
nating with the feminization of men. The generation of bold, adventurous,
brave, virile pioneers who had cleared the path west had been replaced by a
new generation of men, flat-chested, thin-armed, and pencil-necked.

What American men needed was a massive transfusion of strength and
force. In his influential essay "The Strenuous Life," Theodore Roosevelt
decried the "soft spirit of the cloistered life"—a "life of slothful ease"—
and challenged American men to "boldly face the life of strife . . . for
it is only through strife, through hard and dangerous endeavor, that we
shall ultimately win the goal of true national greatness."[14] Roosevelt's sentiment was echoed by bodybuilder Bernarr Macfadden, who in the first
issue of his magazine *Physical Culture* (1899) proclaimed his slogan:
"Weakness Is a Crime."

The new manliness not only rejected the soft, comfortable life, it also jettisoned anything that smacked of femininity. Temperance reform movements, domesticity, Christianity, women, and language itself had a circumscribed place in the new realm of masculinity. A new ideal type, epitomized by the emerging protagonist of western novels, was a man unencumbered —no home, no wife, no church, just a gun and a horse. Unlike a lawyer or a politician, his power came not from the manipulation of language but from the absence of language. He spoke the new language of men, the sparse vocabulary that would become the hallmark of Jack London, Ernest Hemingway, and Norman Mailer. He was silent, strong, independent, and deadly, familiar with saloons, prostitutes, animals, and firearms, but a world away from sentimental expressions of love or abstract debates. What mattered was what he did. Like Sullivan, he was defined by his physical feats.

It was to this new sensibility that John L. Sullivan and prizefighting appealed. Charles Dana of the *New York Sun* had only to look at Sullivan to realize the future of American manhood was safe. "A wonderful specimen is this Sullivan," he bubbled. "He dines like Gargantua. He drinks like Gambrinus. He has the strength of Samson, and the fighting talent of Achilles. When he moves it is with a child's ease, and he hits with a giant's force. . . . If any one thinks that the physique of the human race is degenerating, let him consider the great John L. He should be reassured."[15]

Unintentionally, Dana captured part of Sullivan's attraction. The fighter was childlike. Modern masculinity worshipped the boy's "animal spirit" and impulsive behavior. As Roosevelt wrote in his autobiography, "Powerful, vigorous men of strong animal development must have some way in which their animal spirits can find vent."[16] A man was no longer the opposite of a boy; he needed to release the elemental boy inside of him. Here, again, Sullivan was the cultural yardstick. He was the "Boston Strong Boy," the "Boston Boy," or just the "Boy." To be a boy in a man's body, to be in the prize ring with John L. Sullivan or perhaps alone on an Arizona mesa, riding on the frontier of bare-chested American masculinity—that's what it meant to be a man in the age of TR and John L. Explaining why a man of fifty-five years, a former president of the United States and a father of six children, would want to chuck it all and risk his life on a dangerous jungle trip to trace the River of Doubt's route to the Amazon, Roosevelt wrote, "I had to go. It was my last chance to be a boy."[17] Roosevelt admired the qualities that made a great boxer, football player, cowboy, and soldier. He had tried his hand at each. But always, he just wanted to be "one of the boys." His friend John L. Sullivan would have understood—and so would millions of other American men.

Under the reign of Sullivan, then, the heavyweight championship became the symbol of the toughest man/boy in the world, a symbol that rested comfortably on the brow of an American. At a moment when Social Darwinism was the final word of the pecking order of ethnic groups, when such phrases as "survival of the fittest" and the "struggle for survival" were attached to just about every aspect of life, this was a significant achievement. Early in Sullivan's career an editor for the jingoistic *New York Sun* labeled him the "most phenomenal production of the prize ring that has been evoluted during the nineteenth century."[18] And during his years as champion a rough syllogism took shape: Sullivan is the greatest fighter in the world; Sullivan is an America; ergo, America is the greatest country in the world. Nor did this notion die with the end of Sullivan's reign. In the late 1960s, Black Panther leader Eldridge Cleaver wrote, "The boxing ring is the ultimate focus of masculinity in America, the two-fisted testing ground of manhood, and the heavyweight champion, as a symbol, is the real Mr. America."[19]

Freighting the title with such cultural weight, however, created problems. As long as the heavyweight champion was an American—a white American—the syllogism provided endless opportunities for international and racial bragging rights. But what if a non–Anglo Saxon foreigner captured the crown? Or even worse for millions of white Americans, what if a black American won the title? During Sullivan's years as champion there were several outstanding black heavyweight boxers, including the great Australian champion Peter Jackson, who had once fought a sixty-one-round draw with Jim Corbett. Sullivan, in his usual fashion, attacked the issue head-on. In 1892 he issued a general challenge to fight for a purse of $25,000 and a side bet of $10,000. He preferred to fight a foreign opponent, he said, "as I would rather whip them than any of my own countrymen." But he made one exception: "In this challenge I include all fighters—first come, first served—who are white. I will not fight a negro. I never have and never shall."[20]

In one stroke, Sullivan banned black boxers from the empire of masculinity. He set a precedent—Jim Crowing the most important athletic title at a time when "separate but equal" was becoming the law of the land. The heavyweight crown was too valuable a cultural artifact to risk in an interracial bout. The champions who followed Sullivan reinforced the barrier.

James J. Corbett, Robert Fitzsimmons, James J. Jeffries, Marvin Hart—each, even if they had fought blacks before they won the title, drew the color line once they were champion. The very best African American boxers of the late nineteenth and early twentieth centuries—such men as Peter Jackson, Joe Jeannette, Sam McVey, and especially Sam Langford—were simply erased from the title picture. They were the invisible fighters, there but not seen when it mattered, more often than not forced to fight each other because they could not get a decent payday against a white heavyweight. The legendary black Canadian boxer Langford, for instance, spent much of his brilliant career battling other black fighters for small purses. He fought Jeff Clark eleven times, Jim Barry twelve times, Jeannette fourteen times, McVey fifteen times, and Harry Wills twenty-three times. He fought more than three hundred matches and never saw a title shot. Sadly, by the 1940s he was penniless and blind.

The color line lasted until 1908, when titleholder Tommy Burns concluded that it had a price tag. By then the crown had lost its luster. Even after the change from the London Prize Ring Rules to the Queensberry Rules, Americans had not universally embraced professional boxing. The heavyweight champion, to be sure, was a national icon whose exploits in and out of the ring made news. Millions of Americans admired and respected the champion, and the finest journalists of the day often covered important fights. But professional boxing was still illegal in almost every state in the Union, and reformers clamored to outlaw it everywhere. Oddly, many reformers decried the money in prizefighting more than the brutality of the sport. That an uneducated, semi-skilled man could make thousands of dollars by pummeling another man struck reformers as socially unhealthy. Even Teddy Roosevelt agreed. Although he advocated boxing for boys and young men, boxed regularly while in the White House, and counted a few prizefighters "among his friends," he felt that the "enormous" amounts of money that professionals fought for "are a potent source of demoralization in themselves, while they are often so arranged as either to be a premium on crookedness or else to reward nearly as amply the man who fails as the man who succeeds."[21] His professional friends were not losers, and the idea of rewarding losing offended his sense of competition.

The money, the encouragement of gambling, and the association with drinking and prostitution—everything about prizefighting angered reformers. Whereas once the most important matches were staged in New Orleans and Coney Island, progressive legislation closed legal loopholes that permitted prizefighting there. In the early years of the new century prizefighting had swept west to cities like Los Angeles, San Francisco, and Colma in California; Reno and Goldfield in Nevada; and Las Vegas in New Mexico. It became a thoroughly western sport, a dusty gold-town competition between mostly westerners for the amusement of cowboys, ranchers, miners, and assorted western sports, pimps, prostitutes, and gamblers. Eastern journalists began to lose interest, and after the popular James J. Jeffries retired as the undefeated heavyweight champion in 1904, westerners started to ignore the sport as well. The title passed in an elimination contest to Marvin Hart, a fighter who possessed only one good eye and had difficulty even drawing yawns from the sporting public. When he lost the crown to Tommy Burns, no one cared. To make any money at all—and that was not very much—Burns packed his bags and sailed the high seas, defending his title against mediocre boxers in London, Dublin, Paris, Sydney, and Melbourne. Americans could not have cared less. The heavyweight crown had become a mere bagatelle.

That is, to everyone except Jack Johnson, a magnificently talented black boxer who had followed Burns almost the entire circumference of the globe in effort to get a title match. Repeatedly Burns had drawn the color line, but finally in the heat of Australia he named his price: $30,000. For that sum, and not a penny less, he would give a black man a crack at becoming the emperor of masculinity. An enterprising Australian promoter, Hugh D. "Huge Deal" McIntosh, arranged the money, persuaded Johnson to accept only $5,000, and set the match for Boxing Day, December 26, 1908. The Great John L., old and fat but still opinionated, admonished Burns, sniffing, "Shame on the money-mad champion! Shame on the man who upsets good American precedents because there are Dollars, Dollars, Dollars in it."[22] A journalist for the *Australian Star* was even more concerned, writing, "This battle may in the future be looked back upon as the first great battle of an inevitable race war."[23]

The fight took place in Sydney's Rushcutter's Bay in an arena freshly washed by a cool rain. It wasn't much of a fight. Johnson knocked down Burns in the first round and dominated completely until the referee stopped the fight in the fourteenth. By then, Burns was a battered mess. His eyes were bleeding and swollen, his jaw grossly misshaped, and his mouth bloody inside and out. Johnson later wrote that he had "forgotten more about boxing than Burns ever knew," and no one had reason to doubt his words.[24] Novelist Jack London, covering the fight for the *New York Herald,* reported,

"The fight, there was no fight. No Armenian massacre could compare with the hopeless slaughter that took place in the Sydney stadium today."[25] For London, it was a contest between a "colossus and a toy automaton," between a "playful Ethiopian and a small and futile white man," between a "grown man and a naughty child."

Something more than mere victory drove Johnson. He was a black man lashing out at the thousands of racial insults and humiliations that he had absorbed, affirming his manhood and his superiority and, for want of a better word, his existence. He could have ended the fight earlier, but he wanted to punish and humiliate Burns. Sometimes he hit his white opponent and physically prevented him from falling, holding him up so that he could continue the punishment. Constantly he taunted Burns. Speaking audibly but with his soft, southern accent, he asked, "Poor little Tommy, who told you you were a fighter?" Or, "Poor, poor Tommy. Who taught you to hit? Your mother? You a woman?" Or, referring to Burns' wife, "Poor little boy, Jewel won't know you when she gets you back from the fight."[26] Always Burns was "little Tommy," "little boy," or "Tommy Boy." Johnson repeatedly compared Burns to a woman, emasculating insults that carried as much sting as his blows. For a time Burns attempted to respond in kind, spitting out racial invectives with mouthfuls of his own blood. But as the fight wore on, Burns grew quiet, conserving his energy for survival.

When it ended, thousands of spectators silently exited the stadium. A fight that had been consciously and purposefully promoted as a clash for racial supremacy had ended with the raising of a black man's gloved fist. The crown worn by Sullivan, Corbett, and Jeffries was now on the head of Jack Johnson. Resorting to doggerel, a reporter for the *Daily Telegraph* concluded:

> And yet for all we know and feel,
> For Christ and Shakespeare, knowledge, love,
> We watch a white man bleeding reel,
> We cheer a black with bloodied glove.[27]

But the cheers for Johnson were few. Many Australian reporters portrayed Johnson as a black beast, a shave-headed serpent, an apocalyptic Antichrist extinguishing the light of civilization. Much of the racial heat was not felt—not yet, anyway—in the United States. The American black press celebrated the news. "No event in forty years has given more satisfaction to the colored people of this country than has the signal victory of Jack

Johnson," wrote a reporter for the *Richmond Planet*.[28] The mainstream white press adopted a cautious, wait-and-see position. The general line was that Johnson had not defeated the real champion. Jim Jeffries, though in peaceful retirement and having ballooned to three hundred pounds, was the legitimate titleholder. Until Johnson defeated him he was not the true champion.

Jack London undoubtedly spoke for millions of whites when he asserted, "Personally, I was for Burns all the way. He was a white man and so am I. Naturally, I wanted to see the white man win."[29] Watching the fight he witnessed Johnson's superior performance, accepting fully that the best man won. But he was haunted by Johnson's behavior in the ring, and especially the fighter's gold-tooth smile as he physically beat and verbally assaulted Burns. "But one thing remains," London wrote from Sydney. "Jeffries must emerge from his alfalfa farm and remove that smile from Johnson's face. Jeff, it's up to you."[30]

Suddenly there was a revival of curiosity for a sport Americans had forgotten, a down-on-its-luck, punch-drunk, left-for-dead, relic-of-barbarism sport. Jack Johnson had more than captured their attention; the black fighter had gotten under Americans' skin. Why? What was it about this thirty-year-old, Texas-born son of former slaves that caused such a ruckus? During the next seven years Johnson served as the national racial lightning rod, channeling white America's fears, anxieties, and hatreds into his soul.

"Well, you see, Jack Johnson didn't know his place," a white southerner explained. "See, Johnson was a pure individual. He did everything exactly the way he wanted to. I don't think it ever crossed his mind that he should be anybody else's version of Jack Johnson," a black northerner speculated.[31] What was the proper place of African Americans? That was at the nub of the public debate over Johnson. Americans were obsessed by the debate. It echoed in the editorials in northern and southern newspapers about the "race issue," lingered in the halls of the Capitol where congressmen railed about the "Negro problem," and hung like strange fruit on the trees of the nation beside the hundreds of blacks who were lynched. Booker T. Washington and W. E. B. DuBois addressed it, as did Theodore Roosevelt and Woodrow Wilson. It was the eight-hundred-pound gorilla at the Fourth of July celebrations.

As heavyweight champion, the emperor of masculinity, Johnson insisted on his rightful share of privileges. Like John L. Sullivan, he enjoyed the high life. He had his front teeth capped in gold, wore diamond rings and stickpins, drank champagne and brandy, traveled with fast company, and consorted with scores of women. He was a recognized and accepted "sport"—a fraternity that included certain athletes, gamblers, confidence men, pimps, and other assorted men open for some action and a romp. The sporting ideal involved living fast and walking slow, winning bets and staying out of jail. It was a tightrope life for most, and for a black man it was more like a life on a razor's edge.

Especially where white women were concerned. Nothing—not the gold teeth, diamond rings, champagne, or even victories in the ring—enraged white Americans more than Johnson's choice of women. To be sure, most of his companions were prostitutes—boxers had a long, rich history of involvement with "working women." It was natural. Fighters were a peripatetic breed, traveling about on the rails, living in shabby hotel rooms and dingy training camps, and existing outside the margins of acceptable society. A boxer and a prostitute were the two sides of the same coin. Emerging out of poverty, scraping a livelihood from their bodies, and ultimately arriving at sad ends, the arc of their lives was similar. Johnson, however, took more risks than most other African American boxers and sports. Just as he did in the ring, he crossed the color line.

His choice was a bold assertion of his masculinity. As was the case with John L. Sullivan, evolving notions of manliness gave meaning to Johnson's actions. It is not to say that they expressed manliness in the same ways. Although both drank heavily, boasted frequently, and disdained marriage vows, they differed on other points. Sullivan's and Roosevelt's readiness to give expression to their "animal spirits" and embrace of the idea of being "one of the boys" were not part of the African American sense of masculinity. For a people a generation removed from chattel slavery, and still regarded by many whites as some sort of "incipient species," any talk of animal spirits was objectionable foolishness. And the mere word "boy"—a rebuke that every black male heard thousands of times during his life— stung like the tip of a whip.

Nor did the new guttural vocabulary of the inarticulate man hold the same attraction for Johnson as it did for many white fighters of the time. Although his formal education was meager, he took pride in his self-education. He read Milton and Shakespeare, frequently quoting a line or two during conversations with reporters; he enjoyed listening to opera, and if asked he would accompany the music on the bass viol; he even applied for and was granted several patents, one for a specialized automobile wrench and the other for a "theft-preventing device for vehicles."[32] When in the mood, Johnson was a delightful and voluble conversationalist who dotted his monologues with references to history, literature, music, art, and his own philosophy on life. Although differing dramatically on many points with Booker T. Washington and W. E. B. DuBois, he agreed with the two prominent black spokesmen that education, intellectual growth, and verbal dexterity were essential to advancement.

Even the folklore that mushroomed around Johnson's life emphasized his Brer Rabbit ingenuity. One tale has Johnson speeding in an expensive roadster through some backwater, dusty, red clay section of the Jim Crow South. A local sheriff pulls him over and explains, "You know you were speeding, boy? Goin' way too fast." Johnson acknowledges the fact. "Well," the sheriff says after glancing at the make of the car and the fighter's fine, costly clothes, "That's gonna cost you fifty dollars, boy." Without looking up, Johnson pulls out from his pocket a thick, heavyweight champion's roll of cash, peels off a hundred dollar bill, and hands it to the sheriff. "I can't change that big a bill," he says. "Keep the change," Johnson replies. "I'm coming back same way I went through." In another tale Johnson attempts to check into a Jim Crow hotel located in some small, cracker town. Johnson asks for a room and the desk clerk, hardly raising his eyes, says, "We don't serve your kind, boy." Johnson asks again, and receives the same answer. He asks a third time and the desk clerk angrily retorts, "You heard me, boy, we don't serve your kind." Johnson rolls back his head, laughing, and replies, "Oh, there's a misunderstanding. The room isn't for me. It's for my wife. She's one of your kind."[33]

These tales are not of heavyweight power but of lightweight adaptability, featuring Johnson's intelligence and verbal skills rather than his physical ones. The stories underscore why white Americans considered the champion a threat. They express, implicitly, that this black man can dominate anyone physically *and* mentally. They showcase someone who was his own man, one who drove too fast, spoke his mind, and selected companions to suit his desires. "I am not a slave," Johnson remarked, "and I have the right to choose who my mate shall be without the dictation of any man. I have eyes and I have a heart, and when they fail to tell me who I shall have as mine, I want to be put in a lunatic asylum."[34]

The more white Americans learned about Johnson the more they itched with discomfort. No sooner was he back in the United States than boxing managers and promoters began a search for a "White Hope" who could deliver the championship from his black hands. They scoured the country. Journalist John Lardner wrote that "well-muscled white boys more than six feet two inches were not safe out of their mother's sight."[35] Some carried their search across the Atlantic. Others ventured across the Pacific. Walter "Good-Time Charlie" Friedman, a resourceful talent scout, hunted for a White Hope among Chinese peasants. And White Hopes they discovered. Some were giants—Jim Coffrey, the Roscommon Giant; Carl Morris, the Sapulpa Giant; Fred Fulton, the Giant of the North; and, eventually, Jess Willard, the Pottawatomie Giant. Others were smaller but billed as terribly ferocious. But in the early years of the search, while Johnson was still in his prime, none of the Hopes panned out. In 1909 the champion dispatched a series of them in short order.

Johnson's early victories occurred during white America's "ace-in-the-hole" period. Out West, baling alfalfa—or whatever one did with alfalfa, most journalists were uncertain—was Jim Jeffries, the retired but still undefeated former champion, a grizzly of a man said to pack a punch harder than even the Great John L.'s and to be able to withstand a whack from a poleax. Jack London had called on Jeffries to redeem his race, and so had thousands of other journalists and citizens who wrote about or penned letters to the retired fighter. At first Jeffries refused to budge from his retired status, but he turned out to be a poor businessman. He opened a saloon and launched a fight club. Both went bust, leaving him with unpaid bills. Fighting, it turned out, was the only business he really knew.

Promoter George Lewis "Tex" Rickard put together a package that Jeffries could not resist. He guaranteed the fighters $101,000 and two-thirds of the movie rights to meet in the ring on Independence Day, July 4, 1910. The winner would receive two-thirds, the loser one-third. It was a staggeringly high amount of money, higher than had ever been offered two athletes. Although journalists choked over the money, Jeffries and Johnson quickly signed the contracts. The fight was set for San Francisco, but it aroused a firestorm of political protest in California, forcing Governor J. N. Gillett to push the match out of his state. Without missing a beat, Rickard moved the fight to Reno, a town so soaked in sin that the staging of a prizefight hardly seemed to make a difference. In fact, fighting appeared a fitting companion for the town's divorce, gambling, and prostitution businesses.

Rickard promoted the fight as a racial reckoning. And reporters covered it that way. It was a fight in which people, white and black, felt invested. Whites worried about the implications of the fight. "If the black man wins," a *New York Times* editorialist warned, "thousands and thousands of his ignorant brothers will misinterpret his victory as justifying claims to much more than mere physical equality with their white neighbors."[36] Even in Great Britain, where race and empire had long mingled uncomfortably, the idea of the fight sounded alarms. "It is not so much a matter of racial pride as one of racial existence which urges us so ardently to desire [Jeffries'] triumph," commented an editor of a British boxing magazine. The writer knew that the "coloured races outnumber the whites," and that Japan's victory over Russia in 1905 and Johnson's defeat of Burns in 1908 had sent out signals that the position of whites around the world was not secure. "Does anyone imagine for a moment that Johnson's success is without political influence," he continued, "an influence which has only been checked from having full vent by the personality of Jim Jeffries? Jeff may smash Johnson when they meet . . . and by so doing restore us to something like our old position. We shall never quite regain it, because the recollection of our temporary deposition will always remain to inspire the coloured peoples with hope. While if, after all, Johnson should smash Jeffries—But the thought is too awful to contemplate."[37]

An edgy anticipation marked the Fourth of July celebrations. America's attention leaned toward the sun-baked ring in Reno where thousands of spectators had crowded into a hastily built arena. The sky was crystalline in the desert air, Reno a perfect jewel edged by mountains. Inside the arena a band played "Just Before the Battle, Mother," "All Coons Look Alike to Me," "America," and "Dixie." Like the music, the mood of the spectators was a cross between a traditional Independence Day festival and a Ku Klux Klan gathering. As flags fluttered and racial epithets flew, the fighters climbed between the ropes and prepared to settle the question foremost on everyone's mind.

The fight started at 2:46, and by 3:00 or so it had already settled into a pattern. Perhaps, as Jeffries said later, "I couldn't come back."[38] Perhaps he was too old, had shed too much weight too quickly, or no longer had the reflexes to exploit openings and avoid danger. Perhaps he was just facing a better fighter, one whom he could not have beaten on his best day. Whatever the case, Jeffries could not sustain an offense or mount much of a defense. Patiently, Johnson wore him down, cutting and nearly closing his eyes, breaking his nose, and draining his energy. By round ten the thick pelt of hair that covered Jeffries' body was matted with his own blood. His corner man did not even attempt to wash it off. The ring was stained with blood, and the white shirts of spectators at ringside had red spots. In the fifteenth round, Johnson cut loose. Jeffries, who had never been knocked off his feet, went down one, two, three times. Finally, to save the former champion from the humiliation of a knockout, his manager threw in the towel. The Battle of the Century, as it had been billed, was over. But the fighting wasn't.

Telegraph operators in Reno tapped out the fight's outcome immediately, communicating to every corner of the country the news of Johnson's victory. Black Americans rejoiced. In the black section of Chicago, they banged pots, gave thanks, and chanted, "Jack, Jack, J-A-J! Jack, Jack, J-A-J!"[39] In African American saloons in New York and Boston patrons drank champagne on the house. They danced in the streets in Cincinnati and St. Louis. Bubbling celebrations of victory led some black journalists to discuss the meaning of the fight. The fight demonstrated, wrote an editor for the *Baltimore Times,* that "any negro anywhere may reach eminence in peaceful ways by using the Johnson method in his particular trade or calling."[40] Soon black voices sang a new ballad:

> Amaze an' Grace, how sweet it sounds,
> Jack Johnson knocked Jim Jeffries down.
> Jim Jeffries jumped up an' hit Jack on the chin,
> An' then Jack knocked him down again.

> The Yankees hold the play,
> The White man pull the trigger;
> But it makes no difference what the white man say:
> The world champion's still a nigger."[41]

For the most part the white man did hold the trigger, and even before evening became night he began to squeeze it. There was a long tradition of working-class drinking, gunplay, and disorder on Independence Day, and the news of Johnson's victory added another combustible element to the mix. The results were predictable. In Uvalda, Georgia, a gang of whites attacked a camp of black construction workers, killing three and wounding five. In Houston, a black man openly celebrated Johnson's victory, enraging a white man who "slashed his throat from ear to ear." In New York City a black shouted, "We blacks put one over on you whites, and we're going to do more." A white mob stopped just short of lynching him for his bold exhibition of free speech. And so it continued until dawn. Whites killed two blacks in Little Rock; white assailants killed three blacks in Shreveport, Louisiana; roving white sailors attacked scores of innocent blacks in Norfolk, Virginia; thirty people were injured in a race riot in Pueblo, Colorado. In every section of the country, in big cities and hamlets, pitched battles occurred. Although a number of whites were injured, in far more cases blacks were shot, stabbed, and lynched. Interracial violence resulted in the deaths of at least twenty black Americans. In the reform magazine *Independent*, an editor wrote, "Like the *Hexenlehrling* these apostles of savagery have unchained the demons of disorder whom they are powerless to lay."[42]

Never before had a sporting contest—or any other event—unleashed such powerful waves of hate and violence, and not until the assassination of Martin Luther King, Jr., would another such spontaneous outbreak recur. Nor was there any question, among either white or black Americans, over the cause of the civil disturbances. A black man had defeated a white man for the greatest prize in sports, the heavyweight championship. It was an outcome that raised bile into the throats of thousands of whites, turning a handful into murderers. The burst of destructive energy frightened many middle-class blacks, threatening the gains they had achieved. But several black commentators refused to diminish Johnson's victory by saying that it was *just* a prizefight and did not *mean* anything. William Pickens, president of Talladega College, commented, "It was a good deal better for Johnson to win and a few Negroes be killed in body for it, than for Johnson to have lost and Negroes to have been killed in spirit by the preachments of inferiority from the combined white press."[43]

In victory Johnson had probed the live nerve of American racism. And the Jeffries fight was only the beginning. White America's violent reaction to the fight, and what white authorities interpreted as Johnson's continued provocative behavior, prompted a virtual coup d'état against the emperor of masculinity. The first phase of the campaign attacked the most visible expressions of Johnson's athletic superiority, the moving pictures of his victories. Throughout the early twentieth century, progressive reformers oozed anxiety about the evil influences of both prizefighting and films. Under certain circumstances, they argued, each encouraged vice, contributed to public disorder, and multiplied moral and social corruption. And combined, they had the power to foster incalculable harm.

In 1912, as Johnson prepared to defend his title against "Fireman" Jim Flynn in another Independence Day contest, Congress stirred to action.

Four southerners on Capitol Hill—Thetus Sims (Tennessee) and Seaborn A. Roddenbery (Georgia) in the House and Furnifold M. Simmons (North Carolina) and Augustus Bacon (Georgia) in the Senate—spearheaded a bill "to prohibit the exhibition of moving pictures of prizefights." Roddenbery made no bones about his position on Johnson's mixed-race fights: "No man descended from the old Saxon race can look upon that kind of a contest without abhorrence and disgust."[44] On July 31, only weeks after Johnson's victory over Flynn, President William Howard Taft signed the Sims bill into law. Although the law did not prohibit the filming of a fight or the exhibition of the motion pictures in the same state as the contest was staged, it did outlaw the interstate transport of the film. At a time when championship fights were contested in such sparsely populated locales as Nevada and New Mexico, the law effectively ended the profitability of prizefight films.

The Sims law attacked Johnson indirectly by making it more difficult for him to make money (a standard championship contract gave the fighters a share in the film rights). It hit him in the pocketbook, and might be considered merely business. But the second phase of the government's campaign against Johnson was personal, amounting to an all-out frontal assault against how he lived his life. As the boxer's fame increased, his relationships with white women became an open, festering wound for many Americans. When he married Etta Terry Duryea in January 1911, one of his relationships was sanctioned by the courts. Their stormy marriage ended in September 1912 when Etta committed suicide by shooting herself. Three months later in Chicago, Johnson married again, this time to Lucille Cameron, a white prostitute with whom he had been having an affair for four or five months.

Criticism, ominous and threatening, rained down on Johnson.[45] A group of whites in Louisiana inquired whether the good citizens of Illinois knew what "seagrass ropes are made for." The governor of New York called the marriage a "blot on our civilization." Taking the logic one step further, the governor of South Carolina asked, "If we cannot protect our white women from black fiends, where is our boasted civilization?" Not to be out-bigoted by any governor, Representative Roddenbery cried with indignation on the floor of the House, speculating on the history of race relations and lamenting his own times: "No brutality, no infamy, no degradation in all the years of Southern slavery, possessed such a villainous character and such atrocious qualities as the provisions of the laws of

Illinois, New York, Massachusetts, and other states which allow the marriage between negro, Jack Johnson, to a woman of Caucasian strain." With the applause of the gallery ringing in his ears, Roddenbery continued, "Intermarriage between whites and blacks is repulsive and averse to every sentiment of pure American spirit. It is abhorrent and repugnant to the very principles of a pure Saxon government. It is subversive to social peace. It is destructive to moral supremacy, and ultimately this slavery of white women to black beasts will bring this nation to a conflict as fatal and as bloody as ever reddened the soil of Virginia or crimsoned the mountain paths of Pennsylvania." Concluding, he ranted, "Let us uproot and exterminate now this debasing, ultrademoralizing, un-American, and inhuman leprosy."

Behind the scenes, agents of the Justice Department were feverishly compiling a case against Johnson for violating the White Slave Traffic Act (1910). That piece of Progressive Era legislation, popularly know as the Mann Act after its sponsor, prohibited the interstate transportation of women "for the purpose of prostitution or debauchery, or for any other immoral purposes." It was clearly aimed at commercialized vice, not sexual relations between consenting adults. But its language was as broad as it was vague, leaving ample room for a creative interpretation of the law. To be sure, it could be used to harpoon a madam who was attempting to move some new recruits across the country. But justice officials argued that it could also be employed to gig any man who traveled across state lines with a female who was not his wife and incidentally engaged in sex. "Debauchery" and "immoral purposes" were like the legendary grandmother's nightshirt that covered just about everything.

Jack Johnson became the test case for the alternate interpretation of the Mann Act. In his line of work he traveled often, and he normally took along women. And almost as often he made love—or something close enough for government work—with them. The government's hope to charge Johnson with a Mann Act violation with Lucille Cameron went up in smoke when she married the champion. But it was not difficult to find another companion of Johnson's who was willing to support the government's case. Belle Schreiber, a seasoned prostitute who had plied her trade in Chicago, Pittsburgh, Baltimore, and several other cities, stepped forward and asserted that she had gallivanted about the country with the champion and had had sex with him many, many times. And in fact, she had.

Johnson was duly arrested, charged, tried, convicted, and sentenced.

Judge George Carpenter noted that the boxer was "one of the best known men of his race" and, therefore, in a manner of speaking, he decided to throw the book at him. Instead of just levying a fine, Carpenter ordered Johnson confined to prison for a year and a day and fined $1,000. Before the sentencing a *Cleveland Daily News* headline blared: "BLACK PUGILIST WILL BE MADE AN EXAMPLE."[46] And he was. But what exactly was he an example of? Not of harming anyone, for he had harmed no one. Not of breaking the law, for he had broken no laws. What then? He had won the title, become the emperor of masculinity, lived like the heavyweight champion of the world, and bedded and married white women. He had lived like a free man—and because he was black, he was now going to pay. The federal government, in its own way, had cut off his balls. It had symbolically lynched Jack Johnson.

W. E. B. DuBois saw eye-to-eye with Johnson on very few matters, but he did understand the reason for the champion's downfall. It was not just that Johnson had "out sparred an Irishman" or that he was unfaithful to his wife. "We have yet to hear, in the case of white America, that marital troubles have disqualified prizefighters or ball players or even statesmen." No it was something deeper, an impulse almost primordial. It was the color of his skin, said DuBois. "It comes down, then, after all to this unforgivable blackness."[47]

***

The importance of John L. Sullivan and the persecution of Jack Johnson formed the backdrop for the career of Joe Louis. Johnson's career was particularly crucial for Louis. John Roxborough, Julian Black, Jack Blackburn, everyone in boxing, and most people who had never seen a fight knew what happened to Jack Johnson after his sentencing. He skipped the country, slipping into Canada before sailing for Europe. Then he traipsed about the Western Hemisphere, lost the title to White Hope Jess Willard in 1915, returned to the United States in 1920, and served his year in prison. His title was lost, his money spent, and his chances of a prosperous future squandered. But he remained in the public eye—sort of. Showing up at a flea circus or a traveling show or a major fight, he would flash his golden smile, remind everyone how great he was, and predict that he was returning to the ring and could still lick anybody who laced on gloves. Some people nodded, others laughed, and everyone knew that he was used goods. He had floored the finest white heavyweights, married less than the finest white women, faced a sea of white hostility, and finally got knocked on his ass. Everybody knew that.

They also knew that Johnson had muddied the waters for future black heavyweights. After Willard knocked out Johnson in the scorching heat of Havana, Cuba, a sportswriter for the *Detroit News* expressed what many white Americans felt. "The Ethiopian has been eliminated," he wrote. "There will never be a black heavyweight champion . . . at least as long as the present generation endures."[48] That was why Blackburn had been so reluctant to train Joe Louis. "You know, boy," the trainer told Joe, "the heavyweight division for a Negro is hardly likely. The white man ain't too keen on it. You have got to be something to go anywhere. If you really ain't gonna be another Jack Johnson, you got some hope. White man hasn't forgot that fool nigger with his white women, acting like he owned the world."[49]

To escape the shadow of Jack Johnson, Louis' managers set down some hard-and-fast rules. Johnson had consorted with and married white women; Louis was forbidden from ever having his photograph taken alone with a white female. Johnson had talked loud, boasted constantly, and luxuriated in the nightlife; Louis was instructed never to humiliate an opponent, gloat over a victory, or visit a nightclub alone. He was coached to express little, say even less, and allow his fists to give meaning to his existence. His managers made sure that he was matched against quality fighters and that all his fights were on the level, and they insisted that he live and fight cleanly. Although Louis' "deadpan" expression confused white reporters, it could never be confused with Jack Johnson's "golden smile." Everything Louis did, every image he projected, carried the same message: "I am not Jack Johnson." No verbal boasts, no flashy smiles, no public sexual exploits—just machinelike fighting and Bible-reading innocence.

Repeatedly, John Roxborough told Louis, "You just keep clean so [journalists] can't write you into scandal." If you do not understand a question, do not answer it. If people seem too friendly in a nightclub, get up and leave. If any white woman, anywhere, gets too friendly, run away as fast as you can. The idea was to avoid being known too well, to be a world-beater in the ring and invisible outside of it.[50] Years later poet Langston Hughes captured the essence of Roxborough's instructions to Louis:

"They say" . . . "They say" . . . "They say" . . .
But the gossips had no
"They say"
To latch onto
For Joe.[51]

Roxborough's rules fit Louis' nature as comfortably as an old flannel shirt. The "Joe Louis" Roxborough was intent on crafting was remarkably similar to the Joe Louis who was training in the gym with Blackburn. Still young and uncertain about everything but boxing, Louis was by nature silent. He suffered from a mild speech impediment, was sensitive about his educational failings, and did not enjoy speaking to groups of people or even being too open with his thoughts. All his life he had watched others, observing their behavior, listening to their opinions, feeling no compulsion to voice his ideas. He enjoyed company, loved to laugh, but was not much of a talker. It was a disposition that made him easy for Roxborough and Black to manage and Blackburn to train. And, in just a little more than a year, it made him more acceptable to white journalists and white America.

By the summer of 1934 Louis had mastered the basic rules—the social ones of Roxborough and Black and the pugilistic ones of Blackburn. Although there was more to learn, he knew how to throw a left and slip a punch, say the right thing and avoid the wrong question. It was time to put the lessons to work. On the Fourth of July, 1934, in Chicago, he fought Jack Kracken, a good club fighter who was not overly impressed with Louis' amateur record. "He looked like he had it made, and that bothered me a lot," Louis remembered.[52] Blackburn told him to stay calm and look for the opening, not waste his punches in fits of overexcitement. "One clean shot is better than a hundred punches," the trainer insisted. "Bide your time," Blackburn said. And Louis did. For less than two minutes. He landed a few body shots, and when Kracken dropped his guard, Louis ended the fight with a clean left to the chin. He had won his first professional fight with a first-round knockout. His purse was $59. His managers told him to keep it all. They would take their 50 percent (minus expenses) when the purses became higher.

During the next eleven months Louis fought, on average, slightly more than twice a month. About half of the matches were in Chicago, with most of the rest in other midwestern fight towns. The men he fought are obscure today; their only claim to fame is that they fought Joe Louis on his way up the heavyweight ladder. But many of the fighters were very good journey-men or fighters on the make themselves, hopeful of one day vying for the championship. Very few were bums. *Ring* magazine ranked Adolph Waiter, who went ten rounds with Louis in September, just below the premier heavyweights. Charles Massera, Lee Ramage, Patsy Perroni, Hans Birkie, Reds Barry, and Natie Brown cracked the top ten rankings for heavyweights at various times in the mid-1930s. At a time when the division was loaded with promising contenders, promoters matched Louis with some of the best. And the best were not good enough. In his first twenty-two profes-sional fights Louis won all of the contests, fourteen by knockout in less than three rounds. Only four boxers went the distance with him. By March 1935, *Ring* ranked Louis in the top five heavyweights.[53]

His rapid ascent in the division, however, was not reflected in his purses. For more than half of his first twenty-two matches he was paid less than a thousand dollars, and under four thousand dollars for most of the rest. There were few big purses waiting for a black heavyweight in the Midwest, and his telephone was not ringing for any big money paydays in the East. Blackburn's prediction about the long shadow of Jack Johnson appeared to be true. It would be wrong to say that Louis needed a piece of good luck. Boxing was not a profession that gratuitously rewarded black fighters. What he needed was a new alignment of the stars, one that threw him into the orbit of a more powerful force. As it happened, in the first quarter of 1935 powerful economic forces were reshaping the sport, and as a result, Joe Louis' career would take off.

3

Tethered by Civilization

What happens to a dream deferred?
Does it dry up
Like a raisin in the sun?
. . . .
Maybe it just sags like a heavy load.
Or does it *explode?*
— *"Harlem," Langston Hughes*

New York had pretty much seen it all, but the arrival of Joe Louis on May 15, 1935, at Grand Central Terminal was unprecedented. Never in the city's long history of comings and goings had a black American created such a stir. He arrived like a visiting dignitary, dressed to the nines in a gray overcoat and fedora, white gloves, tan shirt and plaid suit, and green tie, and accompanied by a retinue of managers, trainers, cooks, and bodyguards. To provide security for the twenty-one-year-old fighter, two New York detectives joined counterparts from Chicago and Detroit. To provide spending money, Mike Jacobs, on the verge of becoming the most powerful economic force in boxing, greeted Louis.

The smiles that Louis' presence aroused clashed with the tight security. Faces turned toward Louis as if he were the sun. Some people cheered, others watched with their mouths agape. Railroad porters stood starstruck, ignoring requests to carry a bag or check for luggage. "They were gazing at Joe Louis, their idol," wrote a reporter at the scene.[1] For a photo opportunity a group of accommodating porters and railway workers hoisted Louis off the ground and doffed their caps in salute. Even Louis, whose public displays of emotion were as rare as good stock market advice, proffered a half smile.

The lighthearted mood had drifted away by the time he sat for an extended interview. A writer for the *New York Times* commented on the boxer's "somber aspect," noting that he never permitted "a flicker of expression to change his countenance even when the subjects under discussion were humorous." Louis sat stone-faced, measuring out his words with teaspoons. He doubted if he would have the time to inspect New York's architectural wonders. He had a tight schedule, which started the next day with a one-week engagement at the Harlem Opera House. But, he added quickly, there would be no "song-and-dance" in his act. "I will go through a routine of sparring, shadow boxing and bag punching, and that's all."[2] Joe Louis was no man's Stepin Fetchit or Bill "Bojangles" Robinson. He was a serious man, a fighter, a person who had come to New York City, the mecca of the world of boxing, on a mission.

***

Louis needed to fight in New York to advance his career, but New York needed Louis to enable it to survive as the center of the boxing world. Oddly, in the heart of the Great Depression, New York did not look frayed at the cuffs. Taking stock of the city, writer James Thurber observed that "there is no big parade of the unemployed, stalking the streets, muttering ominously; there are no hungry mobs besieging bread shops; there is not even a pall of gloom hanging heavy over the town."[3]

Instead, the streets had a carnival feel. To attract riders, cabbies painted their taxis in every shade of rainbow colors. Lime-green cabs jerked down Fifth Avenue next to robin's-egg-blue and royal-purple ones. Cabs with diagonal lines and tiger stripes, bold trims and outrageous designs, prowled the streets more swiftly than ever before, especially given the lighter Depression traffic. The best Broadway plays still did fine business, and the movie houses had mostly recovered from their early Depression slump. Marlene Dietrich in *The Devil Is a Woman,* Jean Harlow in *Reckless,* Irene Dunne in *Magnificent Obsession,* and Bette Davis in *Bordertown* garnered millions of Depression dollars. And so it went. On the surface New York still gleamed. Every night its lights flashed bright and garish, perhaps even brighter with the addition of the top of the relatively new, virtually empty Empire State Building.

But the city could not withstand a closer inspection. Life had been scaled back. Although the top theatrical productions enjoyed decent runs, lesser plays opened and closed as silently as sinking ships. Compared to pre-Depression levels, a third to a half fewer plays ran in New York's legitimate theaters, and admission prices for those productions had dropped. The same was true for book sales. Increasingly readers borrowed books from libraries rather than purchasing them. The exception to the steady economic erosion was burlesque. In seedy joints along 52nd Street between Fifth and Sixth avenues strippers undressed in front of packed houses, the process of losing one's clothes serving as a powerful metaphor for the fate of millions of Americans.

Across the city this fog of economic doom was spreading. Fewer out-of-town visitors spelled more hotel vacancies, more empty seats in restaurants, and more problems for New Yorkers dependent on tourism. Real estate prices had slid sharply. The Empire State Building struggled to attract renters. Each night darkened windows in apartments buildings and other skyscrapers signaled the soul-crushing emptiness of the times. So did the "GOING OUT OF BUSINESS" and "FINAL LIQUIDATION" signs on store windows. Merchandise was cheap, but buyers were few. Even Cartier, F. A. O. Schwarz, and Brooks Brothers, stores that stood for quality and toniness, now advertised sales to attract the better-off sorts. For those who still had money and were not scared to death to spend it, Saks Fifth Avenue, Bergdorf Goodman, Jay Thorpe, and Kurzman were fairytale wonderlands, offering the very best at a fraction of their former prices.

In New York City hard times were the sign of the times. Suffering had survived the excitement over the election of Franklin Roosevelt, his first hundred days in office, and his homey fireside chats. Hunger had endured the passage of the Federal Emergency Relief Act and the establishment of the Civilian Conservation Corps. One of FDR's advisors might have been correct when he boasted that "capitalism was saved in eight days," but the hard times that crippled people's daily existence had neither gone away nor shown signs of packing for an extended leave.

Like the real estate or the diamond business, the taxi or the book business, the boxing business stood on rubbery legs, ready to collapse. In a time when masculinity itself was suffering the repeated body blows of unemployment and its associated heartaches, the Empire of Masculinity had lost much of its luster. John L. Sullivan and James J. Corbett were names from a mythical past. Even the great Jack Dempsey, he of the million-dollar gates and the Hollywood patina, seemed as remote from the new realities of American life as the Great Bull Market. Poet Horace Gregory employed the fall of Dempsey as a metaphor for Americans trapped in a dead-end economy. Although the central figure in his poem "Dempsey, Dempsey" is worn out, dead-legged, beaten, and going down for the final count, he pleads, "God save Dempsey, make him get up again."[4]

By the early 1930s the business of boxing was battered and sagging. Dempsey and Gene Tunney, the golden stars of the golden age of the sport, had retired from the ring. George "Tex" Rickard, the gifted showman who had promoted Dempsey's million-dollar gates, had died after a brief illness. Without its leading heavyweights and primary promoter, the sport entered a dark age. It is a truism worth repeating that the wellbeing of boxing as a whole follows the health of the heavyweight division, and after the retirement of Tunney, the heavyweight division was virtually on life support.

The division suffered from a combination of ailments, the most important of which was the absence of a dominant, charismatic champion. The heavyweight titleholders who followed Tunney demonstrated a singular, crippling inability to successfully defend the title. The heavyweight crown, once the most cherished title in all of sports, became something of a flea-market hand-me-down. In 1930 Max Schmeling ignominiously won the title on a foul when Jack Sharkey sank a left hook into his groin. After one successful defense, Schmeling lost the title by decision to Sharkey. Many reporters considered it a bad, hometown verdict, but after the unmanly way Schmeling won the title, they wrote it off as poetic justice. Sharkey proved as careless with the title as he had with his punches. In his first defense he lost the championship to Primo Carnera in a six-round knockout. The fact that Carnera, a huge mob-backed fighter with a feathery, muscle-bound punch, was able to knock out the rugged Sharkey was universally interpreted as the low point in the history of heavyweight championship boxing.

The reign of Carnera lasted less than one year. During that period he defended his title successfully twice and unsuccessfully once. The unsuccessful defense was particularly brutal. Max Baer, a talented, hard-hitting, undisciplined fighter from California, demolished Carnera, knocking down the Italian heavyweight twelve times in eleven rounds. By the last knockdown Carnera's face was cut, bleeding, and grotesquely swollen, and his body—as well as Baer's—was covered with his own blood. Only then did referee Arthur Donovan humanely, but belatedly, halt the contest.

The handsome, powerful Baer seemed to have what Schmeling, Sharkey, and Carnera did not—the right balance of punching ability and star power. But he had no real affection for the sport, trained irregularly, and practiced virtually every vice trainers told fighters to avoid. As a result, his reign lasted only a few days longer than Carnera's. He lost his first defense. James J. Braddock, a once decent light heavyweight who had repeatedly broken his right hand, quit boxing, and gone on the dole before mounting a well-publicized comeback, outpointed Baer. Although the match provided human-interest columns for an army of reporters, it did nothing to restore prestige to the division. Braddock was no Dempsey. He was no Tunney. He was not even a Max Baer. He was an honorable, hard-working, Depression-scared bloke, a family man who enjoyed a beer with friends, but not someone whom boxing fans could hold in awe, the sort of demigod who could, like John L. Sullivan, swagger into any establishment in America and announce, "I can lick any sonofabitch alive."

The decline in the quality of heavyweight champions created an economic crisis in the sport. Attendance at important fights and gate receipts dropped like the Dow Jones average. More than 80,000 spectators paid to watch the 1921 Jack Dempsey–Georges Carpentier fight, almost 121,000 attended the 1926 Jack Dempsey–Gene Tunney match in Philadelphia, and nearly 105,000 witnessed the 1927 Dempsey-Tunney Long Count fight in Chicago. During the 1920s the live gates of five separate Dempsey fights exceeded $1 million. In sad contrast, the Primo Carnera–Jack Sharkey title fight drew only about 10,000 fans, and none of the heavyweight championship contests during the sport's dark age came anywhere near a million-dollar gate.

The declining sport presented an odd paradox. Thousands of Depression-desperate men climbed into a ring to earn a few dollars. During the 1930s in the United States five thousand to six thousand professional boxers practiced their trade annually, compared to half that number worldwide today. And in the nonheavyweight divisions boxing was awash with talent. Such lightweight, welterweight, and middleweight champions as Tony Canzoneri, Mickey Walker, Jimmy McLarnin, Barney Ross, Lou Ambers, and Henry Armstrong were among the greatest fighters in the sport's history. In fact, Canzoneri, Ross, and Armstrong each won world titles in three different divisions. Each had a loyal, passionate following, and they breathed color and life into the profession. Yet in spite of the number of fighters and the quality of champions in lighter divisions, many journalists prophesized the death of the sport. Others scanned the horizon for a heavyweight savior.

Those inclined toward savior searching hoped for another Dempsey—a white heavyweight with a lethal punch, a killer smile, and a common touch. Finding none, they relaxed their requirements. For some people in the fight business, Joe Louis was a pulsating neon sign announcing better times ahead, a powerful, exciting force of nature that promised to blow away the gloom and revive the sport like a cleansing rain. Nat Fleischer, editor and chief writer for *Ring,* the leading boxing magazine, appreciated the importance of Louis to the sport. For him, Louis was the "Savior of Boxing," "a Moses [who led] it out of the wilderness." "Boxing thrived again," Fleischer wrote. "The depression that had caused a lull in the sport and had forced thousands of persons into unemployment was now over so far as pugilism in America was concerned. Joe Louis had shown the way to a new life."[5]

Louis represented a pugilistic trickle-down theory. The excitement he generated flowed downward. Old fight clubs reopened. New clubs mushroomed in cities across the country. Thousands of hopeful, tough young men laced on gloves for the first time. Box office men, ticket takers, ushers, program pushers, and venders returned to their jobs. Promoters, managers, trainers, cut men, and boxers began to earn incomes again. The fight business was back in business, and Joe Louis was responsible. His arrival in New York, then, was more than simply symbolic; it was a visible, palpable sign of the return of happy days. But nothing in boxing is ever simple or clearcut. As Paddy Flood, a boxing insider, testified before Congress, "Let me tell you about boxing. It's the most treacherous, dirtiest, vicious, cheatingest game in the world. . . . That's the nature of the business. It's a terrible business." True to form, the arrival of Joe Louis in New York was the result of the financial dealings, double-crosses, and shifting alliances that characterize the sport of professional boxing.

✳✳✳

Joe Louis' reception in New York was the handiwork of Michael Strauss Jacobs. By 1935 "Uncle Mike" Jacobs had already earned a reputation as a sharp businessman who distrusted everyone and was trusted in return by no one. Barney Nagler, a reporter who watched Jacobs operate for years, recalled that when Uncle Mike wanted something from a person he could be charming and ingratiating to the point of unctuous handshaking and obsequious smiling. At all other times he was a "ruthless predator."[6] A New York character, a figure who seemed to have stepped out of Damon Runyon's *Guys and Dolls,* Jacobs fit Nagler's description. He had the look of a suspicious IRS accountant. Hunch-shouldered, thin-limbed, and bald-headed, he had only two thoroughly memorable features.

Most people noticed his teeth first. They were store-bought, badly fitted, and noisy. Some journalists said Jacobs purchased them cheap, others insisted that they were top of the line. There was a basis for both interpretations because Jacobs went through numerous pairs of teeth. But they all seemed to rattle like bad car engines, and he complained incessantly about each pair.

Jacobs' second distinguishing feature was his eyes. He had small, bird-like eyes, dark and intense, that seemed as if they could penetrate walls. A reporter who knew Jacobs well recalled that he had "no bullshit eyes, and by that I mean that he could look at anyone and tell if the person was full of shit or not. And mostly they told him the other fella was." They were the eyes of a man who knew the bottom line before anyone else did. They aroused the concern of anyone who was negotiating with him. Combined with his noisy teeth, his predator eyes had a destabilizing effect. "When you heard his teeth clack and looked into those dark eyes," boxing writer Dan Daniel said, "you instinctively felt for your wallet."[7]

Jacobs was not a former fighter, displayed no particular fondness for boxers or the sport's numerous offbeat characters, and did not even enjoy watching a good match. In fact, he believed that holding a ticket back for himself in his own promotions was a wasteful indulgence. His interest in boxing was purely business. He was in it, as he frankly admitted, for the bucks.

The accumulation of dollars drove his life. A son of Jewish immigrants, born in New York City in a tough Irish neighborhood close to the Battery, Jacobs learned early the importance of money. He hustled nickels and dimes from an age when it was just barely possible to hustle. As a youth he scored big hawking soda, popcorn, and lemon drops on excursion boats from the Battery to Coney Island. He used to drop a box of lemon drops on the laps of young women with dates and then return to collect. Demonstrating a keen command of psychology, he understood that a young man would rather pay ten cents for a nickel box of lemon drops than make a scene and look cheap in front of his girl.

Jacobs also had a keen eye for the next score. He advanced from selling lemon drops to speculating on excursion tickets and chartering excursion boats. Soon he outgrew the economic and geographic world of the Battery, moving his base of operation uptown and making a play to corner the cutthroat ticket speculation business. Working long hours, mastering the art of obtaining product, Jacobs became the man to see if you wanted a ticket to a Broadway play, a sporting event, or, at the top of the ticket pyramid, the Metropolitan Opera House. "I once paid a grand for a couple of choice locations for one night a week, and sold them to a new rich man for $5,000," he recalled. "It was not a bad business, and I wondered why it had taken me so long to move uptown."[8]

Just as he had in the Battery, he moved from scalping tickets to running operations. He backed Broadway productions and revived dying attractions. Of course, he controlled the tickets to those productions. Jacobs financed events that ranged from six-day bicycle races, the Barnum-Bailey-Forepaugh Circus, and the Buffalo Bill Wild West Show to the annual Society Ball and the Fifth Avenue Fashion Show. He had an almost unerring sense of what people wanted to see, and he was willing to gamble on his hunches. When criticized on his prices, as he sometimes was by a journalist or an irate customer, he asserted, in true robber baron fashion, "I make those attractions possible with my financial backing. Without me, they do not exist. I take the big chances. I should make some profit. How I get my first-class tickets is nobody's business."[9]

In the 1920s he moved more heavily into boxing. As the sport reached its golden age, the public associated it with two men: heavyweight champion Jack Dempsey and promoter George "Tex" Rickard. A master of ballyhoo and hype, Rickard was a natural showman who had a knack for weaving dreams. The most important fights he promoted were never about finding out who was the better boxer. They were symbolic dramas that trafficked in conflicting ideologies. The dynamic Dempsey was Rickard's clay, a fighter that he could refashion to suit different dramas. The Dempsey–Georges Carpentier bout pitted the draft-dodging American against the war-hero Frenchman; the Dempsey–Luis Firpo contest matched the true-blue American against the invading Latin American; the Dempsey–Gene Tunney fights featured the anti-intellectual Everyman against the Shakespeare-reading, Yale-lecturing pug-turned-effete-snob. Each fight surpassed the million-dollar-gate yardstick.

In each fight Rickard received promotional backing from Jacobs, who, of course, gained a corner on the ticket sales for his efforts. Rickard died in 1929 practically broke. He never learned Jacobs' art of accumulating a fortune. But Jacobs discovered, through Rickard, the secret of dreams and boxing promotions. A big fight was a product, and it had to be sold as a product. A soap salesman did not push soap; he sold beauty. A car salesman did not hawk cars; he sold social and economic mobility. People purchased dreams with their mundane products. For Rickard—and Jacobs—a fight was not so much a boxing match as it was a status symbol, a story, and a fantasy.

After Rickard's death Jacobs worked the sidelines of the boxing business. Many journalists and boxing insiders anticipated that he would be named the promoter for Madison Square Garden, Rickard's former position. But the Madison Square Garden Corporation gave the job to Jimmy Johnston, a former manager known as the Boy Bandit who had made slightly fewer enemies than Jacobs. The moment called for a promoter with imagination and long-range vision. Johnston possessed large quantities of neither. Occasionally he looked out for his closest friends, but mostly he just maneuvered to increase his share of the action. The result of his short-sighted greed undermined the Madison Square Garden Corporation's near stranglehold over major fights and gave Jacobs the opening he needed to take over the sport.

Johnston's missteps and Jacobs' opportunity involved the most unlikely, at least for them, of human impulses—charity. In the early 1920s, Millicent Hearst (Mrs. William Randolph Hearst) helped organize the Free Milk Fund for Babies drive. The charity raised money to feed hungry children, and throughout the 1920s and early 1930s it enjoyed great success, and, incidentally, made Millicent a recognized force in philanthropic circles. One of the ways she raised money was through boxing events staged at Madison Square Garden or at one of the other arenas controlled by the Madison Square Garden Corporation. The association with Mrs. William Randolph Hearst and charity had elevated the social position of boxing, a by-product of the relationship that Tex Rickard encouraged. Always eager to link boxing with wealthy and politically important patrons, Rickard treated the Free Milk Fund charity as if it were the closest thing to his heart. He was not concerned with such mundane issues as rents and profits. He saw the larger picture: if Mrs. Hearst was happy, her husband (though estranged) was happy, and if her husband was happy, boxing received good press and the patronage of the "better sorts."

The Boy Bandit had a different read on the Free Milk Fund. With the Garden losing money and Colonel John Reed Kilpatrick, president of the Garden Corporation, breathing down his neck, Johnston raised the rental fee for the Free Milk Fund's boxing shows. Hearst reporters with vested interests in the Free Milk Fund and boxing cried foul, self-righteously charging that the Garden Corporation was quite literally depriving babies of milk and heartlessly contributing to the suffering of millions of infants. Never had the Boy Bandit's larceny appeared so nakedly vile.

Johnston's actions were simply too stupid for Jacobs too ignore. During the early 1930s he kept his hand in the game, controlling blocks of tickets for big fights and helping to keep Madison Square Garden afloat on turbulent economic waters. But Johnston's blunder gave him a chance to cut into the Garden's control of boxing. In late 1934 he chartered the Twentieth Century Sporting Club to promote and stage boxing matches. He assured Mrs. Hearst that he would provide advantageous rental rates for her Free Milk Fund for Babies boxing events. Secretly, Jacobs also enlisted several of Hearst's leading sportswriters to guarantee him favorable press in his planned war with Johnston and the Garden Corporation. Edward J. "Ed" Frayne, sports editor of the New York *American;* Wilston S. "Bill" Farnsworth, sports editor of the New York *Journal;* and Damon Runyon, one of Hearst's most influential and widely read columnists, were central to the promotion of Mrs. Hearst's Free Milk Fund shows.

They met with Jacobs secretly in the Forrest Hotel on West 49th Street, across the street from Jacobs' ticket brokerage office, and struck a bargain. Jacobs provided the money and knowledge of the ticket business. The journalists promised to supply the publicity. Because of the serious conflict of interest and violation of virtually every journalistic code, the sportswriters allowed Jacobs to publicly hold all of the stock in the Twentieth Century Sporting Club. Frayne demanded a letter outlining the partnership. Farnsworth and Runyon accepted Jacobs' word on the deal, or perhaps they simply feared any sort of paper trail. Whatever the case, with the deal done they set their sights on the Madison Square Garden Corporation's monopoly of boxing.

They thrived immediately, and almost as quickly succeeded beyond their greediest dreams. In February 1935 Farnsworth announced that the Free Milk Fund as well as the New York *American's* Christmas and Relief Fund had broken with the Madison Square Garden Corporation and would stage their fights in the major league baseball parks of New York. The promoter for the charity fights, he added, would be "ticket broker" Mike Jacobs. At the time, the Garden still controlled the heavyweight championship through its ties with Max Baer, so Jacobs had to begin his promotional career with smaller boxers. He quickly forged a promotional relationship with Barney Ross, the popular Jewish fighter who had recently lost the welterweight title to Jimmy McLarnin. Jacobs promoted the Ross–Frankie Klick fight in Miami and then in May staged the third Ross-McLarnin match in the Polo Grounds. Refereed by Jack Dempsey, Ross regained his title in front of more than forty-five thousand spectators.

Ross was a game fighter and a popular champion, but Jacobs knew that heavyweights ruled the sport. From his first days as a promoter he kept his eyes open for another Dempsey, a fighter so powerful, a product so rare, that he could be transformed into a dream factory. In Miami for the Ross-Klick match, Ross's co-managers, Sam Pian and Art Winch, told Jacobs about a talented big man they had seen, a kid out of Chicago named Joe Louis. "He's a heavyweight," Winch said. "He'll be a champ."[10]

Jacobs acted immediately. In February 1935 he traveled to Los Angeles and watched Louis knock out the talented Lee Ramage in two rounds. Then he made his pitch to John Roxborough. He stressed two points. First, he said that as a Jew he understood something about discrimination. Eyes tearing with sincerity, which he was always able to summon if he really wanted something, he told Roxborough, "John, you and Joe are colored. I'm a Jew. It's going to be hard for us to do anything. But if you stick with me, I think I can do it." Second, Jacobs told Roxborough of his ties with the Hearst journalists. He could guarantee that the press would support Louis and build him into a championship contender.

Roxborough was in a listening mood. After the Louis-Ramage fight he had talked on the phone with Jimmy Johnston about a big-money Garden fight for Louis. The Boy Bandit had never met Roxborough, knew no one in the Detroit numbers rackets, and could not tell from his voice that the manager was black. He assumed Roxborough was white and made no attempt to conceal his racism. Sure, he could arrange a payday for Joe, but only on his terms. "Well, you understand he's a nigger," Roxborough recalled Johnston saying, "and he can't win every time he goes in the ring." Roxborough answered, "So am I," and hung up. Roxborough was livid. Johnston was unconcerned. As the promoter later told a white associate, "We don't need the nigger."[11]

As usual, Jacobs had taken the perfect line in his negotiations with Roxborough. He might not be able to get Louis a Madison Square Garden fight, but he could arrange a New York City match under favorable terms in a major league ballpark, a summer fight under the lights with the eyes of the sports world on him. And Joe would not have to throw any fights. After facing the racism and hostility of Johnston, Roxborough and Black were ready to sign. They would remain Louis' managers, but Jacobs would collect 50 percent of Louis' purses and guide the fighter's career. Under the terms of the contract, Jacobs had the sole right to chose Louis' opponents and promote the fight. The contract gave Jacobs promotional control of the most important fighter in the world, an arrangement that over time would allow him to dominate the sport.

Joe Louis became Jacobs' Dempsey. It's an open question whether Jacobs immediately realized Louis' potential value. Was the ticket scalper that smart? One thing is certain: From the moment he saw Louis and formed a promotional agreement with the fighter, Jacobs did not take a false step. From the very first he treated Joe Louis as nothing short of the second coming of Jack Dempsey. Louis' arrival in New York, the pomp and circumstance with which he was carried off the train and greeted by the journalistic dignitaries, transmitted a protean message. Heavyweight pretenders were expected to step aside and make way for King Joe, or else face prompt and utter destruction.

***

After his first meeting with Jacobs, Louis' national profile soared. In March, Jacobs paid for a carload of New York reporters to travel to Detroit to watch Joe fight Natie Brown, a slick veteran boxer who knew how to avoid trouble in the ring. The fight went the ten-round distance, but the reporters treated it as another sensational Louis victory. They admired Louis' "jolting" left hooks, "powerful" rights, and "cool and methodical" manner.[12] None of the reporters doubted that Louis was ready for the best in the heavyweight division. Although reporters from the *New York Times* paid scant attention to Louis before the Lee Ramage match, after the contest, and after the signing with Jacobs, they were as enthusiastic as those at the *American* or the *Journal.* In his column, John Kieran noted that "Shufflin' Joe from Detroit" "came over the fence from the amateur ranks only last July and has been going through the field like the boll weevil through a cotton crop. All he leaves is destruction in his wake." But, Kieran added, "the dusky Detroiter" had not yet fought a top contender.[13]

That was about to change. That was the purpose of Louis' imperial entrance into New York City. It was an announcement that Joe's days in the minor leagues, his road show matches in Dayton, Flint, Peoria, and Kalamazoo, were over. From now on he would fight contenders. His sights were set firmly on the title.

From a pool of name heavyweights, Jacobs selected Primo Carnera as the opponent for Louis' first New York match. He set the battle for June 25 in Yankee Stadium. The Italian boxer was an inspired choice. A former champion, Carnera had won the title in 1933 and defended it twice before losing it in 1934. Furthermore, he had engaged in more than eighty bouts, scored close to sixty knockouts, and lost merely seven matches, only one by knockout. His was a championship record, a testimony to his endurance and punching power.

Dubbed the Ambling Alp, Carnera was just a hair under six feet, six inches and weighed 260 pounds. He was not just big, he was colossal. His feet and hands were oversized, and his legs, arms, and chest swelled with muscle. To sportswriter Paul Gallico, Carnera appeared like some sort of mythological man/beast: "His legs were massive and he was truly thewed like an oak. His waist was comparatively small and clean, but from it rose a torso like a Spanish hogshead from which sprouted two tremendous arms, the biceps of which stood out like grapefruit. His hands were like Virginia hams, and his fingers were ten thick red sausages."[14] Proportionately large was his head, his face freakish—wide, sloping forehead; thick, irregular nose; fleshy lips; gummy, snaggle-toothed mouth; lantern jaw. In a boxing ring it was less a face than a target, and perhaps the gentle fighter realized as much. There was sadness in Carnera's eyes, a fragile look of a man who was in the wrong body.

But other factors far overshadowed his record and his size. From the beginning of his career Carnera was more of a dream than a reality, the brainchild of French boxing promoter Leon See, who saw in a traveling circus "strong man" a vision of indestructibility and power. Carnera's size and face were frightening, the kind of nightmare vision that scared children and fascinated the public. Anything that reporters wrote about him, no matter how farfetched, seemed possible to anyone who watched him stride down an aisle and climb inside a ring.

In 1928 Carnera made his professional debut in Paris, and for the next sixteen months he battled mostly obscure opponents in major European cities. But as European economies slid further into depression in the late 1920s, See decided to take his fighter to the United States to find significant purses. Before departing for New York, See signed Carnera to a management deal with Walter "Good-Time Charlie" Friedman, a New York boxing functionary with "important contacts." The management arrangement effectively wrestled control of Carnera's career away from See, making him essentially a well-paid cheerleader, and put it in the hands of several of Friedman's "important contacts." Two gangsters—"Broadway" Bill Duffy, a bootlegger, nightclub owner, and small-time hood with his fingers in boxing promotion, and Owen "Owney the Killer" Madden, a New York gang leader, murderer, and gambler who also had interests in the boxing business—became Carnera's behind-the-scenes managers.

Duffy and Madden marketed Carnera like the tent-show strongman that he was. They billed him more as a freak of nature than a fighter, a man-mountain, rock-fisted, iron-jawed missing link. Their problem was that Carnera could not box, had virtually no punch, and, although brave, did not have a particularly good chin. In any honest fight against a decent heavyweight his chances of winning were as tiny as he was large. But for well connected managers, this was not an insurmountable hurdle. Beginning with his first New York bout in January 1930, Carnera was matched against a series of hand-picked opponents who fully understood that their role was to look frightened and small, not hit the Ambling Alp with any punches that could crack his eggshell chin, and wait for the right moment to take a punch and go down for the count. From that first American contest against Big Boy Peterson, New York boxing writers grasped that Carnera was a fraud, but his story made good copy and they did not ask any serious, investigative questions.

For most of the next three years Carnera engaged in a stiffs-in-the-sticks campaign, fighting mostly pugilistic nobodies in pugilistic nowheres. Newark, Memphis, Oklahoma City, Jacksonville, St. Paul, Grand Rapids, Omaha—Carnera became a traveling road show, crossing America, and once again Western Europe, peddling hokum to the credulous. During those years he seldom fought in New York, and on the few occasions that he did, his opponents were lackluster journeymen who knew perfectly what was expected of them.

Not until February 1933 was Carnera pitted against a named fighter in the mecca of the sport, and only then against a fighter whose career was on a decline. Ernie Schaaf was a ranked heavyweight with several important wins in his seventy-four-fight career, but in August 1932 he had suffered a frightful beating in a bout against hard-hitting Max Baer. Just before the end of the fight, Baer had clubbed him to the canvas, and only the final bell saved him from being counted out. After the Baer fight, Schaaf complained of headaches and appeared listless in the ring. He looked no better in his fight against Carnera. For most of the rounds the two missed and clinched, neither landing very damaging blows. A disappointingly small crowd of nineteen thousand spectators booed and whistled. As the fight progressed Schaaf visibly tired. He shuffled into clinches and at times looked as if he could not lift his arms to defend himself. In the thirteenth round Carnera landed several innocent shots and Schaaf collapsed to the canvas. As suspicious spectators registered their verdict in catcalls, Schaaf was counted out.

Four days later, on Valentine's Day, Schaaf died in New York's Polyclinic Hospital of an intercranial hemorrhage. An autopsy showed that he had entered the ring with a blood clot in his brain, probably the result of his brutal match with Baer. Any punch or movement could have caused the bleeding that killed Schaaf, but the New York State Athletic Commissioners and city boxing writers quickly and mistakenly attributed his death to Carnera's power. Several commissioners trumpeted for the establishment of a "super-dreadnaught" class of heavyweights. A man of Carnera's size and power, they worried, was a clear and present danger for a normal-sized heavyweight. Overnight journalists transformed the Italian dreadnaught heavyweight into a carnival freak and killer.

Four months later Carnera fought Jack Sharkey in the Madison Square Garden Corporation's seventy-two-thousand-seat outdoor Long Island City Bowl for the title. Forty thousand spectators watched the green-satin-robed Carnera scramble into the ring and deliver a stiff-armed "Roman salute" to his cheering Italian American supporters. For five rounds Sharkey outmaneuvered and outhit Carnera, but in the sixth the challenger landed a right uppercut, sending the champion face first to the canvas, where he lay inert while the referee counted to ten. *New York Times* sportswriter James P. Dawson wrote that the "uppercut to the chin . . . almost decapitated Sharkey" and suggested that the fight had not been fixed.[15] Other reporters disagreed, noting that there was a theatrical dimension to Sharkey's fall and unmoving position on the canvas. Gallico, always on the cynical end of the sportswriter spectrum, maintained that the fight was fixed. But perhaps unlike so many of Carnera's other fights, the Sharkey contest was on the level. Perhaps—though it stretched credulity a bit too tightly—his next two title defenses against Paulino Uzcundun, a capable fighter, and Tommy Loughran, a magnificent boxer and a former light-heavyweight world champion, were also on the up-and-up. But his third title defense, against Max Baer in the Long Island City Bowl, had not a whiff of scandal about it.

Some fifty-six thousand spectators turned out to watch Carnera defend his title against Baer, the flamboyant California heavyweight who dated celebrities, fancied himself a budding movie star, and despised his chosen profession. Unfortunately for Baer's career ambitions, fighting was the only thing he did very well, which, as it proved, was also unfortunate for Carnera. The fight was never much of a contest, alternating between tragedy and farce. Its tragedy resulted from the fact that Carnera could not hit Baer or avoid the challenger's thumping right-hand punches. In less than eleven rounds Baer knocked down Carnera twelve times, including three times in the first. His punches cut and bruised the champion's face and body. In some of the rounds, however, Baer transformed the fight into a comedy. He stopped fighting and began conversations with Carnera and people at ringside, becoming a smiling, laughing, clowning ham. But then, just as quickly, he turned vicious. Finally, in the eleventh round, Carnera could not go on. Looking appealingly at referee Arthur Donovan, he signaled that he had had enough. "Carnera asked me to stop the fight, just at the second when I was going to stop it anyway," Donovan told reporters. "He didn't know where he was. He could not continue, and there was no use letting it go on when he was so helpless."[16]

After the Baer fight Carnera was on his own. See had been shipped back to France. Good-Time Charlie Friedman had moved on to other projects. Duffy had been sent to prison, Gallico said, "for some boyish pranks with his income tax," although he would soon return to Carnera's side.[17] Madden had shifted his sub rosa managerial skills to Max Baer. Carnera was abandoned, essentially penniless, and forced to fight without the advantage of backroom deals and prearranged outcomes. All that remained was his reputation as a superhuman specimen and a bona fide killer. He had become, in short, the ideal opponent for Joe Louis' first New York City fight.

***

Jacobs knew that Carnera's reputation as a fighter was overblown, constructed on fixed fights and sportswriters' hype. As for his ability as a boxer and a puncher, there was simply not much there. Carnera was no match for Louis, a heavyweight with exceptionally quick hands, great fighting instincts, and lethal punching power. As an opponent for Louis, Carnera's chief attractions were his size and the fact that he had once held the title. Jacobs' job entailed convincing the sporting public that the Carnera-Louis contest would be, as one journalist said about another bout, "the greatest fight since the Silurian age."[18]

Dozens of sportswriters girded their belts, sharpened their pencils, and went to work. Much of the hype was insider material. A group of reporters questioned Louis' youth and experience, pointing out that his spectacular run of victories had been achieved against inferior talent. Even the better fighters he had demolished—Charley Massera, Lee Ramage, Patsy Perroni, Reds Berry, and Natie Brown, all top-ten heavyweights—were less than marquee names. The bottom line for the anti-Louis camp was: he was a midwestern fighter who had spent most of his time knocking out obscure stiffs or near unproven boxers out in Chicago and Detroit.

One of Louis' most vocal detractors was Jack Johnson. He happily bent the ear of any sportswriter willing to listen, describing Louis as an awkward plodder who suffered from bad instruction and worse technique. His footwork was awful, his balance terrible, and his defensive abilities appalling. Of course, there was a back story to Johnson's opinions. That he disliked and perhaps even envied Blackburn was certain; that he had once campaigned to replace him as Louis' trainer was a distinct possibility. More importantly, Johnson was chronically short of funds, a not infrequent condition of all former boxers, champions or not. It was (and is) understood by virtually everyone in the sport that many prominent fighters and ex-champions can pick up pocket change at a big fight by building up the underdog. Recently crowned heavyweight champion James J. Braddock, for example, also picked Carnera to win the fight. In the years ahead, Johnson would make a second career feeding reporters stories that stressed Louis' many shortcomings and his opponents' almost insurmountable assets. That Johnson and Louis both happened to be black only increased the value of Johnson's statements. The soupçon of intraracial rivalry gave a nice seasoning to his pronouncements.

Other reporters and boxing sages who lacked the imagination to see beyond the obvious asserted that Louis would win. They began by challenging Carnera's record. No world-class heavyweight's record listed more "palookas" and opponents of dubious lineage than Carnera's. Throughout much of his career he had tramped about two continents, fighting in European capitals and American tank towns, facing opponents whose names baffled even veteran sportswriters. And there was more than just a hint of suspicion about many of those "fights." Wilbur Wood, sports editor for the *New York Sun* and frequent contributor to *Ring,* challenged the view of "once a freak, always a freak," suggesting that Carnera had evolved "from freak to fighter." Admittedly, Wood added, the Italian is a "freak fighter, if you will, but a fighter" nonetheless. He had "a fine straight left, a good knowledge of defense, speed that is remarkable in a man of 265 pounds."[19] But Wood's appreciation for "Mussolini's muscle man" was shared by very few sportswriters.

For reporters who looked beyond the relative skills of the fighters and delved into matters sociological, Louis' race was the crucial factor. The race riots that had followed the Jack Johnson–Jim Jefferies title clash had occurred twenty-five years before, but they lingered fresh to many journalists. In fact, Nat Fleischer, the liberal publisher and writer of the *Ring,* addressed the race issue in the first piece his magazine ran on Louis. In his May 1935 article entitled "The Black Menace," Fleischer praised Louis' sensational victories against such rated fighters as Charlie Massare, Lee Ramage, Patsy Perroni, and Hans Brikie, and he admired the fighter's no-nonsense, workman style. "There is nothing of the flashy, colorful style about him," Fleischer wrote.[20] Of course, flashy and colorful had long been code words for Jack Johnson. What Fleischer really meant was that Joe Louis was no Jack Johnson—in or outside the ring. But the writer knew that black fighters of the past, from Tom Molineaux of the early nineteenth century to Harry Wills and George Godfrey of the 1920s, had faced insurmountable discrimination in the sporting world. "Perhaps the 'powers that be,'" he wrote, "will see to it that a fair-play precedent is established in the matter of Joe Louis' progress toward the championship goal. And perhaps not!"[21]

Louis' race certainly was not going to fade into the background if sportswriters had any say in the matter. No sooner was he introduced to the national press than sportswriters began digging deep into their thesauruses for alliterative racial and jungle nicknames. A sportswriter for the *Milwaukee Journal* commented in June 1935 that Louis had already become "the dark destroyer, the central Michigan massacre-rer, the black bomber, the tan torpedo, the Cordovan .44 Colt, the Harlem hammer, the black bullet, . . . the tawny tiger, the polished puma, the African armadillo, the Harlem hippopotamus, the ebony elephant, the panting panther, the chocolate cobra, the oscillating ocelot, the g-nawing gnu, and the Ford factory box."[22] But that hardly completed the list. Others added the shufflin' shadow, the dusky dynamiter, the ebony assassin, the sepia slugger, the mahogany maimer, the saffron sphinx, the saffron sandman, the mocha mauler, the chocolate chopper, the brown bomber, and others to the ever-growing register. The list was so extensive that in 1938 the academic journal *American Speech* devoted an article to it.[23]

The nicknames were important on several levels. On the surface, they were symptomatic of sports journalism in the 1920s and 1930s. Such top sportswriters as Grantland Rice, Damon Runyon, Ring Lardner, Westbrook Pegler, Heywood Broun, John R. Tunis, and Paul Gallico—and scores who followed their leads—approached their jobs more as writers than mere reporters. They attempted to move beyond simply reporting what happened on the field or in the ring and create deeper narratives about the sports and athletes they covered. As much as the athletes, the sportswriters were part of the entertainment business, transforming tobacco-chewing ballplayers and semiliterate boxers into epic figures to rival Achilles, Hercules, Mercury, and other Greek and Roman gods. Their most famous subjects—the Babe, the Manassa Mauler, Big Bill Tilden, "Bobby" Jones, the Iron Horse, the Walloping Wop—transcended their sports, becoming American shorthand for basic values and beliefs. Ruth's innocence, Dempsey's aggression, Tilden's grace, Jones' class, Gehrig's endurance, DiMaggio's majesty—the men and their primary characteristics defined America.

In Louis the sportswriters saw another transcendent athlete, a black one, and they calibrated their stories accordingly, searching for a moniker that would associate the boxer with an accepted characteristic and compelling narrative. For Rice and Gallico and the others, Louis was the Janus Negro—two faced, both lazy darkie and potential disrupter of the social order. He shuffled and he destroyed, was lazy when he trained and a killer when he fought. He was, for white journalists of the 1930s, the primitive black man—a dark, dangerous, primordial, incomprehensible force. Their job was to domesticate him, to make Louis a harmless figure from an Uncle Remus story, someone whom white Americans could laugh at and not be threatened by. Their struggle to give him a nickname was part of their attempt to circumscribe his humanity by defining who and what he was. "Joe Louis, the shufflin' shadow . . . " "Joe Louis, the chocolate cobra . . . " Perhaps the "Brown Bomber," the nickname that stuck and was given to him by a black sportswriter, was the least offensive.

Instinctively, Louis resisted the efforts of sportswriters to classify him. He did not intentionally offend or threaten anyone, but he refused to fit neatly into the "harmless darkie" narrative. In 1981 Red Smith, one of America's finest sportswriters, recalled that when Louis arrived for the first time in New York "some people still saw any black man as the stereotype darkie, who loved dancing and watermelon." Several photographers even tried to convince Louis to pose for pictures eating a slice. He refused, saying that he did not like watermelon. "The funny thing is," a friend told Smith, "Joe loved watermelon."[24] But he knew that the photographers wanted to demean him and rob him of his dignity. In his quiet way, he refused to be a party in his own humiliation.

Consistent with their narrative approach, journalists in the weeks before the Carnera fight debated the Detroit heavyweight's nature, insisting that he was a representative of his race and not a singular individual. H. G. Salsinger of the *Detroit News* asserted that Louis was a scientific boxer, seasoned craftsman, and clean-living athlete. Louis "does not smoke, drink or chew," trains religiously, and lives quietly, wrote Salsinger.[25] Bill Corum, feature writer for the *New York Evening Journal,* had a different read on the Brown Bomber. Corum recounted the high points of Louis' story, from his childhood as a "screaming new pickaninny in [a] shadeless Alabama" shack to his pre-pugilistic days working in a Ford assembly plant. "But there are no medals and music in an automobile plant, and Joe Louis Barrow craved both. At least he wanted excitement and fun and bright colors." Concluding his speculations about the quiet, smooth-fighting athlete, Corum added, "It is doubtful if this husky colored lad, who was born to be a singing cotton picker, could ever have wholly adapted himself to being part of a silent, smooth-running factory machine."[26]

There was nothing exceptional or extreme about Corum's racism. White journalists saw Louis as a jungle animal, often as a large cat, generally sleepy-eyed, relaxed, and silent, but always with a certain ominous potential lurking just beneath the surface. A *New York Sun* sportswriter took a close look at the fighter and observed, "There never was such a dead pan. The eyes never light, not even when he smiles. That smile, too, is queer—just the drawing of the lips into a thin line. Never a change of thought, nor an impulse is reflected in those tawny orbs. Dead eyes; dead from freezing."[27] What was behind those eyes? Was he Sambo or Stagolee, Stepin Fetchit or Jack Johnson? Did they signify a malleable, content African American underclass or a dangerous, broiling mob? The jury was out. But one fact was certain: Joe Louis was more than just another boxer, a sum greater than just another man. If he could be read properly, he was a road map for the geography, the vast unexplored territory, of American race relations.

He was also a window into the wider world. By June 1935, while Louis and Carnera prepared to meet in the ring, a dispute over rights to water wells on the border of Italian Somaliland and Ethiopia (Abyssinia) had led to several violent clashes and threatened to flare into a war. The minor incidents were part of Mussolini's plan to build his new Roman empire at the expense of Haile Selassie's Ethiopian nation. Mussolini's actions were not as much a first act of another world war as the last act of Europe's imperial wars in Africa. Italy had been embarrassed by Ethiopia in an 1895 conflict and was now determined to exact its revenge. During the winter and spring of 1935, relations between Italy and Ethiopia spiraled downward, and the international press treated the story like a morality play, with the tiny, proudly independent black nation refusing to bend to the dictates of the Fascist bully.

The international crisis provided the backdrop for the Louis-Carnera battle. Especially on the East Coast, African Americans followed the worsening situation in the black press. Since the 1920s, when Marcus Garvey's United Negro Improvement Association celebrated racial pride, lectured about Africa's rich heritage, and implored blacks to return to their ancestral homeland, Africa had occupied a central place in racial thinking—especially Ethiopia, one of the last independent black African nations. As Garvey exalted, "Wake up Ethiopia! Wake up Africa! Let us work toward one glorious end of a free, redeemed and mighty nation. Let Africa be a bright star among the constellations of nations." The idea lived longer than Garvey's career in America. As influential black historian John Hope Franklin observed, when Italy threatened Ethiopia "even the most provincial among the American Negros became international-minded. Ethiopia was a Negro nation, and its destruction would symbolize the final victory of the white man over the Negro."[28]

The fact that a smaller black boxer was pitted against a huge white Italian—never mind that neither man was even marginally political—was tailor-made for sportswriters. The stories practically wrote themselves. Syndicated sportswriter Edward J. Neil stated the theme: "Little Abyssinia and big Italy—war in the prize ring instead of Africa—is the lure of Yankee Stadium."[29] Political cartoons portrayed Italy as a gigantic Carnera moving toward a small, black Louis labeled Abyssinia. Reporters suggested that Roxborough and Black had taken the war talk to heart and were feeding it to Louis to fuel his hatred of Carnera. They even invited Princess Heshla Tamanya, first cousin of Emperor Haile Selassie, to Louis' Pompton Lakes training camp, where photographers snapped pictures cementing the ties between the fighter and the beleaguered nation.

Later in his life, Louis remembered talk of Mussolini, Ethiopia, Marcus Garvey, and the racial symbolism of the fight. "Now, not only did I have to beat a man, but I had to beat him for a cause," he said.[30] In truth, in training camp interviews Louis seemed unaware of the political readings of the fight. He seemed mystified by questions that touched on Mussolini's foreign policy, Haile Selassie's predicament, or the fate of black Africa. In his lack of specific knowledge, Louis was no different from most other Americans. More typical was a Harlem resident who said, "Personally, I never heard of Abyssinia until here lately, except for the Abyssinian Baptist Church over on 138th St."[31]

Talk of war between Italy and Ethiopia did, however, stir fears of racial confrontation in America, concerns that always seemed just beneath the surface for many white Americans. Westbrook Pegler and Arthur Brisbane, two of the nation's leading syndicated sportswriters, predicted that the contest would cause an explosion of racial violence in Harlem between blacks and Italians. The combination of white and black, imperialistic Italy and defenseless Ethiopia, with a touch of David and Goliath, was dry tinder, ready to combust at the hint of a spark. Pegler called the fight the "stupidest move in the history of a dumb, rapscallion industry."[32] Brisbane, a veteran of the Jack Johnson era, had always been a harsh critic of inter-racial heavyweight bouts, and Pegler had a well-deserved reputation of being a vocal critic of just about everything. Other black and white re-porters, however, criticized Pegler and Brisbane for stirring racial embers.[33]

Still, Brisbane's and Pegler's predictions were not totally out of line. Just three months before, a minor incident fueled rumors which in turn ignited a firestorm. On March 19, Lino Rivera, a black teenage Puerto Rican, attempted to steal a ten-cent penknife from the Kress Five and Dime on 125th Street. Caught by the store owner and assistant manager, Rivera was threatened with a good beating, but after a policeman arrived, no charges were pressed and the youth was turned loose. Nothing much, in fact, really happened. But rumors were not facts, and shortly the word on the street was that Rivera had been taken into the store's cellar and beaten to death. Why else did the police depart without an arrest? Why else was there a hearse parked across the street from the store? That afternoon the Young Communist League and an African American organization called the Young Liberators held a demonstration outside the Five and Dime. Angry words gave way to vandalism and rioting. Looters smashed the windows of many of the area's white-owned stores and walked away with merchandise. During the riot three African Americans were killed, sixty injured, and more than one hundred arrested. By dawn the riot was over, but the suddenness and violence of the outbreak suggested that Harlem was no longer a happy, jazz-mad haven where whites could go slumming. There was a new mood in Harlem, an angry mix of pent-up frustrations and hostilities. If an unfounded rumor could set off a night of havoc, what might the Louis-Carnera fight unleash?

The Communist Party in Harlem did its best to assuage the strained emotions of black and Italian Americans. Members passed out handbills proclaiming in bold block letters: "FIGHT FAN ITALIAN AND NEGRO! DON'T ALLOW ANY SENSATION SEEKERS TO CREATE ENMITY BETWEEN THE ITALIAN AND NEGRO PEOPLE ON ACCOUNT OF THIS BOUT!" The Communist Party called for the workers of the world—or at least Harlem—to unite and not be swayed by the "sensation mongers" of the Hearst press. It was the residents of Harlem, the "oppressed masses," that cared about Ethiopia, not the "imperialist" media who sought only to divide the workers. The communist plea ended with a call to end discrimination against blacks in sports and the cry, "LONG LIVE THE SOLIDARITY OF THE ITALIAN AND NEGRO PEOPLE!"[34]

By fight day, June 25, the match had become the center of America's attention. One wag claimed that Italy and Ethiopia had suspended all hostilities to allow their people to devote their full attention to the Louis-Carnera match. Sportswriters had devised monikers that matched Louis with virtually every animal inside and outside of a jungle. Oddly, their nicknames for Carnera tended to link him to such inanimate things as mountains or walls. Promoter Mike Jacobs' plans to transform the fight into a Wagnerian opera had succeeded beyond his wildest dreams.

There was no doubt that the contest had aroused more passions than any fight in years. The official weighing-in was a madhouse of pushing, clamoring people. Through the din, State Athletic Commission authorities barked orders and photographers' flashbulbs beat out a blinding show. Carnera attempted a pro forma greeting but Louis ignored him and silently went through his ritualized tasks. He weighed in at 196 pounds, sixty-four and a half pounds less than Carnera. Louis appeared uninterested in the entire affair, ignoring his opponent's bantering with reporters and grinning for his supporters. Surprised by Louis' calmness, Dr. William H. Walker of the Athletic Commission remarked, "He's the closest thing to a wooden Indian I've ever seen."[35] When it was all over Louis could not get through a crowd of thousands of his supporters waiting for him outside the State Office Building. Patrolmen on horses and on foot struggled for fifteen minutes clearing a path.

The mob scene lent credence to Brisbane's and Pegler's concerns. To be on the safe side, New York authorities assigned more than fifteen hundred uniformed police officers to Yankee Stadium for the fight, including two emergency squads equipped with tear gas and riot gear. It was the largest detachment ever detailed to a boxing match. A *New York Times* reporter noted that the police practically formed a cordon around the stadium. Inside, more than three hundred plainclothes detectives kept watch for trouble. In addition, the police presence in Harlem was increased. But the throng of people milling around and entering Yankee Stadium was peaceful and orderly. Many black fans wore yellow rosebuds, a sign of their support for Louis, and they were animated by a sense of real joy.[36]

Thousands of out-of-town spectators, many recently arrived on trains from Pittsburgh, Cleveland, Chicago, and Detroit, showed up early at Yankee Stadium to buy general admission tickets to sit in the bleachers. Most were black Louis supporters. A *New York Times* reporter estimated that fifteen thousand African Americans purchased tickets, probably the most ever to attend a prizefight in the United States. They had paid to see the "new-risen hero of their race," a phrase that surrounded Louis with a messianic air.[37]

By fight time, more than sixty-four thousand people had crushed into Yankee Stadium, making it the largest-drawing nontitle contest in history. As with the great Dempsey matches, the crowd was as conspicuous for its quality as its quantity. Governors and congressmen, movie moguls and industrial titans, and celebrities from the worlds of motion pictures and sports gathered in the rows closest to the ring, exchanging handshakes and smiles. To this virtually all-white congregation were added many of the most prominent black leaders of the day. Duke Ellington, a passionate Louis supporter, sat close to the ring. Not too far away were the Reverend Adam Clayton Powell, Jr.; Walter White; and Ralph Bunche.

The atmosphere was electric. The night was mild, the sky cloudless, and dusk turned to darkness by inches. Spectators searching for their seats struck matches, which made the stadium sparkle in the night. Expectations were palpable, thick in the crowd's nervous laughter and constant chatter.

Shorty before ten o'clock Louis climbed into the ring, where he waited about five minutes for Carnera to follow. He stood under the "brightest of bright lights," a twenty-one-year-old man who would soon engage in a fight that would make or break his career. Sportswriter Heywood Broun, sitting at ringside, could not take his eyes off the fighter. "Joe Louis was as impassive as if he were waiting for a street car."[38] He did not shuffle his feet in anticipation or moisten his lips. He neither spoke to anyone, smiled at anything, nor changed the disinterested look on his face. He was the absolute calm in the eye of the hurricane.

Eventually Carnera lumbered down the long aisle and fumbled through the ropes. He was followed by a handful of champions and former champions, all formally introduced and all quickly forgotten. Then ring announcer Harry Balogh, dressed as though he were going to the opera, grabbed the microphone. He had a loud voice, and a tendency toward malapropisms, neologisms, and overly formal speech. Earlier in his career when a fan in the cheap seats repeatedly screamed, "I want blood! Give me blood!" Balogh announced, "There will be no transfusions for fifty cents!" Another time, after a particularly fine oratorical flourish, an impressed reporter asked Harry if he had really extemporized his speech. Balogh shot back, "Hell, no, I made it up as I went along."[39]

But on this occasion Balogh was not looking for laughs. Before introducing the fighters he implored the spectators "in the name of American sportsmanship" to control their passions. "I therefore ask that the thought in your mind and the feeling in your heart be that, regardless of race, creed, or color, may the better man emerge victorious!"[40] Balogh's plea met with polite applause, but the thoughts in the spectators' minds and the feelings in their hearts were readily and loudly apparent during the introductions of the combatants. For the last several months, journalists—and especially those of the black press—had focused more attention on Louis than on any other black athlete in history. He had become the most famous black man in the country. Now his actions had to redeem their words.

Jack Blackburn had Louis ready to fight Carnera. He had used tall sparring partners in training camp to get his fighter accustomed to the size difference. From the opening bell, Blackburn's strategy was clear. Louis fought from a semi-crouch, accentuating the height difference. Carnera had never been a fluid heavyweight, and he reacted slowly. His best chance was to employ his left jab to keep Louis at a distance and clinch at close range. By fighting out of a semi-crouch, Louis made Carnera extend his jab a few extra inches, forcing him slightly off balance and opening him to counterpunches. Carnera had an added disadvantage. He pushed out his jab stiff-armed, like he was shoving a row of books off of a chest-high shelf. The punch itself had no snap or power; even if it landed it did little damage. This meant that all he could hope to do was to keep Louis away from him some of the time. It was not a defense that could keep Louis away from him for long.

In the first round the course of the fight took shape. For a brief time Carnera pecked at Louis with his jab, but when he adventurously threw a right, Louis launched a counter right of his own, which narrowly missed Carnera. Most of Louis' early counters missed, but their force clearly unsettled the Italian boxer. A left counter caught Carnera smack on the mouth, ripping an ugly cut on his upper lip and forcing him to swallow his own blood for the rest of the fight. It was the sort of gash that no cutman could mend, and it made Carnera appear to be wearing a permanent, inappropriate smile.

After a slow second round, Louis increased his attack, stalking Carnera "like a panther," noted one white *New York Times* reporter who was echoed by many others.[41] Grantland Rice, using the same image, wrote, "Joe Louis was stalking Carnera, the mammoth, as the black panther of the jungle stalks its prey. There was no wasted motion. . . . Louis was crowding in, waiting his chance."[42] Simply put, he was too quick for his opponent. Louis' feints and hard body shots opened Carnera's massive head. Time after time Louis landed crushing straight rights and left hooks. By the fourth round the former champion's face looked like a cut and bruised peach, a skin color unknown outside of Hollywood. In the fifth round Carnera tried to outmuscle Louis in a clinch, but instead the younger fighter tossed him into the ropes. Carnera looked at his smaller opponent incredulously, saying, "Oh, that should be me." Later Louis told reporters, "I knew [then] that I would get him."[43]

He did, in the next round. Early in the sixth he landed another hard right to the face and blood spurted from Carnera's mouth. Carnera was hurt and could not conceal it. Emboldened, Louis pressed forward, dropping Carnera with a clubbing right to the face. Carnera began to rise, fell back down, and then stumbled to his feet in a few seconds, and almost as quickly a right to the jaw sent him down for a second time. Once again he scrambled to his feet, but he was disoriented and frantic. Paul Gallico observed that Carnera was like a fine Spanish bull in the ring. "When wounded he turns all to courageous animal. He has only one instinct in his being and that is to get up and turn to face his own destruction. His great bulk and stricken, bloody face made him look horrible and fascinating."[44] Louis moved in and landed a hard overhand right and a short, punishing left, crashing Carnera to the canvas for the third time. Although he regained his feet, he was through. Looking pleadingly at the referee, his face a mask of blood and pain and fear, he made the slightest of gestures in a signal of defeat, mumbling to referee Arthur Donovan, "Give eet to heem, give eet to heem."[45] Donovan immediately stopped the fight. As Carnera turned away from Louis, Joe reached out and touched him on the back, a sad gesture of sympathy and understanding.

Louis stood in his corner, stoic and immobile, while all around him danced handlers and hangers-on. He appeared oddly unmoved by the dramatic ending of the fight, oblivious to the high-octane celebrations. Once Jack Johnson's golden smile and grinning confidence enraged white sportswriters; now Louis' impassivity drew their complaints. Rice commented that through the entire fight Louis' "expression never changed," adding that he "seems to be the type [of jungle animal] that accepts and inflicts pain without a change of expression." A few sportswriters argued that there seemed something cold and calculating about the fighter's assaults. Even in the locker room afterward the winner appeared unanimated in front of reporters who crowded close to him. "He wastes neither punches nor words, does this human fighting machine," wrote one.[46] Answering questions in an unadorned fashion, briefly and to the point, struck many of the white journalists—and none of the black—as, strangely, not quite proper.

The next day, Davis J. Walsh of the International News Service expressed the disquiet of his white colleagues, writing, "Something sly and sinister, and perhaps not quite human came out of the African jungle last night to strike down and utterly demolish a huge hulk that had been Primo Carnera, the giant. And high above the clamor over the knockout Joe Louis, the strange, wall-eyed, unblinking Negro, administered in the sixth round there rose a cry that smote upon the ear drums and left them shivering. It was the primitive, unnatural shriek of the Harlem belle, reacting to the emotions of centuries." Yes, that was it exactly: the fear that Louis had unleashed something dangerous. Although the spectators were orderly, there was something—a threat, a potential, a portent—oozing beneath the surface. It would take only a spark, perhaps "a careless word or an unthinking gesture to touch it off. Africa, the dark continent, was ready to revel at the slightest notice over this amazing person who has arisen overnight to challenge and defy the white man's innate sense of superiority."[47]

What Davis wrote nearly everyone felt. Joe Louis was a transcendent figure—part common man, part Moses—with the potential for incalculable good and, for many nervous white Americans, an equal amount of harm. After the fight, millions of eyes of black as well as white Americans focused on Harlem, the epicenter of the Louis phenomenon. Almost as soon as Donovan stopped the fight Harlem exploded, "crooning hallelujahs for Joe Louis."[48] The celebrations, commented a New York Times reporter, "outdid New Year's Eve."[49] In fact, added Pittsburgh Courier reporter Floyd J. Calvin under the headline "HARLEM GOES 'MAD WITH JOY,'" Harlem had its "biggest moment since it became the capital of the Negro world."[50] Not since the days of Marcus Garvey had there been such an expression of unity.

The festivities began when Charles Buchanan, the manager of the Savoy Ballroom who was in constant telephone contact with someone inside Yankee Stadium, raced out of his establishment and yelled, "He won!"[51] Buchanan's shout of pure joy was like a starter's gun. Jubilant Harlemites spilled out of Lenox Avenue bars and nightclubs and took over the streets, snarling traffic, yelling with abandon, and crying with joy. Inside the Savoy, people on the dance floor performed the Lindy Hop and the Shim-Sham-Shimmy. When it was learned that Louis was scheduled to make a late-night appearance there, a crowd of people sent a plate-glass door to the pavement in their rush to get into Harlem's most popular dance hall and gathering place.

The scene between 125th and 145th streets, along Lenox and Seventh avenues, swirled with a holiday excitement. Serenaded by blasts of automobile horns, wails of police sirens, clangs of bells, and bleats of whistles, men, women, and children danced in the streets until the mild night gave way to a cool, fresh dawn. Outside of the Savoy Ballroom, on Lenox between 140th and 141st streets, crowds waiting for Joe to make his triumphant appearance began to swell. Ten thousand people gathered close to the Savoy, and another fifteen thousand congregated along 140th Street just hoping to get a look at him. "It was surely something," recalled one observer, "Lindy-hopping Negros, Fletcher Henderson playing the 'King Porter Stomp' at ear-splitting decibels, painted ladies and men dressed just right, and all the joy in the world at arm's reach."

Bill "Bojangles" Robinson, the famous tap dancer and the unofficial mayor of Harlem, cruised slowly along Lenox Avenue trying to calm the crowds, and for a short time it worked. But the warmth and love of the good-natured crowd soon drew Robinson into its orbit. "I'm so happy I could eat a mud sandwich!" he shouted. "Didn't I tell you how it would be? Joe bore down on that old satchel-foot until he didn't know which end was up. I got to collect my money."

Not far away, in an apartment on 153rd Street, Louis—whom *Pittsburgh Courier* sportswriter William Nunn said had carried "the weight of an entire race on his shoulders"—sat relaxing by reading a newspaper. After pummeling Carnera he had no desire to fight the crowds to get to the Savoy. "I got to sleep sometime tonight," he told John Roxborough.[52] He tried, but after a brief nap he was awoken and persuaded to make his promised visit to the Savoy, which he did not long before dawn. He said nothing, stayed for only a short time, and then departed for a well-deserved rest.

Rest was not on the schedule for thousands of other black Americans. Celebrations took place in the black sections of every major northern city. The victory came as sweet partial vindication for the slights and abuses that blacks daily confronted and the battles they daily fought along the color lines of the country. The bold headline "JOE LOUIS WINS!" in the *Pittsburgh Courier* was an expression less of news than of pride and joy. The paper's "Talk o' Town" columnist addressed Louis in a personal manner. "Mr. Joseph Louis . . . Lawd! Bless your sweet soul! If I were near you, I would whisper something in your ear . . . so help me! But, since you are far away, take my word for it, you are everything God intended a good man to be . . . and 11,999,999 sepias agree with me. You are the tops, my boy! Be sweet and keep up the good work."[53] The columnist's feeling were echoed in African American newspapers across the land. Joe Louis *was* something special. A fighter, a deliverer, a source of pride—he was all these and more.

While Joe slept and blacks rejoiced, white journalists began to evaluate the meaning of Louis' victory. The sheer excitement of the celebrations in Harlem and in other "Negro sections," the crush of the crowds, the explosion of energy, and the volume of people and noise frightened many white authorities, reminding them of the riots after the 1910 Jack Johnson–Jim Jeffries fight. What would have happened if Louis had lost? What thin veneer of civilization separated the joyful, dancing, chanting crowd from an angry, howling, violent mob? And, as importantly, exactly who was Joe Louis? Less than two months before the Carnera fight he had been virtually unknown outside the small circle of boxing reporters and fans. They knew him as a heavyweight fighter—a "Negro" heavyweight fighter—sweeping through the West like a spring tornado. They understood his potential but only vaguely sensed his personality. Several reporters had already translated his quiet, restrained dealing with the press as sullen and moody. Others wondered if he was not another Jack Johnson clothed by his handlers and Mike Jacobs to look like a sheep. Was he a threat? Could his actions convert a crowd into a mob?

Louis' handlers moved quickly to calm the wild speculation. With an angry knife scar running down his face, a prison stint for murder, and a well-deserved reputation as being a bad man, Jack Blackburn did not seem the ideal candidate to address character issues. But capturing the essence of the Louis Doctrine laid down the year before by managers John Roxborough and Julian Black, Blackburn tried. "We will see to it that Louis never does anything that will in any way bring about public criticism," he asserted. "There will be no public statements belittling opponents, no gloating over victims, no act of any kind that can be offensive."[54] Louis' associates wanted him to be like Peter Jackson, a turn-of-the-century fighter "respected by everybody." "We will not let Louis follow in the footsteps of Jack Johnson," Blackburn promised. "He will be an example and a help to the colored race."[55]

***

The forces that the fighter let loose were not subject to the same restraints. The celebrations in Harlem were not unique; similar eruptions of joy and pride shook black neighborhoods in Detroit, Chicago, and to a lesser extent other towns large and small. For the hundreds of thousands of celebrants, Louis' victory was so much more than a pugilistic success. It reverberated through black America like a twentieth-century Emancipation Proclamation. Blacks broadly interpreted it as a social triumph, an unequivocal pronouncement that a black man had achieved a milestone. But the meaning of the event, and of Louis himself, remained uncertain.

It was unclear what he meant internationally. Will Rogers, America's leading social comic, sent a letter to the *New York Times* joking that America's "first battle of the next war" was contested in Yankee Stadium. "Big Italy met Little Abyssinia [*sic*] and Mussolini's first Spring drive was halted in its tracks."[56] Rayford W. Logan, one of the most prominent black historians of the day, was not joking at the New England Institute of International Relations Conference when he addressed the meaning of Louis' victory. "I'm afraid that the defeat of Primo Carnera last night by Joe Louis will be interpreted as an additional insult to the Italian flag, which will permit Mussolini to assert again the necessity for Italy to annihilate Abyssinia," he said.[57]

Ultimately, Italy did attack and brutally overrun Ethiopia. The humiliation of Carnera's defeat probably did not play a crucial role. But Logan was certainly correct that the fight and everything about Joe Louis was subject to interpretation. He *signified* something. Margaret Garrahan of the *Birmingham News* saw in Louis something southerners had long feared. "On the surface," she speculated, he "seems to be just a nice, accommodating colored boy. He likes to dance and eat and sleep and takes great pains with his clothes—spends hours dressing, as a matter of fact." But something troubled Garrahan. The idea of Louis dressed in a perfectly tailored suit, his hair "slicked down" just right, jarred with the fighter's "wooden brown eyes, the thick upper lip, the mouth that never smiles." Louis, she wrote, was something dangerous, a "tan-skinned throw-back to the creature of primitive swamps who gloried in battles and blood." Most disconcerting about the boxer, she concluded, were his silence and his lack of expression. She simply did not know what he was thinking, a circumstance that made her squirm. "He is like a wild thing tethered by civilization—a wild thing that somehow doesn't belong to civilization, but that having been born in it and caught in its strands, intends to wring the best from it. And do what his mentors tell him to get it."[58]

Garrahan glimpsed in Louis what she probably feared most, an untethered black population. Columnist Broun saw in the fighter something far more hopeful for the future of race relations in America. "In many respects, Joe Louis is the least colorful of all the recent heavyweights, but paradoxically enough he is likely to be the most interesting," he wrote. Max Baer, Jack Dempsey, Gene Tunney, Jack Johnson—they were heavyweights with larger-than-life personalities, heavyweights whose antics inside and outside the ring provided endless copy for sportswriters. But Louis was different, and "curiously enough" he was the least like Johnson. He defied glib stereotypes and proved "the futility of any dictum which begins, 'All men are . . .' or 'All Assyrians' or 'All Negroes.' For instance, it is some-times held that every Negro has a great capacity for gaiety, that he is emotionally high strung and a natural showman. Not one of these things is true of Joe Louis."[59]

Unlike other writers who characterized Louis as a savage beast, Broun found him "too perfect and finished. I prefer more primitive people." He discovered a "strange irony" in the boxer: "Joe Louis set all Harlem to dancing and jubilating. And he himself couldn't even work up a grin. From the beginning to the end he remained the man in the copper mask."[60] Broun, then, was no more capable of knowing Louis than was Garrahan. Northern and southern white journalists were mystified by a black man who did not conform to their expectations. They failed to answer two central questions: Who was Joe Louis? And what did he mean?

4

He Belongs to Us

John Henry said to the captain,
"A man ain't nothing but a man.
And before I'll be governed by this old steam drill,
Lawd, I'll die with the hammer in my hand,
Lawd, I'll die with the hammer in my hand."

On the South Side of Chicago, in a tavern filled with nervous black patrons, aspiring novelist Richard Wright cupped a cigarette in his right hand and bent his ear toward the radio. He was a member of the Communist Party, but on this particular night he was not interested in the biracial struggle of the working-class masses. It was September 24, 1935, perhaps a half hour before the opening bell of the Joe Louis–Max Baer heavyweight fight, and Wright was pulling for Joe to knock out his white opponent. He was one of millions of black and white Americans across the country, part of the vast sporting republic connected to each other by the invisible empire of the radio, feeling a surge of anticipation, rooting for their man to win, sharing an impulse so primal that it is probably encoded in human DNA.

As fight time drew nearer, Wright became a live wire, a fuse attached to dynamite, ready to explode. From New York, Newark, and Philadelphia, across the Midwest to Cleveland, Chicago, and Detroit, to the West Coast and Los Angeles, Oakland, and San Francisco it seemed that all black Americans old enough to understand what was happening were also gathered around radios. The great jazz musician Miles Davis recalled from his childhood the mood before a Louis match. "We'd be all crowded around the radio waiting to hear the announcer describe Joe knocking some motherfucker out," he later wrote. "And when he did, the whole goddamn black community of East St. Louis would go crazy, celebrate in the streets, drinking and dancing and making a lot of noise."[1] It would explode. Like Richard Wright felt he would do.

Across half a country from Wright, Max Baer felt that he too might explode—or be exploded. Outside his dressing room, Yankee Stadium was electric. This was the fight that America had been waiting for since Jack Dempsey and Gene Tunney retired, a contest between two heavyweights with hand speed, punching power, and that soupçon of something even more special. Both Baer and Louis exuded undeniable, stare-inducing, jaw-dropping charisma. Dubbed the Clown Prince of Boxing, Baer was an easygoing man-child, always ready with an off-color quip and an infectious smile. Critics charged that he was often undisciplined, sometimes mean, and rarely serious, but they also noted that he dominated every space he occupied. Inside and outside of the ring, he was always center stage.

Louis was Baer's polar opposite. New to the national spotlight, he was the most visible invisible man in America. In any public forum he seldom spoke, virtually never smiled, and laughed, genuinely laughed, not at all. Reporters commented on his stone eyes, expressionless mouth, and lockjaw approach to social intercourse. Meyer Berger, in a 1936 *New York Times Magazine* piece on the fighter, commented that Louis "says less than any man in sports history, including Dummy Taylor, the Giant pitcher, who was mute."[2] In fourteen months as a professional fighter, Joe had attracted more attention while revealing less of himself than probably any person who ever lived. That might have been part of the reason he fascinated people in the first place; he was America's great sporting riddle. That, and the fact that he was black and a seemingly relentless, indestructible force of nature that had swept across the heavyweight division like a tsunami, leaving shattered faces and destroyed careers in his wake.

As night swept across the Atlantic to New York, Yankee Stadium stirred awake. Promoter Mike Jacobs, the architect of Louis' career, had realized two weeks earlier that the fight would exceed even his sanguine predictions. He had scaled his tickets for a $500,000 gate, a great night by Depression standards. But the national demand for tickets surprised even the veteran scalper. It was too late to change the ticket prices so Jacobs did the next best thing. He added seats. Jacobs played Yankee Stadium like an accordion, doubling the number of ringside rows. In an action described by Joe Williams of the New York *World Telegram* as "both flagrant and fragrant trickery," Jacobs' new seating scheme left holders of seats in rows six, seven, and eight, for example, howling about their seats in rows forty-six, forty-seven, and forty-eight. As the gate assaulted the million-dollar mark—for the first time since the 1927 Jack Dempsey–Gene Tunney "Long Count" bout in Chicago—Jacobs managed to assuage the violence done to his good name.

The stadium filled in socioeconomic order. At 6 P.M., when the gates opened, men, and a surprisingly large number of women, holding general admission and bleacher seats bounded in and rushed for the best seats, quickly filling the outer sections. Most of the early arrivals were black, part of the estimated thirty-five thousand African Americans who attended the fight, the core divisions of the Joe Louis army. Many had to scrape and borrow to amass the money to buy a ticket for the fight and, if they came from out of town, to pay for the trip. A writer for the *Chicago Tribune* commented that an hour after the gates opened the "outer fringes of the stadium looked like Addis Ababa." For them the evening held the promise of a biblical festival, full of joy, celebration, and even deliverance. Although the fight was still hours from starting, the Louis sections "buzzed," alive with animated greetings, shouted predictions, and whispered prayers.[3]

Sportswriters also arrived early. In the 1930s a top sportswriter was the "aristocrat of the paper," highly paid and widely read, the dispenser of wisdom and the inside skinny. Knowing that they would have to file their stories shortly after the fight, they watched the preliminaries for filler material. But even more importantly, they reveled in the prefight gala. Paul Gallico recalled that he loved the hours before a major fight when he could "hang around and gossip with the gang."[4]

Hundreds of sportswriters filled the press rows. The secular gods of journalism were all there. Grantland Rice, with his seen-everything eyes peering out from under his beat-up, Confederate-gray fedora, was seated close to the ring, a fitting tribute to his status in the profession. But not far from Rice were the other immortals of the golden age of sportswriting—Gallico, secretly suspecting that he was writing beneath his talent; James P. Dawson, depending on his connection to the *New York Times* to give weight to his ordinary observations; Frank Graham, as dedicated to craft and truthfulness as any journalist in the business; O. B. Keeler of the *Atlanta Constitution,* convinced that Louis was a flash in the pan who had fed on nothing but ham-and-eggers.

The inner sections filled more slowly. People with secure seats and no interest in the preliminary matches had little reason to hurry through their meals or rush to the stadium. But after eight o'clock they began to arrive in record numbers, dressed splendidly in suits, gowns, and even tuxedos. The official count exceeded eighty-four thousand but the unofficial number was much higher, perhaps as high as ninety-five thousand. Gate receipts inched above $1 million for only the sixth time in history and for the first time for a match that did not involve Jack Dempsey. And all of this was accomplished with the highest-priced ticket pegged at $25. Never before, or since, had there been a million-dollar gate in which a ringside seat went for $25.

Joe Louis was the reason. For more than a year interest in him had been growing exponentially. At a time when President Franklin D. Roosevelt's New Deal for America was at its height, Joe Louis' New Deal for boxing was producing an economic miracle. Newspapers and magazines detailed his every movement, popular songs trumpeted his achievements, and news-reels presented the fruits of his labor to a nation of Louis-mad viewers. Although there was a vigorous debate over the origins and importance of this Louismania, there was no denying its existence, a palpable, audible hum that on the night of September 24 was centered in the Bronx. Louis, commented a journalist, was a "modern Moses," leading the "manly art out of the depression to a new 'high,'" escorting "boxing back to a big time basis and the million-dollar gate."[5]

Louis' appeal caught the many as well as the special few. The last spectators to take their seats were the elite of show business, politics, and the arts, the famous who came to be seen as much as to see. James Cagney, Edward G. Robinson, and George Raft—the cream of Warner Brothers— exchanged small talk with Cary Grant, George Burns, and Gracie Allen. Governor Herbert Lehman of New York played unofficial host to governors George H. Earle of Pennsylvania, Frank D. Fitzgerald of Michigan, Wilbur L. Cross of Connecticut, Harold Hoffman of New Jersey, and Louis J. Brann of Maine. New York mayor Fiorello La Guardia was joined by his counterparts from Jersey City, Newark, Chicago, and Detroit. Had Uncle Mike Jacobs needed a couple of performers to play and sing the national anthem, Irving Berlin and Al Jolson could have handled the job nicely. Had he asked for someone to punch an obnoxious heckler, ex-heavyweight champions Jack Johnson, Jack Dempsey, Gene Tunney, and Jack Sharkey, and the present titleholder, James J. Braddock, hovered near ringside. Had he desired someone to hit a baseball out of the stadium, Babe Ruth was close at hand. Had he, for some inconceivable literary emergency, cried out, "Is there a novelist in the house?" Ernest Hemingway, fresh from finishing *Green Hills of Africa* and cheering hard for Baer, was there. Had he needed a millionaire to float a loan . . . well, lucky Uncle Mike had his pick of a Vanderbilt, a Whitney, or any one of a dozen lesser sorts. Simply put, Mike Jacobs was a very fortunate man, for anybody who wasn't in Yankee Stadium that night must have felt like a nobody.

They all waited, patiently, joyously, expectantly, for two men, each weighing about two hundred pounds, to emerge from the darkness of the night into the white pillar of light that illuminated the ring. But one of the two, Max Baer, was beginning to have second thoughts about the whole affair. As he pulled on his ring attire he began to suffer from an acute attack of imagination. This can be a fatal malady for a fighter, as terminal in its own way as a glass chin or slow reflexes. A fighter is trained to anticipate and react—not to imagine. The imagination is the graveyard of too many ghosts.

Baer had lived with those ghosts for years. Everyone in boxing agreed that Baer had a killer right. Literally, a killer right. On August 25, 1930, he had fought Frankie Campbell in San Francisco's Recreational Park. Campbell was a talented young heavyweight, like Baer one of the best in California. In the second round, Baer landed a murderous right. Dazed and hurt, Campbell struggled through several more rounds, but in the fifth Baer trapped him against the ropes and scored with a series of hard punches. Too late the referee stopped the contest. Unconscious, Campbell slumped slowly to the canvas in a lazy, terminal fall. For half an hour the fighter lay inert on the canvas. Then his seconds carried him to the locker room, where they waited for an ambulance that was stuck in traffic. Thirteen hours after the fight Campbell died.

It took Ernie Schaaf longer to die. A little more than two years after beating Campbell, Baer administered a terrible beating to Schaaf. Just before the final bell, Baer lashed out with his signature right and knocked his opponent unconscious. Schaaf was never the same. He fought several more fights, but he complained of headaches and seemed much older than his twenty-three years. Six months after the Baer fight, he fought Primo Carnera, and after twelve virtually action-free rounds the Italian boxer landed a light glancing blow and Schaaf collapsed. Some spectators suspected that Schaaf had taken a dive. But he had not. A blood vessel had ruptured in his brain. Reports from the autopsy indicated that latent damage from his match with Baer had caused Ernie Schaaf's death.

More than most fighters then, Max Baer knew firsthand the dangers of his profession. He could imagine that what had happened to Frankie Campbell and Ernie Schaaf could happen to him. He had won and lost matches. He had won and lost the heavyweight title. He was a mortal fighter, probably past his prime and certainly not eager to end his career lying comatose in a hospital bed. The closer the time came to leave the security of his locker room, the more certain he became that the match was a tragic mistake. His pulse raced, his face flushed crimson, and he talked wildly of having a heart attack. He was afraid of what might happen when he was alone in the ring with Louis.

"Fighters know fear," said Jack Dempsey, the former heavyweight champion who was in the locker room with Baer. "It's like a lump in your chest. But you learn how to live with it. You don't talk about it and you try not to show it."[6] Ray Arcel, perhaps the most successful trainer in boxing history, agreed. "Most fighters are afraid. I don't mean they're so afraid they don't want to fight. I mean that most of them know some fear." Arcel recalled a world champion who did not fit Dempsey's stoic sufferer ideal. "This man was more nervous than any fighter I ever handled. He used to give up within himself. He'd be so sick before some fights that you could hardly get him out of bed. You'd have to scream at him and holler at him and abuse him. Yet if ever a man had courage, he had it."[7]

Baer was exhibiting the latter characteristics, forcing Dempsey into the role of a stern father. Baer said he had hurt his hand in training. He could not fight one-handed. Louis would kill him. "I don't care if they're both broken," Dempsey said. "You're not quitting now." Years later Dempsey recalled, "I let him know in very direct language that he had to get out there and fight. No choice. All he had to do was to get into the ring. When the bell rang he would be alright."[8] Finally, like a man who had just eaten his last meal, Baer slipped into his robe and trudged heavily out of the locker room. Heavyweight champion Jimmy Braddock, sitting close to ringside, watched Baer climb into the ring and thought that the fighter whom he had defeated for the title looked like a man going to the electric chair.

In the hours before the bout, while Baer was experiencing the torments of the damned, Louis was napping up on Sugar Hill, Harlem's most prestigious neighborhood. During the 1920s and 1930s such African American notables as Adam Clayton Powell, W. E. B. DuBois, Thurgood Marshall, and Langston Hughes lived on Sugar Hill. Louis was staying in an apartment on the sixth floor of 381 Edgecomb Avenue, the building where Duke Ellington lived. From his window he could see Yankee Stadium coming alive in the distance. Across a stretch of Harlem it seemed to sparkle like the Emerald City.

Waking from his nap, perhaps two hours before the fight, Louis decided to attend to a personal matter before going to the stadium. He had recently become engaged to Marva Trotter, a stenographer for the Chicago Insurance Exchange. Roxborough and Black encouraged the relationship, seeing in Marva a "safe" match for Louis. As Truman Gibson, Jr., Julian Black's lawyer explained, "Marva was beautiful. Came from a large respectable family. She had wonderful brown eyes, and very light skin—but she was black. That was important. She wasn't white, wasn't a gold digger, and wasn't anything like the women Jack Johnson married."[9] Her brother was a minister, and all her dates with Louis had been chaperoned. She had come to New York to see Joe fight Baer and had hoped to witness the fight as Mrs. Joe Louis. Marva and Joe planned to wed, they had just not set the date.

No better time than the present, Louis reasoned. At about 7:45 P.M. the Reverend Walter Trotter married his sister to Joe before a small gathering of friends. Julian Black was the best man; Marva's sister Novella was maid of honor. Jack Blackburn watched the short ceremony and commented that the thought of his wedding night should encourage Joe to knock out Baer early. By 8:10 Louis had kissed his bride, said a few hurried goodbyes, and scrambled into the back seat of a car headed for Yankee Stadium and another engagement.

***

"Baer gleamed white under the hot ring lights," observed a reporter. The comment, of course, drew attention to his race, but it was unnecessary. From the moment Jacobs signed the two fighters, race became central to the match. It was the most important interracial contest since the 1910 Jack Johnson–Jim Jeffries bout, and no article about the match was complete without some remark about one or both of the fighters' race. The day of the fight, for example, Paul Gallico commented that there was something Roman about the entire affair. It was "as though the emperor had said: 'There is news of a new gladiator from Africa, a man whom none can withstand.

Fetch Baer, my Jews. Throw the Jew and the black man into the arena and let them fight.' " Gallico's racial logic moved him to favor Louis in the fight. "Louis, the magnificent animal. He lives like an animal, untouched by externals. He eats. He sleeps. He fights. He is as tawny as an animal and he has an animal's concentration to his prey. Eyes, nostrils, mouth all jut forward to the prey. One has the impression that even the ears strain forward to catch the sound of danger."[10] And Gallico was considered a New York liberal on racial matters. White reporters from the South were not quite so generous in their descriptions of Louis.

Comments such as Gallico's added a hard edge to the fight, undeniably contributing to the interest in and the gate for the contest. It was also what made Richard Wright, Miles Davis, and several million other blacks ready to explode. They had heard it before—all the talk of Africa and Africans and animals. Joe Louis could not win for losing. He trained hard, fought valiantly, competed cleanly and honestly. He was a Horatio Alger morality tale—pluck and luck—up from the cotton fields of Alabama and the streets of Detroit to stand within an arm's length of the heavyweight title. He should have been a great human interest story for all Americans slogging through the Depression, but race had gotten in the way and Alger's *Ragged Dick* had become Kipling's *Jungle Book*. Instead of Joe Louis the American Dream, it had become, according to a white physician, Joe Louis the "primordial organism . . . in temperament, he is like a one-celled beastie of the mire-and-steaming-ooze period."[11]

But in the ring, race did not matter. Louis would not win or lose the fight because he was black and Baptist, any more than Baer would because he was white and Jewish. Baer was slightly bigger and more experienced, but he was also frequently undisciplined, unpredictable, and wild. Louis, regardless of what Gallico and other reporters wrote, was thoroughly disciplined, fairly predictable, and supremely controlled. At the weigh-in ceremony a reporter had commented to Baer that he looked in better shape than he had when he lost the title to Jimmy Braddock. Baer shot back, "Why shouldn't I be? This is one I trained for." That may have been true, but Louis was always in shape. Since turning professional he had fought too frequently to lose his conditioning.

The bell clanged and ninety-five thousand people seemed to take one long breath together. Baer wore a white Star of David on his dark trunks, and, true to Dempsey's prediction, once the bell sounded his fighting instinct took over. In the first round Louis fought cautiously, jabbing effectively out of a closed position. Grantland Rice, adopting the familiar jungle metaphor, wrote, "Dead pan, sleepy-eyed Joe Louis, with the half-lidded look of the jungle cobra, shuffled out to his night's work." Baer was predictably unpredictable. Occasionally he stuck out his left as if gauging the distance between himself and Louis. Sometimes he used his extended left to push Louis a few more inches away from him. Then, suddenly, he launched an amateurish right from long distance. Louis easily sidestepped the unproductive forays. Toward the end of the round the two exchanged hard punches along the ropes, which concluded with Baer hurt in the corner. The first round ended, wrote Rice, "as Baer reeled to the ropes with a fresh flow of crimson coming from his badly battered face."[12]

The second and the third rounds followed the pattern of the first. Louis fought with total control, landing perfectly timed left jabs that snapped back Baer's head. Occasionally his head jerked back as violently as if he had walked into a tree limb on a dark night. Every time Baer moved forward, Louis crushed a left into his face. Every time Baer attempted a looping overhand right, Louis stepped out of reach or moved inside and landed short, devastating counters. Baer looked like a "bloody hulk," bleeding from his mouth, nose, and small cuts around his eyes.[13] Toward the end of the third round, Louis landed a short, chopping right that knocked Baer to the canvas. After rising to his feet, a series of hard right hooks knocked him down again. He was on the canvas when the bell ended the round.

During an exchange in the third, one of the few black sportswriters in the press rows jumped to his feet and called out, "Kill him, Joe . . . Kill him!" Louis' seconds reacted as if they had been doused with icy water, darting angry looks at the miscreant and saying, "Please don't do that. That isn't nice. We don't want that sort of thing. It will do the boy harm." Louis was killing Baer in front of some sixty thousand white spectators. Louis' seconds did not need a sportswriter to announce the obvious. They could see, as Gallico later wrote, the sickened look in the white faces of the spectators, the look of people watching a terrible disaster.[14]

It was clear in the fourth round that Baer had given up any hope of winning the fight. He balled himself into a defensive position, keeping his arms and hands close to his body and face, fighting for survival and to limit the damage. "Fight him, Max—fight him," Dempsey yelled from the corner, but there was no fight left in him.[15] Louis jabbed. Jabbed again. And some more. The powerful jabs connected with frightening dull thuds. Sometimes he feigned a jab and sank a right or left under Baer's ribs near the heart. Baer winced and covered. Then Louis feigned and threw an overhand right that looked like it would cave in the left side of Baer's face. The punch bounced Baer off the ropes, and for a moment he hesitated, reaching out like he was trying to adjust his balance in a carnival's revolving barrel. He ventured a tentative step, but his legs collapsed and he tumbled to his hands and knees. His balance was gone, his legs were gone, his face was a mask of blood and pain and, perhaps, fear. As referee Arthur Donovan began his count, Baer looked at him, sitting on one knee in a familiar resting position of a football player. Then he slid to a sitting position, his legs folded under him. He did not seem focused on anyone or anything. Donovan finished his count.

After the fight reporters speculated that Baer could have gotten to his feet—not that he could have won or competed, just that he could have gotten to his feet and been hit more and bled more. The day after the fight Gallico argued that the point was moot. Baer had taken a "truly terrifying beating" and "could not have been any more helpless had he been pilloried with his arms in stocks."[16] In his dressing room after the fight Baer considered the point and confessed that perhaps he could have beaten the count. "I could have struggled up once more," he mused, "but when I get executed, people are going to have to pay more than twenty-five dollars a seat to watch."[17]

While Baer was pondering such questions as "Could you have?" and "Should you have?" in Harlem, on the South Side of Chicago, in Cleveland's Black Bottom, and elsewhere spontaneous street celebrations erupted. Minutes after Joe Humphreys, the venerated ring announcer, boomed "JOE LOUIS—THE WINNAH!" Richard Wright's South Side exploded. Witnessing the mad scene, Wright wrote, "Negroes poured out of beer taverns, pool rooms, barber shops, rooming houses and dingy flats and flooded the streets." They chanted "LOUIS! LOUIS! LOUIS!" throwing their hats in the air and walking through slums as though they were in a magical kingdom. "They shook the hands of strangers. They clapped one another on the back. It was like a revival," Wright continued. "Really, there was a religious feeling in the air. Well, it wasn't exactly a religious feeling, but it was *something*, and you could feel it. It was a feeling of unity, of oneness." And still more celebrants came. "They seeped out of doorways, oozed from alleys, trickled out of tenements, and flowed down the street; a fluid mass of joy." They went stark, raving "joy mad," clapping their hands and forming long, undulating snake lines. They blocked traffic and hectored white bystanders.[18]

Whites surely must have felt, Wright speculated, "that *something* had ripped loose, exploded." Something they thought was buried so deep in the grounds of oppression that it could never be unearthed. With the joy came bitter memories of past injustices. Some of the celebrants stopped street-cars, smashed a few windows, and expressed what was in their hearts. "Thought Joe was scared, didn't you? Scared because Max talked loud and made boasts. We ain't scared either. We'll fight too when the time comes. We'll win too." Wright was sure he knew what was happening in Chicago— and across America—in the hours after the fight. "A something had popped out of a dark hole, something with a hydra-like head, and it was darting forth its tongue." It must have felt like freedom.

The same scene, with only minor variations, was at that same moment taking place in every city with robust black populations. A front-page report in the *New York Amsterdam News* said the celebrations after the fight were reminiscent of the signing of the armistice ending the Great War. In Harlem, as in Chicago, bars, pool halls, barber shops, and tenements emptied after the fight, and thousands of people choked the streets of Harlem. "Washboards, tin gasoline cans and glass containers, horns and bells and whistles, and most anything else that would yield a sound, were put into use."[19] Spontaneous parades formed along the major avenues, one led by men holding high the flag of Marcus Garvey's Universal Negro Improvement Association. Entrepreneurs hawked postcards and metal buttons with pictures of Louis, and newsboys sold every early edition they could get their hands on.

Arthur Brisbane of the *New York American* described the inconveniences confronted by the "society cream" as they drove through Harlem on the way back to Manhattan. "Rejoicing in what they considered a great racial triumph, Harlem's population of a quarter of a million members of the Colored race laughed good humoredly at the Whites, convinced that they were going home dejected." Some in the crowd scrawled "JOE LOUIS" on the hoods of a few automobiles, but there were no major racial incidents, Brisbane reported.[20] But there easily could have been. He suggested that it might be a good policy to prohibit interracial fights.

After the society cream had maneuvered through Harlem, the celebrations became more frenetic, and there were a few episodes of violence. Someone stabbed Richard Ford in the back; someone else fractured Wheles Hammond's skull; and yet another person stabbed James Abney in the stomach. But even with the violence, an editorialist remarked that "there was something grand, something splendid" in the celebrations. Commenting on the reaction to the fight in Asia, the writer noted that even in Tokyo people "took exceptional delight" in the fact that the "Brown Bomber" defeated the "white idol."[21]

In Detroit and East St. Louis, Philadelphia and Baltimore, and in smaller towns and villages Louis' victory was toasted and celebrated. There were some racial flare-ups, but mostly they were small scale, nothing like the battles that followed the Johnson-Jeffries match. In Oyler Grade School in Cincinnati jubilant black Louis supporters touched off a rock-throwing incident, but a handful of policemen quickly restored order. In Utica, New York, a few interracial fights broke out. On the whole, however, blacks celebrated with each other and whites mostly went to sleep, knowing that next day they could read about the subhuman jungle animal in the local newspaper.

True to form, most of the white sportswriters both praised and damned Louis. They called him a great fighter, yet in the same piece suggested that he was more animal than human. To Grantland Rice he was a "jungle cat" and the "jungle cobra"; to Bill McCormick of the *Washington Post* he was a "panther" whose eyes were brimming with "blood lust."[22] Not to be outdone, Paul Gallico attempted an imaginative leap into Marva Louis' mind: "I wonder if his new bride's heart beat a little with fear that this terrible thing was hers. . . . The thing is macabre. . . . If Baer had offered more resistance, and there had been no rules, or referee, Louis would have killed him with his hands and never so much as blinked en eye, or altered the shape of his half-parted lips."[23] In victory then, Joe Louis was transformed by white journalists into a jungle beast, and worse, a psychopath.

***

Joe Louis cut a different figure in African American culture. By the end of 1935 he had become the most famous black man in the United States, perhaps even the world. Americans, especially black Americans, simply could not see, read, or hear too much about him. It was almost impossible to glance through a black newspaper without encountering Louis' face and dozens of articles touting his exploits. In the second half of 1935, for example, the *New York Amsterdam News* promoted everything from the Joe Louis Boys Club to Joe Louis rings. One advertisement claimed that the fighter's good health, at least in part, was the result of the laxative Fletcher's

Castoria that his mother had administered when he was a child in Alabama. "My mother raised me on Fletcher's Castoria until I was 11 years old," Joe said. "And it sure kept me regular. I can truthfully say that this is one reason why I have never been sick a day in my life."[24] A second advertisement suggested that the famous Louis style was enhanced by the custom-made suits tailored for him by Broadway's Billy Taub. A photograph showed the "famous clothier" measuring Louis for eight new suits, and Marva, his new bride, was so impressed with Taub's skills that she ordered "two unusual and smart suits for her own wardrobe."[25] Day after day, in African American newspapers across the country, Joe's name was associated with scores of assorted products and causes.

Endlessly, it seemed, editorialists turned to Louis to make some point about race. After his knockout of Baer, when Harlem predictably quivered with spasms of brotherhood, stopping cars and turning blocks around 125th Street into an outdoor party, a New York Amsterdam News editor noted that whatever else might be said about the celebrations, "one fact stands out." "Every Negro must feel that his fate is inexorably bound" to the success or failure of Louis. "This apparently holds true from the highest to the lowest Negro in America."[26]

Why was Louis so important? Why were black Americans so invested in a boxer? Because, answered another editorialist, "what he is doing as a fighter will do more to show up the fallacy of 'inherent inferiority' of Negroes than could be done by all the anthropologists in the nation—so far as the ears and eyes of the white masses are concerned. One flash of his mighty brown arm is a better argument than a book—to a great majority of men. His personality is more impressive than a thousand sermons, for he will be felt where no sermon would ever be heard."[27]

What stood out like a neon sign was that Joe Louis had become a grassroots, mass-participation political force. Politically in the 1930s African Americans were being pulled in several directions. On the political left was the Communist Party. Several blacks held important party offices, and worldwide the party proclaimed staunchly anti-imperialist and militantly antiracist positions. More than any other event, the Scottsboro case attracted blacks to the communist cause. Almost from the day the nine "Scottsboro boys" were arrested in Alabama in late March 1931 for the rape of two white women, the Communist Party's International Labor Defense (ILD) opposed the blatant racism and miscarriage of justice. Through a series of appeals and trials, the ILD provided legal defense, contributed financial support, and organized community rallies to aid the youths. Although relatively few African Americans actually joined the party, many appreciated the Communists' efforts.

The National Association for the Advancement of Colored People (NAACP) also received more general encouragement than actual members in black communities. Many blacks considered the biracial organization the mouthpiece for the "talented tenth," those middle-class African Americans for whom an integrated society promised admission to the most prestigious colleges, opportunities for higher-paying professional jobs, and homes in more affluent neighborhoods. They complained that the NAACP was headed by a man named White who looked white, and that its offices were staffed by light-skinned employees. Even the NAACP's primary focus on civil rights fueled criticism. During the worst years of the Great Depression, simple survival was a more pressing issue than admission into segregated graduate and professional schools. To be sure, black newspapers applauded the gains made by such leading NAACP lawyers as Charles Hamilton Houston and Thurgood Marshall, but for impoverished and undereducated blacks trapped in a northern ghetto, the progress of the talented tenth did not put food on the table or coal in the furnace.

More often than not, the most dynamic political efforts were local and issue oriented. Harlem's "Don't Buy Where You Can't Work" campaign produced more jobs than all the editorials in the NAACP, Urban League, and Communist Party publications. Similarly, the 1935 race riot showcased the appalling conditions of Depression Harlem more dramatically and starkly than any peaceful, organized protest. Hungry for immediate solutions to immediate problems, black Americans, like whites, gravitated toward leaders who trafficked in quick-fix answers. In Harlem, Father Divine preached a gospel of hard work, clean living, and racial cooperation. His Peace Mission Movement fed meals to the hungry, provided jobs for some of its followers, and gave hope for a better future. In Detroit, Wallace D. Fard organized the Nation of Islam. As run by his disciple Elijah Muhammad, the Nation rejected integrationist goals and practiced community-centered, racially based economic nationalism. Although Divine and Muhammad were powerless to alter the course of the Depression, they were as important to black America as Dr. Francis Townsend and Senator Huey Long were to white America.

Joe Louis communicated a message more socially ecumenical than those propagated by the NAACP or the Communist Party, and more individually uplifting than those espoused by Elijah Muhammad and Father Divine. More than any man, any force, of the generation, Louis confirmed full black equality—even, some asserted, superiority. In the ring he did not ask for respect or equality; with his fists he demanded and received it. No foundry pay for him. He earned hundreds of thousands of dollars doing to white men what a black man would be lynched for doing outside of the boxing ring. As such, Louis exerted a powerful appeal, symbolically expressing African Americans' struggle for equality and deep-seated yearning for a settlement of past injustices.

Richard Wright, sitting in that bar in Chicago, recognized the meaning of Joe Louis. After the Louis-Baer fight, he wrote, "Four centuries of oppression, of frustrated hopes, of black bitterness, felt even in the bones of the bewildered young, were rising to the surface. Yes, unconsciously they had imputed to the brawny image of Joe Louis all the balked dreams of revenge, all the secretly visualized moments of retaliation, AND HE HAD WON! Good Gawd Almighty! Yes, by Jesus, it could be done! Didn't Joe do it? You see, Joe was the consciously-felt symbol. Joe was the concentrated essence of black triumph over white. . . . And what could be sweeter than long-nourished hate vicariously gratified?" Wright recognized Louis as a political force, understood how millions of blacks interpreted him. "From the symbol of Joe's strength they took strength, and in that moment all fear, all obstacles were wiped out, drowned. They had stepped out of the mire of hesitation and irresolution and were free! Invincible! A merciless victor over a fallen foe! Yes, they had felt all that—for a moment . . ."[28]

The radio was more important than any other force in spreading the gospel of Joe Louis. A dozen years before Louis' fights with Primo Carnera and Max Baer, there was no national radio. There were no national networks, and except for the broadcast of a few isolated sporting events, there were no nationally broadcast news and programs. Overwhelmingly, radio was local or at best regional. By 1935 this had changed. Increasingly, Americans were wired together by a national network of radio broadcasts, ranging from news, suspense, and comedy shows to World Series games and important boxing matches. The solemnity of Roosevelt's fireside chats, the rituals of political conventions, the humor of Jack Benny and Red Skelton, the voice of Bing Crosby, the antics of Amos 'n' Andy, the thrill of World Series games and heavyweight title fights, the endless soap operas, adventure shows, and mystery programs—all were part of a new national culture experienced by tens of millions of Americans at the very same moment.

Louis connected black Americans to the radio mainstream. Many black families purchased their first radios just to hear Joe Louis fights. Those with radios invited friends to their homes to listen to the breathless broadcasts. They would make a party of the evening, celebrating Joe and feeling right about their whole race. "Joe was our avenging angel," remembered actor Ossie Davis. In a decade when it was dangerous for a black man to confront a white man, when there were lynchings and cross burnings, Louis "stated our capacity to defend ourselves if given a chance. He was spiritually necessary to our sense of who we were, to our manhood."[29]

Writer Maya Angelou testified to the social and psychological power of listening to a Louis fight. Although she confused some of the smaller details of Louis' career, she was clear about its impact. On the night of a Louis match she recalled that a congregation of friends and relatives wedged themselves into her grandmother's store in Stamps, Arkansas. Her Uncle Willie would turn up the radio so the children on the porch could hear, and in the main room women sat with babies on their laps and men leaned against shelves or each other. There was laughter and talk and a good warm feeling of fellowship. "He gonna whip him till that white boy call him Momma," a man said, and everyone laughed. Then the fight started. Before long Joe had his opponent in trouble, forcing him to clinch to clear his head. "That white boy don't mind hugging that niggah now, I betcha," someone joked. Everyone in the store listened with one ear, cheered with one voice, and pulled as hard as they could for Joe. Angelou wondered if the fight announcer realized that when he said "ladies and gentlemen" he was addressing "all the Negroes around the world who sat sweating and praying, glued to their 'master's voice.' "[30]

Between rounds some of the listeners bought RC Colas or Dr Peppers, putting their coins on the cash register. But no sales were rung up during the fight. Uncle Willie did not want to miss a word coming out of the box. Almost inevitably Joe's opponent would land a few hard punches. The disembodied voice would get excited. "He's got Louis against the ropes and now it's a left to the body and a right to the ribs. Another right to the body, it looks like it was low. . . . It's another to the body, and it looks like Louis is going down."

Uncle Willie's people reacted as though they were taking the blows. "My race groaned," Angelou recalled. "It was all our people falling. It was another lynching, yet another Black man hanging on a tree. One more woman ambushed and raped. A Black boy whipped and maimed. It was hounds on the trail of a man running through slimy swamps. It was a white woman slapping her maid for being forgetful." It was the worst thing that could be imagined. "This might be the end of the world. If Joe lost we were back in slavery and beyond help. It would all be true, the accusations that we were lower types of human beings. Only a little higher than the apes. True that we were stupid and ugly and lazy and dirty and, unlucky and worst of all, that God Himself hated us and ordained us to be hewers of wood and drawers of water, forever and ever, world without end."

Of course, Joe did not fall. "He's off the ropes, ladies and gentlemen. He's moving toward the center of the ring." In a moment, fast as the glow of a lightning bug, Joe is back on the offensive, moving forward, delivering punishing lefts and rights, knocking his opponent to the canvas. "Babies slid to the floor as women stood up and men leaned toward the radio." Everyone held their breath as the referee counted. And then . . . "ten." "The fight is all over, ladies and gentleman." Angelou remembered the announcer calling Louis the champion of the world. "Champion of the world. A Black boy. Some Black mother's son." It was worth the price of another RC Cola, and a peanut patty or Baby Ruth. Maybe even a cola with a shot of white lightning. Yes, it was worth that—and more. It was worth the world.

The newness of national radio broadcasts, and the refinements of the announcer's craft, contributed to the importance of Joe Louis. In the 1930s radio became the medium of choice for the most momentous national news. Roosevelt's fireside chats galvanized listeners, taking them, as it were, inside the Oval Office and sitting them in front of the president of the United States. FDR was talking to them, not to congressmen or cabinet members. He addressed them personally, in a voice modulated to demonstrate his concern and respect for every American. Radio sports announcers also developed a conversational, intimate style. Such famed boxing announcers as Graham McNamee and Clem McCarthy abandoned the declamatory style for something more personal and individually identifiable. They combined blow-by-blow reporting with down-home color observation. They ranged across a sea of emotions, drawing the listener into the drama of the moment. The very best could make their listeners feel that they were in Yankee Stadium or at the Polo Grounds watching Louis pummel an opponent and experiencing the fight from a ringside seat. They made the fights so real that listeners occasionally died from excitement.

As the broadcasts made Louis mythical, the record industry celebrated his triumphs. No athlete, and probably no person since Jesus Christ, had inspired more recordings. One authority noted that there were at least forty-three songs recorded about Louis, and given the decentralized nature of blues recording there were undoubtedly many more. Several of the early recordings emphasized the fighter's skills. In "He's in the Ring (Doin' the Same Old Thing)," for example, Memphis Minnie, a well-known blues singer, praises Louis' "mean left" and "mean right," comparing one of his punches to the "kick from a Texas mule." And in "Joe Louis Is the Man," Joe Pullum's clear, high-pitch voice warns that "He throws them fists like a .45 throwin' man/He throws it heavy and he throws it slow/ . . . . /And when it hits ya you sure bound to hit the floor." The singers repeatedly recounted the boxer's feats, treating him like a black Hercules or Samson endowed with supernatural strength and power.[31]

The Joe Louis the singers construct transcends Hercules and Samson, however. He is also a role model and a black Moses, sent by some higher being to deliver his people to the promised land. Songs stress his generosity to his mother—"Bought his mother a brand new home on some brand new land"; his clean living—"Joe lives just like a preacher/Don't dip chew or smoke"; and his modesty in victory—"He doesn't smile he doesn't frown/ Just turns around and trucks on down." Louis, the songs imply, was there for every black mother's son—and daughter, too. There to deliver them at some level from the clouds of the Depression and the blues of oppression. Memphis Minnie knew what Joe promised. She sang, in a husky, insistent voice,

> I wouldn't even pay my house rent
> I wouldn't buy me nothing to eat
> Joe Louis said "Take a chance with me
> I'm going to put you back on your feet."
> He's in the ring (he's still fighting)
> Doing the same old thing!

There is an undercurrent of uplift and joy in her song, a sense that life is a boxing match and Joe Louis is her champion. Joe, not FDR, is the true savior for black Americans.

That same sentiment drifts through folktales about Louis during the 1930s. In his writings and speeches Martin Luther King, Jr., told a story about the importance of Louis for African Americans during the Depression. It is a tale of a black convict in a southern prison who was the first victim of a new form of capital punishment. Rather than hanging him, the state executed him in a gas chamber. A microphone was placed in the chamber so scientists could evaluate the victim's reaction. "As the pellet dropped into the container," King insisted, "and gas curled upward, through the microphone came these words: 'Save me, Joe Louis! Save me, Joe Louis!' " Pondering the meaning of the tale, which had no basis in fact but was an established folk legend, King commented, "Not God, not government, not charitable-minded white men, but a Negro who was the world's most expert fighter, in the last extremity, was the last hope."[32]

And in fact, by 1935 Louis had begun to receive hundreds of letters, from men on death row and on the doorstep of the poor house, from women who had young mouths to feed and had lost all hope in social and governmental institutions, saying, in effect, Save me, Joe Louis! The letters, noted the *New York Amsterdam News,* came from Mississippi, Minnesota, Illinois, and most of the other states; from England, Norway, Mexico, and other countries. They came in the hundreds, and then thousands. One man asked for two dollars so he could double it by betting on Joe. A woman wrote to tell Joe that she had named her new bull after him; she included a picture of the bull. Another man asked for the money he needed to travel to New York to watch Joe fight.[33] Most of the correspondents wanted something, usually not much. If they all did not say, "Save me, Joe Louis!" there was an undeniable undercurrent of "Help me, Joe Louis!" They wrote to Joe like Americans wrote to FDR, intensely personal letters composed on the assumption that they would receive individual attention. Louis had become the last hope for the all but hopeless, the black president for the politically powerless.

Assessing Louis' impact on African American culture, scholar Lawrence Levine compared the fighter to folk hero John Henry. Joe Louis, like John Henry, was a "baaad man," a moral hard man who "defeated white society on *its* own territory and by *its* own rules. They triumphed not by breaking the laws of the larger society but by smashing its expectations and stereotypes, by insisting that their lives transcend the traditional models and roles established for them and their people by the white majority." They were both men of physical dominance, of supernatural feats of strength, epic in scope. Both were quietly confident, heroes of great dignity and resolve who allowed their actions to speak for them. For millions of blacks Louis was the modern John Henry, a "representative figure whose life and struggle are symbolic of the struggle of worker against machine, individual against society, the lowly against the powerful, black against white. His victory is shared and his demise is mourned."[34]

As 1935 ended and 1936 began, however, there was no demise of Joe Louis. On December 13, 1935, he knocked out Paulino Uzcudun, an outstanding Basque heavyweight, in the fourth round. A month later, on January 17, 1936, he took out the top-ten ranked Charley Retzlaff in the first round, raising his record to twenty-seven wins, twenty-three by knockout, and no losses. He was John Henry before the steel-driving man's clash with the steam engine. He seemed unbeatable. A Detroit sportswriter expressed mock disappointment with Louis' performance in the Retlzaff bout. He had predicted that Retzlaff would not last a minute. "So when the affair dragged along to one minute and twenty-five seconds we felt that the Chocolate Clouter either didn't have his mind on his work or else was beginning to slip."[35]

But what if he did slip? As historian Thomas R. Hietala suggested, Louis had become like the protagonist in Langston Hughes' poem "Mother to Son."

> So boy, don't you turn back.
> Don't you set down on the steps
> 'Cause you finds it's kinder hard.
> Don't you fall now—
> For I'se still goin', honey,
> I'se still climbin',
> And life for me ain't been no crystal stair.[36]

Louis was ascending toward the championship, and black Americans were taking joy in his climb, celebrating each step up the heavyweight ladder, interpreting his successes as their successes, his rewards as their rewards. In 1935 Ruby Berkley Goodwin, a writer for the *Los Angeles Sentinel*, penned a letter to Louis, explaining that her four sons, like "every Negro lad in America," were enthralled by his exploits. "Don't fail them," she stressed. "Keep your life and your fighting clean. Now, Joe, don't let us down. . . .

Whatever temptation comes, whether wrapped up in a bottle or a skirt, we hope you'll just think of the million little brown and black boys who want to be just like Joe Louis."[37]

***

The day after the Baer fight, the *New York Evening Journal* ran a Burris Jenkins, Jr., illustration of Louis. It shows a post-fight Louis with his hands still taped, sitting and pensively considering a small globe labeled "FIGHT WORLD" that he is balancing in his right hand. The caption reads, "GOTTA HAND IT TO YOU, JOE!"[38] There was nothing ambiguous about the meaning. Although he had not won the title, he controlled the division. Any heavyweight, including titleholder Jimmy Braddock, had to come to Louis for a big-money fight. Even Louis was now convinced. He was never better than in the Baer fight, he later judged. "I've never had better hand speed; I felt so good I knew I could have fought for two or three straight days." For the first time he thought, "Maybe I can go all the way."[39]

Joe Louis was in the catbird's seat. He seemed to have everything. "I had a wife who was a dream, I had money, I had fame."[40] He was living the life—a kid in the candy store, the American Dream. Before he had ever stepped foot in Hollywood he had become what Hollywood manufactured. Joe Louis, born in a shack in Alabama, raised in a ghetto in Detroit, had through hard work, determination, talent, and blind good fortune made it to the pinnacle of his profession. His life was a script. Hollywood beckoned.

After his January match with Retzlaff, Louis took a break from boxing. Since turning professional in July 1934 he had fought at least once in all but three months. The rhythm of his life followed the beat of a speed bag—training and fighting, gyms and arenas, rat-a-tat-tat. That changed in mid-January. He traveled to Hollywood and starred in a low-budget film loosely based on his life.

During the Depression, Hollywood filmmakers fed Americans alternative rags-to-riches stories. Gangster films—from *Little Caesar* (1931), *Public Enemy* (1932), and *Scarface* (1931) to *Manhattan Melodrama* (1934), *Angels with Dirty Faces* (1938), and *The Roaring Twenties* (1939)—featured men who made fortunes outside of the law. They were men from the slums, often immigrant and poorly educated but with drive and ambition, men who saw the Depression as an opportunity and traditional authority as a mere nuisance. Boxing films trafficked in the similar themes. *The Champ* (1931), *Winner Take All* (1932), *The Life of Jimmy Dolan* (1933), *King for the Night* (1933), *The Prizefighter and the Lady* (1933), *Palooka* (1934), *Kid Galahad* (1937), *The Crowd Roars* (1938), *They Made Me a Criminal* (1939), *City for Conquest* (1940)—these and other films portrayed boxing as a fluid, democratic sport, a meritocracy in which what you are and not who you are is what matters. Before film noir claimed boxing as its own in the 1940s, boxing movies in the 1930s emphasized that the American spirit and the belief in the American Dream were surviving hard times.

Spirit of Youth (1938) was intended to capitalize on the 1930s market for schmaltzy boxing films. In the film, Joe Thomas (Joe Louis) moves from his home and closely knit family in Alabama to Detroit, where he begins to box and wins the Golden Gloves. Away from the wholesome influences of his family and his girlfriend, Mary, he falls in with nightclub owners, gamblers, and showgirls. He shirks training, spends nights with a manipulative showgirl, and is knocked out in an important fight. After the fight he rededicates himself to boxing and earns a title shot, which he wins after Mary reunites with him at ringside. In the end it is a redemptive tale. Like many of the era's boxing films, it peddles rural family values and warns against the corrupting influences of cities.

Spirit of Youth was produced by the Globe Picture Corporation as a "race" film, one with a virtually all-black cast aimed at a virtually all-black audience. Lou Golder, the film's producer, surrounded Louis with leading African American performers, including Edna May Harris, Clarence Muse, and the Savoy Ballroom dancers. But the film was hindered by several features, the most important of which was Louis. To label him wooden would suggest flexibility and range wholly lacking in his performance. When the film premiered in early 1938 the reviewer for *Variety* wrote that it "isn't so bad, considering the handicaps entailed in the star's lack of facial and lingual mobility."[41]

The film also ran into problems with the censors. Joseph Breen's Production Code Administration judged the film "questionable from the standpoint of policy, because it shows, among other thing, several scenes of a black man victorious in a number of fistic encounters with white men."[42] Ignoring the reality of Louis' career, Breen believed that the film would face serious distribution obstacles in the South. The idea that a film based on

Louis' career could provide social uplift for blacks was lost on the country's leading censor. The antics of Stepin Fetchit were fine; the example of Joe Louis was dangerous.

In early 1936 Louis was unconcerned about Breen's objections, and he had little interest in the production of *Spirit of Youth*. Rather in a case of life imitating art, he was living the second act of the drama, the part when Joe Thomas forgets what is important. For a young, handsome, famous athlete with time on his hands and money to burn, Hollywood was a wonderland. Though recently married, Louis behaved like a bachelor, and an extremely eligible one at that. "The women, the starlets, white and black, came jumping at me," he remembered.[43] And he did not jump back. He lived like Jack Johnson but in a far less public manner.

Women were not the only passion he indulged. He had found a new love—golf. New York columnist Ed Sullivan had introduced Louis to the country club sport, and Joe took to it immediately. A great boxer and a very good baseball player, he had the basic skills to be an outstanding golfer. He was a fluid, gifted athlete with exceptional hand-eye coordination and near-perfect timing. In addition, he understood the importance of technique and training. He took an interest in the swing, the way a golfer shifts his weight and allows his hand to release toward the target. For a boxer it was a logical and natural movement. And the feeling of a well-struck ball, the intoxicating moment of impact, was a sensation he knew from the ring. He was soon hitting buckets of balls, and in Hollywood there seemed no end of celebrity golfers and teaching professionals who wanted to play a round with Joe Louis. He enjoyed rounds with comedians Bob Hope and Jimmy Durante; singers Eddie Cantor, Al Jolson, and Bing Crosby; journalists Ed Sullivan and Hype Igoe. On the course with a few golfing buddies he would relax, laugh at their stories, and hit the ball, thoroughly enjoying everything about the sociable sport.

If he missed the regimen of training and boxing, he did not mention it. But boxing missed him. He was money in the bank at a time when money was tight. Columnist Damon Runyon called him the "greatest asset to the boxing game that has been produced since Dempsey went into decline."[44] His purses had exceeded $400,000 in 1935, an extraordinary sum for an athlete. As a point of comparison, in 1930 Babe Ruth's salary reached $80,000, which in itself was a fabulous amount. No other baseball player was anywhere near Ruth's number. For the 1941 season Joe DiMaggio made $37,500, and the next year—after hitting in fifty-six consecutive games, leading the Yankees to a World Series victory over the Dodgers, and winning the most valuable player, player of the year, and sportsman of the year awards—he did not receive a raise. What Louis made, like the salaries of Ruth and DiMaggio, was only the tip of the financial iceberg. It is impossible to calculate how much the "Louis phenomenon" earned for others.

Before Louis traveled to Hollywood, Mike Jacobs had signed his next fight, a mid-June engagement against former champion Max Schmeling. It was part of Louis' ex-champions tour—Carnera and Baer were both ex-heavyweight champions—and virtually every journalist believed that Louis would knock out the German fighter as easily as he had the Italian and American ones. In one of his columns, Paul Gallico sent a message: "To my friend Max Schmeling—Stay in Germany. Have no truck with this man. He will do something to you from which you may never fully recover. You haven't a chance. You are wealthy, and have your health and strength. And besides Der Fuehrer wouldn't like the pictures—you my friend, unconscious and standing erect, your conquerer, an . . . ah . . . Untermensch as they say in Germany."[45]

An examination of Schmeling's record could not have inspired anyone to place a wager on him. Strike one—he had begun his professional career in 1924 in Düsseldorf. Few heavyweights of any stature came from the Continent, and none from Germany. Strike two—after winning a few lightly regarded European championships he came to America and fought for Gene Tunney's vacated heavyweight title, winning the crown on a foul. Writhing on the canvas, holding one's groin, was regarded as no way to win the crown that had been worn by John L. Sullivan and Jack Dempsey. Strike three—a year later he lost the title on a controversial decision to Jack Sharkey. He should have been out, especially after Max Baer knocked him out the following year and Steve Hamas outpointed him the year after that.

Schmeling, however, was more than the sum of his wins and losses. If there was a theme to Schmeling's life, speculated German scholar George von der Lippe, it was survival. "He adapt[ed] to the situation, he adapt[ed] to the people he [dealt] with."[46] He was a German Talleyrand, able to adjust his politics and behavior to please whatever group held sway in his country. Weimar Republic, Nazi dictatorship, postwar democracy—Schmeling moved through the ideological minefields with the grace of a gymnast on a balance beam, making abrupt turns and flips, defying the laws of gravity, and always landing solidly on both feet. Never in the history of the sport had a boxer so adroitly controlled his own image, career, and destiny.

During the Weimar years, at the beginning of his ring career, Schmeling was the darling of Berlin's cabaret set. He was in the right place at the right time. Although boxing had shallow roots in German culture, during the 1920s the intellectual elite accurately associated the sport with Jazz Age America. Boxing was democratic, dynamic, glamorous, virile, and violent. It was like America, the new center of world culture, and German avant-garde artists moved toward the ring lights like moths. Boxing was modernism in action, it was multi-ethnic, jazzy, and urban—it was the very definition of *Amerikanismus*. As such, Berlin's fight scene attracted such cultural luminaries as filmmaker Josef von Sternberg, artist George Grosz, playwright Bertolt Brecht, and novelist Thomas Mann. Schmeling, the leading European heavyweight, became a totem for the avant-garde community. Boxing was an art, he said. He too was an artist. It seemed only natural that Grosz painted his portrait, Brecht exchanged opinions about the ring with him, and the doors to the trendiest cafes and salons opened wide for him.

Culture Berlin had, but deutschmarks for big-money prizefighting it did not. The German heavyweight title carried little weight west of the Rhine, let alone on the other side of the Atlantic, where the best heavyweights were earning fortunes. In late 1928 Schmeling sailed to New York, determined to make his way in that world as easily as he had in Berlin. Once again he adapted, dumping the manager who had guided his career in Germany and entering into a managerial arrangement with Joe Jacobs. Everything about Jacobs was fast and loud—his voice, the clothes he wore, and the women he dated. Nicknamed Yussel the Muscle, Jacobs seemed to have been born with a cigar in his mouth, and he maneuvered down Broadway and Eighth Avenue as smoothly as Schmeling moved around Berlin. Schmeling wanted a Jewish manager who could make things happen for him. Jacobs was the man. If there was a promoter, manager, or journalist he did not know, the person did not matter.

Jacobs Americanized Schmeling. He began by pointing out the obvious —Schmeling looked like Jack Dempsey's twin. With their thick necks, high cheekbones, square jaws, dark hair, almost black piercing eyes, and well-muscled bodies, they had the ruggedly handsome looks of a saloon bouncer. Jacobs insisted that Max not only looked like Jack, he hit and fought like Jack. "A killer, dis boy's a killer," he said to anyone who would listen. In a matter of months Jacobs got Schmeling a few major fights. In a little over a year he watched his fighter win the title. Of course, Schmeling won the title while sitting on his stool while Jacobs moaned about the terrible low blow "his boy" had suffered. But no matter, a title was a title.

But Schmeling, like Weimar Germany, flamed out in the early 1930s. By 1936, when Mike Jacobs signed him to fight Louis, Schmeling was damaged goods. He had been beaten up, knocked out, and generally written off. Then he had made a modest comeback in Germany, defeating Walter Neusel, Steve Hamas, and Paulino Uzcudun, but the victories turned few heads in the United States. As bluesman Joe Pullum said in the title of a song, "Joe Louis Is the Man." Max Schmeling was just an opponent.

Schmeling, however, exhibited an odd, almost symbiotic relationship with his country. He was a man not of a career, but of careers. If his first career rose and fell with the Weimar Republic, his second surged with the acquisition of total control over Germany by Adolf Hitler. Like the Weimar avant-garde—but for very different reasons—Hitler extolled boxers and boxing. Boxers were like soldiers, men of strength, determination, and action, men who settled disputes violently rather than peacefully. All German boys and men, Hitler thought, should learn to box. "There is no sport that so much as [boxing] promotes the spirit of attack, demands lightning decisions, and trains the body in steel dexterity," he wrote in *Mein Kampf.* "The young, healthy body must also learn to suffer blows. . . . It is not the function of the folkish state to breed a colony of peaceful aesthetes and physical degenerates."[47]

After his appointment as chancellor in January 1933, Hitler promoted a "purified" boxing program in Germany. As David Margolick has demonstrated so eloquently, Nazi efforts to render boxing free of Jews—*judenrein*—preceded purges in other professions. Within months, both amateur and professional governing bodies banned Jews from boxing. No Jews, even if they had converted, could be associated with boxing, whether as fighters, promoters, managers, trainers, seconds, physicians, lawyers, or dentists. European and American boxing commissions greeted the anti-Semitic measures with a nearly audible yawn. The *New York Times* buried a small wire dispatch about the ban deep in the sports section, below a story about a horse show, and the Berlin correspondent of a British boxing magazine somehow managed to blame Jews for provoking the ban.[48]

Considering the remarkable change in the political winds, Schmeling appeared to be in an awkward position. To begin with, Nazi propagandists favored the purer amateur version of boxing over the greedily mercenary professional one. Professionals fought for themselves, for their own profit and glory, rather than for the honor and glory of the *volk*. And no German professional was as monetarily motivated as Schmeling. Adding to this problem, Schmeling's Jewish manager Joe Jacobs said kaddish for his dead mother and had a Yiddish nickname.

But Schmeling could adapt to the apocalypse. And Hitler understood the propagandistic value of a former heavyweight champion who perhaps could win the title again. In May 1933, before Schmeling departed Germany for New York to fight Max Baer, Hitler invited the German boxer to the Reich Chancellory. There Schmeling met Joseph Goebbels, Hermann Goering, and several cabinet members. He found Hitler "charming," fully relaxed, confident, and friendly. After a brief talk, Hitler said, "I've heard that you're going to America." He then added casually, "If anyone over there asks how it's going in Germany, you can assure the doomsayers that everything is moving along quite peacefully."[49] Schmeling was flattered; no Weimar politician had paid him the least attention. But over time he came to understand Hitler's comment. It was the beginning of an informal contract between the athlete and the politician. Hitler granted Schmeling certain dispensations—travel visas to the United States, a Jewish American manager, the luxury of remaining nominally nonpolitical, and certain freedoms of speech and association. In return, during his American sojourns Schmeling affirmed that all was well in Hitler's Germany. Yes, everything was in order and functioning smoothly. Throughout the rest of the decade both men honored the terms of the bargain.

By December 1935, when Schmeling signed to fight Louis, he and Hitler, that strikingly non-Aryan looking odd couple, had become quite cozy. Schmeling's victories in Germany had erupted with as many cries of "Sieg Heil!" and choruses of the "Horst Wessel Song" as a Nuremberg rally. The Nazi leaders, especially Goebbels, were thoroughly taken with Schmeling's wife, Anny Ondra, a gorgeous blond movie star, and the celebrity couple had enjoyed an afternoon tea with Der Fuehrer. Schmeling had become a German Uebermensch, wealthy, famous, and connected. Perhaps it had all gone to his head, for when he agreed to fight Louis it was not for the money. He was already rich. Perhaps, as he said, he wanted to become the first man to win the heavyweight crown twice. Louis was a final step toward that goal. Or perhaps, as Nazi publications suggested, it was for the Fatherland, for the greater good and the eternal glory of Germany. Either way,

Schmeling believed what few reporters in the United States would even entertain—that he had a chance to defeat Joe Louis.

Schmeling saw something. In Germany he repeatedly watched Louis' fights with Carnera and Baer, analyzing Joe's techniques, the distance from which he liked to throw punches, the way he executed his assaults. He crossed the North Atlantic to watch Louis fight Paulino Uzcudun, witnessing the brutal punch that floored the Basque "as though he had been struck by an explosive bullet." Schmeling's manager looked sick after Louis' fourth-round victory, but Schmeling himself was undisturbed. "I saw something," he said. "I am satisfied."[50] He told sportswriters the same thing, prompting them to quote the German fighter: "I zee zometings."

What he saw was a simple, basic flaw, Schmeling later explained. "After he jabs with his left hand, once, twice, he drops his left arm. The side of his face is wide open for a straight right cross."[51] Schmeling was convinced that he had a shorter, faster counterpunch than Louis. "I know that after I have taken his left, my right hand, which drops from my chin, must land before he can."

Confident in his observations and plan, Schmeling began to prepare for the fight. He knew he had to be in shape to withstand punishment: "Taking Joe Louis' iron left fist in the face ten or fifteen times in a round is not exactly a pleasure." And he needed the stamina to land his right as hard in the fifteenth round as the first. First in Germany and then deep in the Catskills at the Napanoch Country Club he punished his body. Believing that victory depended upon his legs as much as his right hand, he ran mile after mile along mountain paths. During sparring sessions he took hundreds of left jabs to the face, conditioning his mind and body to accept pain. Occasionally, when a reporter politely asked how he hoped to win, Schmeling explained the broad outline of his plan, but the sportswriters paid scant attention. Louis, they had already concluded, was invincible. He had proved against Carnera and Baer that he had the experience and ability to take a punch. Max? Well, Max had a quaint accent, worthy of a quote or two because he probably would not be able to talk after the fight.

Louis shared the general opinion that he was unbeatable. He set up camp on the Jersey Shore in fashionable Lakewood, a decidedly upscale locale. At the turn of the century it was a popular winter resort for wealthy New York City residents. John D. Rockefeller had a rambling estate in Lakewood, as did Jay Gould. Grover Cleveland had been a frequent visitor to Lakewood, and Rudyard Kipling had gone there to recuperate from an illness. With the Depression, however, hard times arrived for the region's hotels and resorts, permitting prizefighters and their associates to walk in the footsteps of Rockefeller and Kipling. Louis trained on the grounds of the Stanley Hotel and lived close by in a mansion. Altogether, it was a setting fit for the "uncrowned king of fistiana."

Louis' lifestyle in Lakewood verged on the royal, with more than a hint of New World decadence. Jack Blackburn, recently acquitted of charges stemming from a gunfight that ended with the death of an elderly man, had begun drinking again, lessening his influence over Louis. For his part, Joe pursued a less intensive training routine than had been his practice. Although he worked out and sparred in front of crowds of boisterous spectators, his mood had subtly altered. Some reporters wrote that he displayed a "new maturity," others that he evinced a "new independence," but whatever the label, he was more than ever his own man. He seemed to lack intensity and focus, going through the motions like a priest who had lost his faith saying Mass. Al Monroe of the *Chicago Defender,* a committed Louis enthusiast, noted that Joe had been "looking terrible in his workouts," swinging wildly, missing targets, and getting hit by "some pretty stiff rights and lefts."[52] But did it really matter? Could anyone stay in the ring with him? Rhetorical questions, even for Monroe. As far as Louis and his legion of supporters were concerned, the answer to both was a resounding no.

Louis exhibited his passions outside of his training quarters. During long, hot afternoons he played rounds of golf with sportswriters Hype Igoe and Walter Stewart at the famed Lakewood course. His game had improved. Although he shot in the 106 range, reporters who walked a round with him said he used a nine iron like "mortals would employ a 4."[53] On the golf course as in the boxing ring, he hit with heavy hands. Blackburn lodged a few mild protests, complaining that golf and boxing used different muscles and that extended exposure to the sun sapped a man's strength. It made no difference. "Good God, I was really in love with the game," Louis recalled.[54] Golf was a challenge—unpredictable and frustrating, but also rewarding. Boxing was a grind—predictable and boring, even more so since he had become a sure bet. He could not resist the temptation to cut short his boxing routine and visit the course.

During the nights Louis ignored the ancient admonition against sexual activity. Marva had rooms in the Stanley Hotel. "What can I say?" he recalled. "I was young, she was younger, and we'd just been married must be nine months."⁵⁵ Eventually Louis' managers forced Marva to return to New York, but the move did not alter Joe's behavior. There were other women, and clandestine rendezvous with a female he was seeing in Atlantic City. The nonboxing activities took their toll. Between golf, Marva, the affairs, and training, Louis lost weight and looked listless. But he was not concerned. After all, Max Baer had knocked out Schmeling— or "Smellin," as Louis pronounced his name—and Joe had destroyed Baer. Louis-Schmeling? The only question was what round Schmeling would fall.

Almost every reporter seemed to agree. Paul Gallico claimed that after talking to Schmeling he picked the German to win between the tenth and twelfth rounds, but that his editor scrapped the farfetched prediction to save the reporter embarrassment. A few reporters, following the lead of Bill Corum of the *New York Evening Journal*, reminded their readers that Louis was "not a sure thing to beat Max Schmeling. He simply is as close to a sure thing as can come along when two able-bodied men of approximately the same size square off against each other." Corum, a friend of Schmeling's, predicted that the German would be "fortunate to hear the bell for the fourth round."⁵⁶ Few reporters dug as deeply for a contrary opinion as Frank Graham. He interviewed Sam Wallach, former manager of Leach Cross, who had quit the boxing business and become a lawyer. Wallach stopped short of predicting a Schmeling victory, but he did say, "Every fighter is human. There is no superman. On dope, Louis should win by a knockout in about four rounds. But, to quote George M. Cohan, 'There is nothing so uncertain as a dead sure thing.' "⁵⁷

***

Showers drenched New York on June 18, the scheduled day of the fight. Jacobs reluctantly postponed the contest until the next evening, giving reporters another twenty-four hours to speculate about the upcoming "public execution."⁵⁸ The promoter moaned about both the delay and the press. All the columns about Schmeling's certain fate, he complained, were killing the gate. Based on the Louis-Baer fight, he had scaled ticket prices to guarantee another million-dollar gate, but sales had been lousy. He expected an attendance of about seventy-five thousand, but by the week of the fight he realized that the turnout would fall far short of expectations. The belief that Louis would dominate Schmeling and a proposed Jewish boycott of the fight over Nazi persecution of Jews undoubtedly took their toll. In an effort to boost the gate Jacobs persuaded several of his sportswriter associates to come out more strongly for Schmeling. It did no good. Sixty million Americans would listen to Clem McCarthy's call of the fight on the radio, but Yankee Stadium would have gaping holes in its rows of seats, holes, as Richard Vidmer later wrote in his *New York Herald Tribune* column, "like divots on a fairway."[59]

Neither Louis nor Schmeling seemed concerned about the delay. In fact, nothing appeared to derail Schmeling's focus. In his dressing room, just before the fight, Schmeling was visited by Tom O'Rourke, a veteran promoter, manager, and longtime fixture on the New York boxing scene. Although O'Rourke had not exactly said Schmeling would win the fight, he was pulling for the German, and a week earlier he had told Runyon that Louis was overrated. John L. Sullivan, O'Rourke asserted, "would have stopped Louis. It wouldn't have taken him long, either."[60] Now, only ten or fifteen minutes before Max would go into the ring, O'Rourke sat down on a stool close to Schmeling, saying, "You know you can win, Max. You've just got to be careful and use your head."[61] With that he fell to the floor, dead from a heart attack. A few people carried O'Rourke to another room, returning with a story that he had just fainted.

Schmeling knew O'Rourke was dead. But at that moment it did not matter. He had other things to consider. Called to the ring, he told Gallico, "Do you know what was in my mind . . . during that long walk through the crowded aisles in the darkness, down to that one bright, white central spot where stood the ring? A curiosity and an excitement. I mean a pleasant excitement. I knew my body was right. Soon I was going to find out whether my brain was good too. I had thought something out. I had made a plan. Soon I was going to find out how good my thoughts were—whether I was right or wrong. It is hard to describe that eagerness to begin."

***

Shortly after ten o'clock, when the bell sounded for the first round, the atmosphere in Yankee Stadium was something close to business as usual. Gallico, in one of the press rows, looked toward the edges of the vast ballpark, dark except for the "ceaseless glow of matches flaring to cigarettes."[62] It reminded him of thousands of fireflies. In his corner, Louis, dancing a slow fighter's ballet, looked impassive, almost bored. As a profes-

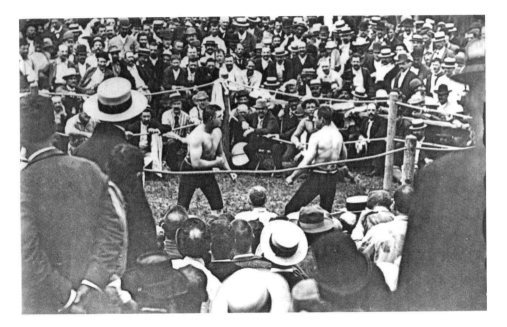

In 1889, John L. Sullivan (left), the Boston Strong Boy, defeated Jake Kilrain in the last bare-knuckle heavyweight championship fight. Celebrated in a poem by Vachel Lindsay, the battle confirmed Sullivan's status as the Emperor of Masculinity. (Library of Congress)

Jack Johnson won the heavyweight title in 1908, becoming the first black champion. Proud, articulate, and defiant, he challenged racial stereotypes. Shortly before the 1910 fight with James J. Jeffries, *Puck* suggested that a Johnson victory would invert the racial order in America. Johnson won the fight, and rioting followed. (Library of Congress)

Joe Louis in 1934 at the beginning of his career. Opponents insisted that he could look straight through them and that he seldom missed an opening. (Chicago History Museum)

In 1935, Louis went to New York to fight Primo Carnera. When he arrived at Grand Central Station, porters and railway workers hoisted him for publicity shots. He would soon prove the savior of boxing. (Bettmann/CORBIS)

On September 24, 1935, Joe Louis knocked out former heavyweight champion Max Baer. Before the fight Baer had feared for his life. After the fight Louis was regarded as the best heavyweight in the world. (Bettmann/CORBIS)

Louis, just after the Baer bout, is at the center of the world of boxing. Although known for his deadpan expression, he here offers a brief smile. (Bettmann/CORBIS)

A few hours before knocking out Baer, Joe Louis married Marva Trotter. They soon became the most famous African American couple in the country. They strolled the avenues of Harlem like royalty, turning heads wherever they went. (Chicago History Museum)

Posed photographs of Marva emphasized her grace, charm, and cultivation. Pictures like this were part of an effort to domesticate the image of Joe Louis. (Chicago Historical Museum)

The Louis legend holds that he used money his mother had given him for violin lessons to rent a locker at a local gym. Taking a break from training for his June 25, 1935, match with Primo Carnera, Louis shows manager Julian Black his violin chops. (Chicago History Museum)

The Joe Louis Brain Trust—from left, managers John Roxborough and Julian Black and trainer Jack Blackburn. Roxborough and Black were numbers men, and Blackburn had served time for murder, but they were devoted to Louis. This photograph was taken in early 1940, at the height of Louis' career. (Getty Images)

Louis' most important
fights were the 1936 and
1938 contests against
Max Schmeling. Schmeling
was a German Talleyrand,
able to adapt, survive, and
prosper in any political
climate. During the 1930s
Schmeling was a popular
draw in the United States,
famed for his resemblance
to former champion Jack
Dempsey. (Library of
Congress)

In the first Louis-Schmeling fight, on June 19, 1936, Louis fought too cautiously, and Schmeling capitalized on that weakness. Two years later Louis did not make the same mistake. (Library of Congress)

The centerpiece of Louis' career was his June 22, 1938, one-round knockout of Schmeling. Harlem exploded in celebration. (Bettmann/CORBIS)

During World War II, Louis was central to the U.S. government's efforts to get African Americans to support the war. He toured bases, appeared in promotional films and on posters, and donated his purses from two title fights to military relief funds. Here he meets with troops at Camp Upton shortly after enlisting in 1942. (Chicago History Museum)

There was nothing gentle about Louis' last fight. On October 26, 1951, up-and-comer Rocky Marciano battered Louis in the later rounds and then knocked him out. (Getty Images)

Where did all the money go? Louis reviews the numbers with accountant Ted Jones. Louis had ignored his finances while he was fighting for enormous purses, and when he retired in 1951 his debts were beyond repayment. (Chicago History Museum)

sional, he had known only victories, and he had become accustomed to throwing punches and knocking opponents senseless. He expected this fight to be no different. In the other corner, Schmeling appeared tense—not afraid, but curious, like a man about to watch a play with an unknown ending. He had a well-conceived strategy for fighting Louis, but it was an intellectual construct. He had yet to experience Louis' hand speed or punching power. "All I feel is excitement and great interest," he wrote shortly after the fight.

The bell rang. Louis moved across the ring like a workman who was in no hurry to finish the job early. His first punch, a left jab, landed high on Schmeling's cheek, and Max countered with a right that fell a touch short. For Schmeling the two punches were the opening notes of a symphony: "The themes are announced, Joe Louis' left jab, my right cross. We will develop those later."

For the forty-five thousand people in Yankee Stadium, nothing of importance was taking place in the ring. For Schmeling, the form of the battle was taking shape, and he was alive with interest. As he moved, he watched Louis work: "Pretty! Fast! Quiet! Smooth! Left jab. Left jab. I am studying. I must study it from the ring. I have only seen it outside the ring and the angle is different again, inside. Left hook! It lands, and it hurts. Next time I will not be hit by that punch. It is not healthy." Incrementally, and certainly not perceptively, Schmeling began to dictate the action. He knew that Louis was the best counterpuncher in the heavyweight division, so he forced him to lead. He noticed that just before throwing a punch Louis paused briefly to set himself. So when Schmeling saw Louis set, he moved a few inches out of reach. He understood that he would have to withstand a number of hard Louis jabs before he would get an opening. And so he waited—rounds one and two went to Louis. Schmeling felt his mouth fill with blood and his left eye begin to close as Louis' jabs found their mark.

Early in the third round, however, Louis jabbed, and as he pulled his left hand back low, Schmeling countered with a hard right. Just one right, and Louis responded by going on the offensive, easily winning the round. But in the corner after the round Max Machon, Schmeling's trusted second and trainer, remarked, "*Du hast ihm da einen schonen geholt*—You fetched him a pretty one." Schmeling nodded his head. "I think I knock him out. I have him where I want him."

In the fourth round everyone in Yankee Stadium saw what Schmeling already knew. Louis jabbed, dropped his left to jab again, and then "pop," Schmeling countered with a perfectly timed right. "He staggers. He shakes. He does that little dance on his heels," Schmeling remembered. That "little dance" was an instinctual attempt by Louis to find his equilibrium and clear his head. But Schmeling moved instantly onto the offensive, punishing Louis with lefts and long, powerful rights. For Schmeling the fight moved almost in slow motion. He could hear the crowd. It was as though someone had switched on microphones plugged into the far reaches of the stadium. He landed a right, then another right with all his shoulder behind it. Louis stumbled backward and fell straight down, his legs under him and his hands hitting the canvas together behind him. It looked like he had fallen onto a spring, for he bounced immediately to his feet. He was up before referee Arthur Donovan reached the count of two. That surprised Schmeling. "A superfighter does not go down, but if he does, he is smart enough to stay down and take a count of eight before he gets up," Schmeling told Gallico. "I think he is just a hurt, bewildered boy who does not know what he is doing at that moment."

Madness reigned in Yankee Stadium. The noise was deafening, loud as the sea in a violent storm. Reporters furiously pecked out their thoughts, trying to describe what none had thought could happen. Grantland Rice admired Louis' survival instincts but saw that Schmeling's rights had left Joe with a "cloudy, muddy brain."[63] In his corner Louis shook his head, trying to clear the fog. The left side of his face felt anesthetized, and it had already begun to puff out, as though his cheek were filled with golf balls. Blackburn leaned in close, repeating, "Keep your guard up, keep your guard up."[64] Louis shook his head and blinked.

Schmeling's corner was frantic. Joe Jacobs said nothing of any value but would not shut up. Machon, as always, was cool and direct. "*So. Den Uebermensch haben wir in unsere Tashche. Nun vorsichtig!*—So, now we have the superman in our pocket. But be careful." Schmeling hardly had to be told to be careful. He knew Louis was hurt but still dangerous. But he now knew that he could win. "I have the upper hand now. I must keep it."

Most fights are over before the final count or bell. After the fourth round, the outcome of the Louis-Schmeling contest was predictable. Louis was badly hurt, his brain numbed, and he moved and punched like he was underwater. Just after the bell in the fifth round Schmeling landed another right, and Louis stumbled to his corner as though he were walking on a boat. Rice thought he looked like a "ship in a storm without a rudder—a punching bag hung up beneath the arc lights for Schmeling to nail."[65] He was simply unable to recover from Schmeling's devastating rights. But he was too well trained and too well conditioned—too young and strong—to go down without a fight. He continued to battle—punching wildly and ineffectively. Several of his punches were clearly low blows, and after the fight Schmeling accused him of intentionally trying to win the fight on a foul punch. There is no evidence for this charge, any more than there is any that Schmeling's punch after the bell in round five was intentional. Both boxers had reputations as clean fighters, but in the heat of the battle both threw punches that were clearly against the rules.

Round after round, Schmeling's right found its mark. Louis' face swelled grotesquely. His left cheek looked like it had been inflated with an air pump, and Schmeling's punches seemed to echo when they made contact. Veteran trainer Steve Acunto said, "There was a pop, pop, every time one of those right hands landed. It sounded like a bag full of water coming down from the second floor of a building: 'POP, POP, POP.'"[66] Marva, sitting at ringside, put her head in her hands and cried, "He's hurt. He's hurt bad."[67] She felt physically sick. Lillie, Joe's mother, fell to her knees and prayed for her son's survival. Soon she left the stadium, weeping that her son was being killed. In the bleacher seats, where many of Louis' supporters sat, blacks, their faces streaked with tears, pleaded and prayed for a miracle. It was as if they wanted Joe Louis to save Joe Louis. As if, like Joe himself, they were living a nightmare that could be wiped away with a few shakes of their head and blinks of their eyes.

The same mood prevailed wherever blacks were gathered around radios. The disappointment was made more bitter and painful by the length of the fight, which allowed a breath of hope to linger long past all promise of victory was extinguished. Singer Lena Horne recalled listening to the fight in Cincinnati's Moonlite Gardens while performing with Noble Sissle's band. The band had a radio behind the grandstand, and during breaks they listened to the broadcast with heightening concern. "I was near hysteria toward the end of the fight when he was being so badly beaten, and some of the men in the band were crying." Joe was the one black man who stood up to whites, beat them in fair contests, and, for Horne, he "carried so many of our hopes, maybe even dreams of vengeance. But this night he was just another Negro getting beaten by a white man." As tears marred

Horne's performance, her mother became outraged. "Why, you don't even know the man." "I don't care, I don't care," Horne yelled. "He belongs to all of us."[68]

On that night he also belonged, in the brutal language of the ring, to Max Schmeling. Between rounds Machon told his fighter, "*Der Ueber-mensch hat ja Gummibeine*—The superman seems to have rubber legs." His legs, his arms, his head—all rubber, all gone. With cold, terminal precision, Schmeling finished the job. In the twelfth round, he landed three more brutal rights. Louis barely moved his hands to block them. "Louis, I think, knows what will happen," Schmeling recounted. "He puts out his left, but it is no more than a push. I smash over it again, and he holds on. Donovan breaks him out, and I follow him to the ropes and throw the right again." Over the radio millions of Americans heard McCarthy make the call: "And Donovan broke them. Schmeling got over two more hard rights to Louis' jaw and made Louis get down, and Schmeling straightening up Louis with hard rights and lefts to the jaw. . . . He has puffed up Louis' cheek, and Louis is down! Louis is down! Hanging to the ropes and hanging badly! He's a very tired fighter, he is blinking his eyes, shaking his head and the count is TEN. THE FIGHT IS OVER! THE FIGHT IS OVER! LOUIS IS COMPLETELY OUT!"[69]

In Germany, millions of Schmeling's supporters who had tuned in to the shortwave radio broadcast of the fight in the middle of the night heard Arno Hellmis' final call: "He's down! Schmeling has knocked him down! He doesn't come back up! He can't come back up! He's shaking his head. He knows he's finished. *Aus*—Out! *Aus! Aus! Aus! Aus! Aus! Aus!*"[70] Listening to the final report, Anny Ondra relaxed for the first time in hours and smiled. She had listened to the fight with a "small but exclusive circle" in a luxurious Potsdam home. The first person to congratulate her was the host, Dr. Joseph Goebbels, Hitler's minister of propaganda.[71]

It was just before sunrise in the Fatherland when the sport of boxing reached a new level of meaning and importance for the world.

5

King Louis I

You can't Jim Crow a left hook.
—*Henry Armstrong*

When Max Schmeling's right sent Joe Louis to the canvas in the twelfth round, the radio was turned low at 2100 McDougall Avenue in Detroit, the home that Joe had bought for his mother. His stepfather, Patrick Brooks, had suffered a stroke the day before and was sleeping in a darkened bedroom. Although Louis' mother, Lillie, was in New York for the fight, several of his brothers and sisters were huddled close to the radio "too stunned and sorrowful to move." "I wish Mother wasn't there to see it," said Joe's brother Lonnie. Dr. J. A. Moore, the family physician who had listened to the broadcast at the home, put a finger to his lips, looking toward Brooks' room. "We won't tell him for awhile," he whispered. "He's too weak, and it might break his heart."[1] Outside the home a crowd had gathered, standing silently, paying respects for the evening's tragedy.

All across America hearts broke as Arthur Donovan finished his count over Louis. Josephine Tandy, a sixty-six-year-old black women listening to the broadcast of the fight in Madison, Indiana, grabbed her heart and fell to the floor dead. In Harlem, at about the same time, Harry Saw, five years younger than Tandy, "fell dead at the radio." Younger still, Robert Gantt of Columbia, South Carolina, was listening to the broadcast with a group of other black Louis partisans when he suffered a heart attack and died. The *New York Times* reported other deaths in Pittsburgh, Memphis, Cassville (New York), and Chicago, as well as in Halifax, Nova Scotia, and Forest, Ontario.[2] As boxing writers liked to put it, the final bell tolled for eleven people who were listening to the broadcast of the fight, twelve if old Tom O'Rourke is included in the group. But for millions of blacks the heartbreak was greater than a few failed hearts. Joe Louis had lost. The impossible had happened.

"The atom has been taken apart," wrote Grantland Rice. "The myth of the superman has been exploded completely."[3] Rice signaled the direction for the vast majority of the white sportswriters. Joe Louis' invincibility was a myth built on hype. Carnera, Baer, and Uzcudun believed the myth and were beaten before their fights with Joe began. But Schmeling was different; he thought Louis was just another boxer, talented but beatable. Schmeling "destroyed a myth," wrote Frank Graham of the *New York Sun*. After the fight, "Nobody paid any attention to Louis. The myth had been destroyed, and he was only a battered and broken Negro boy."[4] Running through the New York sportswriters' descriptions of the match and post-fight columns was a sense of satisfaction, a feeling that the German had reestablished racial order. In a contest of brains against brawn, an agile mind had carried the day; the white Schmeling had outthought and outfought the black Louis. As Rice wrote, Louis' "elemental, jungle cunning was no match for a much superior intelligence that happened to size things up—and act on the situation as it was."[5]

Southern journalists openly celebrated the triumph of white over black. In the weeks leading up to the match, the *Jackson Clarion-Ledger* had barely mentioned the fight, but after Schmeling's victory its headline boomed: "GERMAN STAGES WILD UPSET BY WHIPPING NEGRO." The headline of a *Raleigh News and Observer* article crowed: "HAH! HAH! BOOMS MAX—JOE CAN'T TALK." Veteran New Orleans sportswriter William McG. Keefe commented, "[The] reign of terror in heavyweight boxing was ended by Schmeling. The big bad wolf has been chased from the door. It took the Black Uhlan [Schmeling's nickname] to prove that the black terror is just another fragile human being."[6] For the most part, southern sportswriters had downplayed Louis' march through the heavyweight division. But now they almost universally applauded his collapse, resorting to images of caged panthers and domesticated jungle animals in their stories and illustrations. Historian Jeffrey T. Sammons accurately observed, "In triumph Louis appeared like a threatening animal; in defeat he was just a harmless mortal."[7]

Blacks struggled to come to terms with the result. Theories of why Louis lost began with the conspiratorial. A *Chicago Defender* headline announced: "PROBE REPORT THAT JOE LOUIS WAS DOPED: CHARGE DRUGS, NOT FISTS SENT BOMBER DOWN FOR COUNT." Al Monroe, one of Louis' most persistent supporters, wrote that there was something wrong with Louis in the weeks before the match. He had lost weight, looked lethargic during training sessions, complained about a lack of sleep, and generally was not himself. Then "when he entered the ring he was obviously in a daze—a daze from which he never recovered." A "prominent Chicago toxicologist" told Monroe that "certain tasteless drugs could be put in a person's food or water that would produce just such a condition." Monroe argued that Louis' position on the canvas during the final knockdown suggested a drugged fighter.[8] William G. Nunn of the *Pittsburgh Courier* expressed similar fears. He tried to get to the bottom of the thirty-one and a half "mystery hours" between the official weigh-in and the fight the following night. Who cooked his meals? Where did his water come from? Who was in contact with him? And was there a suspicious syringe?[9]

The rumors and wild speculations disturbed the Louis camp. John Roxborough and Julian Black announced that there was no truth in the drug rumor. Jack Blackburn said, "I had Joe in tip-top shape and I know he wasn't doped." Louis added, "I just forgot to duck."[10] But for weeks after the match, the notion persisted, filling newspaper columns and fueling barbershop conversations. Something had to be wrong. Joe just was not Joe. The calypso performers The Lion & The Atilla captured the deep sense of suspicion in their song "Louis-Schmeling Fight." After Lion sings, "Though his disappointment he has now faced, he has been defeated but not disgraced," Atilla responds:

> As an admirer of Joe Louey—I do appreciate your song,
> But on the night of the fight . . . something was wrong
> It wasn't the same Bomber that we saw
> Smashing Baer and Carnera to the floor
> I wouldn't say it was dope or conspiracy,
> But the whole thing look extremely funny to me.[11]

Other black journalists placed the blame on Louis' marriage. Some wrote that Joe and Marva's ship of bliss had gone off course and was on the rocks. Frank Marshall Davis of the *New York Amsterdam News* reported a rumor that late in the night before the fight Joe and Marva had gotten into a terrific argument over a letter she had received from a former suitor.[12]

Journalist Roi Ottley denied that there was a rift between Joe and Marva—as did Mr. and Mrs. Joe Louis—but recounted stories that the boxer and his wife did attend a party the night before the fight, against the strongest objections of his handlers.[13] Finally, other journalists held that Joe was the victim of a too-happy home life. He had grown soft and domestic, had lost his Spartan edge. All three reports, however, blamed Marva for the national catastrophe, and in the weeks following the fight she received chilly greetings from her husband's legion of supporters. If Joe had been Joe all would have been right with the African American world.

Louis' camp also contributed to the blame game, naming the fighter as the chief culprit. John Roxborough charged that Louis had become "a little 'cocky' and wouldn't listen to anyone. . . . It got so bad that he was beginning to tell Blackburn what to do instead of listening to his trainer." Joe had refused to jump rope or punch the heavy and speed bags, asserting that road work and sparring were enough training. The knockout, the manager mused, should actually make Louis a better fighter. "Personally," concluded Roxborough, "I think it is the best thing that ever happened. All the great fighters suffered knockouts. . . . They all come back to be better fighters and I think Joe will do the same thing." "Yea," Jack Blackburn pitched in, "maybe we can tell him sumthin' from now on. He learned a good lesson."[14]

The theories and excuses, however, did nothing to lessen the impact of Louis' defeat. Sadness enveloped Harlem, the South Side, and the Black Bottom. Almost twenty years later Langston Hughes could still recall the pall of grief that hovered above black Americans. Joe Louis' impact was incalculable—he lightened the bleak realities of the Depression. "No one else in the United States has ever had such an effect on Negro emotions—or mine," Hughes wrote. "I marched and cheered and yelled and cried, too. . . . When Joe Louis lost his first fight to Schmeling in Harlem, I had been part of the hush and the sadness that fell over darker New York. After the fight, which I attended, I walked down Seventh Avenue and saw grown men weeping like children, and women sitting on the curbs with their heads in their hands. All across the country that night when the news came that Joe was knocked out, people cried."[15]

Joe Louis felt their emotional pain. It was worse than his physical suffering, more aching than his cut lips and the horribly swollen left side of his face, more bitter even than the loss itself. In the hours after the fight he said almost nothing. "I didn't know nuthin' after the second round," he told reporters. "Everything was in a fog. I went just as far as I could. I couldn't go no further."[16] He could barely move his jaw enough to mumble the words. After the fight he retuned to the Theresa Hotel, where he spent the night vomiting, allowing only Marva into his room to administer cold and hot compresses. After a few days' rest in a darkened room he returned to Detroit. He wore dark glasses to hide his bruised eyes and pulled up his overcoat's collar to conceal swollen cheeks and lips. Unlike his previous triumphant returns, there was no crowd to greet him, and before photographers could take his picture he was in a taxicab, pulling a straw hat low over his face.

For more than a week the fighter avoided people. A neighbor recalled seeing him riding in the back seat of a car; still in dark glasses, he looked out the window with an unusual sadness. Around the neighborhood Joe had always been open and friendly, but now he just wanted to be left alone. Marva tried to cheer him. "You're a boxer, not a movie star," she said. But Louis blamed himself. He had not trained properly, and he had spent too much time chasing golf balls and women. "I let myself down," he recalled. "I let a whole race of people down because I was some kind of hot shit."[17]

By early July he was back in New York, recovered and rededicated to his profession. "I got careless," he said in a radio interview. "It won't happen again. I am going to prepare for my future bouts just as though the title was at stake in every one of them." When asked if he had watched the films of the Schmeling fight, Louis answered, "No, suh, I saw all of that fight I wanted to that night."[18] For Joe Louis, his first fight with Max Schmeling was history. He was looking forward.

***

Some reporters transformed Joe Louis into a national morality lesson. Joe Williams of the *New York World Telegram* suggested that the Roosevelt administration should consider what happened to Louis. There were disturbing signs of overconfidence in the New Deal management, a "careless kind of 'high-wide-and-handsome' attitude," a burgeoning confidence and an "it's 'all-over-but-the-shouting' psychology."[19] It was not the sort of mentality that would end the Depression or win the heavyweight title. What was called for was a single-minded dedication to get the job done, a well-formed plan and a determined execution. Louis needed to get back to work.

Mike Jacobs and Louis' managers felt the same way. Rest had obviously not agreed with Joe, and as soon as his face and body had recovered from the beating he went back into the gym. Before the Schmeling contest Jacobs had planned to match Louis with the champion James J. Braddock for the title. But Schmeling had ended that plan. "He gave me a good licking," Louis confessed, "and he's earned his chance at the championship."[20]

Oddly, Louis' loss increased newspaper and magazine coverage of him. Before the Schmeling fight his image had been carefully constructed and controlled—it was cardboard, as bloodless as a cartoon figure. In the ring, he was the irresistible force, a superman, winning his matches without real exertion. Opponents fell from his assaults like dominoes in a row. Outside the ring he was a Bible-reading, mother-loving, milk-drinking, puppy-petting idol. Although he said little, nothing he said detracted from his anti–Jack Johnson image. Shortly before the Schmeling fight the publication of Ed Van Every's *Joe Louis, Man and Super-Fighter* confirmed the stained-glass image of Louis. Van Every, a *New York Sun* reporter, wrote that Louis was a "Black Moses" singled out by the "finger of God" for "purposes of His own." He was destined not only to win the title but also to light the way "to a broader tolerance on the part of his white brother."[21] Readers almost felt like bowing before the sheer holiness of Louis' mission.

The loss to Schmeling and the post-fight analysis made Louis into a more compelling character. The aura of invincibility had disappeared. Jack Dempsey argued in *Ring* magazine that "from now on, he'll never improve."[22] Schmeling, Dempsey believed, had conclusively demonstrated Louis' weaknesses, and that his future opponents would know how to beat him. Heavyweight champion Braddock agreed, contributing an article in *Ring* entitled "Louis Bubble Has Burst." Even before the match Braddock said that he and Jack Johnson had seen the same flaw that Schmeling had exploited: "On several occasions Johnson and I trained together, our aim being for me to develop an attack that would take full advantage of Joe's shortcomings."[23] Sportswriters harped on the same themes: Louis had suffered a devastating defeat, he would never be the same, his career was in shambles. Adding a racial slant, they argued that history was clear on one point: black fighters are never the same after a punishing loss.

Louis' character also became more interesting. One question echoed through scores of articles written about the fighter: Does anyone really know anything about Joe Louis? For more than a year white reporters had not ventured beyond jungle animal imagery and plantation Sambo stereotypes to try to understand the man behind the expressionless mask.

Now his relationship with Marva, his managers, and the black community needed reconsideration. And above all else: Did Louis have the character to come back? Or was he, as a popular illustration portrayed him, a boxing god with clay feet?

***

Jacobs wanted Louis back in the ring. He wanted him to fight an effectively toothless boxer with a marketable name. Jack Sharkey, the "Boston Gob," fit the requirements like a tailored suit. He had lost a controversial fight to Jack Dempsey in 1927, won the title on a controversial decision in 1932, and lost the crown on a highly controversial knockout in 1933. Since then he had drifted ingloriously toward retirement, fighting seldom and losing most of his matches. Certainly his 1935 victory over the appropriately nicknamed Unknown Winston inspired no confidence that he was on the comeback trail. The fight gave off such a malodorous whiff of fix that the boxing commission suspended Unknown after the contest.

Understanding his role as a well-compensated sacrificial lamb, Sharkey demonstrated a steadfast disinclination to train and a halfhearted will to fight. *Brooklyn Daily Eagle* columnist Ed Hughes wrote that the thirty-five thousand spectators who paid to see the August 18 fight in Yankee Stadium did not learn much about Louis. The problem was Sharkey. "He put up less resistance than a Bowery bum would if you begged him to wade into a juicy steak smothered in onions." All the fight proved, Hughes commented, was that Louis was not "punch shy" when fed a "set-up." The fight lasted less than three rounds. Sharkey played the role assigned to him. "As 'build-up' stuff for the reconstruction of the Louis world-beater reputation, Sharkey was Grade A material."[24]

On September 22, Louis continued his comeback, fighting Al Ettore in Philadelphia's Municipal Stadium. A popular and capable heavyweight from South Philly, the blond-headed Ettore said before the fight that "all Negroes look alike" and boasted that Louis would not last more than five rounds. Fifty thousand spectators, mostly Ettore partisans, cheered loudly when the Italian American fighter entered the ring, and they continued their support as their fighter attempted wild bull rushes in the first few rounds. By the fourth round, as Louis belted Ettore around the ring, the cheering ebbed, dying almost completely in the fifth when "the Ethiopian" knocked out "the Italian" with two devastating left hooks.[25]

It was not a popular victory in Philadelphia. O. Harrington of the *New York Amsterdam News* described the long route from Municipal Stadium to downtown Philadelphia, which was swarming with Ettore fans and forcing automobiles to creep forward in single file. Exaggerating but making his point, Harrington wrote, "I suppose there were close to 500,000 Ettore fans along the sides after the fight and 499,000 spat on each passing car carrying Negro occupants. Of the other thousand, 900 cursed and threw trash, 50 were policemen and the other 50 were too old to take an active part in the proceedings. Your correspondent had the good fortune to ride in an open car where the occupants were all obviously colored. We stopped on South Street long enough to throw out the dead cats and other oddities."[26]

In Philadelphia race mattered, just as it had across America two months earlier during the Louis-Schmeling bout. For many white Americans it was not an American against a German or an American against a stand-in Italian. It was a black against a white. "Sure I was for Schmeling and Ettore," commented a white Pennsylvanian. "The whole family was. Why? Schmeling and Ettore are white." The racism was not as pronounced or as violent as it had been during the championship years of Jack Johnson, but it gathered like a storm cloud above every Louis contest. In fact, the term "white hope" experienced a revival in 1935 and 1936 as Louis began to dominate the heavyweight division. Jack Dempsey, the legendary heavyweight who had drawn the color line during his championship years, even sponsored a White Hope Tournament to discover a boxer who could defeat Louis.

***

But for Mike Jacobs, dollars always trumped race, and the elevation of Schmeling to leading contender status complicated the heavyweight picture. Put bluntly, Jacobs did not trust the strength of the promotional deal he had signed with Schmeling. To his mind, the German fighter was first and foremost a German, a Teuton, at a moment in history when such a distinction mattered deeply. Interviewed after the fight by German radio, Schmeling asked whether Hitler had listened to the fight, and he ended his remarks with a cheery "Heil Hitler!" At about the same time Schmeling was talking to the German nation, Joseph Goebbels was sending him a telegram, congratulating him on his victory.

With Schmeling's return to Germany, Jacobs lost confidence in his ability to control Max's career. Although Schmeling often referred to the

United States as his "second home," after the fight he could not leave that home soon enough. Within days he was aboard the dirigible *Hindenburg* for the fifty-hour trip to Frankfurt, where he was greeted with Wagnerian pageantry. Crowds of ecstatic Germans cheered, Nazis delivered nationalistic speeches, a Brown Shirt band played rousing songs, and "Seig Heils!" and "Heil Hitlers!" filled the late-afternoon air. From Frankfurt he took a plane to Berlin, where the celebrations were repeated. That night he had dinner with Goebbels, and the next day he watched the film of the fight with Hitler, who cackled and "slapped his thigh with delight" when Max landed a powerful right. It was a film, Hitler proclaimed, that all good Germans should see. Soon *Max Schmelings Sieg—Ein deutscher Sieg* (Max Schmeling's Victory: A German Victory) was playing to packed theaters across Germany. As presented and narrated, it was the story of the resurgence of a boxer and a nation. Placing Schmeling's victory into the proper context, the narrator said that while all the American boxing authorities predicted a Louis triumph, Max never lost faith. As such, the film stands as a "wonderful document attesting to the ability of a will as hard as Krupp steel to accomplish everything."[27]

Will and steel—they were the order of the day in Germany. Schmeling's timing, once again, could not have been more fortuitous. Siegfried was long dead, and Hitler's Germany was in need of a hero as large as the Reich. Hitler, like Schmeling, was in the process of defying world opinion. In late 1933 he had discovered a convenient pretext for pulling Germany out of the League of Nations, steering his country on an independent and reckless course. Three months before the fight in Yankee Stadium, Hitler had violated the Versailles Treaty by remilitarizing the Rhineland. Further ignoring the treaty, he had begun to rearm Germany by expanding the size of the army, acquiring and producing offensive weapons, and establishing an air force. As far as the Western democracies were concerned, the German leader was not playing by the rules of the international game.

Hitler's behavior, his willingness to move into uncharted waters, alarmed Jacobs. What would happen if Schmeling won the title from Braddock? Would New York remain the sun of boxing's solar system? As important, if not more so, would Jacobs continue to promote the major heavyweight fights? He had watched Nazis purge Jews from boxing in Germany, and it did not take a Copernican leap of imagination to realize that if Schmeling won the most important athletic title in the world Hitler would probably find a more "racially pure" promoter for the fighter's future title defenses. As John Kieran of the *New York Times* reported, it was likely that if Max won the crown he would board the *Hindenburg* and take it back to Germany with him.[28]

It is impossible to know exactly when Jacobs decided that there would be no Braddock-Schmeling championship contest. It was probably in his mind by the time Schmeling landed in Germany. It is also uncertain how much of the promotional charade that followed was planned. Undoubtedly most of it was. Hitler may have reigned supreme in the mid-1930s in his ability to bluff and bully other European leaders into giving him what he wanted. But Jacobs was no schmuck in his world, either. He could maneuver, connive, and operate with the best of them. Always could—since he was a boy selling lemon drops on excursions to Coney Island.

No one in the United States or Germany doubted that by knocking out Louis, Schmeling had earned a title fight, and within a month the match was scheduled. Madison Square Garden promoter James J. Johnston and Braddock's manager, Joe Gould, slated the Braddock-Schmeling bout for September 26 in the Long Island City Bowl. But within weeks things began to go sideways. First, Mike Jacobs revealed that he had a promotional deal with Schmeling, just as Johnston had one with Braddock. Then, Braddock hurt his left pinkie while training. Gould announced that an operation would "probably" be necessary, that Braddock had made "tentative arrangements to enter a local hospital," and that in any case the scheduled match would have to be pushed back four months.[29]

All this may have been true. The parties might have entered into the contract in good faith, and Braddock might have injured his pinkie. Braddock certainly had a history of serious hand injuries, though he registered surprise when his manager told him of his most recent problem. Yet before long Braddock's medical issues were linked to serious promotional troubles, and disturbing rumors about a Braddock-Schmeling title match were accepted as gospel along Eighth Avenue. The fight was dead, said sports columnist Dan Parker. It would never happen. In Berlin, Schmeling discounted such loose gossip. He was sure Braddock and Louis would not "chisel" him out of his title shot.[30] To be on the safe side, however, he decided to return to New York. In the second week of December, Max sailed to America and signed a new contract. The bout was now set for June 3. He then sailed back to Germany, where it was announced he would be the guest of Reichsfuehrer Hitler for Christmas.

While Hitler and Schmeling were warming their hands in front of a Yule log, other hands were warming to the plans of Uncle Mike Jacobs. In December 1936 the Non-Sectarian Anti-Nazi League announced a proposal to boycott the scheduled Braddock-Schmeling match. In good faith, the boycotters announced, they could not support any economic activity that would result in transferring dollars to Nazi Germany. Within weeks other organizations and individuals—including Judge Jeremiah T. Mahoney, head of the Amateur Athletic Union—threw in their support. The boycott movement, commented Hearst reporters cozy with Mike Jacobs, was a serious threat to the fight's gate.

There is no record of Braddock actually checking into a hospital for a pinkie operation, but his physical problems were lost in the coverage of the proposed boycott. How could any self-respecting manager, Gould asked, commit his fighter to a match that wouldn't "draw flies"?[31] Well, he answered, he couldn't. In early 1937 Gould announced that Braddock would defend the title on June 22 against Joe Louis in Chicago, outside of the jurisdiction of the New York State Athletic Commission. Using language that Hitler would have understood, Gould suggested that Braddock's contract with Schmeling was "just another scrap of paper," a scrap not legally binding in Illinois.[32] Justifying his about-face, Gould informed reporters that the recently organized anti-Nazi boycott would kill the gate for a Braddock-Schmeling match in New York. He estimated that 75 percent of fight fans at heavyweight championships in New York were Jewish, men and women who had some pretty strong opinions about Herr Hitler and were active in the anti-Nazi boycott. If Braddock fought Schmeling as contracted, it would be a financial disaster, and Gould and Braddock were not in business to fight for pennies.[33]

In Germany a sense of outrage stirred nationalists to action. Amid talk of a "Jewish conspiracy" and "treacherous Americans," Hitler sanctioned an effort to stage a Braddock-Schmeling championship bout at the Olympic Stadium in Berlin. Promoter Walter Rothenburg, with the backing of high-level German authorities, made Braddock and Gould an offer they could not refuse—including $350,000 in a non-German bank, film and radio rights, the choice of a referee, and an American judge. Gould later claimed that negotiations ended when he told a representative of Goebbels that he wanted more money, and, oh yeah, "equal rights for the Jews" in Germany.[34] Undoubtedly, that conversation was a Gouldian embellishment. But the main point was true: he refused the German offer, just as he had wiggled out of the one from Madison Square Garden.

In the end, Mike Jacobs made him the one offer that he could not refuse—50 percent of the gate *and* 20 percent of the net profits from Jacobs' heavyweight championship fight promotions for the next ten years. He gave Braddock and Gould a win-win offer. If Braddock defeated Louis, he won and kept the title. If he lost, he won a percentage of Louis' future defenses. Schmeling was the odd man out. Was it fair? Of course not. But what did fairness and sportsmanship ever have to do with the fight game? In his *New York Times* column John Kieran observed that prizefighting is a very tough business: "Any one who would go into a sordid game like that for anything except money would be a fit candidate for observation in the mental ward at Bellevue. And any one who expects sweetness and light and sportsmanship in the dealing in and around the ring will never pop up as the winner in an I.Q. test, either."[35]

It was a farce, a charade, and continuing along the same lines Schmeling played his part to the last. He insisted that he had a valid contract for a fight, and he was going to honor it. After returning to America in early May 1937 he set up a training camp in Speculator, New York, in the Adirondacks. He diligently performed roadwork, punched bags, and shadowboxed. He avoided coffee, late nights, and anything else that would dull his sharp fighting edge. Then the "plainly peeved" fighter attended a mock weigh-in ceremony, was pronounced fit to do battle, and got his mind right for his phantom shot at the title. Compared to the Schmeling farce, Bill Corum of the *New York Evening Journal* quipped, "the Mad Hatter's party of Alice in Wonderland was a sober meeting of the wise and thoughtful."[36] When the fight did not take place, Schmeling blasted the American system of justice and the powers that be in the world of professional boxing. He had no intention, he said, of attending the Braddock-Louis match. On June 5 he sailed to Germany.

"Scandalous," the chief of the German Boxing Association complained. What the Braddock and American henchmen had done to Max was "degrading," "contemptible and tragic," and "absurd." A German editorialist added, " 'Sport is dead. Long live business.' Under this slogan they cheated Schmeling out of his title bout with Braddock. . . . Such things can only happen in a land of unlimited opportunity. Sport has been knocked out. The victor is business—the hunt for the almighty dollar."[37] Somehow a nation that had enacted blood laws to define citizenship, barred Jews from virtually every profession or trade, and violated international treaties had trouble coming to terms with the injustices of the fight game.

***

While Schmeling had been skipping rope in Speculator, Braddock in Grand Beach, Michigan, and Louis near Kenosha, Wisconsin, had been doing the same thing. Except their training was not the second act in a farce. Oddly, news from the two camps was completely counterintuitive. Braddock had not engaged in a match since June 13, 1935, when he upset the heavily favored Max Baer to win the title. For two years he had done nothing more exacting than box a couple of exhibitions and allegedly hurt his little finger in a light training session. But sportswriters who watched him in Grand Beach reported that he had been secretly sparring for months and that he moved like a world-beater. Such old-timers as George Lawrence proclaimed that Braddock would trounce Louis, mostly because Louis had become rich, fat, and soft. As always, race factored into his opinion. "It is a bad thing for a fighter once he doesn't have to scratch for a living. For a Negro fighter it is ruination."[38]

Even though Louis had defeated Sharkey, Ettore, Jorge Brescia, Eddie Simms, Steve Ketchel, Bob Pastor, and Natie Brown since his loss to Schmeling, reporters insisted that he was not the same old Joe. Something indefinable was missing. Wilber Wood of the *New York Sun* believed that Louis looked slow and uninterested, "sulky because [his managers] have deprived him of his apples and ice cream."[39] A *New York Evening Journal* sportswriter thought Louis did "not possess the mentality to profit by his mistakes" and had "lost his instinct to fight."[40] Even his golfing buddy Hype Igoe admitted, "To be quite honest with you and myself, I do not believe that Joe Louis is half the fighter he WAS. He has slowed up and he has lost a lot of zing to his punch."[41] Virtually every white sportswriter who visited Louis' camp came away with the same thoughts—Joe was an "uninspired challenger," a "cheap and sleazy road company of the original production" who "appears to have lost his verve."[42] Reports from the Louis camp were so bleak that after a few positive notices, Braddock breathed a sigh of relief. "I'm glad you think dat guy is alright again," he said. " 'Cause I don't want you to think I'm picking on a cripple . . . when I belt him out."[43]

Black reporters took a different view of the two camps. By 1937 Louis had become the most visible expression of racial progress. It seemed as if Joe was what every black youth wanted to be when he grew up and what every old man wished that he had been. He was the model of clean living and hard work. Chester L. Washington of the *Pittsburgh Courier* wrote, "Drinking, smoking and carousing still have no lure for Joe. . . . And you can bet your last dollar that Joe will be in the best shape of his entire career for his fight of fights."[44] There was no chance that Louis was going to disappoint his race. Washington compared Braddock on the eve of his title clash with Louis to General George Armstrong Custer on the night before his engagement with Sitting Bull at the Little Big Horn. In 1876 the white Custer was judged superior in brains and strategy, but the darker-skin Sioux demonstrated that racial stereotypes crumbled when put to the ultimate test. As the fight drew closer, the black press displayed total faith in its "champion."

Inside Louis' camp there was an air of inevitable triumph. For three years Jack Blackburn had assumed that white promoters would never give Louis a title shot. "You were born with two strikes against you," he had once told Joe. That was the way of the world, he thought—black heavyweights were not given anything. After the Braddock-Louis match was set, Blackburn became a new man. Until Louis fought for the title he swore off alcohol and devoted himself to preparing his fighter. "All right, you son of a bitch, you made it to here, and I'm going to see you make it all the way. When I finish with you, you're gonna be a fucking fighting machine." He worked on Louis' flaws, his defensive shortcomings, and his predictable offensive maneuvers. By the night of the fight he knew Louis was ready. "This is it, Chappie," he said. "You come home a champ tonight."[45]

For black Americans there were few doubts that Joe would win. The only fear for many influential race leaders was the aftermath of the contest. How would the millions of black Louis supporters react to the victory? And would the many more millions of white Braddock backers accept the new black champion? A front-page editorial in the *New York Amsterdam News* called the match a "milestone in race relations," measuring the "cultural progress of both black and white Americans." It was a moment—a proud moment—in the history of black America, but "with progress goes a definite duty," the editorialist lectured, "and that duty on the night of the fight is for some 15,000,000 Negro citizens to remain sane, respectable, law-abiding persons."[46] The writer offered the same advice to white Americans—enjoy the match, support your fighter, but do not be ruled by your passions.

***

Chicago had been Jack Johnson's town when he ran roughshod over the white American psyche. "The bugaboo of Jack Johnson," as Bill Cunningham of the *Boston Post* said, still "haunted the industry."[47] Thoughts of the black fighter seemed to hover over the Braddock-Louis proceedings like an unlit match atop a powder keg. Johnson smiling, gold-tooth and full. Johnson laughing, not at a joke but at his triumph over white America. Johnson with his heavyweight champion's arm around the waist of a white woman. Louis had been molded and promoted as the anti–Jack Johnson, but on the rainy night before the fight Chicago was once again reminded of the first black champion—and what happened after his 1910 Independence Day title contest. Reports that Jess Willard had come to Chicago for the fight only raised the Jack Johnson ante. Jim Jeffries, Jack Dempsey, and Gene Tunney had come too, all the White Hope ghosts of the past. But Jack Johnson would not be at the fight. Although he had offered to train Braddock, he was anathema to both camps.

With agonizing memories of the 1919 race riot, Chicago authorities prepared for the Comiskey Park title bout. For days the national press had run stories about the "characters" from the nation's "black belts" pouring into the South Side's "Little Hell" district and practicing "every known racket." Perhaps it was the popularity of the "Amos 'n' Andy" radio show. Originally set in Chicago, the show focused on black tricksters and small-time racketeers and wallowed in racial stereotyping. Reporters now suggested that a new Great Migration of black criminals and ne'er-do-wells was rolling into the Windy City. One journalist wrote that Comiskey was in the "worst cesspool of vice and crime known to America," and with the recent addition of "numbers racketeers, agents provocateurs, scalawags, street walkers, daffydills, nymphs, panderers, demimondaines and cadets," the area crawled with evil doings. Remnants of Detroit's Purple Mob, Capone's crime network, and St. Louis' Rats gang, it was rumored, had set up shop in Chicago, and civilization seemed a very thin veneer. Captain John Pendergast of the Chicago police force said his troopers would do what they could. He promised to have ten thousand policemen on riot duty around the ballpark and another four thousand special deputies "throughout the black belt." The plan for Comiskey was to have a policeman stationed every ten feet "to guard against racial conflict."[48]

It might have been the racial gloom and doom forecasts or the high price of the tickets or the feeling that the fight was a mismatch—whatever the reason or combination of reasons, the attendance numbers were disappointing. The paid attendance was less than sixty thousand, and gate receipts below $700,000. But there was no lack of celebrities or Louis enthusiasts in Comiskey Park. Perhaps 30 percent of the spectators were black. They arrived early and filled the less expensive seats in the bleachers in center field and the grandstands in left and right field. The list of the rich and famous filled considerable space in the society pages. Clark Gable led an all-star cast from Hollywood; Kenesaw Mountain Landis, the hatchet-faced commissioner of baseball, was there, someone reported, to make sure major league players did not consort with the throng of gamblers. Perhaps J. Edgar Hoover was doing the same thing, for he was there as well. In what had become a standard line, Chicago sportswriter Arch Ward wrote, "Almost everybody who was anybody from San Francisco to New York was there."[49]

They were there to see two men separated by race but sharing some remarkable similarities. James J. Braddock, the "Cinderella Man," was a Depression feel-good story. In the late 1920s he had been a good, but not exceptional, light-heavyweight scrapper with a fine right hand and not much of a left. In 1929 he got a shot at Tommy Loughran's title, losing in a lopsided decision to the masterful craftsman. After that fight, Braddock sank into pugilistic oblivion. Though always game, he lost more than he won and repeatedly injured or broke his right hand. By the end of 1933 he was just another hard-luck, out-of-work bloke on the dole, his nest egg lost in the stock market crash, his body betraying him, and his future as bleak as the New Jersey skies above his North Bergen home. Then—strike the theme song from *Rocky*—it all turned around. On June 14, 1934, on the undercard of the Carnera-Baer title match, Braddock took out "Corn" Griffin, an up-and-coming southern heavyweight. He followed that upset with more upsets against John Henry Lewis and Art Lasky, making a lightning transition from ham-and-egger to top contender. Finally, on June 13, 1935, as a 10-to-1 underdog he outpointed Max Baer for the heavyweight title. He paid back the dole he had received, bought a house for his wife and kids, and enjoyed the universal good will of the Fourth Estate. He was a thoroughly decent, hard-working, family-loving Irish American pug—what wasn't there to like?

Louis and Braddock were from the same side of the tracks but different sides of the racial fence. Three years before the Braddock match, Joe had been a promising amateur fighting in a Golden Gloves tournament in Chicago. He had come from south of nowhere, accepted the government welfare, and turned professional. Like Braddock, when Louis came into money he paid back his family's dole, bought his mother a house, took care of his brothers and sisters, and become a symbol of all that was right in his race and country. "A credit to his race," reporters had condescendingly begun to write. "A man of honor and decency," a few others commented. Although the trajectory of his career had been straighter than Braddock's, Louis' single loss was crushing, both for himself and for his race. Braddock had achieved his redemption. For Joe Louis, the fight with the Cinderella Man was only a step toward redemption. If he won, Max Schmeling would have to come to him.

At the opening bell, Braddock, his chin tucked close to his chest, rushed across the ring like he had somewhere to go after the fight. He had a plan. He was almost a decade older than Louis and had no chance of outlasting the younger, stronger, harder-hitting challenger. He had decided to gamble, risking everything on a quick knockout. Louis appeared momentarily surprised, unaccustomed to fighters aggressively attacking him. But he adjusted in an instant, more than ready to exchange punches. For much of the first round the fighters traded hard hooks. Braddock's blows seemed to have no effect on Louis, but Joe's opened small cuts on the champion's face. During one exchange Braddock landed a short right uppercut, catching Louis off balance and sending him to the canvas. Arch Ward wrote that Louis "went down like a Texas steer that had been pole axed," bringing spectators to their feet.[50] Actually, Louis was up almost as fast as the spectators, beating even referee Tommy Thomas' count of one. More embarrassed and angry than hurt, he went back on the attack.

Back in his corner, Jack Blackburn put his hand on Louis' shoulder as he gave his instructions. "Why didn't you take a nine count?" he asked. "You can't get up so fast that nobody in the place didn't see you go down."[51] Blackburn then told Louis to fight smart, to grind Braddock down but keep the pressure on. "Don't let that man breathe," he said. Blackburn knew that when Louis was throwing punches he was harder to hit. The champion tagged him because Joe stopped punching. If Braddock wanted a fight, he had one.

Beginning in the second round and continuing through the sixth, Louis forced the action by sliding forward, cutting off the ring, using his left jab, and hooking Braddock's body and head. Braddock's willingness to exchange punches made the challenger's job easier. For most of five rounds the two men fought evenly, but the action and the power of Louis' punches drained the older Braddock. And Louis' punches were tearing apart Braddock's face. By the end of the sixth round his face was a "pulpy mask." A severed artery in his upper lip gushed blood, he was bleeding from smaller cuts around both eyes, one eye was closed and the other puffy, blood was coming out of his left ear, and his arms were bruised and heavy from blocking Louis' blows.[52]

Joe Gould had seen enough. His fighter was hurt and bleeding, complaining that there was something wrong with the lights—he said that he could not see right—and not knowing that what was wrong was with *his* lights. Whitey Bimstein, the great trainer who was in Braddock's corner, recalled Gould saying to Braddock, "That's it, Jim. I'm going to have the referee stop the fight." "The hell you are," Braddock mumbled through swollen lips. "It's time," Gould implored. Braddock had the last words: "If you do, Joe, I'll never speak to you again."[53]

Almost defenseless, Braddock went out for the seventh round. His "spirit was willing but his flesh was weak," wrote Ward.[54] He was a standing target, hardly able to move or defend himself. Louis landed punch after punch, but through pure determination Braddock survived the round. He did not last the eighth round, however. Early on Louis landed two left hooks, the first to the body and the second to the jaw, which he followed with a straight right hand, "driven like a fencer's rapier," to the chin. Louis later recalled the punch: "I laid it solid, with all my body, on the right side of his face, and his face split open. He fell in a face-down dive."[55] "The punch," Jeremy Schaap later wrote, "had knocked [Braddock's] mouthpiece through his lip, opening a cut that would require twenty-three stitches to close and literally scar him for life."[56] Braddock did not so much fall as collapse, like a room at night goes dark when you turn out the lights. At ringside Ward observed that Braddock's "eyes lost their sprightliness. His brain seemed dulled into a stupor."[57] He was unconscious before he hit the canvas.

The referee's count was a formality. Braddock never moved. He lay in the center of the ring for a few minutes in an expanding pool of his own blood. Then his seconds half-carried, half-dragged him to his corner, trailing a thin line of blood along the path. After a few more minutes Braddock sputtered to life. Blinking, uncertain of what had happened, he asked his seconds, "Did I make a good fight?" Bimstein observed, "There may be better fighters than Braddock but there'll never be a gamer one."[58]

Cut man turned writer F. X. Toole once wrote that a fighter's goal is "to take his opponent's heart as mercilessly as an Aztec priest, to leave him blinking up into the lights with his will so shattered he will take the pieces to bed with him every night for the rest of his life."[59] And no fighter ruined as many other fighters, ended as many hopeful careers, as Joe Louis. Braddock's career as a fighter was over in any real sense. But he left the ring with his heart intact. "The exhibition of courage the gallant Anglo-Irishman gave before that final bolt of lightning struck the side of his jaw," wrote Dan Parker of the *New York Daily Mirror*, "awakened admiration and compassion for him in the heart of everyone in that vast crowd."[60]

Parker described the end in racial terms. The crowd accepted it in racial terms. The white faces closest to the ring looked stricken, mourning, silently and reverently, like some sort of pugilistic lost cause, the defeat of "brave Jim Braddock." But a different mood enveloped the outer reaches of Comiskey Park. As Braddock fell, commented a reporter, a "low rumble had started, the distant thunder of the gallery gods heralding a storm. It came from the bleachers far out in center field where many of the Louis adherents were watching. It came from the right and left field stands . . . swelling into a mad roar as tier after tier of spectators caught it up, finally to break in all its fury over the gleaming square where the tense drama of pugilism was unfolding." His language—"low rumble," "distant thunder," "mad roar"—suggested an ominous din of a threatening power. "It was bedlam, nothing less," Ward wrote. For him it was a tableau—Braddock "motionless on the canvas . . . hewn in shining marble against the blackness of the night."[61]

In the ring, as Braddock's seconds worked to revive him, Louis was perfectly calm. "His face was sheepish and solemn, his eyes still on the ground," commented Lloyd Lewis.[62] Interviewed only minutes after his victory by radio announcer Clem McCarthy, Louis was composed. "When did you think you had him beat?" McCarthy asked. "When I took the match," the new champion answered honestly. Even in the locker room Louis was deadpan and direct, hardly celebrating at all. All he recalled saying or thinking was "Bring on Max Schmeling. Bring him on."⁶³ For Louis, the title was only half won.

Beyond Louis' vision, however, black people stirred alive and joyous. Joe Louis, a black woman's son, was the champion of the world. The headlines and stories in newspapers underscored the racial divide. "'WE'VE GOTTA CHAMP NOW!' YELLS HARLEM," read the headline of the *Philadelphia Daily News*.⁶⁴ "CELEBRATION CARRIES LONG INTO THE NIGHT," chimed a *New York Amsterdam News* headline. It was followed by an illustration of a crowned Louis sitting on top of the world. Even more to the point was another *Amsterdam News* headline in bold, large block letters: "KING LOUIS I."⁶⁵

The headlines did not tell any black Americans what they did not already know. As soon as the radio broadcast ended, the celebrations began. Just outside the gates of Comiskey Park it was as if a cosmic clock had struck midnight on a hundred New Year's Eves. In the streets, wrote William Nunn of the *Pittsburgh Courier,* people were "swirling, careening, madly dashing from house to house . . . yelling, crying, laughing, boasting, gloating, exulting . . . slapping backs, jumping out of the way of wildly-driven cars . . . whites and blacks hugging . . . the entire world . . . turned topsy-turvy, this is the Southside of Chicago."⁶⁶ Asked more than a half century after the event to explain what the South Side was like that night, Louis' friend Truman K. Gibson, Jr., began, "It was like this," then stopping to think, he smiled, laughed, and said, "Well, you just would have had to have been there to understand."⁶⁷

Harlem experienced the same rush of joy. "I told you so," was the sentence on everyone's lips. American and Ethiopian flags streamed out of passing taxies, street parades formed out of thin air, and the layers of noise were too many to count. A roving *New York Amsterdam News* reporter observed the pride and passion the community had for Joe Louis. Along Seventh Avenue a "boisterous lad, marching like a drum major," bumped into someone and shouted, "Excuse, mister, it's Joe Louis in me!" Many women, the reporter claimed, were "choked with happiness," too overcome with feeling to talk. "I'm so happy!" one woman finally exclaimed.⁶⁸ Nobody wanted to talk or think about anything except Joe Louis. As a writer for the *Daily Worker* explained, "Joe Louis threw a leather-packed stick of dynamite at Jim Braddock's chin and it exploded in Harlem!"⁶⁹

It exploded in other places as well. "Like a gigantic spring unloosed," the black population of "St. Louis' Harlem" began celebrating "after Joe Louis' hand was raised as heavyweight boxing champion of the world."

They blocked traffic, forming long dancing parades, weaving through the streets shouting "Who won the fight?" and "Who's the champeen?"[70] Thousands of celebrants did much the same thing along South Street in Philadelphia, shouting themselves hoarse cheering for the new champion. The scene was repeated in cities and towns across the country. In Lansing, Michigan, twelve-year-old Malcolm Little swelled with pride during the celebration. Years later, after he had changed his name to Malcolm X and converted to the Nation of Islam, he remembered, "All the Negroes in Lansing, like Negroes everywhere, went wildly happy with the greatest celebration of race pride our generation had ever known. Every Negro boy old enough to walk wanted to be the next Brown Bomber."[71]

The joy experienced by blacks seemed potentially threatening to many whites. British journalist and commentator Alistair Cooke had recently arrived in the United States. On the night of the fight he was in Baltimore's "darktown" watching Fats Waller perform. All at once, a noise from outside of the club overrode the rhythm of the band. "Far off from somewhere came a high roar like a tidal wave. . . . It came nearer, a great singing and cheering. . . . Outside, in the villainously lit streets—they still [had] gaslight in darktown Baltimore—it was like Christmas Eve in darkest Africa. . . . For one night, in all the lurid darktowns of America, the black man was king." The memory of the scene "terrified and exhilarated" Cooke, giving a special meaning to the Marxist phrase "Arise, you have nothing to lose but your chains."[72]

Louis' victory had moved African Americans like few other events in the previous century. There were other black world champions when Louis won the title—John Henry Lewis had won the light heavyweight championship in 1935, and Henry Armstrong had captured the featherweight crown in 1936. But those titles were athletic accomplishments. The heavyweight crown carried social and cultural weight. The number of journalists who compared Louis to biblical and mythological leaders attested to the symbolic meaning of the heavyweight title. In winning it, Louis had become iconic, every bit as much as had John L. Sullivan, Jack Johnson, and Jack Dempsey. But in the black community there was fear that he would squander this cultural capital. After the fight, as Joe and Marva walked to their South Michigan Avenue home, hundreds of people greeted the new champion. They stood outside his home and cheered, demanding an almost royal wave of his hand. They called out to him. "We got another chance." "We're depending on you." "Don't be another Jack Johnson."[73]

6

Red, White, Blue, and Black

One hundred years from now, some historian may theorize, in a
footnote at least, that the decline of Nazi prestige began with a left
hook delivered by a former unskilled automobile worker who had
never studied the policies of Neville Chamberlain and had no
opinion whatsoever in regard to the situation in Czechoslovakia.
—*Heywood Broun, 1938*

Listen to this, buddy, for it comes from a guy whose palms are still
wet, whose throat is still dry, and whose jaw is still agape from the
utter shock of watching Joe Louis knock out Max Schmeling.
—*Bob Considine, 1938*

With his lean face, clenched jaw, and steel-rimmed glasses, Lester Rodney
had a hard, edgy, determined look that shouted political radicalism. He was
a card-carrying member of the Communist Party, class of 1936. If ever there
was a time when it seemed natural for a young, left-leaning New York
University night-school student to become a Communist, 1936 was it. "In
the 1930s on any college campus in New York," Rodney recalled, "if somebody wasn't a Communist, socialist or a Trotskyist or some variation of
radical, they were pretty much brain-dead."[1] From a distance, the Soviet
Union was the light that had not yet failed. It seemed less in the vise grip of
the Great Depression than did the Western democracies, and Joseph Stalin
appeared to be the only world leader who stood irrevocably opposed to
Adolf Hitler. Furthermore, the party had relaxed its single-minded focus

on world revolution. In Moscow, in July 1936, at the Seventh World Congress of the Communist Third International, the Comintern had adopted a broad-based policy toward forming popular fronts with other progressive, noncommunist organizations to combat the growth of fascism. For a brief historical moment in the United States, the CP tried to swim in the mainstream, prompting American CP leader Earl Browder to say, "Communism is twentieth-century Americanism."

The acceptance of the Popular Front strategy altered how the Communists did business in the United States. For one thing, it led to a radical change in the CP's newspapers, the *Daily Worker* and the monthly *Young Worker*. In moving from a superannuated ideological rag the *Daily Worker* became more a newspaper for thoughtful, progressive-minded Americans. This meant that it covered stories that interested normal, working-class Americans, including important boxing matches and major league baseball games. And it did so in a manner that was not too overtly Communist. Before the ideological shift, for example, the *Young Worker* assessed the role of major league baseball: "Through the means of this professional capitalist 'sport,' the capitalists were able to hoodwink the greater part of the American workers to eat, sleep and talk nothing . . . but baseball for a week. . . . Baseball is still a method used to distract workers from their miserable conditions." As for professional boxing, in a piece entitled "Dope Pushers," champions were described as "tools of the bosses in doping the workers to forget the class struggle."[2]

The Popular Front *Daily Worker* took a different tack, and in September 1936 the eight-page paper initiated a sports page. Edited by Lester Rodney, it mixed the action on the field and in the ring with occasional swipes at the ruling capitalist class. The new approach, while never pleasing the old guard Bolsheviks, was nevertheless a huge hit with the struggling masses. *Daily Worker* readers cared about the fate of the Scottsboro Boys, the labor violence at Ford's River Rouge plant, and all the other lefty causes of the mid-1930s, but many also wanted to see the Dodgers win the World Series and the Yankees take it on the chin. And no athlete exceeded the appeal of Joe Louis for American Communists. The paper made abundantly clear that the "quiet, shy, likable Negro boy" was one of them.[3] The son of a sharecropper who had worked in the River Rouge plant of the Ford Motor Company was a member of an exploited race and the working class.

Rodney's editorial fondness for Louis swung toward mania in 1938 as

Joe prepared to defend his title against Max Schmeling. In the year before the Nazi-Soviet Nonaggression Pact, Communists in Moscow and around the world were denouncing Hitler's imperialistic and militaristic advances, imploring other nations to join in the battle against Nazism. For Rodney and American Communists, Joe Louis was fighting on the front lines in the world's most important ideological struggle. Schmeling, Rodney wrote, was a "Nazi Schlager" (thug), a propagandist for "Naziland" sent to the United States to perform Hitler's bidding. Even Schmeling's training camp at Speculator, New York, was a "bit of transplanted Nazi-land, with barbed wire fences, state troopers, and general atmosphere suggestive enough to have earned it the sports writer's title of 'Der Concentration Camp.' "[4] In addition, Schmeling exhibited a " 'professional contempt' for the mentality of the young Negro champion" and a general contempt for blacks and Jews as a whole. He was the representative of the "perverted, bestial national-ism" that was driving the world toward war.[5] The Louis-Schmeling fight, Rodney insisted, had more to do with world politics than sports.

From the pages of the *Daily Worker* Maxwell Bodenheim and Richard Wright seconded Rodney's views. Bodenheim countered the racist tone of white sportswriters' reporting on Louis, arguing that the champion had heroically "fought his way through poverty, discrimination and the lack of education inflicted upon him by our economic system." Wright raged against Schmeling's racist notion that he had a "psychological edge" over Louis because "Negroes never forget beatings." In a time of cynicism and mendacity, Joe Louis was something more, something to arouse the masses' "capacity for loyalty, devotion and exultation." Even the mainstream white press embraced Louis as "America's world champion." For perhaps the first time the conservative Hearst chain and the *Daily Worker* saw eye-to-eye on a story. Richard Wright was correct. Millions of Americans were "pinning their submerged racial and social hopes" on the black champion.[6]

James W. Ford, a member of the Central Committee of the Commu-nist Party and the highest-ranking black Communist in the country, agreed that Louis was a social and political lightning rod. The day before the fight he wired the champion his best wishes against the "Nazi fighter Schmeling": "Millions of both Negro and white American sports lovers and friends of democracy confidently expect you to give an answer via left and right hooks to the Hitler rot of 'Aryan' supremacy."[7] For the first time in American history, a black man had been called on to defend the Ameri-can way of life in a significant, highly publicized symbolic arena. It was the Brown Bomber against the Black Shirt, with racial theories and political world systems riding on the outcome.

***

It seemed the special fate of black heavyweights in the first half of the twentieth century that they had to win two championship fights to capture one crown. Jack Johnson, the first black champion, defeated Tommy Burns for the title, but the sporting public withheld its full recognition until he beat former champion Jim Jeffries. Ezzard Charles, the third black champion, faced a similar task. He defeated Jersey Joe Walcott to win the title, but acceptance as champion came only after he had outpointed former title-holder Joe Louis. Sandwiched between Johnson and Charles, Louis also had to achieve the pugilistic double. He won the title when he knocked out Braddock. But until he defeated Schmeling, the crown rested on his head like a hat he had borrowed only for an evening. Virtually everyone who followed the sport felt this way. And it was the way Louis felt as well. "My only regret," he said in the dressing room after the Braddock match, "is that I did not have Max Schmeling in the ring tonight."[8]

In Germany, Schmeling had other ideas. No German radio station had broadcast the Louis-Braddock fight, regarding it as a contest between unworthy Americans. One fighter Max had knocked out; the other was afraid to box him. A Berlin boxing authority called the Chicago fight a "comedy," affirming that Schmeling was clearly the "world's best boxer." "We can see from the fact that the Negro Louis now is proclaimed world champion how little this American title amounts to," added a German sports official. Resentful of the American domination of boxing, the Nazi mouthpiece *Angriff* charged that "crooked" New York promoters had sacrificed all claims to control of the sport and effectively announced that the heavyweight title was up for grabs.[9]

Nazi boxing authorities hatched a plan to bypass the American Jewish promoters and crown a new heavyweight champion. They arranged an elimination match in London between Schmeling and Tommy Farr, a Welsh boxer who held the British & Empire heavyweight title and had scored recent victories over Max Baer and Walter Neusel. General A. C. Critchley insisted that it was the logical match to settle the muddied heavyweight picture. "I cannot see how the British Boxing Board can refuse to recognize the forthcoming Farr-Schmeling fight as a world title engagement."[10]

Talk of America's "crass materialism" and "dollar mad culture" drifted across the Atlantic, marking the difference between the Old and New World. In Europe, German journalists said that honor and sportsmanship were more valued than dollars. But, as with all things, there were exceptions, and Tommy Farr turned out to be one. When Schmeling refused a rematch offer to face Louis, Jacobs went after the Welshman. For 20 percent of a Yankee Stadium fight gate, Farr agreed to withdraw from his scheduled match with Schmeling and battle Louis. Immediately a legal battle erupted. Schmeling "insisted" that Farr honor his contract, and the British promoter filed a motion for an injunction with the Chancery Division.[11] But within days the motion was dismissed, the British Boxing Board of Control refused to recognize Schmeling as world champion, and Farr sailed for America, land of broken contracts and base materialism. Predictably, the German press compared Farr to Braddock, and Schmeling crabbed about the intercontinental "runaround."[12] After his attempt to outmaneuver Jacobs failed he announced that he would fight the winner of the Louis-Farr contest.

Some thirty-five thousand spectators paid to see 10-to-1 favorite Louis in his first title defense. Few expected much of a fight from a Welshman who had lost well over twenty fights in his career. But he surprised everyone. In the early rounds Louis opened deep cuts near both of Farr's eyes, and the challenger said he had trouble seeing from the mid-rounds on, but he kept punching gamely, "beaten but not disgraced," commented James P. Dawson of the *New York Times*.[13] Repeatedly, Louis hit and staggered Farr, but he could not knock him down. Even money said that Farr would not come out for the bell in round six, but at the end of the fifteenth he was still on his feet. Once again white sportswriters questioned the champion's ability, suggesting that he was "befuddled" by Farr's tactics and "harassed and menaced at every turn."[14] They labeled him "dumb," "stupid," and "overrated." His victory, most agreed, was decidedly "hollow," more an indication of his lack of talent than his invincibility. "He iss not more the same Louis," Schmeling observed.[15] The German did not need to add that he had knocked out the old Louis in twelve rounds.

***

By 1938 the careers of Louis and Schmeling and the courses of the United States and Nazi Germany were moving along parallel tracks. For much of the mid-1930s the shapers of U.S. foreign policy, as well as large portions of the American people, had tragically misjudged Adolf Hitler. Certainly it took William E. Dodd, the American ambassador in Germany from 1933 to 1938, a few years to gauge the direction that Hitler was moving. Dodd's intellectual odyssey in Nazi Germany throws light on American attitudes toward Hitler's regime. The dapper, professorial Dodd, a southerner and a die-hard Jeffersonian who had taken his Ph.D. in history at the University of Leipzig, viewed his appointment as an opportunity to infuse American foreign policy with a dose of Wilsonian internationalism. He traveled to his new assignment believing Germans to be "by nature more democratic than any other great race in Europe," and he considered that they had been unjustly punished at the Versailles Peace Conference.[16] Though he personally opposed Nazi rearmament and blatant anti-Semitism, he insisted that "a people had a right to govern itself and that other peoples must exercise patience even when crudities and injustices are done." Give the Nazis a "chance to try their schemes," he counseled President Roosevelt.[17]

The Blood Purge on the night of June 30–July 1, 1934, changed Dodd's— though not yet other Americans'—thinking about Hitler's plans. The murder of Ernst Röhm, other storm troop leaders, and several high-ranking bureaucrats during the Night of the Long Knives exposed Hitler's willingness to use lies, torture, and murder to achieve total power. After the purge of both right- and left-wing leaders, Dodd wrote of Hitler in his diary, "I have a sense of horror when I look at the man."[18]

During the next few years millions of Americans began to share Dodd's sense of horror. Hitler and the Nazis could not be trusted, Dodd warned, convinced that Germany's goal was "unlimited territorial expansion."[19] Hitler's reoccupation of the Rhineland, Axis Pact with Italian fascist Benito Mussolini, military support for fascist Francisco Franco in the Spanish Civil War, and *Anschluss* with Austria showed that the movement toward war was picking up speed. As Winston Churchill remarked during the Anschluss debate, "Europe is confronted with a program of aggression, nicely calculated and timed, unfolding stage by stage, and there is only one choice—either submit, like Austria, or take effective measures while time remains." During the same years, the movement toward the "final solution" of the "Jewish question" was also gaining momentum in Nazi Germany. From the initial Nazi boycott of Jewish businesses and the removal of Jews from the civil service; to the formation of concentration camps and the expulsion of "non-Aryans" from positions in banks, the stock market, the law, journalism, and medicine; to the Nuremberg Blood Laws and the seizure of Jewish businesses and homes—Jews under Nazi rule were systematically removed from virtually all aspects of German economic, social, and cultural life.

The reality of the "new Germany" spread slowly across America. To be sure, residents of New York City, with its high concentration of Jewish immigrants, registered keen interest in German-Jewish affairs. Jewish as well as mainstream New York newspapers carried feature stories about the Nazi persecutions, and organizations mushroomed to combat anti-Semitism and aid Jewish refugees. But the concern lessened as one moved north, south, and west of New York, and in 1938 American popular culture was only beginning to anticipate and reflect the Nazi menace.

In 1936, shortly after the first Louis-Schmeling match, the Berlin Olympic Games briefly focused the country on Hitler and Germany. Before the games, anti-Nazi groups called for an American boycott. The Committee on Fair Play in Sports, spearheaded by Amateur Athletic Union president Judge Jeremiah T. Maloney, pressed the American Olympic Committee to decline its invitation to the Berlin games. Other liberal organizations supported Maloney's actions. Catholic groups decried the "flagrantly and purely pagan" nature of Nazism; the National Council of the Methodist Church enlisted in the boycott crusade; and the American Federation of Labor supported the efforts because of the Nazi's anti-labor and anti-Semitic stands.[20] "The German government [is] simply terrified," reported a member of the British embassy in Berlin, "lest Jewish pressure may induce the U. S. government to withdraw their team and wreck the festival, the material and propagandistic value of which, they think, can scarcely be exaggerated."[21]

But as summer 1936 approached, more powerful sports bureaucrats trumped the boycott campaign. Charles Sherrill and Avery Brundage, two leaders of the American Olympic movement, visited Germany to gather information. German officials treated them like potentates. Sherrill and Brundage made the job easy for the Germans, for both Americans were looking to like what they saw—and choosing not to see what they did not want to see. Brundage joked that his club in Chicago also excluded Jews, and Sherrill told Hitler that "the Jew LaGuardia" was the real problem. On their return to the United States they argued forcefully that it was a mistake to mix sports and politics. Sherrill even suggested that it was a little churlish of Americans to tell Nazis how to behave. After his trip to Germany and meetings with Nazi Olympic organizers, he was convinced that "at least one Jew" would be a member of the German Olympic team.[22] "As for obstacles placed in the way of Jewish athletes or any others trying to reach Olympic ability," he told reporters, "I would have no more business discussing that in Germany than if Germans attempted to discuss the Negro situation in the American South or the treatment of the Japanese in California."[23]

When the Berlin Games opened the American team was there in full force. Germany staged a festival that set a new Olympic gold standard. The primary object of the Nazi regime was to impress the world. The country of Germany, as much as its athletes, took center stage. Foreigners who attended the games received near-royal treatment. There was no price gouging or any other form of mistreatment. The German government sold its currency to tourists at a reduced rate, and hotel and restaurant owners offered their fare at bargain-basement prices. A magnificent room in a luxury hotel went for about six dollars a night; a large, clean room in a lesser hotel could be had at two dollars. Meals were bountiful, delicious, and inexpensive. For two weeks foreign tourists were kings and queens. *Der Angriff,* the race-baiting Nazi newspaper, told its German readers, "We must be more charming than the Parisians, more easygoing than the Viennese, more vivacious than the Romans, more cosmopolitan than London, and more practical than New York."[24]

The government even declared a Week of Laughter. Mirth and happiness were quite literally the order of the day. The German Labor Front issued the command: "The coming eight days will be days of jollity and cheerfulness. Prior to the strain of the Olympic weeks, Berliners should take stock of themselves, then with merry hearts and friendly expressions on their faces, receive their Olympic guests. None should miss the chance."[25] The Nazis made every effort to show the world what the "new Germany" looked like. The government temporarily suspended the publication of such extreme anti-Semitic newspapers as Julius Streicher's *Der Stürmer,* rounded up troublemakers and threw them in jail, and stationed police—uniformed and plainclothes—around the city to guard against deviant behavior. They did not want a skilled pickpocket artist, legless beggar, or diseased streetwalker to distract anyone from all the joy in Berlin.

The journalists and wealthy foreign visitors—it was, after all, in the middle of the Depression, and few but the rich could afford international travel—saw and experienced exactly what the Nazi organizers wanted them to see and experience. They saw the massive red flag with a black swastika nearly everywhere. At the train stations and at the Olympic Stadium, attached to hotels and in the Olympic Village, along the main thoroughfares and hanging from balconies—the Nazi flag flew with the Olympic flag. But they did not see anti-Semitic posters or graffiti. They witnessed no signs barring Jews from particular hotels and restaurants, no newspaper slogans such as "Jews Are Our Misfortune," and, in fact, hardly anything about Jews at all. If a nosy journalist wished to investigate the "Jewish question" he was told to contact the local Gestapo, who would be most happy to answer all questions and then tail the inquiring writer.[26]

Less snoopy journalists never had it so good. They lodged in the finest hotel rooms, feasted on the best food, and sat in the prime seats at the Olympic Stadium. Everything they needed to practice their craft was at their fingertips. Paper, pencils, typewriters, telephones, publicity shots, darkrooms, secretarial assistants—just ask, it was all there free of charge. How could the journalists not respond generously? They wrote about the "miracle of Germany," told of how the "shadow of the Depression" had vanished from the land, and suggested that Hitler was not such a bad fellow—a little odd, perhaps, but harmless. After all, he had attended many of the events. Laughing, slapping his thigh, and clapping his hands, he looked every bit as merry as the other Germans during the Week of Laughter. Still almost two years away from being named *Time's* Man of the Year, he was clearly Germany's man of the hour.

It took more than a year of American popular culture chipping away at the foundation of the "new Germany" legend to uncover the truth about Nazism. Although liberals and Communists in the movie business formed the Hollywood Anti-Nazi League in 1936, the film industry produced very few films that specifically criticized fascism, and even fewer that took on Hitler and his Nazi pack. A few films, such as *The Story of Louis Pasteur* (1936) and *The Life of Emile Zola* (1937), took tepid swipes at what was happening in Germany, but only someone attuned to the inner language of the Hollywood biopic could have interpreted the messages. The industry was too concerned with anti-Semitism in the United States and its overseas market—40 percent of its total revenues—to move too far out on any political limb.

United Artists' *Blockade* (1938) was the first major Hollywood film to have an unequivocal and understandable antifascist message. But it focused on the Spanish Civil War, not Nazi Germany. "Where is the conscience of the world?" asks the character played by Henry Fonda at the end of the film. Hollywood wanted to be that conscience, and beginning in 1939 with *Confessions of a Nazi Spy* a few studios became more politically adventurous. With fascist markets closed to Hollywood producers, American-based filmmakers demonstrated a new political boldness, poking fun at Hitler in *The Great Dictator* (1940), showing the struggle between good Germans and Nazis in *The Mortal Storm* (1940), exploring the evil nature of Nazis in *Man Hunt* (1941), and demonstrating that there is a fighting man inside all American males in *Sergeant York* (1941). But by the time *Sergeant York* premiered, America was for all practical purposes at war with Germany.[27]

Other forms of popular culture such as radio and comic books were also slow to attack fascism. During World War II, comic book characters from Superman, Captain America, and Batman and Robin to more mortal men, such as Joe Palooka, Dick Tracy, and Tarzan, enlisted or contributed to the war effort. But when Superman made his first appearance in June 1938 he was appealing for world peace and battling "merchants of death" in the arms industry, not warning Americans about the Nazi threat. Similarly, the radio industry was slow to criticize Hitler. Although radio news commentators reported Hitler's march toward war, antifascism was seldom woven into the entertainment programming. Not until January 1938 did an episode of Orson Welles' *The Shadow* feature a German sabotage ring. Like U.S. spectators in Berlin for the Olympic Games, Americans at home—going to the movies, reading comic books, and listening to radio entertainment—were unaccustomed to seeing and hearing representations of Nazi atrocities.[28]

In this regard, 1938 was a watershed year, the moment when the Western democracies realized that only war would curb Hitler's territorial aggression. Of course, such radio commentators as H. V. Kaltenborn, Harold Thomas "Boake" Carter, Elmer Davis, and Fulton Lewis, Jr., put their political brand on news from Europe, though they seldom agreed on what any particular story meant for their American listeners.[29] And *Life* magazine ran photo-essays on the Spanish Civil War, the Japanese invasion of China, and other major world events. But in most of the news on the radio and in mass-circulation magazines, the United States seemed vaguely out of the loop. It was as if violent tremors were rocking a distant planet, an interesting enough event, but for most Americans unconnected to their everyday lives.

The second Louis-Schmeling match connected democratic America and fascist Germany in a compelling, dramatic narrative. The contest focused America's attention on the differences between American and Nazi ideologies, throwing anti-Semitism and racism into sharp relief. Making the matter even more vivid, a black man became the symbol of the American way of life. Joe Louis, the son of a sharecropper, carried the mantle of democracy, racial equality, and the rule of law. On the surface, the fight would settle once and for all who was the rightful heavyweight champion. But just beneath the surface, visible to all, swirled important political, social, and cultural issues. The fight trafficked in conflicts between political orders and world systems, between shining goods and indescribable evils. As America and the world pitched toward war, Joe Louis became one of the iconic images, the irreducible core, of the conflict.

***

Before 1938 Max Schmeling had enjoyed sympathetic treatment from American sportswriters. He was an ingratiating man who made it his business to curry favor with influential people. Life in Germany had taught him how to get along with wildly different types, and he used his skills to good advantage in the United States. Paul Gallico knew him better than any other American journalist. Gallico, who spoke German and served as the boxer's ghost for newspaper and magazine pieces, wrote in his memoir of his years as a sportswriter, "Of all the prizefighters I have known, the German seemed to have come the closest to being a sportsman and a decent fellow."[30] Nat Fleischer, editor of *Ring* magazine, agreed. He had met Schmeling in Weimar Germany, and over the next decade he had become the boxer's outspoken advocate. "Max was wonderful," he recalled years later, "just wonderful—if he wanted you to like him. But he had another side as well. Not mean or offensive. It was just that I'm not sure anyone really knew him."[31] But after signing for a rematch with Louis, Schmeling—Gallico's and Fleischer's "good German"—became freighted by his Nazi connections.

Part of Schmeling's troubles was a natural product of his success. The Germans, short on international sports heroes, gloried in Schmeling's achievements, celebrating his victories with the same enthusiasm as black Americans did Louis'. After signing a contract in September 1937 to fight Louis the following June, Schmeling began to prepare for the match. He had not fought since his June 1936 victory over Louis, and he needed several tune-up matches before facing the champion. Between December 1937 and April 1938, he engaged in three fights, knocking out Harry Thomas in New York and then returning to Germany where in two Hamburg contests he outpointed Ben Foord and knocked out Steve Dudas. The fights enthralled Germans, capturing the mood of the aggressive, goose-stepping nation jerking toward war.

By the end of 1937 it was virtually impossible to separate Nazi policy from Nazi athletic achievement. The American press followed the mounting horrors in Germany: the arrest and imprisonment of anti-Nazi theologian Martin Niemoeller; the opening of Buchenwald, the fourth concentration camp in Germany; the enormous 1937 Nuremberg rally, at which virulently anti-Semitic Julius Streicher claimed that the Talmud gave Jews the right to kill non-Jews; the court case that ruled that German children could be taken from parents who refused to endorse Nazi teaching. In his decision the judge affirmed that any education imparted by a parent had to conform to the "fashion that the nation and state expect."[32] The same standard applied to sport. Athletes like Max Schmeling had become instruments of the state.

Because of this symbiosis, American liberal groups called for a boycott of the Schmeling-Thomas match. The president of the Non-Sectarian Anti-Nazi League wrote Mike Jacobs that his organization would boycott the fight, not because it had anything against Schmeling, but because it would result in a flow of dollars into Germany. Their logic was impeccable. Germany was cash-poor and desperate for foreign currency. The best way to influence Hitler was through economic, not diplomatic, policy. But there was nothing logical about a fight crowd, and the appeals for a boycott garnered only a few inches of filler space in New York newspapers.

Outside of Madison Square Garden a handful of citizens with placards picketed the contest. Crude caricatures of Hitler and signs claiming that Schmeling was a pawn of the Nazis bobbed up and down, all but invisible to spectators eager to get out of the frigid evening. Inside, the Garden was packed for the Schmeling-Thomas match, the largest indoor gathering for a fight in two years. Using his right as he had against Louis, Schmeling chopped down the "stout-hearted Minnesotan" like a tree.[33] As the pro–German American crowd cheered, Schmeling knocked down Thomas six times in the eighth round before referee Arthur Donovan stopped the contest.

The cheers for Schmeling in the Garden paled compared to the noise throughout Germany. Once again Germans stayed awake to listen to the radio broadcast of the fight. One more time, fans gathered in bars and restaurants to celebrate Max's victory, exchanging toasts and belting out drinking songs. Brown Shirts from the Rhine to the Oder were happy and contented. Hermann Goering, Joseph Goebbels, and Rudolf Hess wired Schmeling their congratulations. Hitler personally called Anny Ondra.

The celebrations continued when Schmeling returned to Germany. An official reception was held in Berlin for Max and Anny. His match against Ben Foord was staged on January 30, the fifth anniversary of Hitler's ascension to chancellor of Germany, a date so fraught with symbolism that simply the decision to hold the contest that day created a link between the dictator and the boxer. The event grafted a Nuremberg-style rally onto a boxing match, creating a Wagnerian evening surfeit with speeches and salutes that ended with a rather lackluster twelve-round boxing match. A few months later, during the tense weeks after the Anschluss, Schmeling knocked out American Steve Dudas amid even more political symbolism.

But Schmeling's success in the ring—and the political capital that the Nazi regime made of it—was not the only issue that disturbed millions of Americans. Simply put, Schmeling had become excessively cozy with the Nazi leadership. He never joined the Nazi Party, however, which would have rendered him verboten in American boxing circles. But when in Germany he sure seemed to look, walk, and talk like a Nazi. In September 1937 the *New York Times* reported that he "stole the show" at a tea with Hitler, Benito Mussolini, and four hundred of "Germany's most beautiful motion picture and stage actresses."[34] During the Anschluss referendum Schmeling encouraged all Germans to participate and was photographed voting "Ja!"—one of the 99 percent of Germans and Austrians who voiced their official approval of the union between German-speaking peoples. Then, less than a week later, on April 20, 1938, he was part of the daylong festival celebrating Hitler's forty-ninth birthday. Sitting next to Der Führer, Schmeling, in formal dress, explained how he defeated Dudas and reviewed the film of the match. Later that evening he was part of a select few who previewed Leni Riefenstahl's four-and-a-half hour documentary on the

Berlin Olympics. Contrary to what the boxer would later claim, he was a part of that group.

While Schmeling was boxing and socializing in Germany, Louis was itching for revenge. He defended his title twice, knocking out Nathan Mann in Madison Square Garden and Harry Thomas in the Chicago Stadium. Neither boxer offered much competition. The major attraction of the Thomas match was that it offered a point of comparison. In less than four months Thomas had been repeatedly knocked to the canvas by Schmeling and Louis. As for his opinion of the upcoming title clash, the Minnesotan announced that he planned to bet his entire purse from the Louis match on the champion.

Even when he was not in a ring, Louis was still in the news. Journalists, and particularly African American ones, detailed his every public appearance. He went on tour with the Detroit Brown Bombers, a softball team he subsidized and that was composed mostly of his friends. Crowds of blacks mobbed the ballparks, hoping to get a peek at their champion playing first base or just watching the game. In Philadelphia in late September the stands of the Passon Ball Park filled well before game time, but thousands of Louis gawkers pushed into the park, trying to wedge into the stands close to where Louis was standing at first base. Some spilled onto the field, and twenty thousand to thirty thousand people were outside the ballpark. It was a mob scene. "Women were fainting by the scores," reported the *New York Amsterdam News.* The police were helpless. After two sections of the grandstands collapsed, an umpire called the game.[35]

Louis had become the black Clark Gable, supernatural in his power to attract crowds. When he went to a series of premieres of *Spirit of Youth,* theaters were packed with people who had come to see him—not on the screen, but simply sitting in the darkened movie house watching *himself* on the screen. The film received tepid reviews, accusing Louis of displaying a "paucity of acting ability" and never transcending "his own unsophisticated self." But no viewers complained. Seeing Joe was their only goal. It was what mattered when he appeared in a nightclub, turned up in New York, Chicago, Detroit, or Hollywood, went to a Detroit Tigers game, or just strolled along an avenue with Marva. Any Joe Louis sighting was enough for a headline. Even the *New York Times* took note when Joe Louis and Joe DiMaggio bumped into each other at Pompton Lakes, New Jersey. "Two Famous Joes Meet to Talk Shop," the headline announced. The article claimed that the two celebrities "spent most of the day chatting," but it is difficult to imagine what the two most famously silent athletes found so engrossing.[36]

Louis made news even beyond the public gaze. Journalists speculated endlessly about the state of his marriage, a union that, from the moment Joe and Marva said "I do," seemed on the verge of collapsing like the stands at Passon Ball Park. In truth, their marriage had problems. Joe spent weeks on end in training camps and on tours of various kinds, and still other times he just disappeared with his friends, leaving Marva alone. Generosity was his strong suit, not consideration. The gifts he showered on Marva only went so far in healing the pain he caused. The result was that she usually seemed just a step away from walking out, which led to the constant rumbling of rumors. In the language of gossip columnist Walter Winchell, Joe and Marva were perpetually just on the outskirts of "splitsville," or at least Joe was residing in "alonesville."[37]

***

By the second week in May, however, talk of splitsville became little more than a murmur in the press as journalists sharpened their pencils to write the big story. Even before Schmeling arrived in the United States, members of the Non-Sectarian Anti-Nazi League had begun to prowl the sidewalks outside Mike Jacobs' offices in the Hippodrome on Sixth Avenue between 43rd and 44th streets. The huge building with the twin illuminated sparkling globes in its towers had seen boxers and dancing elephants, actors and opera singers walk in and out of its doors, but never had it been a venue for international political affairs. The Anti-Nazi League members passed out pamphlets that in effect accused the Jewish Jacobs of supporting "Nazi propaganda" by promoting the fight. Jacobs, his store-bought teeth rattling, denied the charge. If anything, one of his office staff added, Jacobs was in the American propaganda business. "Those folks are crazy," he said of the boycotters. "They ought to be shilling for the fight. Joe Louis will knock Schmeling as flat as a German pancake, and what will Herr Hitler do then, poor thing? His shining knight in Nazi armor chopped into mincemeat by a Negro!"[38]

A few reporters from the more staid newspapers argued that a fight was just a fight, that it had nothing to do with politics. "It seems rather silly to vision a prizefighter as a political propagandist," wrote John Kieran in his *New York Times* column. "Herr Schmeling may be a Nazi. He probably is. . . . But over here Schmeling is just a prizefighter when in the ring and a quiet, inoffensive foreigner outside the ropes. . . . The notion of making a prizefighter stand forth as the shining representative of a race, a creed or a political program verges on the fantastic."[39] Myrtle S. Weigand in a letter to the *Times* agreed that Americans should not mix sports and politics. "Leave the European problems on the other side," she advised. "Schmeling has nothing to do with the government of his country."[40] But Kieran's notion that sports were not symbolic and Weigand's idea that Max had nothing to do with Adolf were voices from sport's mythical past, echoes, perhaps, from the playing fields of English public schools. Since early in the twentieth century sport and politics had been thoroughly mixed.

On May 9, with four dollars in his pocket, Schmeling arrived in New York harbor aboard the *Bremen*. He expressed no concern about his bankroll: "I can always call on Uncle Mike. He's not exactly what you would call a poor man." He showed no more concern about the champion. "Louis may not even know it himself," Schmeling explained, "but he'll always be afraid of me. . . . He's the kind who will always hold a man who has beaten him in some sort of superstitious fear."[41] During his conversations with reporters Schmeling attempted to soft-pedal political issues, but few journalists considered him anything other than a representative of Nazi Germany. If the German wins the fight, speculated Henry McLemore of United Press, he "would go back to Berlin to rival Horst Wessel as a Nazi hero. Der Fuehrer Adolf Hitler might be at the Kaiserhof Station to welcome him. . . . All the Nazis would 'Seig heil!' 'Seig heil!' 'Seig heil!' until their throats were sore."[42]

McLemore and scores of other journalists recognized that the Louis-Schmeling rematch transcended boxing. It had more to do with politics than prizefighting, world systems than sports. Although Schmeling was loath to admit it, Louis was willing to articulate the stakes. In a ghost-written article—a standard practice for athletes and other celebrities—Louis noted, "I fight for America against the challenge of a foreign invader, Max Schmeling. This isn't just one man against another or Joe Louis boxing Max Schmeling. It is the good old U.S.A. versus Germany."[43] An apocryphal story of a 1938 meeting between Louis and President Franklin Roosevelt added to the "us" versus "them" sentiment. In the tale, which was widely believed and is still often reported as fact, Roosevelt felt Louis' muscular right arm and said, "Joe, we need muscles like yours to beat Germany."[44]

In this lightning-charged political atmosphere the two fighters retired to their training camps. Louis retreated to Pompton Lakes, his favorite site. He went without golf clubs or Marva, and he stayed without late-night trips to New York or Atlantic City or any other nonpugilistic distractions. He trained harder than he had for any match since the one with Primo Carnera. Blackburn and recently hired assistant trainer Mannie Seamon employed an outstanding group of sparring partners to push Louis to his limits. They told the sparring partners to throw as many right hands as they could. They wanted Louis to get used to blocking rights and countering with his left.

Blackburn and Seamon also devised a fight plan that took advantage of Schmeling's weaknesses. The German was a cautious, defensive boxer—an intelligent, patient fighter who waited for his opening. He tended to set himself before throwing his trademark right hand, and he fought his best in a slowly paced contest. Blackburn's plan called for Louis to fight like Henry Armstrong and take the fight to Schmeling, forcing him to react quickly without analyzing the match. The idea was to get inside Schmeling's defenses and knock him out. The fight would not go the distance, because the pace would be too fast for a heavyweight to survive. "They might as well tell the judges to stay home," Louis said, "because this fight is going to end in a knockout just as sure as green apples will give you stomach misery."[45]

The mood of Louis' camp and the champion could not have been different. The sleepy resort town of Pompton Lakes stirred alive during the weeks before the fight. On some days close to four thousand people turned out to watch Louis train, most sitting on the bleachers surrounding the ring. They paid a dollar each, sometimes in the old envelope size, pre-Roosevelt bills, the ones that had been put away long ago for such an occasion. Talking, laughing, shouting people who could not find a seat in the bleachers crowded around the ring, perched on tree branches, and scampered onto rooftops to watch the champion exercise and spar. When Louis walked by they fell silent, "in a state of deep awe," noted Richard Wright.[46] Just watching Louis jump rope or wallop the heavy bag elicited cheers and groans. Some just looked on dumbstruck, admiring Louis as if he were an inconceivably beautiful work of art. And for many blacks Joe Louis was just that—

a creation whose very existence imparted joy. Although white journalists continued to describe the champion in racist language, their words failed to diminish the meaning of Joe Louis for blacks.

Louis was oblivious to the thousands of eyes that followed his every movement. He trained with a single-minded intensity. It was as if every sit-up, every medicine ball slammed into his gut, every murderous hook to the heavy bag mattered. Trainer Marshall Miles visited the camp a few days before the match and noticed the seriousness of his manner. "Joe, when he got into shape like he was getting into shape then, he didn't talk to people. You can tell a few days before the fight, he gets mean, he gets nasty, and he don't hardly talk to anyone. That's the way Joe was." Shortly before breaking camp, Blackburn told Miles, "Well, Marshall, I did all I could. He's as good as hands can make him." Assessing his fighter's condition, Blackburn told sportswriter Edward Van Every, "He been a good boy, a very good boy this time, and so he's good enough for me, which means he'll be too good for Schmeling."[47]

Schmeling was just as focused as Louis, but his camp lacked the joyous ambiance of the champion's. The Speculator, New York, training quarters had all the charm of an alpine concentration camp. Together with his attendants, he had turned the delightful Adirondack Mountains site into a patch of the Black Forest. His cook, a plump restaurateur named Willy Lehmann, was German. When a visitor told him he had the same last name as the governor of New York, he was apt to say, "Ja! Ja! But I am not Jewish."[48] Schmeling's trainer and staff were German. Armed state troopers, with their black leather jackboots, served as bodyguards; fences were topped with barbed wire; a couple of German shepherds patrolled the grounds. It was as if mirth had been outlawed, thought reporter Francis E. Stan, and even the fans at Schmeling's training sessions watched grimly. Traveling from Louis' camp to Schmeling's, wrote the *New York Daily Mirror's* Dan Parker, was "like stepping from this enlightened republic into one of the totalitarian states. The flavor of Nazi Germany permeates Schmeling's camp. . . . One expects to see brown-shirted soldiers popping out from behind every telephone pole with a 'Heil Hitler!' challenge, and the feeling exists that someone's going to turn you in to Der Fuehrer if you don't salute."[49]

Even the normally affable Schmeling was snappish in his police state in the Adirondacks. He sat for selected interviews, tried unconvincingly to reaffirm that he was just an athlete, and even occasionally mustered a smile and a joke. But he never quite pulled it off. Parker and other reporters sensed an air of condescension. It seemed "as if the Superman from the Superstate were giving an ordinary mortal a break, instead of a heavy-weight pugilist from a foreign country coming here to fight for the title with an American boy for American money."[50] For Parker and others it was a case of waving the flag and supporting the red, white, and blue, even if the Stars and Stripes were draped over the shoulders of a black fighter. Nationality and ideology had finally trumped race.

Schmeling knew the fight was being politicized. He understood the process, having benefited from it in Germany. Years later he argued a bit disingenuously that he was a helpless victim of the times, refusing to acknowledge that in his own small way he had contributed to the temper of the age. "Joe Louis, who had yesterday been celebrated by Harlem as a hero of the underclass, was now suddenly transformed into the symbol of freedom and equality for all people and races against the Nazi threat," Schmeling explained. "Joe, the black man, found himself cast in the unexpected role of national hero for all Americans." And Louis, Schmeling said, had accepted the role and had "worked himself into a rage of retribution."[51]

News of the upcoming battle raged through the national and international press, exposing fault lines in America and the world. Quite simply, virtually everywhere the match was accepted as a fight between America and Germany, democracy and fascism, pacifism and militarism. Joe Williams of the *New York World Telegram* accurately dubbed the match the Battle of Awesome Implications.[52] Although lingering attitudes about race shaded opinions, even in the South many whites accepted Louis as a representative of the American way of life. Even the residue of racism that always clouded the mainstream reportage about Louis did not obscure the main story line that Joe was an American success story. One basic theme roared through hundreds of newspaper and magazine articles: Only in America could a poor black lad from the South achieve wealth, status, and fame. Only in America could Joe Louis become a symbol of America.

The story line was so powerful that both fighters were scrutinized in the weeks before the title fight. Reports from Speculator were countered by reports from Pompton Lakes. Max looked good in camp; Joe overpowered his sparring partners. Max was a craftier and more intelligent boxer; Joe had the outrageous advantages of youth. Max had psychology on his side; Joe didn't even know "Cy what-you-calls-him."[53] Max said that Joe would never be able to forget the punishment he received in the first fight; Joe claimed he was basically out after the second round and couldn't even remember the rest of the fight. Back and forth reporters paddled their stories. As writer David Margolick accurately observed, in the race for "news" stories from the camps "there were . . . conflicting reports about the conflicting reports."[54]

***

In New York City the fight's politics dominated the news. Actually, from the first proposed boycott the Non-Sectarian Anti-Nazi League faced problems. On one hand, millions of Americans—and especially New Yorkers—recognized that the league had a valid point. Hitler was a threat, and it seemed silly to support any endeavor that put more money into the Nazi treasury. But on the other hand, the oddsmakers listed Louis as a two-to-one favorite to knock Schmeling on his Nazi ass. Most observers concluded that that outcome was worth allowing a few dollars to sail across the Atlantic. A Louis victory would prick the Nazi racist balloon, deflating Hitler's theories of Aryan supremacy.

Mike Jacobs did his best to reduce the Anti-Nazi League's ambitions. In a nice bit of political infighting he went cause-for-cause with the boycotters. Except for Mrs. Hearst's Free Milk Fund for Babies, Jacobs had never been much of a cause guy before 1938. His standard line in all business deals was, "What's in it for Uncle Mike?" Yet just weeks before the title bout he experienced his road to Damascus moment. He did not convert to Christianity, but he did embrace a cause—the Refugee Aid Committee, which helped Europeans on the run from Nazi persecution. In a letter to the organization, Jacobs promised to donate 10 percent of the net profits—or not less than $7,500—from the match to ease the terrible plight of Jews and political refugees fleeing European fascism. Overcome with concern for his fellow man, Jacobs expressed hope that his humanitarian gesture would inspire others to open their wallets for the worthy cause.[55]

A spokesman for the Anti-Nazi League was understandably nonplussed. "This just wasn't what we expected," he told reporters. "It casts a different light on the situation. . . . If we go through with our picketing and campaign work, we will be in the position of boycotting an event that is contributing to a fund allied with our organization. Where would that put us?"[56] Perhaps it would put the organization right were Jacobs wanted it, figuratively in his pocket and out of the newspapers. In the end the Anti-

Nazi League and its allied associations pursued an ad hoc approach to the boycott. Some members continued to support the boycott, and others rooted hard and bet their money on Louis. One Jewish newspaper contributed a telling nugget when it mentioned that an Anti-Nazi League official had purchased a block of tickets for the match.

By June 22, the day of the fight, any news of a boycott had been shoved so far back in the newspapers that it amounted to no more than a speck of agate type in a sea of stories about the match. The combatants had left their camps, the pundits had made their predictions, and the journalists had filed their last prefight stories. From New York to Los Angeles and from London to Tokyo, daily life was put on hold until after the fight. A cartoon in the *Toronto Daily Star* captured the moment: In the foreground is a bespectacled globe labeled "TROUBLED OLD WORLD AFFAIRS" and a man labeled "John Citizen." In the background is a ring with two boxers. Pointing toward the ring John Citizen tells the world, "I have an **important conference**. Wait—I'll be right back."[57] Similar cartoons featuring a globe looking toward a ring appeared in other newspapers. To suggest that the match would be the Battle of the Century, commented Joe Williams, was to diminish its scope. It would be bigger than that. "It might properly be called the Battle of the Ages."[58]

***

The night was perfect, a cool breeze drifting off the East River toward Yankee Stadium, which was gleaming almost white from the thousands of lights. The sprinkles of the afternoon had passed, leaving an evening so fine that even a few jaded reporters took note. "No promoter could have asked for a more ideal night," commented Fred Van Ness. "It was just cool enough to make a light wrap comfortable for the women, who were in their Summer finery." The night felt like something out of the 1920s, perhaps a Jazz Age Scott Fitzgerald novel. "If the country is in the grip of a recession it was not evident at Yankee Stadium last night," Van Ness wrote.[59]

The stadium was almost filled. Nearly seventy thousand people gathered inside the House that Ruth Built. A number of factors distinguished the spectators, one of which was the vast number who were not from New York. Thirty thousand or more out-of-towners came for the fight, the greatest collection of visitors in the city since the mid-1920s. They filled New York's hotels and restaurants, pumping dollars into the economy in amounts not seen for over a decade. Several thousand had arrived on ocean liners from Germany, others on trains from Philadelphia, Chicago, Detroit, and Los Angeles. More than most crowds, they comprised a cross-section of America. Rich and poor, black and white, and famous and infamous were gathered in one place for one defining event. Hollywood stars and prominent politicians could always be counted on to attend an important fight, but Louis summoned forth the black elite as well, from Cab Calloway and Bill Robinson to Louis Armstrong and Duke Ellington to Jack Johnson and Henry Armstrong. Yankee Stadium was dripping in diamonds, furs, and hopes.

Two black writers and civil rights proponents, Richard Wright and Roy Wilkins, had made their way to Yankee Stadium to watch a fight that they believed would help to define what it meant to be black in America. In his prefight coverage in the *Daily Worker,* Wright emphasized that he perceived no separation between sport and politics. The fight was ideological, pure and simple. It was black America defending the notions that white Americans held dear—democracy, equality, and tolerance—even during a time when those very ideals were not practiced in much of the country. It was an irony painful in its contemplation. It was also a black American battling for his people, for their place in the national polity. The drama of the event, Wright observed, "manipulated the common symbols and impulses in the minds and bodies of millions of people so effectively as to put to shame our professional playwrights." For millions of black Americans, Louis "symbolized the living refutation of the hatred spewed forth daily over radios, in newspapers, in movies, and in books about their lives. Day by day, since their alleged emancipation, they have watched a picture of themselves being painted as lazy, stupid, and diseased. In hapless horror they have suffered the attacks and exploitation which followed in the wake of their being branded as 'inferiors.' . . . Jim Crowed in the army and navy, barred from many trades and professions, excluded from commerce and finance, relegated to menial positions in government, segregated residentially, denied the right of franchise for the most part; in short, forced to live a separate and impoverished life, they were glad for even the meager acceptance of their humanity implied in the championship of Joe Louis."[60] For twelve million Americans—for W. E. B. DuBois listening to the fight in Atlanta and Miles Davis listening in East St. Louis and all the others—Joe Louis, at that moment, embodied their hopes and promises and tomorrows.

Roy Wilkins sensed this in his bones as well. After putting the NAACP's magazine *The Crisis* to bed in Albany, he rushed to the station and boarded a train to New York, telling the conductor to "step on it." When he got off the train in the heart of Harlem at 125th Street, he latched hold of his hat, flagged a cab, and raced for Yankee Stadium, arriving just after the start of the fight. For him, as for so many others, Yankee Stadium at that moment was the center of the world.[61]

Beyond Yankee Stadium, across America and the oceans, millions more people dialed their radios to the fight. About one hundred million people listened to the contest, sixty million of them Americans. No event had ever attracted an audience that large—not a sporting event, a political speech, or an entertainment show. Perhaps as many as twenty million people were listening to the broadcast at 3 A.M. in Germany. They sat in bars and barracks and private homes, most pulling with all their psychic might for Max. Several other million people in the path of Hitler's march listened to the fight, many entertaining hopes for a very different outcome.

Throughout Europe, where the sounds of war could almost be heard, the fight mattered terribly. It was equally true in America, where the winds of war were still a whisper. On the afternoon before the fight the challenger received an international wire: "To the coming world's champion, Max Schmeling. Wishing you every success. Adolf Hitler."[62] That night many members of the Nazi leadership would listen to the fight. So would southerners who had watched the rise of Joe Louis with vague forebodings. As the time for the fight drew closer, a group of blacks living outside Plains, Georgia, walked quietly to the home of a local peanut and cotton farmer. Earl Carter owned a radio and said his field hands could listen to the match with him. He expected three or four to show up, but about forty arrived. Mister Earl's largess stopped at the front door. Just before the opening bell he propped his radio near an open window and went outside near a mulberry tree and listened to the match with his employees and his son Jimmy. Such scenes, multiplied by the millions, were taking place everywhere there was a radio.[63]

At shortly before 10 P.M. the voice of Clem McCarthy began to fall like a blanket across the nation. Activity inside restaurants, movie theaters, baseball parks, and other public places stopped as people leaned into the airwaves. Out on the nation's streets traffic quieted to a whisper as McCarthy's voice drifted through raised windows into the summer night. Woody Guthrie, whose songs were the conscience of Depression America, recalled walking through the narrow alleys and streets of Santa Fe that evening, listening to the broadcast of the fight. But nowhere were citizens listening more intently than in the black neighborhoods across the country, places where Joe Louis was the embodiment of hope and accomplishment and where his picture hung next to FDR's in thousands of homes.

Listening to the broadcast, many blacks noticed something different from the calls of Louis' previous matches. McCarthy and his color man seemed to emphasize Louis' American roots a touch more, and there was something new in their voices. When describing Louis, it was almost as if they were talking about someone in their own families. Future comedian and civil rights activist Dick Gregory recalled listening to the fight with his family in St. Louis. Almost seventy years later he could still recall the voices of the announcers: "There was a difference in announcers' voices. That night it sounded like they loved him. Sounded like he wasn't a nigger to them. Joe had become an American."[64]

Conscious of his importance to black as well as white Americans, Louis prepared to leave his locker room. Earlier in the afternoon he had confessed to a friend, "I'm scared." Surprised, the friend repeated, "Scared?" "Yeah," Louis answered. "Scared I might kill Schmeling tonight.' "[65] He was a man who normally fought coldly, without rage or anger, but not on this night. Schmeling's claims that he had fouled him in their first match, and Hitler's racial exhortations against blacks, had gotten to the champion. He had what Jack Blackburn always wanted in his fighters—"blood in his eye." As Blackburn had told Louis years before, "You just gotta throw away your heart when you put on those boxing gloves, or the other fella'll knock it out of you."[66] On this one night, Blackburn did not have to say anything.

Louis was determined to make the German pay. In his locker room he shadowboxed for an extended period, working up a good sweat so he could enter the ring hot and ready to fight. To keep the heat in his muscles, he put on a white flannel robe and his blue silk robe over it. Every detail was magnified by the importance of the match. So much depended on him—the weight of his race and democracy seemed more than just symbolic. Jacobs felt the weight too. Thinking about the Jewish boycotters when he visited Louis' locker room shortly before the fight, he said, "Joe, I told these folks you're going to knock that German out. Don't make a sucker out of me, and make it a quick knockout."[67]

The weight was also on Schmeling. He was nervous. Although always popular in New York, he knew that the public had turned against him, and perhaps it clouded his memory of the moments before the fight. All reports suggested that he received a fair, generous reception from the crowd, but he remembered wading to the ring through a river of hate. "As I became visible to the crowd, all hell broke loose," he wrote. "It was like walking a gauntlet. Even though I was flanked by twenty-five police officers, I was still hit by cigarette butts, banana peels, and paper cups, so that I had to pull a towel over my head just to reach the ring safely."[68]

***

If Schmeling believed that he would find safety in the ring he must have been singularly disappointed. "Kill that Nazi, Joe! Kill him!" someone yelled as the bell rang for round one.[69] Intent on a quick victory, Louis moved directly toward Schmeling, landing several stiff jabs and a leaping left hook. The punches were less important than the pace of the action. Driving Schmeling against the ropes and closing the distance, Louis forced the fight, affording the challenger no time to get set. Schmeling tried one overhand right, but it just grazed the champion's face as he rolled with the punch. It caused no damage. With a left jab that was more probing than forceful, pushed forward like a man reaching out in the dark to check his distance from a wall, Schmeling had no weapon to force Louis backward.

Before the round was a minute old, Louis lashed out with a right hook that landed flush on Schmeling's jaw, buckling his legs and forcing him to grab the top rope to keep from falling. In an instant the champion attacked, throwing devastating punches to the German's head and body. His legs too rubbery to escape, Schmeling clung to the rope, turning to his right and holding the top rope with his right hand. He was defenseless against a fighter who was too well trained and too smart to allow his opponent to survive. Schmeling's arms and hands were high, hugging the rope like a lifeline, so Louis widened his stance to get maximum power and threw rights to the German's exposed side. Crushing rights—the kind of rights that he threw in training against a heavy bag, the sort that leave dents in the heavy canvas sack. One sank into Schmeling's side, causing him to pivot even more to his right, and a second landed hard against Max's left side, breaking chips off of a vertebra and two ribs and driving his third lumbar vertebra into his kidney.

The pain was blinding. Schmeling screamed, a sound so unusual to come out of the mouth of a fighter that several spectators said that it made them physically ill. It was high-pitched and vaguely nonhuman, like the desperate cry of an animal in a slaughterhouse. It sounded like Schmeling was not just being beaten—he was being murdered. "The scream just went through the stadium," said Louis' friend Truman Gibson.[70] "Schmeling cried out in agony and the look on his face indicated that he wanted no more of this," noted Richard Wright.[71] Sitting close to ringside, Lester Rodney got a good look into Schmeling eyes: "He was in a state of fear."[72]

There was no one to save him—at least not yet. A hard kidney punch can momentarily paralyze a fighter, and Louis' froze Schmeling. The German clung to the ropes, his expression a mix of pain and fear, while Louis clubbed him with overhand rights and left uppercuts. For a moment it appeared that Max would fall, but once again his grip on the ropes saved him. Anticipating a knockdown, referee Arthur Donovan stepped between the fighters and gave Schmeling a one count. Schmeling blinked hard and looked around, but before he could focus on anything in particular or regain his scrambled senses, Louis was on him. A perfect right hand snapped Schmeling's head around like it was on a pivot and sent him to the canvas. He rolled over once and instinctively rose to his feet. By then he had no idea where he was or what he was doing.

Too dazed to remember to take an eight count—just as Louis had been in their first fight—Schmeling was up at two and Joe was back in front of him, ripping more punches through Max's crippled defenses. Schmeling went down again, this time just enough for both of his gloves to make contact with the canvas. One second passed, maybe two, before Louis had resumed his attack.

It seemed as if only Louis had any wits about him. Spectators were on their feet screaming wildly, most unable to follow the high-octane action in the ring. Wright, who said the German looked like a "soft piece of molasses candy left out in the sun," remarked that Louis was punching Schmeling "so rapidly that the eye could not follow the blows. It was not really a fight, it was an act of revenge, of dominance, of complete mastery."[73] McCarthy's broadcast painted the action in bold, dramatic brushstrokes. Later criticized for missing knockdowns and mangling the sequence of punches, he was in truth blameless. No announcer could have faithfully described the action. How could anyone put into words the furious events that took only seconds? What came across the airwaves was a rapid-fire list of punches and images, a machine gun of lefts and rights and "Schmeling *is* down!"

On his feet again, Schmeling's eyes were unfocused, his feet unbalanced, his hands useless appendages. He looked like he was in a stupor, lost in a world of his own. The end was swift. A pawing left, a couple of rights, and then the final straight, heavy-bag right that corkscrewed Schmeling's head and knocked him to the canvas for the third time. After the knockdown, Louis pivoted and made a slight, lightfooted skip as he went to the neutral corner.

Schmeling's trainer, Max Machon, tossed a towel into the ring, the European symbol that his fighter had taken enough. But by New York rules only the referee could stop a fight. Donovan picked up the towel and quickly shoveled it underhanded, like a boy tossing a beanbag, toward the ropes, where it latched on to a strand and hung like a limp white flag of surrender. Donovan then began his count, which was temporarily interrupted by Machon's futile dash into the ring to save his fighter. Donovan pushed Machon aside and resumed his count, reaching five or six before he waved the match over. Schmeling was not going to get up. The fight was over. The official time was two minutes and four seconds. In Hitler's Third Reich time, it was a thousand years.

Most of the fans in Yankee Stadium had some inkling that the fight was over, but it had ended so quickly that time seemed disjointed. Of course there were some who had arrived late or looked down at the wrong time and missed everything. Count Basie dropped his straw hat as the fight was starting, and it rolled out of reach. "I'm bending down there looking for my hat so I can settle back in my seat and watch Joe take that cat apart," he recalled, "and everybody started jumping to their feet, hollering, and I looked up and the goddamn fight was all over."[74] Bob Hope also missed most of the fight. Just as it began someone called his name and he looked around. When he looked back Schmeling was on the mat. "I missed half the fight!" he said. "It was that quick."[75] Roy Wilkins also missed the first minute of the fight. He reached his seat just as Louis began to land his best shots. Wilkins did not have time to sit or even remove his coat, but he saw the last minute. And all things considered, he believed that it "must have been the shortest, sweetest minute of the entire thirties."[76]

The hundred million people listening to the fight on the radio were even more mystified about the exact order of events. McCarthy's call of the match was exciting in its generalities but wholly lacking in specifics. He came across like an auctioneer on amphetamines—short, staccato sentences delivered at warp speed, sounding to Americans like "Schmeling's hit. Schmeling's hurt. Schmeling's down. Schmeling's up." It was like that until he announced that the fight was over. It was worse in South America, where the Spanish and Portuguese feeds got crossed and several million listeners heard the call in the wrong language. The German broadcaster, Arno Hellmis, made the call in the right language but in an utterly incomprehensible manner. He was so close to Schmeling personally and so invested in the fighter's career that his call of the fight sounded more like the sufferings of a close friend than a dispassionate professional broadcast. But by the time Hellmis went off the air and the German broadcast ended with the "Horst Wessel Song" and "Deutschland über Alles," the Third Reich had learned at least the general outline of what had happened in Yankee Stadium.[77]

∗∗∗

The night now belonged to the millions of celebrants. Outside Mister Earl's house the black field hands thanked him for sharing his radio. Their tone was proper and mannerly, perhaps all the more so since Mister Earl was "deeply disappointed in the outcome." Young Jimmy Carter remembered that they had listened to the fight without a word spoken or a cheer uttered, then filed away quietly, crossing a dirt road and a railroad track and entering a house out in a field. "At that point, pandemonium broke loose inside that house, as our black neighbors shouted and yelled in celebration of the Louis victory. But all the curious, accepted proprieties of a racially-segregated society had been carefully observed."[78] Mister Earl's "boys" knew "their place," but in some way and for some period of time, Joe Louis had liberated them. He had taken them to another place.

The feeling was shared by colonial peoples struggling for freedom and Jews living in the footprints of Nazi jackboots. The result of the match was lamented in Italy and Japan and celebrated by the men and women who were dominated by the two expansionist powers. Throughout the Caribbean, where Louis was a popular figure, the rejoicing and dancing lasted until daybreak. In Holland, where the championship was viewed as a contest between pro-Nazi and anti-Nazi ideologies, Louis' triumph was met with nearly universal joy. The same was true in Poland, Czechoslovakia, Austria, and much of the rest of Eastern Europe, especially among the Jews in those countries. Writer Frederic Morton, who in 1938 was a young Jewish boy named Fritz Mendelbaum living in Vienna, listened to the fight with his father. It was a liberating experience. "It was a sense of jubilation that we had, my father and I, and for the first time there was an inkling that Hitler might somehow be stopped."[79]

For black Americans that inkling mixed with another hunch—that the entire racist edifice was nothing more than a bundle of myths and lies. Celebrations had become common after Louis' victories. But this night was different in intensity and scope and meaning. The eruption of joy after the fight had occurred instantly and simultaneously in hundreds of places. In Detroit thousands of blacks, and a "sprinkling of whites," marched thirty blocks through the streets of Paradise Valley behind a banner proclaiming, "JOE KNOCKED OLD HITLER COLD."[80] In Chicago, New Year's Eve arrived almost six months early as blacks on the South Side fired guns into the air, set off firecrackers, and beat on whatever would make a loud, sharp sound. In Pittsburgh's Hill District, anti-Nazi demonstrations and Joe Louis celebrations brought together blacks and whites, Jews and Christians, all shouting, "Hail Joe Louis, the people's champion." "They understood," wrote a local journalist, "that now once and for all the stupid, vicious Nazi race theories, the 'aryan' superiority that Schmeling had so blatantly expressed to reporters before the fight, was completely blasted, completely discredited."[81] In Cleveland the celebrations turned violent and the police used tear gas to "quell a riotous crowd."[82] A man was shot, scores were injured, a streetcar was stoned and several others overturned, and a few policemen were hit by bricks. But there were even more peaceful scenes of dancing and cheering. Later a few reporters speculated that the police had caused more violence than they had prevented.

And so it went across the country—a celebration in one town, a confrontation in another, and a little of both somewhere else. But the epicenter of black America was in Harlem, just blocks away from Yankee Stadium. There, Richard Wright commented in an article in the *New Masses*, "a hundred thousand black people surged out of taprooms, flats, restaurants, and filled the streets and sidewalks like the Mississippi River overflowing in flood time. With faces to the night sky, they filled their lungs with air and let out a scream of joy that seemed would never end, and a scream that seemed to come from untold reserves of strength."[83] They rejoiced with all their might. Ben Davis, Jr., wrote in the *Daily Worker*, "There was never anything like it. . . . Take a dozen Harlem Christmases, a score of New Year's eves, a bushel of July 4th's and maybe—yes, maybe—you get a faint glimpse of the idea."[84]

It was a cross between a midsummer Mardi Gras and a political rally. Homemade confetti drifted down like snowflakes from open windows and roofs of tenement buildings, landing on smiling dancers and demonstrators carrying U.S. and Ethiopian flags and banging trashcan lids and metal pots. African Americans, Latinos, and Jews hugged and danced together. "White anti-fascists from within—and without—Harlem walked arm in arm with Negro workers, teachers, doctors, and ministers to express their boundless happiness and solidarity at this symbolized victory over Hitlerism," noted a reporter. They carried banners and placards that announced their political positions: "JOE LOUIS WINS, HITLER WEEPS"; "WHO SAID ARYAN SUPREM-ACY"; "PASS THE ANTI-LYNCHING BILL"; "FREE THE SCOTTSBORO BOYS"; "DEMOCRACIES MUST FIGHT FASCISM EVERYWHERE." For communist writ-ers covering the event for the *Daily Worker* or the *New Masses,* it was noth-ing short of heaven: "Nothing is more indicative of the power of Negro and white unity for progress and democracy—once it hits full stride."[85]

Even mainstream white newspapers grasped the meaning of the cele-brations. "It may have been a bleak night on Berlin's Unter den Linden—but all was star-spangled brightness in Harlem," commented a *New York Daily News* reporter.[86] Joe Louis had transformed black into red, white, and blue. Probably never before in American history had a black man received so much praise in the mainstream press. In a moment of democratic peril, with Japan on the move in China, and Germany talking about annexing the Sudetenland, Joe Louis had with his fists made a bold, direct statement about the vitality of democracy. He had done what American, English, and French politicians had failed to do—achieve a victory, even a symbolic one, against Hitler. A cartoon in the *Chicago Daily News* made the essential point: It showed a plane named the Brown Bomber dropping a bomb next to Adolf Hitler. No caption was needed.[87]

White Americans, white journalists explained, had to accept that blacks were Americans too, capable of contributing to a shared democracy. Unlike Jack Johnson a generation earlier, Joe Louis was portrayed as an ally, not a threat. He represented millions of other black Americans advancing toward a fuller equality. It was nothing to fear, suggested prominent Democratic politician General Hugh S. Johnson. "These black boys are Americans—a whole lot more distinctly so than more recently arrived citizens of, say, the Schmeling type. There should be just as much pride in their progress and prowess under our system as in the triumph of any other Americans. For all their misfortunes and shortcomings they are our people—Negroes, yes, but our Negroes."[88]

It was not the sort of endorsement that could be found in the *Daily Worker,* but it probably represented the feeling of many millions of white Americans. In his locker room after the fight a reporter asked Louis how he felt. "Now I feels like the champ," he answered.[89] And so he was—America's champ.

7

The Last Perfect Night

"You got a fight tonight, Joe."
"I knows it."
—*exchange between Billy Conn and Joe Louis*

It had come to this. Joe Louis, the great Joe Louis, sitting in his corner after the twelfth round, his arms heavy at his sides, his legs feeling ancient, his face swollen and discolored, his title slipping away like a boat in the night. Across the ring, Billy Conn, the young, thin, confident, white matinee-handsome challenger, smiled. "This is easy," Conn told his manager Johnny "Moonie" Ray. "I'm going to take this son-of-a-bitch out this round." He could feel it. He knew with the same dead certainty that Louis had known so often that the end was near, that he had broken his man, that all that remained was the final punch and a ten count. Pittsburgh's own Sweet William was, perhaps, only a minute or two away from ending the reign of Joe Louis.[1]

Louis breathed hard, his face masking any feeling. The twelfth had been a bad round, ending with fifteen unanswered punches to his face and body. Jack Blackburn leaned close to Louis' ear, shouting instructions above the din of screaming spectators. "Chappie," he said, "you're losing. You got to knock him out." The trainer had a plan. Conn was overconfident. Blackburn saw it in Conn's smile. Nobody smiled when they fought Louis. He had often seen opponents look nervous when they came face to face with Joe, and on more than a few occasions he had glimpsed fear in their eyes. But they sure as hell didn't smile like some damned boy out on a date with the best-looking girl in the class. Blackburn tapped Joe on the shoulder to get his attention. Conn was full of himself, he said. He was going to come at Joe hard. He was going to take chances. He was going to throw a looping left. Joe had to watch for the looping left. When he saw it coming he had to be ready to step inside and deliver a right. A Joe Louis right. Watch for the opening. Throw the right. Blackburn was not the sort of man who liked to see fighters in the opposite corner smile.

The bell rang for the thirteenth round. The steel-and-concrete stands of the Polo Grounds quaked as 54,487 spectators cheered and whistled and hooted and stomped their feet. Like Louis and Conn and Blackburn and Ray, they knew that something special was about to happen.

***

In retrospect, it almost seemed as if the gods of sports were preparing for World War II, as if they were offering up an unparalleled cornucopia of performances for fans to cherish and remember during the lean combat years ahead. In 1941 there were only three money sports that mattered—baseball, boxing, and horse racing. All other professional sports were afterthoughts. Basketball was mostly a high-school sport played in drafty auditoriums and armories and still occasionally behind chicken-wire netting; football was primarily a college sport that had not yet found a popular professional outlet; golf and tennis were basically games for rich kids; and car racing was primarily a once-a-year event held in Indianapolis. It was baseball, boxing, and horse racing that sold newspapers and filled the radio airwaves.[2]

In horse racing, 1941 was the year of Whirlaway. Even taking into account the marvelous performances of Seabiscuit, no horse had ever captured the public's imagination as Whirlaway had. Sired by Blenheim II at Kentucky's Calumet Farms, he was a beautiful chestnut stallion blessed with unnatural speed and handicapped by a temperament that ranged from erratic to crazy. When the gates opened, nobody—not trainer Ben A. Jones, jockey Eddie Arcaro, or anyone else at the track—knew what the horse would do. The only certainty was that Whirlaway would not run an orthodox race. Often he veered to the outside rail; sometimes he doddered at the back of the pack. Then at the last possible moment, when the race appeared lost, the horse would perk up his ears, swing back to the inside, shift into another gear, and begin passing the other horses like they were pulling plows. The drama of a Whirlaway race was breathtaking, as exciting in a radio broadcast as it was live at the track. In 1941 the three-year-old Whirlaway became the first Calumet Farms horse to win the Triple Crown. Along the way, as thoroughbred experts speculated about how to manage the horse and psychiatrists advanced theories to explain his equine quirks, Americans fell in love with the oddball animal.

Baseball's answer to Whirlaway was Theodore Samuel "Ted" Williams. He was "The Kid," temperamental, erratic, quarrelsome, and singularly talented with a baseball bat in his hands. His 1941 season began like a train wreck. He missed the opening day of spring training because, he explained, he had become so engrossed in a wolf hunt in the forests of Minnesota that he had lost track of the date. Then in a spring training game he chipped a bone in his right ankle. But toward the end of May he was moving well and swinging the bat with an unworldly precision. In a late-May series against the Yankees his batting average edged over .400. It remained there for all of June, and at the All-Star break in July it stood at .405. As a preview for the second half of the season, Williams hit a two-out, ninth-inning home run to win the All-Star game.

At the end of July, Williams' batting average was .409, and after the dog days of August it slipped only to .407. Throughout September, millions of Americans turned to the sports pages to see if Ted lined a hit before they read the alarming news from the Russian front and about the deteriorating American-Japanese relations. And The Kid, like the Russians, rose to meet the challenge. Going into the last series of the season, against Connie Mack's Philadelphia Athletics, Williams' average was .401, and after going one-for-four in the first game of the series it dipped to .39956. Rounded off, that's .400, but baseball is a game of cold numbers, and .39956 is in fact .39956, a hair below the magical .400. As an Associated Press reporter accurately noted, he had "only two games left in which to re-enter the select class." The operative word was "re-enter."

Boston's doubleheader in Philadelphia on September 28, 1941, was one of baseball's greatest days. Legendary home plate umpire Bill McGowan set the tone before Williams' first at-bat. As he brushed in front of Williams to sweep off home plate, he observed, "To hit .400, a batter has got to be loose."[3] The Kid responded with a drive down the first-base line for a hit. And he continued to hit, going four-for-five in the first game and two-for-three in the second, finishing the season with a .406 batting average. It had been eleven years since any major league player had hit over .400. No hitter has repeated the feat.

Nor has any player matched or exceeded Joe DiMaggio's 1941 record. On May 15, with Williams hitting only .339, DiMaggio singled off Chicago White Sox's Eddie Smith, finishing the day one-for-four. The same day Williams went one for three in Cleveland. It was the beginning of hitting streaks for both men. Williams' ended at twenty-three games. DiMaggio's concluded in immortality. It took a while before Americans began to pay much attention to DiMaggio's streak, but virtually every baseball fan was aware that the Yankee Clipper's hitting had almost single-handedly pulled his team out of a slump and put it into the pennant race. As the streak moved past the twenties into the thirties, Americans' interest piqued. When it reached the forties, close to "Wee Willie" Keeler's record of forty-four, DiMaggio's name was on everyone's lips. Journalists wrote millions of words about him, Tin Pan Alley songwriters composed tunes about him, vaudeville comedians added gags about him, and politicians paid homage to him.

By the time the streak ended at fifty-six on July 17, when Cleveland Indian third-baseman Ken Keltner's backhand stabs robbed DiMaggio of two hits, the Yankee Clipper had become the most celebrated athlete of his generation. Along with Williams, he had helped turn Americans' attention inward, away from snowballing world events. Whirlaway, Williams, and DiMaggio, more than any politicians or news commentators, defined what was special about America. America was the freedom to be irascibly eccentric and the will to finish strong. It was about the sun on your face at a baseball game and the dirt flying up behind a horse's hoofs. It was a thousand simple pleasures and a handful of basic beliefs. While President Franklin Roosevelt spoke in Wilsonian abstractions, a horse and two baseball players touched the soul of Americans, making them cheer, dream, and wonder.

***

In the first half of 1941 Joe Louis seemed to have lost the power to inspire. It was not his fault. He was still the peerless champion, the same Brown Bomber, knocking out one challenger after another. Back in 1935 blues singer Memphis Minnie, her husky voice reaching for joyous notes, had compared Louis' left and right to a "kick from a Texas mule" and a "jolt of dy-nee-mite." She expressed a singular note of pleasure in the song's refrain that "He's in the ring . . . / Doing the same old thing!"[4]

THE LAST PERFECT NIGHT 177

When he won the title in 1937, Louis had promised to be a "fighting champion." No boxer had ever been more faithful to a pledge. He had defended his title three times in 1938, four times in 1939, and another four times in 1940. Reporters began to refer to each challenger as the Bum of the Month, but they were never bums. They were the best fighters in the heavyweight division. It was just that the gap between them and Joe was too wide to bridge, and in only a few of the matches—the 1939 fights against the flamboyant Tony Galento and the popular Bob Pastor, and the fights against Arturo Godoy—was the interest of the general public aroused.

But never during his championship years was Joe more often in the ring, doing the same old thing, than in 1941. It was the third year of the "Bum of the Month Club." At the end of January he knocked out Red Burman; in mid-February he made short work of Gus Dorazio; in March he took a bit more time to dispatch Abe Simon; in early April he finished off Tony Musto; and in May he defeated Buddy Baer on a disqualification. January, February, March, April, May—the popular saying in African American neighborhoods was that black schoolchildren learned the months by following Louis' career.

But even for Louis the pace had become frenetic. His life had become a cycle of training camps and boxing arenas. He was a pugilistic road show: the Great Joe Louis Traveling Boxing Tour—buy a ticket and see the champ knock out a white stiff. In the first half of 1941 he fought opponents in New York, Philadelphia, Detroit, St. Louis, and Washington, D.C. No heavyweight champion had attempted such an exhausting schedule, and none has done so since. Spectators bought their tickets, but, as in all lengthy road shows, the headliner paid the steepest price. Pictures of Louis in 1941 show a man visibly aging. His hair was thinned, his waist was thickened, and his face, always difficult to read, displayed a disturbing weariness, the look of a fighter who had stepped into one too many rings.

Why? The triumvirate of Mike Jacobs, John Roxborough, and Julian Black controlled the career of the most important fighter in the world. These seasoned boxing men had magnificently handled Louis, astutely guiding him to the heavyweight championship and helping to revive the entire sport along the way. Louis' purses reflected the triumvirate's success —$240,833 for the Max Baer fight, $140,959 for the first Max Schmeling contest, and $349,228 for the Schmeling rematch. But Louis' purses for his first five matches in 1941 totaled less than $120,000. He was proving the law of diminishing returns, fighting more and more for less and less.[5]

Tex Rickard, Jacobs' mentor, had shown his protégé how to avoid the law of diminishing returns. In the 1920s he had made boxing history—and pocketed millions of dollars—arranging a series of Jack Dempsey's heavyweight championship fights. Rickard had used a simple formula: give the people what they want, but don't give it to them too often. Between 1921 and 1927, Rickard promoted the first five million-dollar gates. They all featured Dempsey, and in each one Rickard carefully orchestrated story lines, characterizations, and subtexts. They were his masterpieces, his Mona Lisas, his Davids, his Taj Mahals.

Jacobs had witnessed Rickard's magic. More than that, Jacobs was present at the creation of the masterpieces, helping to finance the million-dollar gates and taking his healthy cut of the ticket sales. He had learned how to promote a match. He knew that it took time—months of careful planning, hundreds of planted stories, and through it all a consistent, relevant, compelling story line. Jacobs' masterful promotions of the Louis-Carnera, Louis-Baer, Louis-Braddock, and Louis-Schmeling fights had demonstrated that he understood the formula. Even during the hard times of the mid-1930s, when the Roosevelt promise was wearing thin and men were still lining up for bread, Jacobs had promoted two million-dollar-gate fights featuring Louis. But the receipts for the Burman, Dorazio, Simon, and Musto fights were hardly $50,000 each, and the gate for the Baer contest was barely over $100,000.

Why, then, for so meager a return, squander Louis' talents and risk serious injury or the off-chance that a lucky punch would strip him of the title? The answer could be read daily in the newspapers. Europe was at war, and after the November 1940 election the United States was heading in that direction. In a December 1940 fireside chat President Roosevelt described America as the "arsenal of democracy" and pledged material support for the countries battling the Nazis. In January 1941 he asked Congress to pass a lend-lease bill to aid the Allies. In March he signed the bill into law. In April the United States took control of Greenland to make sure it did not fall under Nazi control. In May Roosevelt ominously announced that an "unlimited national emergency exists" and promised full aid to Great Britain. "The delivery of supplies to Britain is imperative," he said. "This can be done; it must be done; it will be done."[6] Nowhere did the drums of American intervention beat louder than in New York. Jacobs was not deaf. He knew that once the United States entered the war, Louis' title would be worthless.

And so Joe fought for what he could get. It resembled a heavyweight fire sale, the greatest fighter in the world battling before small crowds in secondary arenas for insulting purses. Five defenses in five months, and a sixth scheduled for the next month. On June 18, 1941, Joe would fight Billy Conn, the former light-heavyweight titleholder who was actually on the light side of even that division. But Conn was a popular fighter. He was good-looking and good copy, a talker with a fresh face, quick smile, charming eyes, and an air of confidence.

***

Jacobs had his reasons for sending Louis into the ring. Joe had his reasons for going in. It all boiled down to money. Jacobs, a parsimonious, careful manager of money, wanted more. Louis, a profligate, careless spender, needed more. Between the desire for more and the need for more was the ring.

Truman K. Gibson, Jr., a lawyer who by 1941 had known Louis for a half-dozen years and would later become very close to him, understood Joe's psychological makeup as well as anyone. After Louis was dead and buried, Gibson was interviewed by Chris Mead, a Yale-educated young man who was writing a biography of the champion. The old black lawyer looked at the young white scholar and chose his words carefully, attempting to bridge the wide cultural gap. "The thing you have to understand about Joe is that he lived every day." Mead understood: "I went to school, I planned for the future, Joe Louis lived every day."[7] Louis did not dwell on yesterday any more than he planned for tomorrow. He just *lived* every day. And living came with a steep price.

By 1941 Louis was bleeding money. His spending seemed to increase with his fame and fortune. It was not so much that the more he made the more he spent; for him, the more he made the more he overspent. Since he had begun to make serious money in late 1935 his retinue of friends, associates, hangers-on, and glad-handers had swelled to epic numbers. It was not unusual for Louis to begin a day with $400 or $500 in his wallet and run short of cash by noon. He treated often, tipped heavily, and gave the rest away. He was an easy mark for a hard-luck tale or an oddball request.

What loose money his "friends" did not take, his opponents did. Not his boxing opponents but his golfing "buddies." By 1941 Louis had developed a fluid, heavy-handed swing and become a decent weekend player. He could pound drives, hit long irons, and score fairly well. He played as often as his tight schedule allowed, and, according to his friend Sunnie Wilson, developed an addiction to "that little white ball."[8] But, like many other celebrity golfers, he was not nearly as good a player as his partners told him he was, and their habit of giving him three- and four-foot putts contributed to a deceptively low handicap. It left him vulnerable to golfing gamblers with deceptively high handicaps, men whose games became very good indeed when the stakes moved into the thousands of dollars. As Louis later recalled, "I was betting heavily on my game, but, damn, I was losing a lot of money."[9] But he kept playing—and gambling and losing. "Sometimes Joe would break the sticks and say, 'Get rid of 'em, they're a bad habit,'" said Wilson. "He was like a man with alcohol. It was an addiction."[10]

He lost far bigger sums through careless spending and poor investing. He was the embodiment of the American Dream, a rags-to-riches story, and he lived his life Hollywood style. He dressed the part. Clothes, for Louis, may not have been the sum of the man, but they were definitely an important part of the equation. He had closets of suits, armoires of shirts, racks of ties and shoes, drawers of underwear, socks, and all sort of accessories. Everything was inventoried, catalogued, and perfectly stored. He kept track of what he wore when, making sure not to duplicate outfits too often or commit an unforgivable breach in fashion etiquette. He purchased his clothes at the "right" men's shops, and he designed outfits that he imagined but could not find. It was not uncommon for him to change clothes two or three times a day.

Added to the clothes was his real estate. He kept apartments in Chicago and Harlem, costly places in prime locations. But he spent even more putting a roof over the heads of his horses. Joe and Marva enjoyed horseback riding. In 1938 they joined other members of the black American aristocracy in staging the inaugural United States Negro Horse Show at the Utica Riding Club. In August 1939 Louis paid $100,000 for Spring Hill Farm in Utica, Michigan. Built in the 1830s and a stop on the Underground Railroad, Spring Hill Farm was a rolling 477-acre estate. Louis converted it into a riding academy and stable, replete with a white frame lodge, restaurant, dance hall, and show ring. Spring Hill Farm became a showplace, drawing vacationers from Detroit, Chicago, and other parts of the Midwest. They sat in the bleachers and watched trainers put the horses through their paces. Sometimes they dined in the restaurant, but more often they ate picnic lunches on the lawns of the estate.

Reporters commented that Joe had become a "country squire," suggesting that Spring Hill Farm was his Tara. And in fact Louis, in a rather abstract fashion, was proud of the estate. During his infrequent visits to Spring Hill Farm he greeted visitors with a wave and a smile and took long pleasant rides across the grounds. But from the first, the place was a mismanaged, poorly conceived money pit. If it was a country retreat, Louis' schedule seldom allowed him to spend more than the occasional day there. If it was an investment, it cost far more money to run than it returned.

Louis' problems in 1941 stretched beyond the merely financial. For being Joe Louis meant living large, a combination of spending freely, satisfying his desires discreetly, and ignoring the consequences of his behavior. Most of his actions were relatively harmless, and there always seemed to be more money somewhere when he needed it. But he had only one wife, and his behavior was threatening to reduce the number to zero.

The problem was that the demand for Louis' attention was high and his ability to say no was low. Marva understood most of the claims on her husband's time. She accepted that he had to spend months every year in training camps, travel widely for special appearances, disappear now and then to Hollywood for a part in a film, and generally make himself available for a wide range of unspecified activities. But one of the unspecified activities that she found difficult to countenance was his habit of playing loose and easy with his marriage vows. From the start of their marriage Louis was a serial philanderer.

A son of one of the champion's close friends put it this way: "My father said that Joe was a 'road man.' He had an itch, and a sort of wanderlust. The easiest way for him to satisfy the itch was to get into a car and hit the road." Throughout his adult life Louis remained a road man. Sunny Wilson, one of Louis' closest friends, said that on one occasion Joe and Marva and he and his girlfriend were dining at the Brown Bomber Chicken Shack in Chicago. Joe had recently bought a new Mercury, and he said to Wilson, "Let's try this car out."[11] The two women remained in the restaurant. The two men drove to Toledo to see a traveling revue featuring a dancer Joe knew. They then followed the revue to Cleveland, Pittsburgh, back to Cleveland, Buffalo, and finally to Albany. There was no master plan. Along the way Louis had to borrow money and buy clothes. Certainly he never informed Marva about his extended romp. On a whim he simply took off and did not return for a "good two weeks."

It was a pattern: Joe would get up one morning, go out on some task or just to visit a friend, then simply disappear for a few days or weeks. He had lovers in Detroit, Chicago, Toledo, New York, and various other cities across the country. Some were penniless showgirls, others wealthy society women. Most were black, some were white. As a group they did not conform to any particular pattern or look. They were simply females who saw something in him—and in whom he saw something in return.

Vernon E. Jordan, Jr., the former president of the National Urban League, provided a glimpse of how women regarded Louis. When Jordan was a college student in Atlanta he was friendly with a waitress named Elsie, an older, experienced woman whom his mother would have called a "hussy" but whom he considered "VERY SEXY." He once asked her: "You've had a lot of boyfriends. Who's the most exciting man you ever met?" She answered without hesitation: "Joe Louis." It was not so much the answer that impressed Jordan, "it was the way she said JOE LOUIS. The body language was there. And could she generate body language. She was quite something in those days."[12]

Louis' attractions were obvious. The fact that he was the wealthy, generous heavyweight champion of the world, the visible symbol of strength, power, and masculinity, gave him a leg up on the field. Added to those advantages, he had a nearly perfect build and was good-looking. His coffee-and-cream complexion, freckled broad cheeks, and almond eyes were striking enough, but his expressions added to his charms. Joe Louis' public face was almost emotionless, a mask that featured seemingly glued lips and cold, lifeless eyes. But the face his friends saw was wholly different. Both his mouth and eyes burst with expression. He smiled often and laughed— an almost youthful giggle—frequently. Away from the public's gaze he relaxed easily.

Beyond the title, the money, the body, and the face, Joe Louis was nice. He did not seem terribly impressed with himself, treated almost everyone he met decently, listened more than he talked, and had a deadpan, quick sense of humor. For a man whom white reporters claimed lacked intelligence, he repeatedly displayed an ability to speak volumes in a few words. Both inside and outside the ring he was adept at sizing up a person or a situation. He did not always make the best decisions, but he never fooled himself. He did what he wanted to because he wanted to.

And he wanted to be a road man. He was unfair to Marva—and he knew it—but that did not prevent him from having affairs with singer Lena Horne, figure skater Sonja Henie, actress Lana Turner, and hundreds of other women. Marva may not have known about all of Louis' affairs, but she knew about enough of them. She was increasingly resentful, and the diamond rings, closets of dresses, show horses, and other presents her husband lavished on her failed to heal the insults and arguments.

Ironically, life as Mrs. Joe Louis had become lonely. Joe and Marva were the most famous black couple in America. Journalists reported on their every appearance, photographers snapped them walking down a street or riding horses, and they were welcome guests at the best clubs in New York, Chicago, and Los Angeles. But it was all, really, about Joe. Marva understood that she was always in his shadow, almost at times invisible. Years later Louis described his outings with Marva: "People followed us everywhere we went. If we went to the movies, we'd have to leave before it was over; if we went to dinner, we'd have to leave before dessert. . . . The girls were still coming at me as if Marva wasn't there. They'd just push her aside; crowds would mess up her hair and clothes."[13]

The glamour of being the wife of the heavyweight champion faded after three or four years. Joe freely gave away money and jewelry; more than once he literally gave away the shirt off his back. Possessions seemed to mean nothing to him. But he was possessive of Marva. "All you have to do is just be beautiful, gracious, a good mother, and a good wife," he told her. "Just be my doll-baby."[14] When he was training for a fight or off on the road, he insisted that she wait at home for him. When she traveled with him, Joe told her what to wear and how to behave. He even expected that she would associate only with her family and the wives of his friends.

"Eventually, you tire of it," Marva recalled of her life with Joe, "the crowds knocking your hat off and pushing you out of the way to reach him. Fame is the most difficult thing that can happen to a relationship. . . . Your life is just not your own. You always have to be up and on the scene. . . . And Joe was very proud. 'Oh, Marva, you're not going to wear that. Change your clothes.' You see, you represent them, and they want you to be tops. At least, Joe did."[15]

Like Joe, Marva was forced to live a double life. Publicly, both had become important symbols of African American achievement, progress, and dignity. More than any other black couple they represented the American Dream and validated the American success ethic. Privately, they lived very different lives. Joe enjoyed himself, disappearing when he chose, seeking the arms of other women and the comforts of welcoming black communities. Marva stayed in her perfectly furnished home, which was filled with dream possessions. Increasingly she was wealthy, comfortable, and lonely. Shortly before the Conn fight she told Joe that she wanted a divorce.

***

By the summer of 1941, then, Louis was being pressed hard from all sides. Marital problems, money troubles, physical concerns, and the unstable international situation—he had to make money while he could. And the only way he could make money was to climb into the ring and risk his title. The problem was that there was not much money to be made when the risk was negligible.

Conn seemed to offer Louis an opportunity for a good payday without a substantial risk. Although a central axiom of prizefighting holds that a good small man can beat a mediocre big man, it is almost equally certain that a good small man cannot defeat a great big man. And that was the salient feature of the Louis-Conn matchup. Conn was a fine light-heavyweight, if somewhat on the small side. He was hardly old enough to get his driver's license when he began boxing professionally. For the first four years of his career he seldom battled outside his hometown of Pittsburgh, but he fought often and he earned a reputation as a slick, if not particularly hard-punching, boxer. At the end of 1936 he decisioned Fritzie Zivic, a future welterweight champion who had a well-deserved reputation as a crafty, dirty fighter. In the next few years Conn put on a few pounds and defeated several very good middleweight and light-heavyweight boxers. In 1939 he beat Melio Bettina for the light-heavyweight title and then successfully defended his crown three times. In 1940 he concluded that the light-heavyweight purses did not warrant his efforts, and he voluntarily relinquished the title. He decided to fight as a heavyweight for the same reason that Willie Sutton supposedly chose to rob banks—because that's where the money was.

Other light-heavyweight champions of the period had arrived at the same conclusions and failed to escape their graveyard division. Maxie Rosenbloom, John Henry Lewis, and Gus Lesnevich tried and failed. Conn, however, was set apart by something that few fighters in any division had. Before the word had entered everyday American speech he had charisma, the sum total of talent, good looks, ready wit, and charm. In a sport that glorified the Irish American fighter, Billy Conn was perhaps the most appealing boxer to wear a shamrock since the Great John L. Sullivan himself.

Part of his appeal was that, except for his busted nose, he did not look like a fighter. He had the angular face and the lean, muscular body of a matinee idol. His hair swept back from his forehead in masculine curls and his chin jutted forward just enough to accent the line of his jaw. But it was his blue eyes and smile that attracted everyone's attention. He looked as if he was always reacting to or thinking of some slightly off-color joke. Adding to his looks was his full-bodied, hard, exotic Pittsburgh accent. Journalist Frank Deford once claimed that no one raised in Pittsburgh could "correctly pronounce any of the vowels and several of the consonants," insisting on calling the University of Pittsburgh a "cawledge" and legal tender a "dawler."[16] Certainly Conn swallowed syllables whole, added random "r's" to words like wash and Washington, and greeted groups of men with expressions like "Watch younz guys doin'?" Altogether, he was a hard person for anyone to resist.

Even Mike Jacobs succumbed to Conn's personal charms and box office appeal. In late 1938, after Conn had spent his entire career fighting west of the Appalachian Mountains, he got a phone call from New York City. "Jacobs here," said the most important voice in boxing. "Let's work something out."[17] Boxing in the 1930s featured ethnic rivalries, and the promoter was always on the lookout for a promising Irish banger. He matched Conn against Fred Apostoli, an Italian boxer who was generally regarded as the best middleweight in the sport. Conn upset Apostoli in early January 1939, then repeated the feat in February. Then Jacobs matched Billy against Solly Krieger, a top Jewish contender. Conn scored a convincing twelve-round decision.

New York fight fans adored the brash fighter, and Jacobs, who seldom watched the fights he promoted, developed a genuine fondness for Conn. On the nights Conn fought, Jacobs perched at ringside, cheering and imploring, grimacing when Billy was hit and throwing his hat when he scored a combination. Jacobs invited Conn to his country manor on the Shrewsbury River in Rumson, New Jersey, his Miami Beach estate, and his Central Park West duplex. He gave the fighter custom-made suits and a cream-colored roadster. As writer Mike Vaccaro observed, "Joe Louis was Jacobs's meal ticket, but Billy Conn was rapidly becoming his surrogate son."[18]

By the summer of 1940 Conn was through with middleweights and light-heavyweights. He liked the world that Jacobs inhabited, a land of silk suits, flashy cars, and expensive homes. He had also met and fallen in love with a beautiful blond, a hometown Pittsburgh girl. He wanted to marry her, though her father had vowed she would never marry a two-bit pug. By the summer of 1941, riding a twenty-three match win streak, confident to the point of charming arrogance, Billy wanted it all—the girl, the money, the title. He wanted what Joe Louis had.

On June 3, 1941, in Jacobs' crowded Twentieth Century Sporting Club office on Worth Street, just off Broadway in lower Manhattan, Conn and Louis signed a contract to fight for the heavyweight title. For New Yorkers it was a sad day. Further uptown, first at the Church of the Divine Paternity on Central Park West and Seventy-Sixth Street, and then a few hours later at the Christ Protestant Episcopal Church in the Riverdale section of the Bronx, thousands of mourners had silently filed past the casket of Yankee great Lou Gehrig. Men, often with their sons in tow, stood for hours to say their farewells. Some had faces streaked with tears, others talked quietly to those next to them in the slow-moving line. But in Jacobs' office, Billy Conn could still muster a smile and a crack. Jacobs announced that the fight would take place in the Polo Grounds on the night of June 18. He did not have to tell the boxing writers what that meant. A night fight in June, especially in the Polo Grounds or Yankee Stadium, signaled the premier match of the year. Louis had slaughtered Primo Carnera, in his first big New York fight, in June 1935. He had been knocked out by Max Schmeling in Yankee Stadium in June 1936. He had won the title from James J. Braddock in Chicago in June 1937. He had pulverized Schmeling in their rematch in the "Fight of the Century" in Yankee Stadium in June 1938. And even in more recent years, when it was difficult to find a real challenger for Louis, he had fought highly publicized fights in New York with Tony Galento in June 1939 and Arturo Godoy in June 1940. Now it was Billy Conn's turn to take a shot at the champion on the biggest date on the pugilistic calendar.

Louis, as usual, was decidedly on the perfunctory side. The two fighters exchanged few words:

> "You look good, Champ," Billy offered.
> "You do too, Billy. You gainin' weight?"
> "You bet I am."
> "Looking forward to seeing you in a few weeks, Bill."
> "You too Champ. I'll be there."[19]

What they said was unimportant. The meaning was between the lines and in the delivery. Louis' comment about Conn's weight implied that the light-heavyweight was out of his class, that he had no idea what it was like to absorb heavyweight punches. Conn delivered his lines with smiling confidence. He just did not look all that concerned. "I'll be there," he said. He meant, "I'm not afraid of the great Joe Louis."

Normally Conn trained for his New York matches in the city, at the Pioneer Gym. Keeping with the tradition of fighting for the heavyweight title, however, he altered his routine, setting up camp in Pompton Lakes, New Jersey, a rustic retreat in the hills of Passaic County. In a white frame house surrounded by a picket fence Conn seemed a world away from the grimy streets of Pittsburgh, but the change in surroundings did not alter his behavior. Conn thrived in chaos, and one reporter noted of Billy's bucolic retreat, "The joint is jumping" day and night. Never had so many sportswriters chronicled his activities, and he bathed in the attention. "Gosh, ain't it grand?" he said. "Don't let any of 'em leave. Why, I used to fight before crowds that were smaller than this."[20]

And why should they leave? Billy Conn was a sportswriter's dream. Unlike the laconic Louis, who measured his words with a thimble, Conn could not keep his mouth shut. He talked about the champ: "Louis is not the fighter he was a year ago, and as for his punching—well, he ain't going to hit me with those sucker punches."[21] He and his trainer Johnny Ray elaborated about how "they" were going to win the title. Referring to the old and repeatedly invalidated belief that black fighters had weak stomachs, Ray told reporters that Louis was an old twenty-seven: "He won't be able to take it downstairs for long." Conn added his own racial jab: "Louis is just a big, slow thinking Negro."[22]

In truth, Conn seemed different from Louis' recent challengers. He approached the fight with a charming bonhomie. It was not the nonchalance of a man who felt that you can't kill him because he is born to hang. It was more the relaxed disposition of a man who just did not worry much about anything. He referred to Ray as his "vice president in charge of worrying," and Ray explained that his fighter's confidence was sincere. "Conn hasn't been talking just to hear himself talk," Ray told reporters. "He just feels he's going to be the champ."[23]

Louis, training in the Catskill Mountains resort of Greenwood Lake, provided less copy. He listened closed-mouthed to the latest news from Pompton Lakes, to Ray's anthropological theories and Conn's quips. He ran in the early mornings and punched speed bags, heavy bags, and sparring partners in the afternoons. He trained and he listened. Shortly before breaking camp he ventured an observation: "That Conn boy talks too much." As for the fight, Louis commented, "Well, the way I look at it—if Conn wants the title, it ought to be worth fighting for—and if he fights me, I'm liable to knock him out in a hurry, 'cause if he comes to me I can get a full shot at him—and if I get a full shot—well, he just ain't gonna be there long." And if Conn decided not to fight toe-to-toe and use his exceptional footwork, Louis had an answer for that as well: "He can run, but he can't hide."

Banter was common in the weeks and days before a fight. John Kieran wrote in his column in the *New York Times* that all big fights follow the same pattern: The champ is old and slow, the challenger is young and hungry; the champ has "no brains," the challenger is "no Phi Beta Kappa key-holder himself"; the champ is mad at the challenger's ill-chosen words, the challenger is angry at the champ's anger. "They are very angry. Each one is tremendously irked by the gross insults of the other. It will be a grudge fight. It will be a ghastly thing to see. They will try to tear one another apart. Buy an expensive seat, right up close, to get the best view of the horror." Kieran believed that the only thing missing from the usual prefight antics was that neither Conn nor Louis had "rescued some hapless child from drowning."[24]

Kieran, however, wrote too soon, and he concentrated too much on the fighters' words. Doubtlessly, Conn was a better talker than most, but what he said was only part of his appeal. In 1941 his life was a soap opera—a dramatic, constantly evolving story of love, death, and the American Dream. In an age when sportswriters scoured alleys for copy and fought pitched battles for ephemeral scoops, Billy Conn stories virtually wrote themselves.

To begin with, there was his family. He had a brother, Jackie, who was fond of loud suits and street fighting. He had a father, Billy Conn, Sr., who had worked so long for Westinghouse that Billy Jr. and everyone else in the family called him "Westinghouse." Westinghouse, Billy told reporters, was a "fighting Mick," and he was more than happy on any occasion or none at all to validate his son's words. When he traveled to New York to see his son fight, Billy told reporters, "Give him a day or two here, and he'll find some guys to slug it out with."[25] Billy also had a manager-trainer, who wasn't family but might as well have been, named Johnny Ray. It was a good Irish name, but his real name was Harry Pitler, which, as it happened, was a good Jewish name. Ray was his nom de guerre. But that hardly mattered because Billy, who had a different name for everyone close to him, called him Moonie. Like Jackie and Westinghouse, Moonie was a character. He had introduced Billy to boxing, taught him everything he knew about the sport, and loved him like a son. Moonie, however, had a problem with the bottle. For the Louis fight he had gone on the wagon, but the lack of alcohol had frayed his nerves.

Rounding out Conn's family was his mother, Margaret McFarland Conn, whose parents both hailed from County Down, just off the Irish Sea. Billy called her Maggie. She had come to America in third-class steerage, sang like an angel, filled the Conn household with Irish melodies and love, and displayed a true Irish mother's fondness for her boys. And her boys loved Maggie, none more so than Billy. As Conn prepared to fight Joe Louis, Maggie remained home in Pittsburgh dying of cancer. It was a fair bet whether she would live long enough for her son to fight for the title. On several occasions Conn returned to Pittsburgh to visit Maggie. They sat and talked for hours. The last time he saw her before the Louis fight he said, "Maggie, I gotta go now, but the next time you see me, I'll be the heavy-weight champion of the world." "No, son," Maggie replied, "the next time I see you will be in Paradise."[26]

There was more. Billy Conn had a girlfriend—Mary Louise Smith, blond, beautiful, wholesome, and vivacious. Billy called her "Matt." She was from a well-to-do Irish American family, educated at Our Lady of Mercy in Pittsburgh and Rosemont College in Philadelphia, and definitely not the sort of female normally associated with boxers. But Billy knew her father and through him met Matt in the summer of 1938 in Ocean City, down on the Jersey Shore. Matt was fifteen, summer tan, and carefree. Billy, just shy of his twenty-first birthday, fell immediately in love, telling Matt, "Someday I am going to marry you."[27] She laughed, but secretly, behind her father's back, she continued to see the Pittsburgh boxer.

Her father, "Greenfield" Jimmy Smith, was not the sort of man who liked things happening behind his back. Greenfield Jimmy, named after the section of Pittsburgh where he was raised, was a self-styled tough guy, as quick with his mouth and fists as any of the Conn tribe. He had once played baseball for John McGraw's New York Giants, and he spent time with the Pittsburgh Pirates, Baltimore Terrapins, Boston Braves, Philadelphia Phillies, and Cincinnati Reds. Frank Deford claimed the word on Greenfield

Jimmy was "good mouth, no hit." In eight seasons in the Big Leagues he heckled opposing pitchers, insulted opposing batters, and swore at opposing fans while compiling a lackluster .219 batting average. But he did earn—or, at least, receive—a World Series ring as a member of the Cincinnati Reds team that was on the fixee end of the 1919 series.

After his playing days he returned to Pittsburgh and made a small fortune providing illegal and legal booze to thirsty Steel City men. He made an effortless transition from running a speakeasy to, after the repeal of prohibition, owning and managing The Bachelor's Club, the swankest drinking and gambling establishment in Pittsburgh. He became legit, even semi-respectable, a pillar of Pittsburgh's male subculture and a man of considerable influence and means. As fitting a man of ambition and airs, his children went to good schools, learned proper manners, and prepared for a more elevated social world than the one Smith was born into. On one point, he was decidedly clear: he might know and consort with gamblers, mobsters, boxers, and sporting men of all types, but his Mary Louise was not going to marry any of them.

By 1941 Matt had decided to accept Billy's proposal of marriage. She was eighteen, of legal age, and the two had taken blood tests and received a marriage license. They planned to marry after the title fight. Greenfield Jimmy had other ideas. He told whoever wanted to listen that if Conn tried, he, Greenfield Jimmy, age forty-six, "would kick that Mick fighter's ass."

The day before the fight Greenfield Jimmy drew himself up to his full five feet, nine inches and issued a challenge. "Champion or no champion, I'll punch the hell out of that fellow, and he'd probably be the first one to say I could do it. I hope he wins, but I want him to stay the hell away from my family. . . . My little girl has just turned eighteen and that's just a baby to me."[28]

Billy Conn smiled when he learned of Greenfield Jimmy's challenge, but Westinghouse interpreted it as an insult to the entire Conn clan, maybe even a slight to his ancestors dead and buried in Ireland. Jimmy might lick Billy, Westinghouse announced, "but I'll be damned if he can lick me. Who does this guy think he is? There is one thing for certain, he ain't ever punched a Conn. And it'll be a sorry day for him when he tries. . . . Listen, this guy never punched anybody without having a couple of guys hold the other fellow's arms. He was even a light hitter with a baseball bat."[29]

Threats followed threats, Irish fighting words precipitated Irish fighting words. The potential Smith-Conn donnybrook threatened to push the Louis-Conn title fight into the agate type. Up in Greenwood Lake Joe Louis minded his own business and observed strict neutrality regarding the Smith-Conn internecine squabbles. He had his own family problems, though they did not seem to weigh heavily on his mind. More importantly, he had a title defense scheduled for the Polo Grounds.

***

As the family drama unfolded, occupying the attention of inquiring journalists, hard news about the actual fight was scarce. Mike Jacobs refused to release any details about ticket sales, although reporters suspected that it would be the largest gate since the second Louis-Schmeling fight. Concerns about Conn's failure to put on weight circulated widely, and when Jacobs announced that there would not be a public weigh-in, it fueled widespread speculation that Billy was barely over 170 pounds. The chairman of the New York Athletic Commission, Major General John J. Phelan, in line with established policy, refused to announce the referee for the fight. It seemed that the only person willing to say anything new about the contest was Lou Nova, the California heavyweight who was next in line to fight Louis. "I expect to meet the champion in September," he smiled.[30]

Jacobs' decision not to hold a public weigh-in ceremony proved prescient. Commenting to reporters that he had to keep a lookout for Greenfield Jimmy, Conn reported to the weigh-in on time at 11:45. He wanted to get the affair over with and return to his hotel room for a nap. Louis kept him waiting. Fifteen, thirty, and finally forty-five minutes passed. Angered, Conn barked, "I'm not waiting any more. Weigh me and let's be done with it."[31]

Conn stripped, stepped on to the scale, and watched as it settled below 170 pounds. But before Conn's weight was officially announced Jacobs chimed, "One-seventy-four-and-a-half!" As he did so he nudged Conn off the scale. In truth, Conn was just a few pounds over the 160-pound middleweight limit, a sobering thought given that in a matter of hours he was going to face the most dangerous heavyweight in the history of the division.

Louis arrived just as Conn was leaving. The two fighters brushed past each other like strangers on a crowded New York street. A member of Louis' camp explained that the traffic from Greenwood Lake had delayed the champ's arrival, but Louis did not seem particularly interested in the excuse or anything else. Never much concerned with the empty ritual of heavyweight weigh-ins, he stepped on the scale and paid no attention to the results. He weighed 202 pounds, but Jacobs, assuming that what he gave so casually he could just as easily take away, announced an official weight of one-ninety-nine and a half. At the moment it must have sounded much less than two hundred.

As Louis and Conn disappeared into their hotel rooms to rest for the fight, the sporting world in New York buzzed with activity. It was June 18, 1941. Less than a month before, the British battleships *King George V* and *Rodney* had caught and sunk the German terror of the North Atlantic, the battleship *Bismarck*. In the weeks since the naval engagement the United States' relations with both Japan and Germany had become dangerously strained. But the upcoming battle in the Polo Grounds occupied the attention of millions of Americans. Fight fans from Pittsburgh, arriving in New York by train aboard the Ham and Cabbage Special, roamed the city dressed as if it were St. Patrick's Day, looking for tickets and fights, though not always in that order. Back in Conn's hometown, the Pirates' management announced that the game that night in Forbes Field would have a particularly long seventh-inning break—regardless of the inning—so that the fans could listen to the P.A. radio broadcast of the match. In towns and farms across the land it was the same thing. Joe Louis trumped all other news.

***

It had rained during the day and there had been a chance for more in the forecasts, but on the night of the fight the dark skies above the Polo Grounds threatened no rain. Temperatures were mild, and the crowd of some fifty-five thousand spectators was loud but good-natured. Since the 1920s, major heavyweight title fights had become the meeting place for the famous, wealthy, and powerful. Joe DiMaggio and Bob Feller, Al Jolson and Bob Hope, J. Edgar Hoover and Pennsylvania governor Arthur James— they joined hundreds of other celebrities in "ringside seats" that stretched back for rows. Tens of millions more Americans participated in the event, absorbing the excitement and atmosphere of a championship title fight, by tuning in to the Mutual Radio Network broadcast. Altogether about fifteen million radio sets across the country were tuned to the fight, and around each was huddled a group of family and friends. Undoubtedly the largest single group of listeners was at Forbes Field. There, with the Pirates leading the Giants 2–1, the umpires suspended the game and ordered the WCAE broadcast to be patched in over the public address system.

When Americans in the Polo Grounds, at Forbes Field, and in living rooms and bars across the nation had taken their seats, the fight started. It was Joe Louis' eighteenth title defense, and during the early rounds it seemed fairly predictable. Conn appeared overmatched, and like other challengers for Louis' crown before him, he moved as though he realized it. As soon as the bell rang the challenger beat a hurried and disorderly retreat. Sportswriter Vincent X. Flaherty observed that Conn "looked like Oliver Twist invading the den of the 40 thieves with a cap pistol."[32] He moved backward for no other purpose than to avoid serious injury. Occasionally he flicked out a harmless jab, but mostly he just endeavored to stay out of the champion's way. At one point in the first round he slipped to the canvas when his mind went one way and his feet went the other. He survived the round, but surviving was not the same as competing.

The second round was like the first. Louis attacked and landed a few good shots, but Conn was fast enough to stay out of serious trouble. In the third round, however, the tempo of the fight began to change. Conn continued to retreat, but it was more orderly, interrupted at strategic moments with counterattacks. No longer did he move with the frantic jerks of a frightened rabbit. Now he glided like a seasoned fighter—in and out, left and right, landing a jab here and a hook there, making Louis miss and slipping punches. By the end of the sixth round the fight was even on the scorecards, and Conn was fighting with steadily increasing confidence.

Not since his first fight with Max Schmeling had Louis faced an opponent who had a strategy and the skills to defeat him. Years later, Conn explained how he planned to defeat Louis. The main thing was "not . . . to get hit. That's the game. Get out of the way. I knew that [I] had to keep moving from side to side and keep him off balance and never let him get a good shot at [me] because he was a real dangerous man. Keep away from him. Just move in and out. Feint him out of position and whack him and just keep going. Left hook and a right cross, a left hook to the body and a left hook to the chin—all in the same combination, bing, bang, boom! Real fast, like a machine gun, then get the hell out of the way. . . . You look straight at [him] and you just take the lead away from him. You try to mix him up, to befuddle him. Then you take the whole combination of shots at the same time—one, two, three, four, bing, bang, bing and you get the hell out of there real fast. Then when he goes back you get him to drop his hands, feint him out of position, then you can hit him. But every time that you lead with one hand you have to know to keep the other one up so you don't get hit. You can't let him get set to get a clear, good shot."[33]

As the bout went into the middle rounds, Conn's "retreating attack" had begun to frustrate the champion. Louis was not a slow heavyweight, but he moved in patterns. Generally he moved forward with a half step with his left foot and two quick quarter-steps with his right, always working to move his opponent backward and to the short side of the ring. But Conn refused to fight along the straight Louis lines. He consistently feinted to one side, drew Louis in that direction, then darted to the other side, forcing the champion to regroup and mount another attack. "Billy," observed Pittsburgh sportswriter Regis Welsh, " . . . made Joe look as though the champion were trying to wing a hummingbird on the fly with a baseball bat."[34] Occasionally Louis landed a punch. One opened a cut over Conn's right eye. But the champion's strength had always been his knack for landing punches in combinations, and Conn's shiftiness made him almost impossible to catch, trap, and hurt.

From rounds eight to twelve, Conn fought flawlessly. Although Louis was the nominal aggressor, Conn dominated the action. He moved back and forth, side to side, drawing Louis forward and out of position, then lashed out with stinging left and right hands. When Louis threw a counterpunch, more often than not Conn was gone, vanished like some sort of pugilistic phantom. Occasionally he exchanged words with Louis. After landing a hard combination he said, "You got a fight tonight, Joe." Louis answered honestly: "I knows it."

It was difficult not to know. By the tenth round Louis' nose was bloody and his eyes were beginning to swell. In his corner, Louis' managers were beginning to get desperate. Louis' close friend Freddie Guinyard recalled Julian Black and John Roxborough asking, "Oh my God, he's way behind. What's he going to do?"[35] But there was nothing he could do. Conn was too fast, too well conditioned, and too confident. Not only was he out-boxing the champion, but by the ninth round he was out-hitting him as well.

By the twelfth round Conn's confidence was surging toward overconfidence. As he saw Louis tiring, he took the offensive, fighting more flat-footed and throwing power shots. Two sweeping left hooks followed by a hard left to the heart midway through the round staggered Louis, who had to clinch to stay on his feet. "He hurt me pretty much in the twelfth, and I was hoping that he'd lose his head pretty quick, because I knew I was losing the title," Louis told reporters after the fight.[36] Perhaps all those thoughts went through his mind, but one thing was certain, he was hurt "pretty much." Conn abandoned boxing and began swinging for a knockout. Shaken, Louis held on, tying up Conn's arms and smothering his punches. He fought like a hurt boxer is supposed to fight—avoiding further damage and surviving the round.

Conn was so full of adrenaline at the end of the twelfth that he started to go for Louis' corner and had to be turned around and pointed in the right direction. Billy laughed as reached his corner, full of himself and his impending victory. "I'm going to knock this son of a bitch out. Don't worry about it," he told his manager. "No, no, just box," Moonie told Billy. "You've got the fight won, just stay away from him."[37] But there was no talking to him. Conn was beyond wise counsel, out of the range of sage advice. In his mind he was a good left hand away from being the new heavyweight champion of the world.

Conn went out for the thirteenth round thinking he was facing a hurt opponent. Louis started the thirteenth clearheaded, still strong, and looking for one good chance to hit Conn. For half the round the two fought evenly—both aggressive, both flat-footed, both looking for a knockout. Conn had stopped dancing from side to side and had adopted Louis' straight line assaults. Then, as Conn began to throw a left hook, Louis moved forward and delivered a short, perfectly timed right hand that landed solidly. Conn's knees buckled, but he stayed upright. Instinctively, he fought back. It was absolutely the wrong tactic. Although he landed a few punches, he gave Louis the opportunity he needed. While Conn launched wild, looping punches, Louis threw short, straight ones, catching the challenger with several devastating uppercuts and punishing body blows. With less than fifteen seconds remaining in the round, a combination of punches, ending with an ax-like right hook, knocked Conn to the canvas.

Confusion reigned. But Louis strode calmly to the neutral corner, and referee Eddie Joseph moved toward Conn and picked up the timekeeper's count. At seven Conn struggled to a sitting position and focused on Joseph's count. Somewhere between "nine" and "ten" he stood up, ready to commence the contest. But Joseph waved the fight over and wrapped his arms around Conn. Dazed and confused, Conn offered no protest. He was counted out at 2:58 of the thirteenth round.

Spectators in the Polo Grounds reacted wildly to the swift, dramatic conclusion of the fight. For twelve and a half rounds Conn appeared on his way to taking Louis' crown. Then, as Conn might say, bing! bang! boom! The fight was over and the champion was still the champion. At Forbes Field the stands went silent when young announcer Don Dunphy exclaimed, "Conn is *out!* Joe Louis is *still* the champion of the *world!*"[38] Silently the ballplayers trudged back on the field, resuming a game for which neither the fans nor the players had much heart. It was finally called a 2–2 tie after the eleventh inning.

The same shock that struck the Polo Grounds and Forbes Field echoed across the country. The fight was so damn dramatic that it killed people. In Philadelphia three people died from heart attacks. One, Andrew Burke, was rushed to the hospital, and before dying he declared, "It was a great fight." Another person, Delia M. Griffin of Buffalo, suffered a heart attack during the fight and was revived after a fire department squad worked two hours on her. Her first question was, "Who won the fight—Louis or Conn?"[39]

Billy Conn's injuries were minor. He had cuts above and below his right eye, another across the bridge of his nose, bruises on both sides of his face, and a heart that ached from contemplating what might have been. In his locker room after the fight he smiled and answered reporters' obvious questions. Shaking his head, he said, "I tried awfully hard. Louis didn't hurt me but he certainly throws a hard punch, doesn't he." It was not until after he showered and had time to think about how close he had been to winning the title that he sank his head into his hands and began to cry. "I lost my head and a million bucks," he moaned. "That's all right," Johnny Ray said comfortingly. "Go ahead and cry if you want to, it'll do you good."[40] But within minutes his irrepressible smile had returned.

Later, in front of an army of newsreel cameras, he famously elaborated on the fight's outcome. "What happened, Billy?" a reporter inquired. "You had it in your pocket and all you had to do was hold him off for three more rounds." "After the twelfth," Conn explained, "I thought I had him and I simply couldn't do anything else but go after him. Then it happened. . . . What's the sense of being Irish if you can't be dumb."[41] It was a line that would endear Conn to millions of people and cement his place in the history of boxing. A generation later he said, "You only get one chance. Of all the times to be a wise guy, I had to pick it against him to be a wise guy. Serves me right. He should have killed me. What a bastard I was."[42]

Louis, as usual, praised his opponent. "He knows what it's all about in there," Louis said. "And if he only could have kept his temper down he might have been the champion."[43] A few years later, after the two became friends, Louis gave a more detailed explanation to Conn. "Jesus, Joe," Conn wondered, "couldn't you have let me borrow your title for just a little while? Just for six lousy months?" "Billy," Louis answered, "I let you have it for twelve rounds, and you didn't know what to do with it. What makes you think you could have kept it for six months?"[44]

There should have been a rematch in six or so months. Conn's domestic dramas abated somewhat. His mother died less than two weeks after the fight, and a few days after that he married Mary Louise. But his relations with Greenfield Jimmy remained iffy at best. In the spring of 1942 they tried to patch up their differences, but it did not take. A kitchen discussion about the responsibilities of being a husband, a father, and a Catholic turned into an all-out lecture from Greenfield Jimmy that Conn found generally lacking. Billy held his temper until Greenfield added, just for good measure and apropos of nothing, that he could, if and when he chose, still "kick his son-in-law's ass." That seemed a mite strong to Billy, who at the time was sitting on the stove. He came off it like he had been burned and threw a looping left hook at Greenfield Jimmy. The punch landed on the father-in-law's skull and broke Conn's hand. When other members of the kitchen conference pulled Billy back, Greenfield Jimmy attacked and administered some minor bumps and bruises. The result of the blowup was that Conn lost his chance for a big-money rematch with Louis before they both went off to war.

Louis was highly amused by the domestic imbroglio. For decades whenever he crossed paths with Conn he asked, "Is your father-in-law still beating the shit out of you?"[45]

What Louis and Conn and most of America did not realize on the night of June 18, 1941, was that an era had ended. There would not be another classic heavyweight title fight before World War II. During the next six months the movement toward war pushed aside the sporting celebrations of American innocence. Louis, DiMaggio, Williams—they and thousands of other athletes would soon be in uniform. Nor would Joe Louis ever be as great as he was that night. Against Conn he still had the ability to create pugilistic magic. He stepped to the edge of defeat, watched his title slip away, and then, with a sure, perfect punch, snatched victory. It was a wonderful, memorable night that thrilled America. And it was Joe Louis' last great fight.

8

Uncle Sam Says

Well, airplanes flying 'cross the land and sea
Everybody flying but a Negro like me
Uncle Sam says, "Your place is on the ground.
When I fly my airplanes, don't want no Negro 'round."
—*Josh White, "Uncle Sam Says," 1941*

It is impossible to create a dual personality which will be on the one hand
a fighting man toward the foreign enemy, and on the other, a craven who
will accept treatment as less than a man at home.
—*William Hastie, 1941*

Josh White longed to be the Joe Louis of the blues guitar—better than
Robert Johnson, better than Leadbelly, the best. Beyond wanting to reach
the top of his profession, White shared several other biographical similarities with the boxer. Born in the Deep South in 1914, in the same part of
the country and the same year as Louis, he had had painful experiences
with Jim Crow and other southern ways. As a child he had witnessed his
father, Dennis White, being "beaten to a pulp" by a 280-pound sheriff and a
deputy for the infraction of throwing a white bill collector out of his
house.[1] The man had spit on the floor and disrespected White's wife. The
sheriff judged White to be crazy to challenge a white man and sent him to
an insane asylum, where he died.

Like Louis, White grew up fast. He learned to sing and play the guitar
by acting as a traveling guide to a series of blind bluesmen, moving across
the dusty back roads of the South, always trying to anticipate danger and

stay a few steps away from angry or drunken white southerners. While Louis moved to Detroit and then Chicago and became famous for his ability to knock out white opponents, White eventually drifted to Chicago and became known as a musician. Promoters called him the Sensation of the South, and he earned respect as a star of "race" records.

By 1940 the two men had developed different public styles and voices—personas, really, that represented the two faces of black America. Louis by inclination and indoctrination was an earth smoother. He said as little as possible in public. He answered questions in a soft, unthreatening but direct southern accent, often by doing little more than turning a question into a statement. Question: "How do you feel, Joe?" Answer: "I feel good." At times, glimpses of humor broke through his stony facade, small indications that an alert mind was at work, but the occasional flashes were usually ironic in nature, never threatening or insulting.

White looked at life through unblinking eyes and wrote songs that—again like Louis—never pulled a punch. In his 1941 album *Southern Exposure: An Album of Jim Crow Blues,* he and his collaborator Waring Cuney described life on their side of the color line. The title song describes the economic and political plight of a black sharecropper:

> Well, I work all the week in the blazin' sun,
> Can't buy my shoes, Lord, when the payday comes.
>
> I ain't treated no better than a mountain goat,
> Boss takes my crop and the poll takes my vote.[2]

Other songs capture the racial realities of FDR's America. In the "Defense Factory Blues," for instance, he underscores the discrimination in government jobs:

> Went to the defense factory, trying to find some work to do
> Had the nerve to tell me, "Black boy, nothing here for you."
> My father died, died fighting 'cross the sea.
> Mama said his dying never helped her or me.
> I'll tell you brother, well it sure don't make no sense
> When a Negro can't work in the national defense.[3]

In song after song White explores issues bitterly familiar to Joe Louis, but ones the champion almost never mentioned in public. Yet increasingly, as the United States approached the brink of war, issues of justice, democracy, and opportunity nagged at the soul of black America. Against the background of Nazi oppression, the racial status quo in America no longer seemed tenable. The notion of fighting a war for democracy abroad when most black Americans lived out of reach of democracy at home bedeviled black America.

Even President Roosevelt sensed that the customs of the southern wing of his party were contrary to the times. After listening to *Southern Exposure,* FDR invited White to perform for a small gathering in the White House. Before a room full of "bigwigs," White sang "Uncle Sam Says," "Defense Factory Blues," "Bad Housing Blues," "Jim Crow Train," and the other songs on the album, throwing in a few spirituals to make the white listeners feel more at ease. Afterward, he had a private meeting with the president. "Who are you talking about when you're singing 'Uncle Sam Says'?" FDR asked. "You're the president, you're Uncle Sam I was singing about," White answered. "Well, you know, the president can be vetoed; he can't do everything," the president mused.[4]

Roosevelt's comment, a variation on the creed that we can't move too fast, tasted stale for many black Americans. "Why die for democracy for some foreign country when we don't even have it here?" asked an editorialist in the *Chicago Defender.*[5] It was the nub of the "Negro problem" facing American policy makers at the beginning of World War II, and the essence of the "war debate" dividing black Americans. What exactly would be the place of American blacks in the Great Crusade? "Though I have found no Negroes who want to see the United Nations lose the war, I have found many who, before the war ends, want to see the stuffing knocked out of white supremacy," said racial activist A. Philip Randolph. "American Negroes . . . are confronted not with a choice but with the challenge both to win democracy for ourselves at home and to help win the war for democracy the world over."[6] Few black Americans—and a good portion of white Americans—would have disagreed with Randolph, but there was considerable argument over emphasis. Both goals were eminently desirable, but which mattered most? Race or war? War or race? It was a debate that would occupy leading government officials and civilian leaders for the entire course of the war. And Joe Louis, the world's greatest fighter, would play a crucial role in the Gordian "Negro problem."

***

The presidential race of 1940 provided an inkling of the growing importance of Louis. Running for a third term, Franklin D. Roosevelt faced opposition from outside as well as inside his own party. The Republicans chose Wendell Willkie, a relative political novice from Indiana whose plainspoken Hoosier charm and success in corporate America led a Roosevelt supporter to label him a "simple, barefoot Wall Street lawyer."[7] Faced with conservative, discontented southern Democrats, grumblings about the propriety of running for a third term, business community assaults against the New Deal, and a dynamic Republican opponent, FDR sensed trouble. Democratic strategists predicted that black northern voters might well be the key to a third Roosevelt term. Fully understanding the political importance of Louis' popularity, they courted the boxer's support.

Willkie campaign organizers reached the same conclusions, and they were in a better position to win Louis' favor. Trying to end the inroads that Democrats had made with black voters, the Republican platform stressed the need for an anti-lynching law and universal suffrage for blacks. It was enough to win the endorsement both of the *Pittsburgh Courier* and the *Baltimore Afro-American*. In addition, Charles Roxborough, a Republican state senator and major politician in Michigan who was the brother of Louis' manager, had a direct line to the champion. Although Louis admired Roosevelt, he was impressed with Willkie's sincerity and he respected Charles' judgment.

Several weeks before the election Louis announced that he was "in Willkie's corner," encouraging people to vote for the Republican "because I think he will help my people."[8] Immediately he was stumping for the Republican candidate, appearing in major northern cities and calling FDR to task. Before a large African American gathering in St. Louis he criticized Roosevelt's civil rights efforts. "Roosevelt had two terms to do what he could do, but didn't give us an anti-lynching law," he told a cheering audience. Balancing his remarks between humility and militancy, he added, "I am just Joe Louis. I am a fighter, not a politician. This country has been good to me, has given me everything I have, and I want it to be good for you and give you everything you need. I am for Willkie because I think he will be good for my people. I figure my people ought to be for him too."[9]

Sensing that Louis was winning votes, Republicans featured him during the last week of the campaign. Arriving in New York by plane on the morning of October 31, he was rushed from one Republican meeting to the next. He admitted that he had never voted in a presidential election—he had been in California 1936 and too young in 1932—but added, "I was born a Republican. My mother was always a Republican—Republican and Baptist." Eight years of Democrats, he reaffirmed, had hurt blacks. Not only had Roosevelt failed to pass an anti-lynching bill, the National Recovery Administration had allowed employers to discriminate against blacks, forcing more of them onto relief rolls. "I think Mr. Roosevelt is making a lot of lazy people out of our people," he argued. "They sit around waiting for the $15 a week" relief check.[10]

At each of a dozen or more stops across the city Louis spoke haltingly, unsmilingly, but concretely about the failure of Roosevelt and the New Deal to help African Americans. Louis labeled FDR's appointment of Benjamin O. Davis as the only black brigadier general—one of the sops to critics of his racial policies—tokenism. The champion found little in the record that supported the claims of the Democratic Party that it was the new party for black Americans. His criticisms were valid, and at each stop he was enthusiastically cheered.

Democratic politicians countered the champion's speeches with celebrity boxers of their own. Popular former heavyweight champion Jack Dempsey endorsed FDR and called Joe Louis and labor leader John L. Lewis "damn fools" for supporting Willkie. The current heavyweight champion was a "traitor to his race and people," and the CIO head a "disgrace to the workers he claims to represent," Dempsey announced.[11] "Two Ton" Tony Galento, whom Louis had knocked out the previous year, also weighed in on the presidential race, predicting that FDR would "beat Willkie just as bad as I'll beat Joe Louis the next time I catch up with the bum."[12] Although Galento's statement only drew skeptical smiles, Dempsey's attack on Louis prompted Gene Tunney, another former heavyweight titleholder, to respond. "I think [Louis] performed a patriotic service. Personally, I am and always will be a Democrat, but I'd rather go down to hell with Wendell Willkie than to the White House with Roosevelt."[13]

By the time Tunney came to his defense, Louis was in Chicago telling black political rallies that a vote for Willkie "will mean freedom from the WPA and freedom for American Negro rights."[14] At every stop supporters applauded his speeches, beseeching him for autographs and crowding close to shake his hand or touch his sleeve. Louis' activities in the election signaled the growing acceptance of boxing. In the election, entertainers such as boxers Louis and Dempsey; writers Booth Tarkington, Robert E. Sherwood, and Carl Sandburg; and performers Irving Berlin, Benny Goodman, and Bill Robinson were celebrity political spokesmen. They energized the campaigns, guaranteed packed meetings, and added luster to traditional stump appearances. Arthur Krock of the *New York Times* called the election of 1940 a "campaign of amateurs." "Never have the fine and the very liberal arts plunged more heartily and conspicuously into a political campaign."[15] Never had glamour and politics mixed so thoroughly.

Krock was uncertain about what impact celebrity would have on the election's outcome, but he was sure that the entertainment factor had become crucial to American politics. In the far more important conflict already convulsing Europe and Asia, such celebrities as Joe Louis, Irving Berlin, and Benny Goodman—as well as John Wayne, Bing Crosby, Superman, and a host of others—would play vital political roles. For Louis, the 1940 campaign introduced him to his new civic responsibilities. It also demonstrated to politicians the symbolic power he packed.

***

A year later, in the fall of 1941, Americans were edgy. World politics seemed to be fulfilling "The Second Coming" promise of William Butler Yeats—"The best lack all conviction, while the worst are full of passionate intensity." The Nazis had increased their persecutions of Jews in Germany, Poland, and the Soviet Union. Hitler's armies had reached the gates of Leningrad and swept across the plains of central and southern Russia. The winds of war were howling in Asia and Africa. United States merchant ships sailed in peril in the North Atlantic, and millions of Americans, listening to the isolationist harangues of Charles Lindbergh and his American First supporters, feared that the Roosevelt administration was dragging their country into another world war.

It was in this anxious atmosphere that Louis' role as a national icon increased in importance. With the Primo Carnera and Max Baer matches in 1935 he became the central black icon, and with the second Max Schmeling contest in 1938 he became the crucial symbol of America's opposition to Nazi racial theories and expansion. Now, with war only months away, his role as a black cultural and political icon was increasing.

Toward the end of September 1941, *Time* magazine published a cover story about the champion, then preparing for a title fight against Lou Nova. The cover illustration presented a close-up of Louis' face and neck, a painting that suggested unusual physical strength and moral determination. It was the image of a black American warrior—grim-faced, clenched-jawed, and forward-looking. The accompanying article, entitled "Black Moses," also suggested the importance of the champion to black Americans. Louis' managers, the journalist wrote, had shaped him to be a "black Moses leading the children of Ham out of bondage" and "an ambassador of racial good will." In a well-intended if patronizing tone, *Time* affirmed that the champion had become both: "Joe makes no pretense of being a leader of his race. He knows his limitations. He is a good and honest fighter and a simple-minded young man. But intelligent Negroes are grateful to him for remaining his own natural self and thereby doing much to bring about better racial understanding in the U.S.—doing more, some of them say, than all the Negro race-leaders combined."[16]

While managing in a few sentences to insult both Louis and "Negro race-leaders," the writer went to the heart of the "Negro problem" in America. He insisted on portraying Louis in paternalistic language. The champion was a "lugubrious fellow," "as mischievous as a child," an "un-sophisticated, overgrown kid." In contrast, Marva was a "socially ambitious Chicago stenographer" who now "likes to hobnob with the Negro upper crust."[17] For the white journalist, Joe and Marva were caricatures, images of black America culled from movies and novels, a bit of Stepin Fetchit here, a touch of Butterfly McQueen there. They were largely imaginary, divorced from the realities of African American life. Similarly, the "Negro problem" was in truth a "Caucasian problem," centered on how whites perceived blacks.

Racial issues, however, were not on Louis' mind as he prepared to fight Lou Nova, a top-rated boxer from California. After his narrow escape against Billy Conn, sportswriters had begun to write off Louis as a fighter on the decline. Although he was only twenty-seven, a prime age for a heavyweight, he had fought more often than any other titleholder. Since winning the crown in 1937 he had defended it eighteen times, averaging more than four defenses a year for four years. Dempsey had held the title from 1919 to 1926 and had defended it only a total of six times. Adding to the problems of age and overwork, Nova was a talented, six-foot-three-inch heavyweight with victories against such respectable fighters as Max Baer, Tommy Farr, and Lee Ramage. Considered by reporters as an oddball, he called himself the Man of Destiny, practiced yoga, preached a line of Far Eastern mysticism, and threw a particular punch—which he had dubbed the "cosmic punch"—that he claimed came straight from his seventh vertebra, the center of balance.[18] Photographs of the tan, strapping heavy-weight sitting in a lotus position, arms folded, created a stir in the sports community at a moment when events on the eastern side of the Pacific had riveted millions of Americans.

Nova later claimed that his philosophy brought a wonderful calm to his September 27, 1941, match against Louis, an ability to follow the action in a detached, out-of-body manner. Before more than fifty-six thousand spectators in the Polo Grounds, the challenger strove to prolong the fight, hoping to tire out the champion. Louis, wary of Nova's cosmic punch, also avoided trading punches. The result made for a few tame cat-and-mouse rounds. There was a spirited exchange in the fourth, but for most of the first six rounds there was more posing and feinting than punching. A white reporter, still employing animal metaphors when describing Louis, said "the Brown Bomber, the Dark Destroyer, the Alabama Assassin" stalked "his prey like a jungle beast."[19]

Then in the last minute of the sixth round, Louis landed an explosive right to Nova's jaw. The challenger, wrote James P. Dawson, "deflated like a balloon, his body aquiver, his nervous system paralyzed, his mind blank."[20] Nova drifted to the canvas in a slow, sinking fall. There he stayed until referee Arthur Donavan's arm was dropping for a ten count, at which point he scrambled to his feet. He later said he felt no pain, heard no cheers, and experienced nothing but cosmic peace. Perhaps so, but he also experienced Joe Louis in full pursuit. The champion chased Nova across the ring, landing lefts and rights and tearing open a gash above the challenger's left eye. Nova swayed, staggered, and began to sink to the canvas again but somehow stayed upright. Donovan had seen enough. A second before the bell sounded he stopped the match, creating minutes of confusion. But Nova did not complain. "It would be ridiculous for me to say that Dono-van had no right to stop it when he did," he said.[21]

After the fight a few reporters asked Louis about the cosmic punch. The champion thought a few seconds then replied, "That cosmic punch is just a fairy tale."[22] But there would be nothing enchanted about the champion's next opponent. Earlier in September, a Chicago Selective Service Board had removed Louis' 3-A deferment and reclassified him 1-A. He had been deferred because he supported several dependants. He had the right to appeal the new classification, but he immediately announced that if drafted he would serve in the Army, reasoning, quite rightly, that he could not argue that he had to remain a civilian to pay for Marva's housekeeper.

"I don't want any favors," he said.[23] In fact, he welcomed the opportunity to serve his country. After the fight the black press—but not the white— quoted Louis as saying, "Maybe my next fight will be against Max Schmeling in no-man's land. I won't be pulling any punches."[24] In the meantime, he accepted Chief of Staff General George C. Marshall's offer to make a series of appearances in army camps in the Midwest VI Corps area.

Shortly before the Nova contest Louis remarked that he probably would enlist in the Army rather than wait to be drafted. "I'm anxious to do anything the Government wants me to do," he told reporters.[25] If the United States were to enter the war, he was ready to fight. At the time the United States had instituted a peacetime draft and was rapidly expanding its forces, inducting thousands of men in their twenties. Reports of Schmeling's parachute exploits in the European war caused Louis to say that he also could "do anything in a parachute or behind a gun that Max Schmeling has done."[26] But both black and white officials thought that the champion could better serve his country on a stage or in a ring than behind a gun. Soon after the reclassification story broke, the National Negro Congress encouraged Secretary of War Henry L. Stimson to give Louis the "fullest opportunity" to use his talents to strengthen the morale of American troops. Louis, a spokesman for the Negro Congress said, represented the "highest expression of our country's democratic traditions" and had become the "idol of American youth regardless of race, creed or color."[27]

Already a new image of Louis was taking shape. Even before the United States declared war on the Axis powers, Louis had emerged as a "champion of democracy" whose ability to forge biracial unity could "become a key factor in giving America the strength to administer a knockout blow to the forces of Hitlerism."[28] As in the second Schmeling fight, he was transformed into a black defender of America. As he toured military camps in the Midwest, thousands of troops turned out to watch him spar and hear him speak. "We all have to do our bit," he told the soldiers.[29] They all, he said, had to prepare to serve Uncle Sam.

***

As a black icon Louis inevitably faced the dilemma so perfectly labeled by W. E. B. DuBois as "double consciousness." DuBois wrote of "this sense of always looking at one's self through the eyes of others, of measuring one's soul by the tape of a world that looks on in amused contempt and pity." Life lived glancing into the mirror of a different culture, DuBois wrote, created a sense of "two-ness," of being "an American, a Negro; two souls, two thoughts, two unreconciled strivings; two warring ideals in one dark body, whose dogged strength alone keeps it from being torn asunder."[30] For Joe Louis in the last days before the war and then through the years of the conflict, the "two-ness" involved being both an American icon and a black icon, a symbol of the vitality of his country's democratic traditions and a witness to the nation's painful racial reality.

Louis' announcement that he planned to donate his earnings from an upcoming title defense to the U.S. Navy Relief Society demonstrated the impossibility of the balancing act. Of course the singular act of generosity had a backstory that was not quite so munificent. Simply put, by late 1941 Louis was badly in debt. He owed at least $81,000 to the U.S. government in back taxes, and probably even more to Mike Jacobs, who was always advancing the champion money against future earnings. The advances put Louis in Jacobs' pocket, exactly where the promoter wanted to keep him. But by the end of November it was obvious to most Americans that their nation would soon be pulled into the war. The passage of the Lend-Lease Act, the signing of the Atlantic Charter, the freezing of the Axis Powers' assets in America, and U.S. participation in British convoys across the Atlantic—all were signs of the swift movement toward war. Even the American people had come to accept the idea. In a November 1941 Gallup poll, 68 percent of Americans said that defeating Nazi Germany was more important than staying out of the war.

What would happen to Jacobs' business once the United States went to war? Louis would go into the Army. That was certain. No champion fighter could sidestep the nation's biggest fight, especially after the brouhaha over Dempsey's war record that almost destroyed his career in the 1920s. The war might very well lead to the suspension of boxing, as well as baseball, football, and other peacetime sporting activities. Seeking to make money while the nation was still technically at peace, Jacobs came up with an idea that would put money into the coffers of both Uncle Sam and Uncle Mike. In early December he called Louis, who was playing golf and spending money in Los Angeles, to ask if he would defend his title and give the purse to the Navy Relief Society. There would be nothing in return but the satisfaction of helping the families of sailors killed or disabled in action. "Fine," Louis instantly replied.[31]

In the African American community the United States Navy was a hot wire. Blacks rightly considered the Navy one of the staunchest bastions of racism. Throughout the 1930s the Navy followed an ironclad policy of racial segregation. Although blacks sailed on virtually every ship, they did so only as part of the Steward's Branch, cooking and serving meals and acting as servants for white officers. Like Filipinos and Chamorros (natives of Guam), they were barred from the officer ranks. Josh White accurately conveyed black attitudes toward the Navy in "Uncle Sam Says." After describing the segregation of the Army Air Corps, he sang:

> The same thing for the Navy when ships goes to sea
> All they got is a mess boy's job for me
> Uncle Sam says, "Keep on your apron son.
> You know I ain't gonna let you shoot my big Navy gun."[32]

By 1940 the Navy had become a powerful American icon. From the White Fleet at the turn of the century to the white dress uniform of the officers, whiteness and power went white-hand-in-white-glove in the Navy. During the first three decades of the twentieth century the Navy had experienced two trends: the number of southern officers had increased and the number of black enlistees had decreased. By 1940 only 2.3 percent of all naval personnel were black.

For many white sailors and officers that percentage was still too high. It was 0 percent in the Marines, prompting Marine Commandant General Thomas Holcomb to say, "If it were a question of having a Marine Corps of 5,000 whites or 250,000 Negroes, I would rather have the whites."[33] Secretary of the Navy Frank Knox felt basically the same. Toward the end of 1940, in a meeting with President Roosevelt and a group of civil rights leaders, Knox asserted that he would resign his office rather than integrate the Navy. Southern whites would simply not tolerate such a measure. In 1941 he reaffirmed the point, arguing that "men live in such intimacy aboard ship that we simply can't enlist Negroes above the rank of messman."[34] A Navy board appointed to look into the matter agreed with Knox: "Enlistment of Negroes for general service would immediately create a situation which would destroy internally the efficiency of the Navy."[35]

The obstinacy of the Navy brass had become a cause célèbre in the black community. That their champion, the most famous black man in the country, would fight for the Jim Crow Navy rubbed many blacks the wrong way. A writer for the *Pittsburgh Courier* suggested that Louis donating his purse to the Navy was akin to the NAACP "donating half of the funds it collects to the Ku Klux Klan."³⁶ Dan Burley of the *New York Amsterdam News* went even further, writing, "No institution of the United States Government officially draws the color line as rigidly as the ocean going forces of Uncle Sam. No institution operating under the Constitution of the United States has, with the open sanction of the Government, practiced every art of discrimination, segregation and ridicule toward a subject citizenry as has the U.S. Navy in its attitude toward Joe Louis' people."³⁷ The Navy had done nothing for blacks, Burley commented, but when it needed Joe Louis, it expected him "to cringe, show his teeth and grin and come bouncing like the sorriest Uncle Tom to do its bidding—giving it everything, receiving nothing." Burley advised Louis not to "sell out his race."

Other black journalists applauded the champion's actions. They admitted that the Navy was a vile, Jim Crow institution, but Louis had the opportunity to influence its policies by his bigheartedness. He had the chance to shine the "white light of justice on the forces of racial hate and prejudice."³⁸ Many black writers followed the line established by Mary McLeod Bethune, the president of the National Council of Negro Women and a leading civil rights proponent. For all of the problems in America, she told blacks, "we feel that the fight against fascism is our fight, too."³⁹ White Americans had to know that whatever lay in the future, black Americans would share in the struggle and sacrifice.

Louis' views echoed Bethune's. He was not fighting for Secretary Knox or the white southern officers or even the Navy itself. He was fighting for America. He told reporters that he would always be loyal to his country and his race, and he refused to split hairs between the two. Of course the country had problems, but it was *his* country. "No place else in the world could a one time black cotton picker like me get to be a millionaire. I love this country like I love my people."⁴⁰ On this subject Louis was eloquent. When Roi Ottley of the *New York Amsterdam News* asked him why he would risk his title and fight for nothing, the champion replied, "I'm not fighting for nothing. I'm fighting for my country."⁴¹

The debate over the Navy Relief Society fight ended on the morning of December 7, 1941. It went down with the USS *Arizona* and the other ships sunk in Pearl Harbor. Now his scheduled defense against Baer looked like an act of perfect timing, a moment when the country could show its unity in the wake of tragedy. "For America . . . this is no time to quibble," wrote Wendell Smith, the sports editor of the *Pittsburgh Courier*. "And for the Negro this is no time to turn his back to the United States of America." The time for the best strategy to achieve racial ends had passed. "Joe Louis must fight Buddy Baer for the benefit of the Navy. The color question, discrimination and segregation now become secondary. There is only one thing that counts . . . America! And because we are part of it, we must agree that it comes first, last and always."[42]

A month after Pearl Harbor, Louis met Baer for the heavyweight title. Not even after the second Schmeling fight had the nation so fully embraced the champion. "The more I think of it, the greater guy I see in this Joe Louis," wrote Jimmy Powers of the *New York Daily News*.[43] It was the first majestic gesture of the home front, and it came at a moment when the country was reeling from bad news. The Japanese had swept through American, British, and Dutch settlements in the Pacific, overpowering forces at Guam and Wake Island and moving into the Philippines, Malaya, and the Dutch East Indies. In the West, Germany occupied much of the Soviet Union, and its Wolf Pack submarines trolled the Atlantic and the waters off the coast of New England. All the news was bad—and it seemed to be getting worse. Louis' act of generosity and patriotism bolstered the flagging American spirit and affirmed basic American values.

Madison Square Garden, dressed like a political rally for the fight, reinforced Louis' message. American flags hung from the rafters, a sailor and a marine sounded bugles, and Lucy Monroe, a patriotic song specialist outfitted in a blue dress with a red, white, and blue sash, sang "The Star-Spangled Banner." Prominent politicians and uniformed servicemen were everywhere, although Secretary of Navy Knox had another pressing engagement and instead sent the assistant secretary and his best wishes. Before the fight, Wendell Willkie paid tribute to Louis. "Joe Lou-ee," he concluded, "your magnificent example in risking for nothing your championship belt, won literally with toil and sweat and tears, prompts us to say, 'We thank you.' And in view of your attitude it is impossible for me to see how any American can think of discrimination in terms of race, creed, or color."[44]

After the enormous buildup, the fight was a trifle anticlimactic. Louis' opponent was Max Baer's younger brother Buddy, a six-foot-six-inch, 250-pound slugger from California. Joe and Buddy had fought the previous year. The champion won on a disqualification when Baer's manager—in a pointless protest to a late Louis punch—refused to allow him to come out for the seventh round. In the rematch Louis seemed more concerned with Jack Blackburn than Baer. The trainer's health was declining and he told

Joe that he did not think he could make it up and down the steps to the ring for many rounds. Louis assured him that the fight would be short. As he had earlier told a reporter who wanted to know his strategy for the match, "I'm fighting for nothing, so I don't expect to fight long."[45]

The fight lasted two minutes and fifty-six seconds. After the bout Baer explained that "when Joe hit me with a left hook on the head my left hand became numb, and I could hardly lift my arm."[46] The champion twice knocked down the challenger with rights, then finished him with a left-hook, right-uppercut combination. For five seconds Baer lay inert on the canvas, then his muscles "twitched convulsively" and he struggled to get up. At the count of eight he reached one knee, but he tumbled forward and was counted out. After the match Louis told reporters, "Felt like I had 20,000 people in my corner and I wanted to end it quick."[47]

***

Two numbers increased Louis' status. On January 13, 1942, the champion, accompanied by his managers and Mike Jacobs, presented a check for $89,092.01 to the Navy Relief Society. It was one of the largest charitable donations raised by a boxing match or any other sporting event. The donation came the day after Louis had enlisted in the U.S. Army at a pay rate of $21 a month. In a ceremony held on Governors Island, Louis traded in his hand-tailored civilian clothes for a khaki uniform. Asked his occupation, the champion answered "fighting." "I feel better now with that guy fighting for us," remarked another recruit.[48] Throughout the country Louis' induction ceremony received headline treatment. America's greatest fighter was now in America's greatest fight. The champ expressed no doubts about the eventual outcome of the war. "Them Japs is all light-weights, anyway," he told reporters. "They don't have any heavyweights."[49]

George McArthur, Louis' chauffeur, drove the champ from the Hotel Teresa in Harlem to Camp Upton on Long Island, where the boxer began his basic training. Stepping out of the car, squinting into the low winter sun, Louis sloshed through the mud and melting ice to the reception center. Someone said, "Well, Joe, I see you made it," and he replied, "Yeah, I made it." Then, merging with other recruits who had arrived by train, he disappeared into the reception center. For the rest of the morning he plodded along behind other recruits, doing what he was told and saying nothing of consequence. "Yet it was eloquently plain," noted a *New York*

Times reporter, "that none of the Negro soldiers who had been worked up by the prospect of having their idol as one of their own, was the least bit disappointed."[50]

The comment provided just a trivial piece of information, but embedded in the mundane fact was the significant detail. The Army that Joe Louis signed up for was not just the United States Army, it was more accurately the United States Negro Army. As historian Thomas Doherty put it, "At the level of epidermis, wartime tolerance reached its limits."[51] Although civil rights exponents had labored to move the Army away from its segregated structure, both Stimson and Marshall refused to budge. Stimson was decidedly old school. A graduate of Andover, Yale (Skull and Bones), and Harvard Law School, and a member of one of New York's most illustrious families and most prestigious law firms, he considered himself more honorable and a cut above almost everyone in the government. And he wore his racial paternalism as comfortably as his Yale tie. During the war, for example, when it was officially decided that the uppercase word "Negro" should be used instead of "negro" in all correspondence, Stimson reluctantly complied in his reports, though no fiats or prompting could wean him away from using "colored" when he spoke.

Stimson and Marshall set the tone for the rest of the Army. Both men were fond of quoting the relevant passage of the service's position on the issue of segregation. Colonel Eugene R. Householder, representing the adjutant general's office, proclaimed, "The Army is not a sociological laboratory; to be effective it must be organized and trained according to the principles which will insure success. Experiments to meet the wishes and demands of the champions of every race and creed for the solutions of their problems are a danger to efficiency, discipline and morale, and would result in ultimate defeat."[52] In short, only a segregated army could win the war. Marshall, a scion of a distinguished Virginia family and a graduate of the Virginia Military Institute, consistently stonewalled any attempt to alter the official policy. There would be no racial experimentation in his army, no messing with the natural order of things below the Mason-Dixon Line. In a memo to Stimson he wrote that a more aggressive movement toward integrating the armed forces "would be tantamount to solving a social problem which has perplexed the American people throughout the history of the nation. The Army cannot accomplish such a solution and should not be charged with the undertaking. The settlement of vexing racial problems cannot be permitted to complicate the tremendous task of the War Department and thereby jeopardize discipline and morale."[53]

The result of Marshall and Stimson's intransigence was an army that reflected the lowest American racial thinking, an army that in theory would be separate but equal but in practice was separate and thoroughly unequal. The ideal called for blacks to make up 10 percent of the armed forces. The government's plan called for blacks to be enlisted, quartered, trained, and assigned in a manner that limited contact with white soldiers, although white officers would command black soldiers. Once again, Josh White's "Uncle Sam Says" captured the government's intentions:

> Got my long government letters, my time to go.
> When I got to the Army found the same old Jim Crow.
> Uncle Sam says, "Two camps for black and white."
> But when trouble starts, we'll all be in that same big fight.[54]

Although the 10 percent goal ultimately proved logistically impossible, during the war 2.5 million black men registered for the draft and one million served in the conflict.

The war they experienced could never be described as the Good War. Most of the blacks from the North confronted a level of racism that at best was horrible, at worst deadly. Many of the training camps were in the Deep South, and Jim Crow reigned on and off the bases. Whites were normally quartered in wooden barracks, blacks in tents or deplorable barracks far from the central parts of the posts. Mess halls, recreational facilities, and theaters were segregated. On some posts white facilities were painted white and black ones tarpapered. Advancement for black officers was rare; the idea of a white soldier saluting a higher-ranking black was viewed like something from *Alice in Wonderland*. Jim Crow even extended into the operating room, where whites received only the blood of other whites and blacks only that of other blacks. Even though the surgeon general said that the practice was "not biologically convincing," he sensed that it was "psychologically important in America."[55] Black blood was just not considered good enough to save a white soldier's life.

The case of Benjamin O. Davis, Jr., underscores the nature of the Jim Crow Army. Davis graduated from the U.S. Military Academy at West Point in 1936, after four years of being shunned by his classmates. At West Point he never had a roommate and ate by himself. Commissioned upon graduation as a second lieutenant, he was sent to Fort Benning, Georgia. Although there was an officers' club on the post, his wife was not permitted to use it. Nor was such discrimination limited to the South. In 1941 Davis' mother received the same treatment at the officers' club at Fort Riley, Kansas. At the time, her husband, Benjamin O. Davis, Sr., the first black general in the U.S. Army, was the commanding officer of 4th Brigade, 2nd Cavalry Division at Fort Riley. Racism simply seeped into every aspect of base life. It was so ingrained, in fact, that white officers in black units had to be officially instructed not to use such terms as "boy," "darky," "uncle," and "nigger," and to avoid pronouncing "Negro" as "Nigra."[56]

Life for blacks on the posts was paradise compared to life outside the camps' gates. The entire notion of blacks in uniforms, training to shoot guns and engage in combat, bred an atmosphere of unrest and hostility in southern towns. Acts of white violence against black soldiers were common, and lynching far from rare. Even before the war there were deadly incidents at Fort Bragg, North Carolina, and near Gurdon, Arkansas, and in early 1942 there was a full-scale race riot in Alexandria, Louisiana. The attacks on blacks caused civil rights activist Roy Wilkins to write, "Off the military reservations our fighting men have been treated so viciously by their own fellow Americans that many of them have wondered whether the enemy is really across the seas or here at home."[57]

Truman K. Gibson, Jr., a black official in the War Department, dealt with scores of racial incidents. The nub of the problem, he wrote in a memo during the war, was "Negro troops on the one hand are being trained as combat soldiers. On the other hand, they are generally told to 'remain in their place' in the South."[58] The results were as predictable as they were bloody. Years later Gibson wrote, "During the 1940s, so many black soldiers were bludgeoned or shot to death by white police, deputies, and civilians in the South that it might be only a slight exaggeration to say more black Americans were murdered by white Americans during the course of World War II than were killed by Germans."[59]

The beatings and the murders were generally ignored or condoned by post officials, but they were fully covered in the black press. Newspapers such as the *Chicago Defender,* the *Pittsburgh Courier,* and the *New York Amsterdam News* printed hundreds of letters from black soldiers and published thousands of articles on the treatment of blacks in the military. The tenor of most of the pieces was summarized in a letter from a black soldier at Camp Lee, Virginia, to the *Pittsburgh Courier:* "The [German] prisoner of war gets much better treatment than we do when they go to the dispensary or hospital and it is really a bearing down to our morale as we are supposed to be fighting for democracy. Yet we are treated worse than our enemies. . . . If something isn't done quick, I am afraid a great disaster will surely come."[60] The steady stream of negative press, the endless flow of scathing letters and reports, was a constant source of irritation for the War Department.

But the letters and articles fed the African American demand for America to embrace its own ideals. In January 1942, the same month Joe Louis defended his title for the Navy Relief Society, James G. Thompson, a black cafeteria employee at the Cessna Aircraft plant in Wichita, Kansas, wrote the *Pittsburgh Courier,* suggesting "that while we [blacks] keep defense and victory in the forefront . . . we don't lose sight of our fight for true democracy at home." Invoking Winston Churchill's famous "V" sign, he continued, "The V for victory sign is being displayed prominently in all so-called democratic countries which are fighting for victory over aggression, slavery and tyranny. If this V sign means that to those now engaged in this great conflict, then let we colored Americans adopt the double VV for a double victory. The first V for victory over our enemies from without, the second V for victory over our enemies from within. For surely those who perpetuate these ugly prejudices here are seeking to destroy our democratic form of government just as surely as the Axis forces."[61]

The *Courier* immediately launched a national Double V campaign. More than any other symbol it captured the black American fight and the "two-ness" of their culture. The Double V was both patriotic and personal, a call to defend America and their race. It promised deliverance from fascism abroad and at home. Ultimately, it added another freedom to Norman Rockwell's "Four Freedoms"—Freedom of Speech, Freedom of Worship, Freedom from Want, and Freedom from Fear. The fifth freedom —the Double V freedom—was Freedom from Racism. As the editor of *The Crisis* wrote in an open letter to President Roosevelt, generations of black Americans had proved their loyalty to their country. "But we are loyal to the ideals of this nation, not to the practices which meet us on every hand. Our boys, to the last one, are not fighting—and are not offering to die—to perpetuate those practices. . . . They and we would be heartened and strengthened anew if you, Mr. President, would speak out, notifying the foes of liberty *everywhere* exactly what America expects to buy with the blood and billions she is expending."[62]

Josh White, who also had the ear of Mr. President, put it another way:

> If you ask me I think Democracy is fine.
> I mean Democracy without the color line.
> Uncle Sam says, "We'll live the American Way."
> Let's get together and kill Jim Crow today.[63]

But it all added up to the same thing, the persistent and insistent demand from black America to destroy Hitlerism abroad and at home.

***

The demand presented President Roosevelt with a perplexing problem. After considerable pressure he had issued Executive Order No. 8802 outlawing discrimination in defense work or government service because of "race, creed, color, or national origin," but he could not—or would not—so simply end segregation and discrimination in the armed forces and the country at large. What his administration could do, however, was try to minimize the damage through a comprehensive, well-coordinated propaganda campaign that substituted symbols for substance and rhetoric for reality. In this campaign of deception, Joe Louis, perhaps unwittingly, assumed a central role.

In the first year of the war Louis' life changed dramatically. Entry into the Army was the least of the changes. More importantly, the most influential people in his professional life began to disappear from it. John Roxborough, the manager who had nurtured and mentored Joe from the time he was an amateur, was caught in a political bribery investigation. In January 1942, former Detroit mayor Richard W. Reading and twenty-five other political employees and gamblers were convicted in a gambling and bribery scheme. Reading received a sentence of four to eight years; Roxborough, named as the Number 2 man in Detroit's policy racket, received a sentence of two-and-half to five years. Three months later, Jack Blackburn, Louis' trainer and friend, died of a heart attack. When the news reached him at Camp Upton, Louis said that he had lost "my closest friend." The boxer knew his trainer was ill. "We kidded a little bit," he told reporters, "and I thought sure Old Chappie was on the way to recovering. I can't figure it out—how he come to die."[64]

Roxborough and Blackburn were gone—and Marva might just as well have been. The celebrity couple whose marriage for years had been rumored to be on the steps of the divorce court, definitely was by the early 1940s. In 1941 Marva filed for divorce, but she was convinced by Joe and his handlers to withdraw the filing. Though they stayed married, they were apart most of the time. In 1943 Marva gave birth to a daughter—Jacqueline, named after Jack Blackburn—but the addition did nothing for the marriage. In any way that mattered, Louis led a bachelor's life, and mostly for appearances' sake Marva held off filing for divorce until toward the end of the war. In March 1945 she was granted a divorce.

Roxborough's imprisonment, Blackburn's death, and Marva's alienation removed the crucial stabilizing influences in Louis' life. The combination created a void that the government did its best to fill. Uncle Sam said that Joe could help win the war, and for most of the next four years Louis answered the call, doing what was asked, trying to balance the demands of propaganda with his concerns for race, and finding plenty of opportunities to live like a heavyweight champion on his $21 a month.

The government's agenda was clear. The Office of War Information (OWI), the Treasury Department, and the War Department labored to present a picture of American unity to the nation and the world. Defining World War II as a "people's war" to create a "new world," government censors tried to beat the film, radio, and newspaper executives into line. They wanted journalists and producers of popular culture to show the small sacrifices on the home front as well as the heroic sacrifices on the battle front. Arriving at a party with your own sugar, carrying your own parcels, giving your seat on a train to a serviceman, planting a victory garden, living on your ration cards—each was to be portrayed as a step toward ultimate victory. In addition, there was to be no whiff that America was divided along racial, class, ethnic, or gender lines. America was a nation united, not one torn apart by strikes, race riots, and religious bigotry. In Hollywood every filmmaker was to ask only one question: "Will this picture help win the war?"[65] In the newspaper, magazine, and radio businesses, the question was the same.

Obviously a segregated armed forces and brutal treatment of black soldiers and sailors sent the wrong message to America and the world. The film industry, the leading source of entertainment in the country, attempted to avoid stereotypes. The slow-shuffling, dimwitted Stepin Fetchit character, a staple of the 1930s, was gone from the screen, replaced by more noble and patriotic types. In such films as *Sahara* (1943), *Stormy Weather* (1943), and *Lifeboat* (1944), black actors and actresses received parts, as

Lena Horne commented, that portrayed them as "normal person[s]."[66] But just as often they received no parts at all. In an effort to maneuver around the stereotypes, many filmmakers just eliminated black characters from their films about the home front and refused to make any productions about black military units.

In the government's and the mass media's search for an authentic black icon, one who was heroic but did not really threaten the racial status quo, Joe Louis became the gold standard. As heavyweight champion he already carried considerable street credentials, but even more importantly, nothing in his past lowered his public image. He was the nation's original brown-eyed handsome man—soft-spoken, modest, and generous; a mother-loving, Bible-reading, and heavy-punching hero. The fact that he knocked Hitler's superman silly in one round—sending Schmeling to a hospital and forcing him to limp out of the United States—added to his aura.

Everywhere he was praised and showered with awards. In January the staff of the Calvin News Service listed its annual "ten outstanding Negroes" for 1941.[67] Louis finished second to A. Phillip Randolph, the civil rights leader and labor organizer. The same month the Boxing Writers Association of New York honored him with the Edward J. Neil Memorial Plaque for service to his profession. In a black-tie ceremony, former New York mayor Jimmy Walker recounted Louis' distinguished career and public service. Commenting on his fight for the Navy Relief Society, Walker gushed, "Joe Louis, that night you laid a rose on the grave of Abraham Lincoln."[68]

At another public gathering to raise money for the Navy Relief Society, the champion's words made news, leading advertising man Carl Byoir to write the poem "Joe Louis Named the War" for the *Saturday Evening Post*. Navy organizers staged the event in Madison Square Garden, placing the dais in the middle of the ring. Before a full house of twenty thousand people, the leaders of New York politics and American culture spoke and performed, all "on the house." "The only profiteer of the evening," commented the *New York Times*, "was the Navy Relief Society itself."[69] Walter Winchell, the influential columnist and one of the hosts of the evening, received a rousing cheer when he announced that the show had raised $156,000, including a $5,000 check, made out to the Army Emergency Fund, signed by Joe Louis.

Asked to say a few words, Louis, in full dress uniform, rose uncomfortably, looked straight ahead, and began to speak "like a schoolboy reciting in assembly." His speech was unrehearsed. Haltingly he thanked Winchell, saying, "I'm really happy that I'm able enough, that I'm able to do what I'm doin', what I have did and what I'm goin' to do. I'm doin' what any red-blooded American would." Pausing for a moment, he added, "We're gonna do our part and we'll win 'cause we are on God's side."[70] The line caused the vast audience to stand and cheer.

Louis had expressed the mood of the country, and the phrase "we'll win 'cause we are on God's side" became, almost overnight, as familiar as "remember the Maine" or "the Yanks are coming." It appeared in newspapers and magazines, in war bond advertisements and posters. Most famously, it adorned a poster of Louis himself, dressed in a combat uniform and striking a fighting pose, lunging forward with a bayoneted-rifle in his hands. "Pvt. Joe Louis says—'We're going to do our part . . . and we'll win because we're on God's side,'" the poster proclaimed. Throughout the country, World War II had become "God's war."

The poster itself suggested Louis' iconic status. At a time when the government censored, and mainstream newspapers commonly refused to print, pictures of black soldiers in uniform, let alone shots of them holding rifles, Louis' image—in uniform, armed, and aggressive—was slapped up on the walls of recruiting stations and government buildings in every section of the country. The tagline as well as his accepted persona had deracialized his image, transforming him into a symbol of patriotism. And not just black American patriotism—American patriotism. Under the stress of a national emergency, for a brief period Joe Louis succeeded in erasing the color line. During the war years he would enjoy a dignified popularity unknown for a black man in the United States.

This popularity, enhanced by his fight for the Navy Relief Society and his war bond benefit appearances, became a wartime commodity. After seeing what the civilian boxer had done for the Navy's most popular fund, Secretary of War Stimson decided that for Pfc. Joe Louis, one good turn deserved another. On March 27, 1942, he defended his title in a second charity bout, this time against Abe Simon, and donated his purse to the Army Emergency Relief Fund. Before the fight Louis was once again praised for his patriotism. The announcer stressed the number of tickets the champion had bought for fellow servicemen, and the undersecretary of war, Robert F. Patterson, employed Louis as a symbol of the common soldier when he spoke to American servicemen on bases across the country. "It is an army of champions," he told radio listeners. "It is engaged in a championship fight, and it's going to win. We pay special tribute to Private

Pvt. Joe Louis says_

"We're going to do our part ... and we'll win because we're on God's side"

During World War II, Joe Louis became the symbol of a racially unified America. Although virtually all black soldiers were forced to accept appalling discrimination, Louis became the poster image of unrealized ideal. (Courtesy of the National Archives)

Joseph Louis Barrow. He is truly a great champion. He is a credit to the ring and a credit to the Army."[71]

No longer merely a credit to his race—the stock journalist line for Louis—he had become a credit to everything masculine in America. In the ring against Simon the announcer blurred the line between boxing and war, saying, "Louis keeps moving in all the time, the American way." Fighting—in the ring and out—had become the occupation of the American male. And in the hierarchy of fighters, Joe Louis as heavyweight champion was at the zenith. Simon was not just facing a great fighter and champion. He was matched against the symbol of American masculinity, the emblem of the U.S. Army, the wartime spokesman of the American people. For Simon, the thought must have been as sobering as Louis' punches. Although the bell saved Simon in the second and the fifth rounds, Louis finally knocked him out in the sixth. Finding a wartime message in the action, the announcer proclaimed, "We won't stop punching, just as Louis does, till we win."[72]

Financially, the fight was a success, raising $64,980.02 for the Army Emergency Relief Fund. And it further enhanced Louis' reputation for sportsmanship and patriotism. Even in the South the champion was hailed as a model citizen and a "credit to the great American people." An indication of the wartime importance of Louis was an article published in *Liberty* magazine shortly after the Simon match. It was by Paul Gallico, Schmeling's friend and former collaborator who had been one of the leading exponents of the "Louis, the ruthless jungle animal" school of journalism. A paean to the champion, the piece recounted Louis' career and spiritual growth from a child in a "cabin on Buckalew Mountain" to a "denizen of the Detroit Jungles" to the heavyweight champion, who won a smashing victory over Max Schmeling. Louis had once been a "mean man," a "primitive puncher," and "cocky," wrote Gallico, but always a "simple, good American." And he had matured. "Somewhere on the long hard row from rags to riches Joe Louis found his soul," Gallico wrote. And when he enlisted, "it was this, almost more than his physical person, that he handed over to his country. It was a beautiful gift."[73]

***

The question for the Army was what to do with the "beautiful gift." The position of both the relatively liberal Office of War Information and the decidedly conservative Army Department was clear. Both wanted to win the support of black America for the war effort without changing the racial status quo. Philleo Nash of the OWI expressed the goal of the government, stating, "Granting small concessions [to black Americans] . . . does not imply any intent on the part of the Federal Government to make the largest concession of all . . . to break down the pattern of social segregation." To win the support of blacks, both the OWI and the Army opted for a symbolic approach, arousing patriotic fervor with "parades, rallies, glorified heroes, posters, radio and motion picture appeals." Although a racial advisor for the OWI claimed that a "postage stamp with the picture of a Negro author or parades and music will not be enough to improve morale" of blacks, the Roosevelt administration refused to make any fundamental changes, working through smoke and mirrors to give the illusion of social movement when there was in fact none. Louis—a glamourized, celebrated, but depoliticized Louis—was central to the government's public relations campaign.[74]

The day-to-day use of Louis was the job of an office in the Army that was itself part of the government's public relation campaign to win the support of black Americans. In 1940, in the last weeks of his campaign against Willkie, FDR made several political moves to win black votes, including announcing that black aviation units would be formed, promoting a black officer to the rank of brigadier general, and appointing blacks to advisory positions in defense-related agencies. Against the wishes of Stimson, Roosevelt created the position in the War Department of civilian aide on Negro affairs. William Henry Hastie, a distinguished black lawyer, dean of Howard University's School of Law, and a member of the New Deal's informal "Negro Cabinet," was appointed as the first civilian aide on Negro affairs. Truman K. Gibson, Jr., a black Chicago lawyer with ties to Joe Louis, was named Hastie's assistant.

From virtually the first day it was clear that Hastie was the wrong man for a public relations job. The position was created to give the illusion that the War Department was interested in the opinions of black Americans and that it was open to constructive criticism and change. In fact, the War Department was fundamentally uninterested in the opinions of blacks and was closed to any changes that altered its Jim Crow organization. Hastie, however, attacked his job as if Stimson had cracked open his door to change. In report after report he articulated every aspect of the problem. "Much of the difficulty being experienced in arousing the nation today is traceable to the fact that we have lost that passion for our ideals which a people must have if it is to work and sacrifice for its own survival," he wrote in one of his first efforts. "So long as we condone and appease un-American attitudes and practices within our own military and civilian life, we can never arouse ourselves to the exertion which the present emergency requires."[75] The report, passionately stated and full of concrete recommendations, was just as passionately rejected by Stimson and Marshall. They considered Hastie a PR man—what Tom Wolfe would later call a "flak catcher"—whose job was to stall the African American press.

Before long Hastie got the message. In the summer of 1942 the War Department created a special committee on black soldiers, but it was a month before Hastie learned about the board. He was not privy to its creation and was not a member of it. Hastie recognized that Stimson had no interest in black soldiers or the views of the civilian aide on Negro affairs. On January 6, 1943, he resigned. "It has seemed to me that my present and future usefulness is greater as a private citizen who can express himself freely and publicly," he wrote Stimson.[76] Gibson was promptly elevated to Hastie's former position.

Younger, less established, and more eager to please than Hastie, Gibson was more in step with the demands of the job. He saw his role as supporting the war effort and working for incremental improvements for black soldiers. And he wanted to use Louis to support his agenda. In Chicago, Gibson had worked closely with Julian Black, was a friend of John Roxborough's, and had performed legal tasks for Louis. Gibson's partner in Chicago, a certified accountant named Ted Jones, even did Louis' taxes. But Gibson was not yet especially close with the champion. He found the boxer a "difficult person. He didn't open up to people he hadn't known for a while or those he hadn't come to trust. . . . Joe was a guy for activity, not for talking."[77] Years later, he recalled, "In the days before the war, before I really got to know Joe, I thought he was the quietest man I ever met. You could sit next to him for an hour and he would never say a word. It was like you were not even in the room. Joe would eat an apple, read a story in a newspaper, stretch out for a nap, and never even look at you."[78]

Louis and Gibson's relationship changed during the war as the political appointee became the conduit between the U.S. government and the heavyweight champion. Gibson's initial plan was to ease the Army's racial troubles by assigning Louis to the Morale Branch of the Army and getting him in front of as many black and white troops as possible. As one of the nation's premier celebrities, Louis was the perfect goodwill ambassador for race relations. To that end, the Army formed a traveling boxing troupe to visit bases in America and Europe. In addition to Louis, Sugar Ray Robinson, Archie Moore, Sandy Saddler, and Jackie Wilson—all either champions or championship-caliber fighters—and Joe's longtime sparring partner George Nicholson formed the heart of the troupe. All the boxers were black, and Louis refused to perform before a segregated audience. The tours were enormous successes. "Can you picture the reaction a soldier would have to see Joe Louis and other great fighters fly across thousands of miles of enemy infested lands and waters, just to put on a show for them?" Mary McLeod Bethune wrote a colleague. "Just picture the feeling it would give a man to see Joe Louis in action anywhere and under any conditions. . . . That will create a fine reaction and make a soldier glad to be fighting for a country so thoughtful of him."[79] During almost four years in uniform, Louis boxed ninety-three exhibitions in the United States, England, France, Italy, North Africa, and the Aleutian Islands. Almost two million soldiers witnessed the champion box during the war.

Like jazz riffs, the exhibitions followed an improvisational pattern. In a hundred-day tour of the United States that began in late August 1943, for example, the "world's greatest boxing show" included exhibitions between Louis and Nicholson and Robinson and Wilson, but as the occasion moved him, Sugar Ray was apt to belt out a song or slide into a classic soft-shoe dance. For Sugar Ray, they were "shows," not mere boxing exhibitions. Then Joe and Ray would answer questions about opponents and life in Hollywood, and no matter what they said, the troops would howl and clap and whistle. *Life* magazine called one exhibition a "quiet parable in racial good will," and while the tour traveled through northern camps, performances went off without a hitch. On the weekends Louis and Robinson obtained furloughs to visit their favorite haunts in Manhattan, and regardless of his official income, Joe could always get a loan from Uncle Mike Jacobs. In the Deep South the mood was not always as free and easy. Black soldiers grumbled about Jim Crow life in the Jim Crow Army. On one base in Mississippi, a black soldier told Robinson that Jim Crow regulations would prevent him from seeing the exhibition. "Isn't this the United States? Isn't this America?" Robinson replied angrily. "No, man," the soldier said, "this is Mississippi." Louis and Robinson made sure that all of their exhibitions were open for all soldiers, but they could do only so much about the persistence of Jim Crow conditions.[80]

The impact of Louis on the troops was best conveyed in a visit he made to a field hospital shortly after D-Day. "No movie star has been greeted by our fighting men with more enthusiasm than that displayed when the Brown Bomber got into action," wrote a G.I. who watched Louis perform. When he visited the wounded troops, one G.I. whose eyes had been seriously hurt in the fighting asked a nurse to remove his bandages. "Let me have just one look at him," he pleaded. "I'll take my chance with my eyesight."[81]

During his visits Louis spent time with black troops, listening to their complaints and working behind the scenes to ameliorate some of their problems. With an open line to Gibson, he was in a position to solve some thorny issues. His relationship with UCLA athletic star, future baseball Hall of Famer, and civil rights spokesman Jackie Robinson illustrates how Louis worked to achieve small racial changes. In 1942, when Louis and Robinson were both stationed at Fort Riley, Joe heard that Jackie and other qualified blacks had been turned down for Officer Candidate School (OCS). Louis immediately called Gibson, who promptly visited the Kansas post and settled the problem. Robinson and almost a score of other blacks were admitted to OCS.

Before Robinson completed OCS, Gibson also claimed that Jackie took exception to a white captain referring to a black soldier as a "stupid black nigger son of a bitch." "That man is a soldier in the U.S. Army," Robinson told the captain. The white officer shot back, "Oh, fuck you; that goes for you too."[82] Seeing that the officer was immune to his reasoning, Robinson tried a different tack. He knocked out the captain's front teeth. Once again Louis intervened, summoning Gibson back to Kansas to save Robinson from a court-martial and prison sentence. Years after the war Gibson recounted how Louis tactfully bribed the commanding officer to overlook Robinson's actions. Robinson returned to OCS and graduated.

Arnold Rampersad, Robinson's biographer, maintains that the incident never happened, though it was reconfirmed in Gibson's 2005 memoir.[83] Ultimately, however, the truth is less important than what the story says about Louis. It is another variation of the "Save me, Joe Louis! Save me, Joe Louis!" tale. During World War II, Louis was perceived as a savior of African Americans, a sort of black Superman who would swoop onto the scene just in the nick of time to save the day. Jackie Robinson needed help. Joe was there. Some black mother's son needed a loan or a word of encouragement. Joe was there. The United States of America needed a few uplifting words. Joe was there, again. Joe Louis, America's champion, was there when he was needed with a smile, a hand, and words of comfort. Often he was there in the flesh. Always he was there in spirit.

Later in the war, Gibson claimed, Louis was there again for Jackie Robinson. Gibson's rendition of the story is filled with high drama. Stationed at Fort Hood, Texas, Robinson had a run-in with a white bus driver. As Robinson boarded the bus, the driver ordered, "Nigger, get to the back of the bus." "I'm getting to the back of the bus," Robinson replied. "Take it easy." Angered, the driver said, "You can't talk to me like that." The words quickly escalated and the driver reached for his revolver—but not as quickly as Robinson reached for him. Gibson later wrote that Robinson "wrestled the pistol away and massaged the driver's mouth with it, depriving him of many teeth."[84] Once more Louis called Gibson, but it proved unnecessary. The post commander recognized both the justice of Robinson's action and the probability that he would never conform to life on and off a southern post. In November 1944 Robinson was honorably discharged from the Army.

The truth was a smidge less dramatic. Robinson did have a confrontation with a white bus driver and several white officers, and he did stand up for his rights as an officer and a man. There most probably was no gunplay or intervention by Joe Louis. But Robinson did face a court-marital, at which he explained his actions. He had been called a "nigger," he said, and he reacted accordingly. Asked to define the word, Robinson said that his grandmother, who had been born a slave, told him it meant "a low, uncouth person, and pertains to no one in particular; but I don't consider that I am low and uncouth. . . . I do not consider myself a nigger at all, I am a negro, but not a nigger." He was subsequently acquitted and ultimately "honorably relieved from active duty."[85] Again, Joe Louis has become part of the folklore of Jackie Robinson because blacks saw him in the role of the savior. And Jackie Robinson never begrudged him that role. Robinson later credited Louis with his baseball career. "I'm sure if it wasn't for Joe Louis," Robinson argued, "the color line in baseball would not have been broken for another ten years."[86]

Louis helped other black soldiers as well. Most of his good deeds were small and personal—behind-the-scenes help for a single individual or aid in solving a common post problem. He did not address the issues in the press or write accusatory letters. In his trips across the Southwest and the Deep South, where most of the Army posts were located, he brought some of the more outrageous examples of racism to Gibson's attention, and Gibson proved adept at finding solutions. Louis even quietly helped to desegregate Army buses. Assessing Louis' value to the Army, Captain Fred Maly, the organizational officer in charge of the troupe, wrote, "There is no question but that thousands of white soldiers drew a fairer and better evaluation of the negro soldier upon seeing and talking with Louis."[87]

Not all of Louis' work took place on bases. To get the champion before an even wider audience the Army assigned him to appear in several films. In early 1943 he was sent from Fort Riley to Hollywood to work on a film version of Irving Berlin's musical *This Is the Army*. Produced by Hollywood veterans Hal Wallis and Jack Warner and directed by Michael Curtiz, the Warner Brothers film made life in the Army look like an extended Holly-wood Canteen production. It was loud, over-the-top entertainment, but it contained higher production values than most of the films of the war. By 1943 Hollywood was making films on the cheap. The slogan "Use it up, wear it out, make it do or do without" had resulted in films that lacked the production qualities of the prewar era. In its sets and production, *This Is the Army* is a cut above films of the war-rationing period, and it became the top grosser of 1943. Featuring Ronald Reagan, George Murphy, George Tobias, Alan Hale, Joan Leslie, Kate Smith, and a host of secondary per-formers, it presented life in the Army as a song-and-dance summer camp.

The Army planned the film as a morale booster, and the cast included actors and performers who were in the Army. The Army also presented itself as inclusive, a cross-section of America that included citizens of dif-ferent nationalities, religions, and races. Jewish Americans, Irish Ameri-cans, and African Americans are featured prominently, suggesting that the U.S. Army was on the cutting edge of ethnic and racial harmony. One song-and-dance number is devoted to black Americans and features Joe Louis. It is a self-contained, stand-alone piece, a standard practice that allowed southern censors to cut objectionable material without losing the film's continuity. Just before an all-black troupe of tap dancers performs the number "That's What the Well-Dressed Man in Harlem Will Wear," the central character in the film asks Louis if he is worried. "I quit worrying the day I got into uniform," Louis answers. "All I know is I'm in Uncle Sam [*sic*] Army and we're on God's side."[88] Then, during a dance sequence that traffics in prewar racial stereotypes, Louis punches the speed bag.

The racial images in *This Is the Army* do not wear well. In front of a massive painting of zoot-suited black dancers—images suggesting selfish-ness and a lack of patriotism—African American soldiers in khaki and olive drab sing and dance and mime. But in 1943 the fact that blacks were included in the production at all was applauded by reviewers. Al Monroe, a feature writer for the *Chicago Defender*, commented, "Our boys are given a fine chance to display their wares in 'This Is the Army,' and they more than make good." Led by Sgt. Joe Louis, he wrote, "they march right sprightly."[89] Other black and white reviewers agreed. The appearance of Louis in the film and at various premieres achieved the Army's purpose. Black Ameri-cans were portrayed as part of the war effort, even if—as in the one song-

and-dance number—they are segregated from white performers. All Americans, the film seemed to say, were singing the same song, just not in the same choir.

The Negro Soldier (1944) was a far more serious effort to portray inclusiveness, and once again it used Joe Louis as the central image. By 1944 it was a message that was sorely needed. The combination of segregation in the armed services, discrimination on the home front, and the disjuncture between American ideals and American realities during the war had created frustration and unrest. Racial violence on southern bases was common, reported and discussed almost daily in the black press. By the summer of 1943 American cities were seething with racial unrest. Competition for jobs and housing and anger over white police violence against blacks were common in cities with large defense plants. In Detroit a racial incident exploded into one of the worst race riots in the country's history. It took six thousand federal troops to restore order, but not before thirty-four people had been killed and more than seven hundred injured.

The Negro Soldier was intended to help soothe the nation's racial anxieties. Produced by Frank Capra as part of the U.S. War Department's *Why We Fight* series, it was directed by Stuart Heisler and written by Carlton Moss. The film eschewed Hollywood stereotypes, presenting black Americans as thoughtful, patriotic, responsible, orderly, and spiritual. They seem more a part of Andy Hardy's small-town America than Sportin' Life's corrupt ghetto world. The film begins in a stone Gothic church and unfolds as a sermon, following the preacher's biblical text, "Make thine name be remembered in all generations."[90] It is at its core a wartime lesson in black history, from the death of Crispus Attucks at the Boston Massacre to sacrifices of blacks in the Spanish-American War and the digging of the Panama Canal to their contributions as soldiers in World War I. It ends with a staged scene of a black steward manning a gun at Pearl Harbor, a sequence inspired by the real-life heroics of Dorie Miller. The tone of the film is somber, the mood serious, the purpose edifying. Although the Army primarily made *The Negro Soldier* to show to black troops, it was also shown to white troops and distributed, sometimes in a shortened version, for commercial viewing in theaters across America.

Louis was central to the film and its message. The minister, played by Moss, begins his sermon with a recollection of seeing the 1938 Louis-Schmeling fight. "In one minute and forty-nine seconds an American fist won a victory," he says as the film cuts to scenes from the match. "But it wasn't the final victory. No, that victory's going to take a little longer, and a whole lot more American fists. Now those two men who were matched in the ring that night are matched again. This time in a far greater arena—and for much greater stakes." Overcut with images of Schmeling and Louis training for war, the minster discusses what hangs in the balance, quoting from *Mein Kampf* to emphasize the ideological nature of the battle. Admitting that life is not perfect for blacks in America, the minister again turns to Louis. "There's nothing wrong with America that Hitler can fix!" Louis says.[91]

The war, then, is framed by Joe Louis. It is characterized as a boxing contest, a fight between men who represent different racial ideologies. The quote from Hitler denigrates America because it is a country in which a black man can succeed, a place where he can rise to become a lawyer. Louis' victory over Schmeling symbolizes and validates an American ideology of equal opportunity and individual initiative, a civic nationalism that contrasted with Nazi beliefs. Once again, Louis' image is associated with patriotism and service, devoid of any hint of racial unrest or controversy.

Ignoring the patently propagandistic presentation of the film and the irony of its message, most black reviewers applauded *The Negro Soldier.* "Every citizen, white and black, should see this picture," commented one civil rights spokesman. Langston Hughes, reviewing the film for the *Chicago Defender,* labeled it the "most remarkable Negro film ever flashed on the American screen." He said the blacks with whom he screened the production considered it "the most important film of Negro activities yet brought to the screen."[92] But Hughes was not blind to the reality of racism in the Army. In the same issue as his notice for *The Negro Soldier* ran, the *Chicago Defender* published another Hughes article on the mental trauma suffered by black troops stationed in the South.

The Negro Soldier had unintended results. Portraying dignified, respectable, honorable black Americans raised the question of why the Army insisted on segregated forces. The logic of the Army film challenges Army policy. As Moss later explained, he decided to "ignore what's wrong with the army and tell what's right with my people," a decision that led to the film's inescapable subtext that segregation in the Army and civilian life was a grave injustice.[93] The racism of prewar Hollywood films permitted, even excused for some whites, a certain moral laxity on race. But *The Negro Soldier* permitted no middle ground. Robbed of stereotypes—the last refuge of racist thinking—the film allowed for no response short of tolerance.

In a fitting irony, Joe Louis' carefully manicured, noncontroversial image became the centerpiece for the loudest cry for racial justice and set the tone for the later civil rights movement.

***

The alteration of Louis' image, it bears repeating, was unintended. Throughout the war Truman Gibson labored to protect Louis as diligently as Roxborough, Black, and Jacobs had done before the war. Louis' affairs with Hollywood starlets, his occasional brushes with Jim Crow in the South, and his worsening relations with Marva were mostly screened from the press. Nor were journalists eager to dig too deeply into the hero's personal life. He was a valuable national resource, the recognized emblem of racial unity and wartime masculinity, and reporters, accustomed to their roles as team players, helped to enhance the champion's image. From his position in the War Department, Gibson steered Louis away from potential controversies. He approved many of the Treasury Department's requests to have Louis appear in War Bond drives and radio broadcasts, but he denied requests for the champion to appear at any function that was in the least controversial. After the Detroit riot, the Army became even stingier with Louis' services. The Army brass did not want him associated with any organization that challenged its conservative positions on race. Louis' government guardians kept the NAACP and liberal organizations far from the boxer.

Gibson even tried to control the people close to Louis. In 1943, for example, a black member of the Women's Army Corps requested an assignment as a secretarial assistant for Louis' American boxing tour. She noted her ability to act "under military discipline and control." She had sterling recommendations, but Gibson denied the request, noting that he wanted men to work as Louis' aides. "I am afraid that even your resistance, built up over years of battling life on your own, would be melted away by the Sergeant's charm with the ladies," Gibson wrote.[94] No detail was too small to be overlooked by the champion's guardians.

In 1945 Gibson also helped Louis get an early discharge from the Army. He arranged for him to receive the Legion of Merit, the highest nonmilitary medal awarded to military personnel. Louis certainly deserved the award. He had defended his title twice for military benefits, fought nearly a hundred exhibitions for troops around the world, appeared in two military-related films, and generally did everything asked of him. Unlike Joe DiMaggio, his counterpart in baseball, he did not expect special treatment or grouse constantly about military life. Louis took a special interest in black soldiers, performed scores of unpublicized acts of kindness and generosity, and honorably served his country.

On September 23, 1945, before one thousand spectators at Fort Hamilton, New York, Major General Clarence H. Kells presented Louis with the Legion of Merit, calling the fighter a "model soldier in training and an inspiration to soldiers everywhere."[95] He had risked his career and his life, aiding the recovery of injured troops and entertaining others stationed far from home. Receiving the Legion of Merit made Louis eligible for immediate discharge. A week later he was out of the Army. His first civilian act, he said, would be to go to Detroit to see his Tigers beat the Cubs in the World Series. Then he planned to go to California to get back into ring shape. After that, maybe Billy Conn again.

The war was over. Louis had emerged unscathed, even more of a hero in 1945 than he had been in 1938 when he had knocked out Schmeling. In the fall of 1945 hundreds of thousands of soldiers and sailors were receiving—or waiting for—their discharge papers, dreaming of bright futures in a world without Hitlers or Tojos. The champion's future was muddier. He was thirty-one and had taken a career's worth of punches. As a fighter he was near the end of the line, he had recently divorced Marva, and he had debts that he could never pay.

9

An Old Man's Dream

An old man's dream ended. A young man's vision of the future is opened wide. Young men have visions, old men have dreams. But the place for old men to dream is beside the fire.

—*Red Smith*

Rose Morgan was about to set up the projector for a visitor when her husband walked into the apartment with a few friends. Rose was Joe Louis' second wife, but they had divorced three years before and she had married a successful lawyer, a "short, portly, manicured man" who was in form and personality as different from the former champion as was possible. Rose, however, was exactly the sort of woman Joe liked. Stunningly beautiful, perfectly groomed and dressed, she was a practical, successful business woman who, a half decade before, thought she could domesticate Joe but failed utterly. But there were no hard feelings. She and Joe remained close friends. In fact, she was also on very good terms with Joe's first and third wives, leading one of them to say, "Joe Louis never cuts off a woman. He just adds another to his list."[1]

"I'm just showing Joe's fight film," Rose said to her husband as she dug out the projector and put on the first Louis-Conn fight. Uncomfortably, the visitor said that she didn't have to go to the trouble. "Oh, it's *no* trouble," she answered. "Is it alright with you if we watch it?" she asked her husband. "Yes, yes, it's alright with me," he said just above a whisper as he went to mix drinks for everyone. "It was obvious that he was just being polite, and would rather not have to sit through it," noted the visitor.

One of the other guests remarked that Louis was the "greatest of all time." "There was a time when nothing was more important to colored people than God and Joe Louis," he said. By then the film was flickering and it was 1941 in the living room of the apartment. Louis and Conn were still young men, fighting like everything in the world was riding on the outcome. Rose followed the action like she was at ringside. "Mummmm," she let out every time Joe landed a good shot. "Mummmm. Mummmm." Rose's husband watched silently and sipped his Scotch.

The screen flashed Round 13. "Here's where Conn's gonna make his mistake," someone said. "He's gonna try to slug it out with Joe Louis." And so he did, just as he had done in 1941. "Mummmm, mummmm," Rose exhaled. Conn was down, struggling to get up, making it to his feet just a hair of a second late. "I thought Conn got up in time, but the referee wouldn't let him go on," Rose's husband said. It was a valid, if debatable, point.

Without a comment, Rose finished off her drink in a hard, short gulp.

***

It was one of the many ironies of Joe Louis that he excelled in an intentionally violent, primarily urban sport and he loved a totally peaceful, bucolic one. Since he began to play golf before the first Schmeling fight, he had been singularly devoted to the game. He played it steadily during his prewar glory years, whenever he could during his army days, and compulsively in the last half of his life. After his ring career ended it was common for him to tee off in the late morning and play eighteen holes at one country club and then do the same thing in the afternoon at another club. Or if he had a bad first eighteen, he would head to the driving range and hit buckets of balls. Sometimes, pounding ball after ball out toward the yardage markers, something would click. He would discover the secret, returning home happy, telling his wife, "Well, sweetheart, I *finally* got it today! After all these years playing golf, I just realized what I been doing wrong." Then the next day he would be ready to quit the fickle game. "But, honey, you told me yesterday you *had* it!" his wife would say. Joe would answer, "I *had* it, but I didn't *keep* it!"[2]

It was the story of his life. He *had* it but he didn't *keep* it. He let it slip away. It was like a driver with a slick, wet grip that he just couldn't keep in his hands. Between 1935 and 1945 Louis had it—a beautiful wife, the heavyweight title, money enough for several lifetimes. But he did not keep it.

When he took off his uniform in 1945 he was already deeply, irrevocably in debt. In 1942 the Internal Revenue Service had assessed him $117,000 on his 1941 income, an amount that remained frozen but unpaid during the war years. In 1942 he also owed Mike Jacobs $59,000 and John Roxborough $41,000, amounts that did not remain frozen. By the end of the war his debt to Jacobs had climbed to about $170,000, and he owed Marva $25,000 as part of their divorce settlement. Louis' estimated earnings between 1935 and 1942 were in the neighborhood of $4 million. Yet he began his new civilian career owing nearly $350,000—a figure that would soon shoot upward as a result of several disastrous investments and accounting decisions.

A number of people, from Roxborough and Julian Black to Jacobs and Marva to accountants and lawyers, helped Louis squander his fortune. But neither then nor later did he blame anyone but himself. He had spent the money, spent or given away every dollar he made and then asked for loans so that he could spend more. When the income of professional athletes began to skyrocket in the 1960s, a journalist asked Louis if he wished he could have held the title in the age of closed-circuit television and fabulous endorsement deals. "I ain't sorry I fought when I did," he answered. "In my time, I made $5,000,000, wound up broke, and owe the Government $1,000,000 in taxes. If I was fighting today, I'd earn $10,000,000, would still wind up broke, and would owe the Government $2,000,000 in taxes."[3] To his way of thinking, fighting when he did put him a million dollars ahead of the game.

In 1945 Louis was not trying to recoup his fortune. That was impossible, especially with the wartime tax codes with the top-end 90 percent rates in effect. He just needed to reduce his debt, and the only way to accomplish it was to go back into the ring. While in the Army he had "fought" hundreds of exhibition rounds, but they were for the troops. Louis and his boxing partners did not take the fighting seriously. It was not like real fighting or even real training, just going through the motions, pulling punches, and having a beer and a steak afterward. Louis was forty pounds over his best fighting weight, badly out of shape, and past his prime. Had he been at all concerned about his health and legacy, he would have retired. Instead, he went back into training.

When Jacobs began to consider who to match against Louis, he had few choices. Exciting new contenders had not emerged during the war when fighters had been expected to fight overseas against Nazis and Japanese, not in boxing arenas in the United States. The best match, as far as

Jacobs was concerned, was the fight that Americans had wanted to see since June 19, 1941—the rematch between Louis and Billy Conn. Jacobs had tried to arrange a rematch before the war but Conn had broken his hand on his father-in-law's head. Then, the promoter had attempted to arrange the fight after Pearl Harbor, but Secretary of War Henry L. Stimson had scuttled it because he believed the fighters, both now serviceman, would make unseemly amounts of money. But in 1946 both men were free of fathers-in-law and Stimson, and Jacobs set the date for June 19, 1946, in Yankee Stadium.

Louis went back into training, hating the grind of camp life. He talked to reporters more than he had before the war, perhaps simply to break the monotony of his daily routine. "He can run but he can't hide," he said of Conn.[4] But as it turned out, Conn could neither run nor hide. On a cool, pleasant night, under a starless sky, more than forty-five thousand spectators, paying close to $2 million, turned out for the match. The attendance and gate receipts were modest disappointments but were enormous by past standards. The fight was a disappointment by any standards. For seven rounds Louis plodded after a retreating, occasionally stumbling, Conn. It was as if Conn were trying to make up for the thirteenth round in their first fight by staying away from Louis in this one. He attempted few telling punches, landed almost none, and demonstrated to virtually everyone watching the match in Yankee Stadium or on television in bars in four selected cities that he had lost his prewar skills. In the eighth round, Louis, breathing heavily, finally caught Conn with several left-right combinations. Conn fell hard, stretching out on his back and rising to a knee only in time to hear referee Eddie Joseph say "ten."

"I'm convinced I haven't got it any more, so I'm quitting," Conn told reporters after the match.[5] And, save for a couple more matches of no consequence, he did. Louis, however, interpreted his victory differently, admitting that he was rusty but encouraged that he could still fight like a champion. He heard the spectators' boos during the first seven rounds but convinced himself that it took two men to make a good fight, and Conn had not held up his end. With more training, a few tune-up fights, he would be back in top form. Louis was always supremely confident. In the back of his mind he knew that if he kept fighting someday, against some younger fighter, he would lose. But he went into every fight thinking, "not this guy, never tonight."[6] He was still the champion, he rationalized, and his victories could still cause celebrations that snarled traffic in Harlem.

Three months after the Conn match, Louis fought Tami "The Bronx Barkeep" Mauriello, a relatively short heavyweight who was an aggressive fighter. It was an ideal match for Louis. Mauriello would come to fight and Louis would not look slow and awkward chasing him. True to form, Mauriello attacked from the opening bell, landing a right and hurting Louis. But the challenger was slow to follow up on his advantage. When he moved forward again, Louis hit him with a combination, knocking him to the canvas. Two knockdowns later The Bronx Barkeep was counted out. Mauriello was devastated by the loss, saying in a controversial live post-fight radio interview, "I got too god-damned careless," and then crying in his locker room, repeating, "The first god-damned round! The first god-damned round!"[7] Louis kept his composure. Later he recalled, "I really felt like my old self. I had complete control, energy, and power. I wonder sometimes if that wasn't my last great fight."[8]

It was not a great fight, though it was the last fight that allowed Louis to even think that he was still a great fighter. In his next match, journeyman fighter Jersey Joe Walcott revealed the truth. Born Arnold Raymond Cream, about as unpugilistic a name as can be imagined, Walcott's record did not inspire awe. He had been knocked out by Al Ettore and Abe Simon and lost decisions to more than a half dozen lesser fighters. In 1936 he had even served as one of Louis' sparring partners for the first Schmeling fight. Although a crafty boxer and a good counterpuncher, Walcott was simply not in the champion's class—at least before the war.

After the war was a different matter. Once again the champion went back into training, but it was not the same without Jack Blackburn, John Roxborough, and Julian Black. Blackburn was dead, Roxborough in prison, and Black and Louis had parted ways after a disagreement over a $25,000 loan (Louis wanted the loan and Black refused to give it). Louis' new trainer, Mannie Seamon, and manager, Marshall Miles, were devoted to him, but the mood of his postwar camp was different. Before the war, camp life had been fun. Someone was always playing a practical joke or telling an amusing story. Now there was no youthful joy. Louis was different as well. Training bored him—the 5 A.M. roadwork, bland diet, and monotonous routine. The Army had made him weary of a regimented life. And as the Conn fight showed, his skills had declined.

His reflexes were eroding as well. Dr. Robert C. Bennett, Louis' physician, noticed it first. While playing table tennis with Louis he observed that the fighter reacted more slowly to a ball hit to one side than to the other.

Further tests revealed evidence of reflexive deterioration. "Joe is through," Bennett told Miles. Concerned about his fighter, Miles advised Louis, "Quit now. You shouldn't fight anymore."[9] Championship boxing was no sport for a man whose heart was not in it. Louis considered the suggestion. Miles sensed that Louis knew he was right. But Louis decided to go through with the Walcott fight, though he later admitted, "I didn't feel like myself."[10]

When they met in Madison Square Garden on December 5, 1947, Walcott convincingly exposed Louis' decline. He knocked him down in the first round with a solid right, and sent him to the canvas again in the fourth round with an uppercut. He cut the champion's eye and mouth. Louis struggled to come back but was flat. "I didn't have the strength," he said. "I didn't have a punch that night. I was ashamed."[11] He later gave a convincing description of what it is like to be an over-the-hill fighter. "I could see the openings, but my right hand couldn't see them. The right wouldn't move out by itself like it had before. I had to tell it to move, and by then it was too late."[12]

All Louis could do was try. He pressed the fight, landing few substantial punches but making an impression on the judges. In the last few rounds Walcott fought not to lose, moving defensively and staying away from Louis' power. It was no way to win the heavyweight title. "A man knocks a champion down," Louis explained, "he's supposed to come after him. If he don't want the championship bad enough to come and get it, he don't want it bad enough to win it."[13] Still, when the bell rang at the end of the fifteenth round, Louis, feeling that he had lost, tried to leave the ring before the decision. His eyes and jaw were swollen, his head full of cobwebs and pain. Knowing that Louis would be disqualified if he left the ring, Marshall Miles made him stay. As boos rained into the ring, the announcer read the scorecards giving Louis the split decision. The judges agreed that the man who took Louis' crown would have to *take* it, heavyweight champion style. Immediately the switchboards at NBC studios began to light up with callers complaining about the decision and holding the network personally responsible. "I'm sorry, Joe," Louis told Walcott before he left the ring.[14] He was sorry for his performance—not the decision.

There were no more questions about Louis' ability. It was time to retire. Less than a week after the fight he sat in darkened room in apartment 8E, at 555 Edgecombe Avenue—an apartment building near where he had married Marva in 1935—with Barney Nagler, a sportswriter who had worked with Louis on several magazine articles. His left eye was still closed, his face misshapen, his pride deflated. The telephone rang and Louis tensed, like it was the sound of a bell for another round. He allowed it to ring. He was wearing a striped black-and-white bathrobe and was in a somber, reflective mood. "It was tough the other night," Nagler said. "I made it tough," Louis answered. "I saw openings I didn't use. Man get old, he doesn't take advantage of them things as fast." He said he wanted to fight Walcott again. "Next time I'll knock him out," he said, as though he was trying to convince himself. "I'll beat him and retire." Nagler, now eager to leave with his scoop, said, "It's a good story for me." "It's true," the champion said matter-of factly.[15]

Louis just did not want to leave the sport after such a pathetic effort. One more fight, and then he would hang up the gloves. In the rematch, Walcott again got off to a fast start, knocking the champion down in the third round. After that moment of excitement the two fighters feinted and moved or stood and held, subtle tactics that failed to please the forty-two thousand spectators in Yankee Stadium. Between several rounds referee Frank Fullam visited the corners and urged the two boxers to fight. In the tenth round Walcott, ahead on points, began to tire. In the eleventh round Louis landed a right to the jaw that "shook Walcott to the toes."[16] Finally, after twenty-five rounds over two fights, Louis had an opening. Moving close to the challenger he threw short, hard lefts and rights and forced him against the ropes. Walcott crossed his arms against his head in defense as Louis kept punching. A right to the jaw broke through Walcott's defense. He pitched forward, landing on his face and turning over to his back. At the count of seven he struggle to one knee, and with a blank, lost expression, he uncomprehendingly watched the referee finish the count. By the time he made it to his feet the fight was over, but Walcott did not know it.

It was Louis' twenty-fifth successful title defense, the twenty-second to end in a knockout. No heavyweight had defended his title more often; in fact, Louis had defended it seven times more than the previous eight champions combined. It was a magnificent record, and a nice round number to end on. He was too honest to deceive himself or anyone else. In his locker room after the fight reporters crowded about him and asked the inevitable question. "Yes," he answered. "That's my last fight. I've been around a long time and I think that it's about time to quit. And I'm glad to quit with the title still mine."[17]

Rumors that Louis planned to retire had circulated widely before the match, but now that the words were out of the champion's mouth, the sportswriters peppered him with questions. What about light heavyweight champion Gus Lesnevich? Would Joe fight him? Or Ezzard Charles of Cincinnati? "I'm retiring. Tonight's my last fight," the thirty-four-year-old champion insisted. "The last fight."[18]

***

Champions before Louis had said the same thing. They were done with boxing, through getting up for roadwork in the faintest early morning light, through pounding speed bags, heavy bags, and sparring partners, through having their brains scrambled and their faces cut, through pissing blood and enduring blinding headaches after tough fights. And most mean it—at the time. There was always the catch, however, the void between intention and action. After they retired, where did they apply for the job that paid hundreds of thousands of dollars for a single night's work? Where would they find another occupation that took place in a stadium filled with screaming, adoring fans? What position carried the same status at Toots Shor's as being the heavyweight champion of the world? Did Toots come over and embrace a banker or a bond salesman and say, "Anything you want, Champ. It's on the house."

Louis was not immune to the psychic rewards of being heavyweight champion, but even more importantly, he needed money to pay his mountainous debts to the IRS. With his purse in the Conn fight he had paid the money he owed to Jacobs, Roxborough, and Marva, but he had not made a dent in his tax bill, which, with interest, penalties, and additional irregularities, was growing daily. The champ in the ring was a chump when it came to taxes. He was understandably mystified by the entire process, and the advice he received was uniformly bad. For the September 1946 Mauriello fight, for instance, his manager told Jacobs not to pay Louis his $103,611 purse until January 1947. It was a tax ploy to shift the money from his 1946 to his 1947 taxes. When the IRS audited his 1947 return they disallowed the maneuver, creating more back taxes, penalties, and interest. Louis had spent his career receiving purses from which no taxes had been withheld and then spending the proceeds as if all the money was his. Paying taxes was something to be avoided, if not forgotten all together. Now he was being forced to pay the piper, who was going by the initials IRS.[19]

After the Walcott rematch Louis was open to any legal, and some shady, schemes to make money. He endorsed beer and cigarettes, something he had refused to do in the prewar years. He fought exhibitions across the United States, receiving payments above and below the table. He accepted virtually any offer, traveling as far as Mexico, Hawaii, and South America for boxing exhibitions or personal appearances. Louis lived on the road, played golf when he could, and permitted his financial advisors—who were often also his business partners—to make disastrous decisions on his behalf. From the soft drink Joe Louis Punch to the Joe Louis Restaurant and Bar in Harlem, his association with any business venture was tantamount to a kiss of death. Boxing was the only business that could hold his attention.

Louis even arranged to sell the heavyweight title. The deal was not with a person but with an organization, the International Boxing Club (IBC). The deal had a long, complex gestation period, but its essentials included: 1) Joe Louis, represented by an entity called Joe Louis Enterprises, Inc., would obtain an exclusive services contract with the four leading heavyweight contenders; 2) Louis would officially resign his title; and 3) Joe Louis Enterprises, Inc., would assign the exclusive services contracts to the newly formed International Boxing Club, headed by James Dougan Norris and backed by Arthur M. Wirtz, a millionaire owner of sporting venues in the Midwest. For their part in the deal, the IBC gave Louis 20 percent of the stock in the promotional corporation, $150,000, and an annual salary of $15,000 (later increased to $20,000). Those, in any case, were the reported amounts; there may also have been some unreported money that exchanged hands. The IBC would become infamous for transactions that took place off the books. In return, Louis provided the IBC with control of the heavyweight championship, a position they would use in the next half decade to gain a monopoly over professional boxing.[20]

***

And the best part of the deal was that Louis did not have to take a punch. He officially abdicated his crown on March 1, 1949, after eleven years and eight months as heavyweight champion and twenty-five title defenses. His life, however, did not change dramatically. He continued to box exhibitions, make personal appearances, play golf, and live as peripatetically as a hobo. He had no family life. In 1946 he had tried marriage again to Marva. But even though they had a son, Joe Louis Barrow, Jr., Joe was no better a husband the second time around than the first. In February 1949, Marva divorced him for the second and last time. "Much as I love

Joe," Marva said, "our marriage never worked simply because I never had a husband or a home I could really call mine."[21] That was a nice way of saying that she often did not know where Joe was or which woman he was with.

As his boxing career moved toward its natural conclusion, the sad truth of Joe Louis' life came into sharper focus. He remarked about Billy Conn, "He can run but he can't hide"—a line that cuts to the heart of his own personality. All his life Louis ran, relentlessly, moving constantly, from Alabama to Detroit, training camp to training camp, fight to fight, city to city, woman to woman. He never stopped. Between fights, when he could have stayed put, he didn't. After his boxing career ended, when he could have settled down, he wouldn't. He roamed compulsively.

He was equally compulsive about avoiding commitments. Marriage and family did not imply any sort of demand on him. He was a casual visitor in his own domestic circle. When he made it home for a few weeks he had been perfectly willing to share a part of his life with Marva—that is, between daytime rounds of golf and nighttime engagements with "friends." But Marva knew that at any moment, and without warning, he could disappear for days or weeks. He showed even less concern for his two children. He seemed to like them in a distant, abstract way, but he never allowed a birthday party or graduation ceremony to interrupt a golf game.

As Louis began to control his own schedule, it became clear that he would not adapt well to a nonregimented life. For most of the previous twenty years his days had been carefully planned by managers, trainers, promoters, and military officials. Now, at the age of thirty-five, he was making his own day-to-day decisions—and he had begun to drift. He was like Huck Finn—out on a raft, floating down his own private Mississippi River, staying free, avoiding commitments, distancing himself from women, children, and tax problems, always ready to light out for the wilderness of American irresponsibility.

"He can run but he can't hide." Joe said it, and in his bones he knew it was true. His marriage with Marva had been full of episodes of his being caught with other women. As he began to slow down in the ring, his opponents had caught him as well. Walcott had knocked him down, closed an eye, and bruised his face. Divorce ended his problems with Marva. Retirement spelled the end of batterings in the ring. But there was one problem that would not disappear, one trouble he could not run away from and hide: his tax bill. It kept growing, and IRS agents dogged him across the country. In 1950 the government finally examined his 1946 taxes and issued another lien, this one for $246,056 (roughly $2.2 million 2010 dollars). Nineteen forty-six, the year he fought Billy Conn and Tami Maurillo, had been the best moneymaking year of Louis' life. In two fights and various other endeavors, he had grossed more than $700,000 and netted $448,465 after paying manager's fees and other expenses. From this amount, he should have paid federal taxes of $362,048 and New York state taxes of $28,695, leaving him with $57,722, an admittedly disheartening percentage of the whole. But he had misreported his net income as $163,419 and paid only $115,992 in federal taxes, leaving an unpaid tax burden of $246,056.

The $246,056—call it a quarter million—did not include the back taxes he owed on his income from before 1946. Nor did it include the irregularities that the diligent government accountants would later discover in his 1947, 1948, and 1949 returns. In round figures, after the 1950 audit the IRS informed Louis that he owed $500,000 (roughly $4.5 million 2010 dollars). Not to put too fine a point on it, but in 1950 if the Internal Revenue Service had had a Top Ten Wanted List, Joe Louis would have been their equivalent of John Dillinger and Bonnie and Clyde. And sheepishly saying that he was broke and that he was sorry—terribly sorry—was not going to get him out of his jam. The IRS informed him in the strongest official language that they expected him to pay what he owed.

Only by returning to the ring could Louis even begin to settle his debt. In the summer of 1950 he announced his comeback, and the IBC immediately matched him against Ezzard Charles, the Cincinnati heavyweight who had defeated Jersey Joe Walcott in an elimination fight to claim the title. Louis had fought more than seventy-five exhibition matches since defeating Walcott in 1948, but he was in no shape to contend at a championship level. But Norris, the head of the IBC, was eager for an outdoor, financially lucrative bout. Charles, a small but talented heavyweight, suffered from comparisons to Louis, and his title defenses had been financial duds. If anyone could infuse badly needed glamour into the sport and revive the division, it was Louis, even an old, faded version of the original. As an acknowledgment of Louis' appeal, he received the champion's 35 percent share of the gate. The match was set for late September in Yankee Stadium, giving the thirty-six-year-old Louis only six weeks to train for the encounter.

Other great heavyweight champions had attempted to regain the title. All had failed. "They never come back," was the ring truism. But none had ruled the division like Louis, whom the bookmakers made a two-to-one favorite. But the former champion was not the exception to the rule. From the first round, Charles dominated the match. James P. Dawson of the *New York Times,* writing what he assumed would be the obituary to Louis' career, praised the great fighter's determination and heart but accurately noted his long absence from the ring. "Everybody knew his reflexes must have suffered. That's inevitable. Few suspected his coordination would be what it was, so amazingly lacking that it was non-existent."[22] In his prime, Louis' timing, balance, and hand speed had set a heavyweight standard. Against Charles he seemed to plod stiff-legged, like Boris Karloff in *The Mummy.* He looked unsteady, falling off balance into the ropes and stumbling as he threw awkward punches. He would laboriously set himself to throw a punch only to see Charles dance out of reach before he could let it go. He tried to block, slip, or pick off punches as he had done before the war, but he lacked the quickness. Instead, he stopped Charles' sharp punches with his face. By the middle rounds his face was battered. His nose was bleeding, his lips bruised, and both eyes were puffed, discolored lumps. He lasted to the final bell but lost a lopsided decision.

In his locker room after the fight, Louis soaked his left hand in a bucket of ice, though he did not seem to have landed a punch solid enough to have injured it. Then, slowly he began to dress, mumbling answers to questions in a low, tired voice. He thought Charles was a capable boxer, but not the best he had ever faced. He knew early that he could not win. "I just didn't have it," he said in way of an explanation. He added, politely but incongruously, "I enjoyed the fight and want to thank you all. I done my best." As for his future in boxing, there was none. "I'll never fight again. Positively."[23]

For Louis, everything about the fight was a disappointment. It was bad enough that he got beaten up, but he took the punishment in front of a small live audience for just over $100,000, not nearly enough to make a difference in his tax burden. Promoters blamed the pathetic turnout on television. About twenty-five million people watched the match, many more people than had seen Louis fight live during his entire career. Most had listened to radio broadcasts of Louis' classic fights, receiving an image of him painted by colorful broadcasters. In their minds, Louis was the real American Superman, a near flawless fighter who always caught and took out his opponent. What they saw on small, grainy, black-and-white televisions was an aging, balding fighter, a ponderous, plodding boxer who lacked grace and punching power. For millions of Americans, television smeared their memories of the once-magnificent champion. The dominant image of Louis, wrote Tim Cohane in *Look,* was of a "raked, swollen hulk, wearily, if gallantly and proudly, groping for the top ring rope."[24]

Once his body began to heal, Louis resumed his comeback as if he had never mumbled the word "positively." Old fighters are masters of the art of self-deception. They can explain away the most dismal performance. "I knew I'd gone back some, all right, but I never really believed I'd gone back as far as I had," Louis explained. "You can't do what you want in there, so you tell yourself that you trained down too fine or didn't train fine enough; that you ate too much the day of the fight or didn't eat enough. Mostly, you tell yourself that you just need one more fight to get your timing back."[25] Louis knew all the excuses, and maybe in the part of the mind that preserves an athlete's memories of their youth, he believed them. In a series of matches against second-rate heavyweights in late 1950 and the first half of 1951, he kept alive his dream of again fighting for the title.

The dream ended on the night of October 26 in Madison Square Garden. Louis' opponent was Rocky Marciano, a tough street-style brawler from Brockton, Massachusetts. Unlike Louis' other opponents since 1946, Marciano was a postwar fighter. His first professional match was in 1947, and since then he had fought and won thirty-seven times, all but five by knockouts. Most of his bouts had been against third-rate opponents, but he had recently begun to fight ranked boxers, promising fighters like Roland LaStarza, the darling of early television boxing, and Rex Layne. Marciano had outpointed LaStarza, knocked out Layne, and physically battered both. He was a study in contrasts. Almost nothing about him looked right for a heavyweight. He was too short, his arms were too stubby, his defense was too porous, and he had begun boxing too late in his life to master the finer points of the sport. Sportswriters tended to write him off, assuming that as he moved up in class, some ring-wise veteran would take him apart. But Marciano had qualities that balanced the scales. Relentlessly aggressive and unconcerned about taking punches, he had an overhand right like a club. When it made contact, it hurt. Fighters who blocked the punch with their arms or shoulders said it broke blood vessels, sapping their strength and destroying their will. Marciano was not the fighter Louis should have been facing in the twilight of his career.

Louis was Marciano's idol. He recalled growing up listening to Louis' matches on the radio and wildly daydreaming about fighting the champion for the title. As the two men stood next to each other receiving—but not listening to—the referee's instructions, Marciano looked at his idol. "I remember standing in the ring and thinking how big Louis was," he recalled. "I never remembered Louis being such a big guy. The top of my head seemed to just reach the bottom of his chin."[26]

But when the fight started, size seemed less important. For most of the first round the fighters moved cautiously in circles, judging their opponent's quickness, hand speed, and tendencies. Then, just before the round ended, Marciano landed an overhand right and Louis' legs buckled. He grabbed Marciano to keep from going down, and the bell mercifully ended the round. "Are you alright? Are you alright?" Mannie Seamon asked Louis in the corner, pressing ice to the back of the boxer's neck.[27] The answer was no, but it was too late to matter. In the opposite corner, Marciano's trainer was grinning. Thinking it over later, A. J. Liebling, the renowned boxing essayist, observed, "I think that punch was the one that made Joe feel old."[28]

After the first round, Louis began to exploit Marciano's rawness. His jab kept Marciano away from him, and an occasional right cross threw beads of sweat off Rocky's head. The jabs opened small cuts near Marciano's eyes. "It was like getting hit in the face with a hammer," Marciano recalled, but if so, it was a padded hammer.[29] The punches, Liebling wrote, "didn't sicken Marciano, as they had sickened Louis' opponents from 1935 to 1940."[30] Louis piled up points with his jabs but did not hurt Marciano, who seemed as fresh in the fifth round as he had been in the first. And while Marciano was losing most of the early rounds, he was winning the fight by wearing down the former champion and bruising him with sledgehammer shots to the arms, sides, and hips. In the fifth, Marciano landed a hard punch under Louis' heart, causing him to gasp for air. Joe had landed his best shots and had hardly made Rocky blink. Louis knew the fight was over. All that was left was "to go out like a man."

"In the sixth, things started to go sour," Liebling observed. "It wasn't that Marciano grew better or stronger; it was that Louis seemed to get slower and weaker. The spring was gone from his legs—and it had been only a slight spring in the beginning—and in the clinches Marciano was shoving him around." In the seventh, Marciano mauled Louis, landing punches to the arms and body and pushing him around the ring. Liebling thought—hoped, really—that Louis would last the fight. "Three rounds don't seem forever, especially when you're just watching."[31]

Before the eighth, Marciano's trainer said, "Get him now!"[32] Marciano's attack had taken its toll, and Louis' right hand had fallen further and further down, opening him to a left hook. Marciano knocked Louis down with that punch. Joe rose slowly, his face registering, ever so slightly, not pain or fear but a sort of infinite sadness, an ennui about his profession. Marciano moved toward Louis. He did not rush over excitedly, as is often the case, but he advanced like a seasoned workman with a job to perform. He pushed Louis against the ropes, his body rolling as he threw rights and lefts, Joe trying to fend off the punches. A left hook snapped Louis' head back and made his arms fall to his sides. For a moment—a fraction of a second—Louis' head fell to the left, resting on the top rope like he had decided to take a quick nap. At that moment, Marciano threw an overhand right, bouncing Louis' head off the rope and knocking him to the canvas.

"I saw the right coming, but I couldn't do anything about it," Louis said after the fight. "I was awfully tired."[33] The right knocked him most of the way through the ropes, and he landed on the ring apron, one leg dangling between the ropes and the bald spot on the back of his head facing spectators in ringside seats. He was done. His head lolled on the canvas as he rolled from right to left. Sportswriters supported his head to keep him from tumbling to the floor. Referee Ruby Goldstein, a friend of Joe's, waved his arms without a count, and then reached through the ropes to help him back inside the ring. In a moment, the ringside physician and his corner men were by his side, cradling him in a scene from some pugilistic pietà. Arthur Daley, in the lead of his next day's New York Times piece, wrote, "The moment everyone had dreaded finally arrived last night. . . . Old age and Rocky Marciano had simultaneously caught up with the old champion. He was the champion no longer, though. But he was, oh, so old." He concluded his story on the same note: "It had to happen some time and it happened last night."[34]

The heavily pro-Louis crowd was stunned by the finish. Sitting next to Liebling was a tall, blond woman who had come to the fight with a Marciano backer. As the fight began she yelled, "I hate him! I hate him! I think he's the most horrible thing I've ever seen." When Louis fell through the ropes she began to sob. "Rocky didn't do anything wrong," her date said. "He didn't foul him. What you booing." "You're so cold. I hate you, too," she replied.[35]

The blond spoke for much of America. It had to end this way, but few people wanted to see it. Joe Louis had become an American institution. He represented hope and courage for black Americans during the hardscrabble years of the Depression, and for all Americans during the worst dark days of World War II. His public image was one of decency, honor, strength, and patriotism. He was the country's black Uncle Sam. There seemed to be something terribly wrong about the sight of his balding head rolling on the ring apron.

The day after the fight, Arthur Daley considered what Louis had meant to America and boxing. The fight had been a "strange, unpleasant, nasty sort of dream," he wrote. "Joe Louis, the symbol of invincibility, of dignity, of class and of compelling majesty had suddenly vanished." And it was not just Louis that had vanished. So too had the youth of Americans who had thrived on his success since the night in 1935 when he knocked out Primo Carnera in his first New York fight. As long as Louis won, they stayed young. Daley reflected that perhaps he should write more about Marciano, that he should latch on to the rising star. But the dream of what Louis had been, back before the war and television, lingered. "This reporter has been carrying the torch for Joe much too long to start any new flirtation. It's still love. In this corner Louis losing is more important than Marciano winning."[36]

Daley, and scores of other sportswriters, expressed profound sadness over Louis' defeat. A great fighter—a great man—had fallen. Youth had been served. In their columns and their laments, race played no role. Long ago, it seemed, Louis' race had ceased to matter for them. There were no cheers for the Great White Hope, no idle anthropological speculations on the relative merits of whites and blacks, no hyperbole about Italian Americans and African Americans. The fact that Louis' run as an icon had begun with a fight in New York City against Primo Carnera and ended with another in the same city against Rocky Marciano—the simplistic symmetry of race and nation—played no part in their stories. The mainstream sportswriters, still almost all white, had accepted Joe Louis as a significant, endearing icon. He was, even in defeat, the abiding athletic symbol of their age.

***

Louis' locker room was a melodrama of tears. Mannie Seamon and Marshall Miles were both crying. So was Sugar Ray Robinson, who had come to comfort his friend. Even reporters, their voices breaking as they asked questions, choked back tears. Only Louis seemed untouched by the emotions of the moment. "What's the use of crying? The better man won," he said in a flat voice.[37] He accepted the end of his career like he accepted his tax troubles—it was what it was. With his left hand in an ice bucket, angry welts disfiguring his face, and his boxing career lying on the floor next to his frayed robe, he played the hand he had been dealt. As he compared Marciano to Schmeling, he paused for a moment and a faraway look came into his eyes. It had been a hell of a ride.

Louis was thirty-seven years old. Physically and financially he was in worse shape than when he took his first boxing lesson in Brewster Recreational Center. Then, he had nothing. Now, he had much less. In between he had had it all. He had come up from desperate poverty, made millions of dollars, walked down the avenues of America like a god, and heard his name praised from New York to California. Joe Louis, the champion of the world. He had been written about and talked about more than any athlete in America, maybe more than anyone in America. There could be no encore, not even a second act, to his life in the ring.

F. Scott Fitzgerald wrote of his fictional creation Tom Buchanan that he was "one of those men who reach such an acute limited excellence at 21 that everything afterward savors of anticlimax."[38] It is the common lament of great athletes. How do you replace the feeling that comes when eighty thousand people chant your name? What must Louis have felt like in the minutes, the hours, the days after the second Schmeling fight? In his prime, when he was defending his title every two or three months, the champion had developed a satisfying custom. The day after the fight he would show up at Mike Jacobs' Madison Square Garden office to pick up his check. He was not that interested in the money—it would be gone soon enough—but he enjoyed lounging on the promoter's large, red leather chair and fielding reporters' questions. He would smile, eat an apple, glance at the funnies in the paper, and try to explain what he had done in the fight. Although he never had exactly the right words, he would give them a glimpse of what it was like to be Joe Louis. Everyone was relaxed and happy. The previous day's anxieties were gone—the fight for Joe and the deadlines for the reporters. Louis loved those days of just the guys, softball questions, and all the good stuff off the record. And now it was all over, those afternoons of innocence and laughter.

Although there would be plenty of fine days—and nights—ahead, there would be more problems. The most immediate ones were financial. If he just had been broke it would not have been a tragedy. Joe Louis could still make money. He received $15,000 a year from the IBC just for allowing them to use his name, and he could pick up many thousands more for endorsing products, making personal appearances, or attending boxing matches. The name Joe Louis was a brand worth a small fortune. The problem was that he needed a gigantic fortune.

During the next few decades his debt grew at an astonishing rate. Not only was there the standard 6 percent interest charge, but audits of his 1947, 1948, 1949, and 1950 returns uncovered serious and expensive irregularities. Sixty-six thousand dollars deducted from one of his purses that he had paid to Marva "in lieu of alimony" was disallowed. (Evidently it would have been allowed if the wording had been "in lieu of alimony and support.") Thousands of dollars repaid to Jacobs had been deducted as "business expenses." When IRS officials investigated those "business expenses," they discovered receipts for mink coats, diamond rings, and other lesser baubles and bangles for the champion's legion of lovers. The tax people ruled that Louis was just repaying a loan that had nothing to do with any business they recognized. Louis' tax bill climbed higher as his ability to make money suddenly sank lower.

In 1950, before his return to the ring, he had received a bill for $246,056. In 1955, he received the bill for his 1949, 1950, and 1951 audits: $507,610 (roughly $4 million 2010 dollars). Trying to discover in 1956 exactly how much he owed from the various assessments, Louis wrote, "I owe the Government well over $1,000,000 in back taxes. I don't actually know how much the total is, and I don't think the Government does either. Almost every other week I seem to get a new bill."[39] The IRS was fairly certain that in 1957 he owed $1,243,097. By 1962, when a deal was reached between Louis and the IRS, he owed in excess of $1.3 million (in the ballpark of $10 million 2010 dollars). The deal was that the IRS tacitly acknowledged that Louis could never pay his tax bill and stopped harassing him for it. But the government did not officially forgive the debt. It was about $2 million when he died.

Attempts to recover the money between 1951 and 1962 made Louis' life a financial hell. Agents wrote him letters and called him on the phone. They attached trust funds set up for his daughter and son, and swooped in to garnish the lion's share of any money he earned. The people closest to Louis recalled that the constant tax headache took its toll on the former champion. "Joe wasn't much of a complainer," said Truman Gibson, "but, God, it got to him. It was depressing. If it hadn't gotten to him he wouldn't have been human."[40] At one point, with tears in his eyes, he told his friend Jesse Owens that the government was going to send him to jail.

In 1956 the need to make money sent Louis back into the ring—the wrestling ring. Promoter Ray Tabani made him a $100,000 guarantee to go onto the professional wrestling circuit. Like boxing, wrestling was one of the featured sports of the 1950s television schedule. Everyone knew it was all an act, but that did not matter. It was inexpensive programming, and it came with readymade heroes and villains; props and plots; drama, action, and suspense. Altogether, it satisfied the television trinity of advertisers, producers, and consumers. In the late 1940s and 1950s a number of former boxers cashed in on the act. Jack Dempsey regularly refereed wrestling matches, and "Two-Ton" Tony Galento and Primo Carnera were main attractions. Louis, the most popular athlete of his era, was a natural as a good guy.

It was fine with Louis. The money was good. "Beats stealing," he said to critics that called it demeaning.[41] But it was unsettling, a bit like Pavarotti singing in a striptease joint. Rose Morgan, whom Louis had married on Christmas Day in 1955, was definitely cold on the idea. "To me, Joe Louis was like the President of the United States," she told a journalist. "How would you like to see the President of the United States washing dishes? That's how I felt about Joe wrestling."[42]

In any case, Louis' wrestling career was short-lived. Early in a tour that saw him partnered with "bad guy," 320-pound Rocky Lee, either Joe or Rocky made a mistake. Lee jumped on Louis when Joe was not prepared, breaking several ribs and causing a cardiac contusion. After that injury Louis confined his wrestling activities to refereeing matches for $500 a night, decent money for a person who did not owe more than a million dollars to the government.

Arriving at middle age did not ease Louis' financial burdens or quiet his restlessness. He was still on the move, from one city to the next and from one small-time deal to another. Along the way there were plenty of late nights with his old boxing friends and his various lovers. In 1958 his marriage to Rose ended in an annulment. The next year he married Martha Jefferson, a successful Los Angeles lawyer. Martha was remarkably tolerant of Louis' lifestyle—the endless hours of television, golf, and nighttime activities—but she worried about him.

By the 1960s he had begun to change in subtle, hard-to-detect ways. In

1962 journalist Gay Talese began to investigate the former boxer for an *Esquire* piece entitled "Joe Louis: The King as a Middle-Aged Man." He discovered what virtually every other journalist had discovered long ago, a remarkably unaffected, decent, considerate, humorous man. Perhaps Talese expected to find Gallico's and Rice's "stalking tiger" or some other jungle beast or, perhaps, some punch-drunk, down-at-the-heels pug who could not mumble a coherent sentence. He had read stories of Louis standing up for Jimmy Hoffa and trying to do public relations work for Fidel Castro. "And so it was with some unexpected elation that I found Joe Louis to be an astute businessman in New York, a shrewd bargainer, and a man with a sense of humor often quite subtle." Illustrating his point about Joe's sense of humor, Talese recounted how a beautiful Harlem nightclub singer "swished right up to Louis and wiggled close to him." Without missing a beat, Louis said, "You get any closer, I gonna have to marry you." On another occasion when Talese complained about the price of a first-class ticket from New York to Los Angeles, Louis explained, "First-class seats are up in the front of the plane, and they get you to L.A. faster." Talese's observations were all true—as far as they went.[43]

What Talese and the other journalists did not see were the terrors that haunted Louis' nights. At some point in the late 1950s he had begun to use drugs. He was never very clear on the when and how, and by the early 1960s he probably did not know himself. Later he would claim that some woman —perhaps a prostitute, maybe a lover—he was involved with shot him up with heroin when he was asleep. It felt good, making him forget his tax troubles, the recent death of his brother Lonnie, and the other nagging problems of his life. And the cocaine, which came later, made him feel even better, like it was 1937 and he had just knocked out Jimmy Braddock to win the heavyweight championship. Rationalizing the use of drugs, Louis noted, "I kept telling myself that nothing could be wrong with feeling that good."[44] For most of the 1960s he was not an obvious drug user. He showed no signs of being strung out or addicted, but it was part of his world.

That world in the 1960s had increasingly become Las Vegas. It was the place where famous athletes mixed with movie stars, musicians, gamblers, and high rollers out for a good time. In no other place in America was the 1940s more alive in the 1960s than Las Vegas. There should have been signs at the airport and on the highway when you entered town: WELCOME TO LAS VEGAS. TURN YOUR WATCH BACK TWENTY YEARS. Frank Sinatra and Dean Martin, Nat "King" Cole and Sammy Davis, Jr., "Come Fly with

Me" and "Fly Me to the Moon," broads and blackjack, the Sands and the Tropicana—Las Vegas was a shrine to a time when Joe Louis was the Man. And like Joe himself, it was a town that didn't pass judgments. Run your scams, work your deals, risk it all, and accept the consequences. Las Vegas was the perfect spot for Joe Louis, and Joe Louis was the perfect man for Las Vegas. What gambler in what casino would not jump at the opportunity to shake hands and exchange a few words with the Champ? What member of the Rat Pack would refuse the Champ a favor? Refuse? Hell, he wouldn't even have to ask.

Ash Resnick, looking for all the world like the original model for the wise-guy clothing line, was Joe's man in Vegas. Resnick said he had met Joe when they were both inducted into the Army in 1942 on Governors Island. They had stayed in touch. Saw each other from time to time. In 1960 Resnick was running the casino at the Thunderbird, one of the few places that allowed blacks in the main rooms. It was where Sammy Davis, Jr., and Sonny Liston stayed when they were in town. When Joe was around, Resnick would give him a few thousand house dollars for gambling. It was no big deal. Louis, who always treated money like it was going out of fashion, could be counted on to lose every dollar back to the house. But having him at the tables, losing with such a carefree air and friendly smile, was great for business. Who wouldn't want to roll the bones next to Joe Louis?

When Resnick left the Thunderbird for Caesars Palace, he eventually gave Louis a permanent job as a greeter. It was a good deal—$50,000 a year in salary, house money to gamble with, nice place to live, all the golf he wanted, whatever spending money he needed—about anything, really, and Joe didn't even have to ask. Once again he was great for business. Everybody seemed to love Joe, and he was kind and generous with everyone. His decency became legendary. One time a middle-aged female tourist saw him in the lobby at Caesars, exclaiming, "I know you. You're Don Newcombe. My grandson will be thrilled to have your autograph." Not wanting to disappoint the woman, he took her pencil and autograph book, then turned to a friend and said quietly, "How do you spell Don Newcombe?"[45]

Billy Conn recalled another night when he was at Caesars with Louis talking about old times. "He had a pocket full of black chips and a pocket full of green chips," Conn explained. "A bum comes up to him. He gave him a black chip. I said, 'Why don't you give him a green chip?' A black chip's a hundred dollars and a green chip is twenty-five. He said, 'What the hell's the difference? I'm going to lose it anyway.' "[46] Resnick was right. What wasn't there to love about Joe Louis?

But during the same years—the late 1960s—Louis began to lose touch with reality. He was fine during the days, but the nights were something else. "They're after me. They're trying to kill me," he told his wife. When Martha asked who "they" were, Louis answered that it was the woman who gave him the shot of heroin (or at least some woman) and her Mafia contacts, and, maybe, Martha or whoever else was on his mind at the time. He was convinced that Mafia hit men, especially one known as just "the Texan," would probably use poison gas to do the job, so whether he was sleeping in his Los Angeles residence, his Las Vegas guest house, or a hotel on the road, he would tape cardboard over heating and air-conditioning vents and electrical outlets. One evening, Martha was shocked to see grease spots on the ceiling of a Miami hotel room where Joe was lodging. It was a brand new hotel. "I was stopping up the cracks," Louis explained. "The poison gas is coming through them." When she quizzed him further, he said, "I got this mayonnaise out of the refrigerator and smeared it over the cracks. They can't get gas through there."[47]

Even worse was what he had to do to sleep. Fearful of being killed in his bed, each night he built a cave out of mattresses, headboards, dressers, mirrors, and whatever else caught his fancy. Then he would crawl into the homemade cave, fully dressed, with his shoes on, and try to sleep. Of course he usually got very little sleep, worried as he was about "the Texan" and his cronies, who were watching him through the windows.

Eventually his paranoia plagued him during the daytime as well. Wherever he was, he thought people were spying on him. It began to concern Ash Resnick at Caesars. There were incidents. "A friend of Joe's was playing blackjack," Resnick remembered. "Joe was watching. This guy was playing for high stakes and Joe just stood near him, looking over his shoulder. Now there was this other fellow standing behind Joe, looking at the game, an absolute stranger. All of a sudden Joe turned around to the guy and says, 'I know you're following me. You better get out of here. I'll knock you right on your ass.' " A few days later he said the same thing to a woman watching several blackjack players. "I really got concerned, you know," said Resnick, "because I felt, God forbid, if any violence showed up in Joe, it was time to do something."[48]

By early 1970 Martha Jefferson Louis was feeling the same way. In

January she had gone to Birmingham with Joe to attend an induction ceremony at the Alabama Sports Hall of Fame. The previous year he had been the first man inducted into the recently created hall. Now it was the turn of one of Louis' best friends, track and field great Jesse Owens. Before the ceremony Owens visited Martha and Joe in their suite. He was surprised to hear Joe mumbling, "I ain't scared. I'm Joe Louis, heavyweight champion of the world. . . . I ain't scared."[49] Louis was in the process of detaching a vent to get inside an air-conditioning system. His room was a mess. The lamp had been taken apart, and the bed had been rearranged into some sort of tent. Lamps, bed, vents—Louis always followed the same order. Mess up, he indicated, and the poison gas would get him. He explained to Owens that the Texan was out there waiting for a chance to strike. Later, when she was alone with Owens, Martha told him that Joe was losing his mind.

Martha decided that she had to seek help for her husband. Taking advantage of a Colorado law that grants a probate court the authority to commit a person to a psychiatric hospital for a period of three months for observation, diagnosis, and treatment, Martha and Joe Louis Barrow, Jr., arranged for Louis to be placed in the Veterans Administration Hospital. On May 7, 1970, when the local sheriff and a few deputies arrived at Martha's Denver home to escort Louis to the hospital, he was suspicious. He claimed there was nothing wrong with him, and then tried to call President Richard Nixon to help him with the authorities. When he could not get through to Nixon, and several other delaying attempts failed, he went along quietly.

Even when he was in the hospital, struggling to find reality, Louis was easy to love. His major concern was the other patients. Every day Martha brought him five dollars' worth of fruit, which he passed out to the other patients as if he were Santa Claus. No patient seemed to listen as closely as Joe to the stories of the other patients during group sessions. "They talk a lot about suicide," he told a visitor. "But I think 90 percent of them think about getting back home with their families and back into life. And then you get some talking about suicide. . . . I tell each one, talk them out of the idea of trying suicide, give them hope they will be back with their family. I have a lot of discussions about that."[50] Sometimes, of course, Louis was too full of the heavy tranquilizer Thorazine to care about anything, but whenever he was thinking at all clearly, he would ask Martha to bring something extra special that one of the other patients needed.

The stay in the hospital and the medications helped. By January 1971 Louis was back at Caesars, a little slower and more apt to disappear mentally but in good enough shape to listen to other people tell him stories about his life. The kind of tales that began, "I remember the night you fought Schmeling." He had heard all the variations of the stories—listened to them thousands of times—but his ingrained decency allowed him to look as though he were honestly interested. It was funny what he remembered. Occasionally a man would approach and say that he had been part of a foursome with Joe on some golf course somewhere—not one of Joe's usual tracks. Suddenly Louis' eyes would brighten and he would say, "Oh, yeah, is so-and-so still the professional there? Give him my best." He would know the pro's name. It was locked in his memory. Other times, perhaps on a slow day, an old reporter would show up and Joe would talk for hours about the 1930s and 1940s, retelling all the classic tales of his life.[51]

Louis still got around the country some, showing up here and there for a major fight or some other event. His name still meant something, and wherever he was introduced, he received the loudest, longest ovation. Although outside of Las Vegas a new racial order had emerged—one Louis had helped to shape but was no longer a part of—people still revered the Champ. The sportscaster Howard Cosell recalled being on the same flight as Louis when the plane hit a patch of serious turbulence. Cosell felt like it was touch and go, that there was a chance that the plane could crash, killing everyone on board. The one thought that kept going through his mind was that he would not be in the headline of the story. Cosell would die and the headline would read, "Joe Louis Killed in a Tragic Plane Crash." Who could trump Joe Louis?

Louis' life unwound in the 1970s. Thorazine and other prescription drugs helped him through the days and nights. He played golf, enjoyed the sun on his face, played blackjack and shook hands at Caesars, and was surrounded by his friends. Several journalists wrote that Louis had become a glorified doorman, a sad, pathetic fixture of a racist society. But they missed the point. Louis did not feel sorry for himself. He honestly loved his job at Caesars. Every so often "the Texan" came looking for him, but not on a regular basis. All things considered, it was a good semi-retirement, until his heart started to fail.

In November 1977, Dr. Michael E. DeBakey, the renowned heart surgeon, operated on Louis' aortic valve. A stroke followed, leaving Louis confined to a wheelchair and in low spirits. He never really recovered. His heart continued to weaken, and in December 1980, physicians implanted a pacemaker. It kept him alive for several more months, time enough to be wheeled into a few more arenas to witness a few more fights. His skin, wrote Dave Kindred, was "yellow-gray, the color of old newspaper clippings."[52] Louis had become a clipping, a memory, an artifact of another time. A decade before Barney Nagler had written, "He is a man of history, transcending time, reaching beyond the limits of the sports world in which he first became famous."[53] That may have been true—but what remained in the wheelchair was more history than man, and the pained expression on his face seemed to say that he knew it.

On April 11, 1981, Louis attended the Larry Holmes–Trevor Berbick heavyweight title match at Caesars. Sitting in a wheelchair, a big cowboy hat on his ancient head, he looked as out of place at a sporting event as a man in a blue-and-white seersucker suit at Studio 54. The following morning he died of a heart attack. He had been lingering for years, but this time he went quickly.

In the next few days, sportswriters, athletes, politicians, and other pundits wrote about Joe Louis' greatness. "Not once in 66 years was he known to utter a word of complaint or bitterness or offer an excuse for anything," wrote Red Smith.[54] Ira Berkow steered away from platitudes and just reminisced. He recalled a time when a major league baseball player, a sportswriter, and Louis shared a cab to Grand Central Station, where all three were catching a train for an awards dinner in Rochester. Louis took the front seat and the other two settled into the back seat. It was in the sixties, before long hair came into vogue, and the baseball player spouted loud cracks about the length of the young cab driver's hair. Louis said nothing and stared straight ahead. The ballplayer complained about "hippies" and "sissies," and the weird music playing on a portable radio in the front seat. Louis stared straight ahead. "Hey," the ballplayer finally demanded, "turn that damn hippie music off."

Quietly, without turning around, Louis said, "That's Greek music."[55]

***

For the sending-off ceremony celebrating the life of Joe Louis, his body was placed in a copper casket and displayed in a ring at the Sports Pavilion of Caesars Palace, the same arena where he had watched Holmes outpoint Berbick a few nights before. It was fitting. "I insisted on having the service in the ring, because Joe's life was in the ring. He would have wanted it that way," Martha said. "It seemed appropriate." Louis had achieved fame and won a fortune in the ring. It was at the center of the Madison Square Garden ring where in 1942 Louis had said, "We'll win because we're on God's side."[56]

Three thousand people gathered for the ceremony.[57] Frank Sinatra, who quietly picked up the tab, said a few Chairman of the Board words: "It's kind of nice to know that the man who never rested on canvas now sleeps on clouds." Sammy Davis, Jr., sang "Here's To the Winners," and Dannibelle Hall added a gospel rendition of "Bridge Over Troubled Waters." Jesse Louis Jackson—born in 1941, a few months after the Louis-Conn fight, and named for Jesse Owens and Joe Louis—delivered a stirring eulogy. Standing at a podium in the middle of the ring, directly behind Louis' casket, Jackson's voice cut through the somber atmosphere. "This is not a funeral, this is a celebration. . . . We are honoring a giant who saved us in a troubled time," he began. Moving into his familiar rhetorical style, Jackson said, "With Joe Louis we had made it from the guttermost to the uttermost; from the slave ship to the championship. Usually the champion rides on the shoulders of the nation and its people, but in this case, the nation rode on the shoulders of the hero, Joe."

Jackson continued, reviewing Louis' career—his fight against Schmeling, his service to the nation, but most of all, what the fighter meant to millions of black Americans struggling in a land too often lacking in equality and opportunity. "God sent Joe from the black race to represent the human race. He was the answer to the sincere prayers of the disinherited and dispossessed. Joe made everybody somebody. . . . Joe, we love your name." Moving toward the end of his oration, Jackson stood tall, pushed out his chest, physically swelling with pride, and proclaimed, "We all feel bigger today because Joe came this way. He was in the slum, but the slum was not in him. Ghetto boy to man, Alabama sharecropper to champion. Let's give Joe a big hand clap. This is a celebration. Let's hear it for the champ. Let's hear it for the champ!"

Three thousand people were on their feet, clapping, cheering, waving, and shouting, following Jackson's exhortations, giving Louis his final ovation. "Joe, we love your name," he repeated. "Let's give the champ a big hand."[58]

***

They buried Joe Louis in Arlington National Cemetery, a long way from the shack in Alabama where he had been born. A military guard fired three rifle volleys across his coffin. Then a minister, drawing from the New Testament, said: "I have fought the good fight. I have finished the race. I have kept the faith." Several hundred people showed up for the burial. Some were boxing celebrities—Billy Conn and Jersey Joe Walcott, Joe Frazier and Muhammad Ali among them. But most were people who just wanted to say goodbye to a man they had never met, a man they knew only from stories. "I remember my mama crying when Joe lost to Max Schmeling in 1936," said a seventy-two-year-old black man. "We were all gathered around the radio, and she said, 'There goes the savior of our race!'"[59]

The old sportswriters, the men who had covered Louis in his prime, wrote their columns, extolling the dead king. They all loved him, this hero of their youth. They wrote about how good and decent he had been, about his sense of humor and his legendary generosity. But they also wrote about his greatness as a fighter. Joe had been the heavyweight champion, Red Smith noted, "in an era when heavyweight champion of the world was, in the view of many, the greatest man in the world."[60] The title was shorthand for masculinity itself, the incarnation of what it meant to be a man. And Joe Louis had not just been a heavyweight champion. He had been *the* heavyweight champion, reigning for twelve years and defending his title twenty-five times. Harry Markson, a matchmaker at Madison Square Garden who had seen virtually all the great champions, wrote that Louis "was the best I ever saw in close to a half century in the boxing business."[61]

The younger sportswriters mostly said nothing about the passing of Joe Louis, or worse yet took cheap shots at what they considered his sad post-boxing life and his garish Las Vegas memorial service. For them, Louis had lived past his time, like the unlucky runners in A. E. Housman's poem "To an Athlete Dying Young" whose "name died before the man." A new sort of black athlete had emerged to dominate the scene. Proud, articulate, defiant athletes, represented by basketball players Bill Russell and Oscar Robertson, runners John Carlos and Tommie Smith, baseball players Curt Flood and Bob Gibson, football player Jimmy Brown, and tennis player Arthur Ashe. And, of course, Muhammad Ali—the proudest, most articulate, and most defiant of them all. For the younger sportswriters Ali was *the* heavyweight champion. For them, Joe Louis was a relic of another time and another America.

And so he was. Louis had seldom taken intractable public stands on the racial issues of his day. Occasionally he worked behind the scenes for change, but mostly he just kept his mouth shut and allowed his performance to speak for itself. He was a man of action, not words. What he did in the ring spoke more eloquently of equality than anything he could possibly have said. And no black American living in the 1930s and 1940s could have missed the meaning of his victories. In celebrating Louis' victories over Carnera, Baer, Braddock, and Schmeling, they were rejoicing in the destruction of Jim Crow myths of racial superiority. Joe's quiet dignity, the hint of a smile that occasionally cracked his public face, said it all. He was a stone-hard man—a man, not a "boy," the heavyweight champion of the world.

Joe Louis died less than three month after Ronald Reagan became president of the United States. It was a time before the notion of the Greatest Generation had taken shape, let alone received the name from Tom Brokaw. But as much as any man, Joe Louis was a hero and symbol of that generation, a man who had known the poverty of the Great Depression and had done his duty during World War II, a man who had come from nowhere Alabama and become the "king of the world." As much as Franklin D. Roosevelt, he gave hope to Americans during a troubled time.

NOTES

Preface

Epigraph: Ernest J. Gaines, *The Autobiography of Miss Jane Pittman* (1971), 203.

1 For the Lipsyte story, see Interview with Robert Lipsyte; Thomas Hauser, *Muhammad Ali: His Life and Times* (1991), 80.

2 Eldridge Cleaver, *Soul on Ice* (1968), 85.

3 Jules Tygiel, *Baseball's Great Experiment: Jackie Robinson and His Legacy* (1983), 75.

4 Hans J. Massaquoi, *Destined To Witness: Growing Up Black in Nazi Germany* (1999), 114–124.

CHAPTER 1 A Land Without Dreams

Epigraph: Hazel Rowley, *Richard Wright: The Life and Times* (2001), 250.

1 For Smith's comments, see *American Experience: The Fight* (PBS, 2004); Ronald K. Fried, *Corner Men: Great Boxing Trainers* (1991), 126–127.

2 Nat Fleischer, *"Jolting Joe" and "Homicide Hank,"* vol. 2 of *Black Dynamite: The Story of the Negro in the Prize Ring from 1782 to 1938* (1938), 12.

3 Interview with Nat Fleischer.

4 For Louis' trip back to his birthplace, see Joe Louis, as told to Meyer Berger and Barney Nagler, "My Story—Joe Louis," *Life*, November 8, 1948, 127.

5 Ibid., 128.

6 Greil Marcus, *Mystery Train: Images of America in Rock 'n' Roll Music* (3rd ed., 1990), 126.

7 For early Alabama stories of Louis, see Floyd Tillery, "Untold Chapters of the Life of Joe Louis," *Ring*, May 1936, 12–15.

8 Quoted in C. Vann Woodward, *The Strange Career of Jim Crow* (3rd rev. ed., 1974), 68.

9 Ibid., 68–69.

10 Melton A. McLaurin, *Separate Pasts: Growing Up White in the Segregated South* (1987), 21.

11 Quoted in Melvyn Stokes, *D. W. Griffith's* The Birth of a Nation: *A History of "The Most Controversial Motion Picture of All Time"* (2007), 278. The book provides an insightful treatment of all aspects of the film.

12 Quoted in ibid., 111.

13 Quoted in Dan Streible, *Fight Pictures: A History of Boxing and Early Cinema* (2008), 257.

14 Louis R. Harlan, ed., *The Booker T. Washington Papers*, vol. 3 (1974), 586.

15 Louis, "My Story," 129–130.

16 Joe Louis with Edna and Art Rust, Jr., *Joe Louis: My Life* (1978), 9.

17 Tillery, "Untold Chapters of the Life of Joe Louis," 12–15.

18 Ibid.

19 Quoted in Richard Bak, *Joe Louis: The Great Black Hope* (1996), 11.

20 Blind Arthur Blake, "Detroit Bound Blues," 1928.

21 Louis, "My Story," 130.

22 Ibid.

23 John W. Roxborough, "How I Discovered Joe Louis," *Ebony*, October 1954, 65.

24 Louis, "My Story," 130.

25 Ibid.

26 Louis, *Joe Louis*, 20.

27 Louis, "My Story," 132.

28 Louis, *Joe Louis*, 20.

29 Dave Anderson, *In the Corner: Great Boxing Trainers Talk About Their Art* (1991), 228–229.

30 Ibid., 229.

31 Ibid., 232.

32 Bak, *Joe Louis*, 36.

33 Louis, *Joe Louis*, 29.

34 Ibid., 32.

35 Quoted in Bak, *Joe Louis*, 42; Roxborough, "How I Discovered Joe Louis," 66.

36 Truman K. Gibson, Jr., with Steve Huntley, *Knocking Down Barriers: My Fight for Black America* (2005), 72.

37 Louis, *Joe Louis*, 34.

38 Quoted in Ronald K. Fried, *Corner Men: Great Boxing Trainers* (1991), 113.

39 Ibid., 117.

40 Gibson, *Knocking Down Barriers*, 72.

41 Ibid.

42 Fried, *Corner Men*, 129.

43 Quoted in ibid., 121.

44 Ibid.

45 Quoted in Chris Mead, *Champion Joe Louis: Black Hero in White America* (1985), 4.

46 Quoted in Fried, *Corner Men*, 121–122.

47 Ibid., 130.

48 Ibid., 129–130.

49 Quoted in Mead, *Champion Joe Louis,* 6.

CHAPTER 2 **Emperors of Masculinity**

Epigraph: Joyce Carol Oates, *On Boxing* (1972), 72.

1 Dale A. Somers, *The Rise of Sports in New Orleans, 1850–1900* (1972), 185.

2 Elliott J. Gorn, *The Manly Art: Bare-Knuckle Prize Fighting in America* (1986), 144.

3 Quoted in ibid., 152.

4 Quoted in Adam J. Pollack, *John L. Sullivan: The Career of the First Gloved Heavy-weight Champion* (2006), 40.

5 Quoted in Gorn, *Manly Art,* 215

6 Michael T. Isenberg, *John L. Sullivan and His America* (1988), 206.

7 Ibid., 244; " 'John L.,' Last of the Bare-Fisted Fighters of the Ring," *Literary Digest,* February 23, 1918, 60.

8 Vachel Lindsay, "John L. Sullivan, the Strong Boy of Boston," *New Republic,* July 16, 1919, 357–358.

9 Except where noted, for details of the Sullivan-Kilrain fight, see Pollack, *John L. Sullivan,* 170–198; Isenberg, *John L. Sullivan and His America,* 257–280.

10 *New York Times,* July 9, 1889.

11 Quoted in Isenberg, *John L. Sullivan and His America,* 318.

12 Gorn, *Manly Art,* 227.

13 Theodore Dreiser, *A Book About Myself* (1922), 150–151.

14 Theodore Roosevelt, "The Strenuous Life," Speech Before the Hamilton Club, Chicago, April 10, 1899, in *The Strenuous Life: Essay and Addresses* (1900), 8, 20–21; also see John Higham, *Writing American History: Essays on Modern Scholarship* (1970), 78.

15 Quoted in Isenberg, *John L. Sullivan and His America,* 276.

16 Theodore Roosevelt, *Theodore Roosevelt: An Autobiography* (1913), 42.

17 Quoted in Joseph R. Ornig, *My Last Chance to Be a Boy: Theodore Roosevelt's South American Expedition of 1913–1914* (1994), 3.

18 Quoted in Somers, *Rise of Sports in New Orleans,* 160.

19 Eldridge Cleaver, *Soul on Ice* (1968), 85.

20 Quoted in Isenberg, *John L. Sullivan and His America,* 301.

21 Theodore Roosevelt, "The Recent Prize Fight," *Outlook,* July 16, 1910, 550–551.

22 Quoted in Al-Tony Gilmore, *Bad Nigger! The National Impact of Jack Johnson* (1975), 27.

23 Quoted in Richard Broome, "The Australian Reaction to Jack Johnson, Black Pugilist, 1907–9," in Richard Cashman and Michael McKerman, eds., *Sports in History: The Making of Modern Sporting History* (1979), 352–353.

24 Quoted in Geoffrey C. Ward, *Unforgivable Blackness: The Rise and Fall of Jack Johnson* (2004), 123.

25 *San Francisco Call,* December 27, 1908.

26 Quoted in Randy Roberts, *Papa Jack: Jack Johnson and the Era of White Hopes* (1983), 63.

27 Quoted in Broome, "Australian Reaction to Jack Johnson," 356.

28 Quoted in Gilmore, *Bad Nigger!* 32.

29 Quoted in Ward, *Unforgivable Blackness,* 132.

30 *San Francisco Call,* December 27, 1908.

31 Ken Burns, *Unforgivable Blackness* (PBS, 2005).

32 Ward, *Unforgivable Blackness,* 409.

33 Variations of the folk tales are still told today. See discussion in Williams H. Wiggins, "Jack Johnson as Bad Nigger: The Folklore of His Life," *Black Scholar* (January 1971): 4–19.

34 Burns, *Unforgivable Blackness.*

35 John Lardner, *White Hopes and Other Tigers* (1951), 27.

36 *Current Literature,* June 1910, 606–607; Roberts, *Papa Jack,* 97.

37 Quoted in Ward, *Unforgivable Blackness,* 164–165.

38 Ibid., 211.

39 Ibid., 213.

40 *Literary Digest,* July 16, 1910, 85; Roberts, *Papa Jack,* 110.

41 Quoted in Gilmore, *Bad Nigger!* 48.

42 *Independent,* July 7, 1910, 85.

43 Quoted in Gilmore, *Bad Nigger!* 71.

44 62nd Cong., 2nd sess., *Congressional Record* (July 19, 1912): 9305; also see Dan Streible, *Fight Pictures: A History of Boxing and Early Cinema* (2008), 245.

45 For the reaction to Johnson's marriage see Roberts, *Papa Jack,* 158–160; "Messrs. Blease and Johnson," *Crisis,* January 1913, 123–124; 62nd Cong., 3rd sess., *Congressional Record* (January 30, 1913): 502–504.

46 Quoted in Gilmore, *Bad Nigger!* 121.

47 Quoted in Ward, *Unforgivable Blackness,* vii.

48 Ibid., 381.

49 Joe Louis with Edna and Art Rust, Jr., *Joe Louis: My Life* (1978), 35–36.

50 For the shaping of Louis' image see Mead, *Champion Joe Louis,* 51–55.

51 From Langston Hughes, "Joe Louis," *Montage of a Dream Deferred* (1951), quoted in Kasia Boddy, *Boxing: A Cultural History* (2008), 282.

52 For the Louis-Kracken fight, see Louis, *My Life,* 37–38.

53 *Ring,* March 1935, 50.

CHAPTER 3 **Tethered by Civilization**

Epigraph: Langston Hughes, "Harlem," in Arnold Rampersad, ed., *The Collected Works of Langston Hughes,* vol. 3: *The Poems: 1951–1967* (2001), 74.

1 *New York Herald Tribune,* May 16, 1935.

2 *New York Times,* May 16, 1935.

3 James Thurber, "New York in the Third Winter," *Fortune,* January 1932, 41.

4 Horace Gregory, "Dempsey, Dempsey," *Poems, 1930–1940* (1941).

5 Nat Fleischer, *"Jolting Joe" and "Homicide Hank,"* vol. 2 of *Black Dynamite* (1938), 31.

6 Barney Nagler, *James Norris and the Decline of Boxing* (1964), 9.

7 Interview with Dan Daniel.

8 Daniel M. Daniel, *The Mike Jacobs Story* (1949), 36.

9 Ibid., 39.

10 Quoted in Nagler, *James Norris and the Decline of Boxing,* 10.

11 Barney Nagler, *Brown Bomber: The Pilgrimage of Joe Louis* (1972), 43. *American Experience: The Fight* (PBS, 2004).

12 *New York Times,* March 30, 1935.

13 Ibid., March 10, 1935.

14 Paul Gallico, *Farewell to Sport* (1937), 57–58.

15 *New York Times,* June 30, 1933.

16 Ibid., June 15, 1934.

17 Gallico, *Farewell to Sport,* 66.

18 *Chicago Tribune,* September 15, 1923.

19 Wilbur Wood, "Hardly a Circus Freak," *Ring,* July 1934, 4–5.

20 Nat Fleischer, "The Black Menace," *Ring,* May 1935, 14.

21 Ibid., 45.

22 *Milwaukee Journal,* June 1935, Joe Louis Scrapbooks, Archives Center of the National Museum of American History, Smithsonian Institution (hereafter JLS).

23 Eugene S. McCarthy, "Alliteration on the Sports Page," *American Speech* 13 (February 1938): 30–34.

24 *New York Times,* April 13, 1981.

25 *Detroit News,* June 25, 1935.

26 *New York Evening Journal,* June 6, 1935.

27 *New York Sun,* May 17, 1935.

28 John Hope Franklin, *From Slavery to Freedom: A History of Negro Americans* (1974), 365.

29 *Buffalo Courier,* June 25, 1935.

30 Joe Louis with Edna and Art Rust, Jr., *Joe Louis: My Life* (1978), 58.

31 *New York World Telegram,* June 25, 1935.

32 Ibid., May 17, 1935.

33 Ibid., June 25, 1935.

34 Reprinted in Mark Naison, "Lefties and Righties: The Communist Party and Sports During the Great Depression," *Radical America* 13 (1979): 46.

35 *New York Times,* June 26, 1935.

36 Ibid.

37 Ibid.

38 *Cleveland Press,* June 28, 1935.

39 "Harry Balogh Sports Memorial Day," STL All Sports (online).

40 *Boston Herald,* June 26, 1935.

41 *New York Times,* June 26, 1935.

42 *New York Sun,* June 26, 1935.

43 *New York Times,* June 26, 1935.

44 *San Francisco Chronicle,* June 26, 1935.

45 JLS; quoted in Frederic Mullally, *Primo: The Story of "Man Mountain" Carnera, World Heavyweight Champion* (1991), 156.

46 *New York Sun,* June 26, 1935.

47 *St. Louis Star-Times,* June 26, 1935.

48 *San Francisco Chronicle,* June 26, 1935.

49 *New York Times,* June 26, 1935.

50 *Pittsburgh Courier,* June 29, 1935.

51 For the reaction of Harlem to the fight, see *New York World Telegram,* June 26, 1935; *New York Times,* June 26, 1935.

52 *Pittsburgh Courier,* June 29, 1935.

53 Ibid.

54 *Baltimore Evening Sun,* June 26, 1935.

55 *Boston Transcript,* June 26, 1935.

56 *New York Times,* June 27, 1935.

57 Ibid.

58 *Birmingham News,* June 28, 1935.

59 *Cleveland Press,* June 28, 1935.

60 Ibid.

CHAPTER 4 He Belongs to Us

Epigraph: Quoted in Lawrence W. Levine, *Black Culture and Black Consciousness: Afro-American Folk Thought from Slavery to Freedom* (1977), 424.

1 Miles Davis and Quincy Troupe, *Miles, the Autobiography* (1989), 19.

2 Meyer Berger, "Portrait of a Strong, Very Silent Man," *New York Times Magazine,* June 14, 1936.

3 *Chicago Tribune,* September 25, 1935.

4 Paul Gallico, *Farewell to Sport* (1937), 275, 285.

5 *Pittsburgh Courier,* January 4, 1936.

6 Interview with Jack Dempsey.

7 Quoted in W. C. Heinz, "Most Fighters Are Scared," *Saturday Evening Post,* June 24, 1950, 36–37.

8 Jeremy Schaap, *Cinderella Man: James J. Braddock, Max Baer, and the Greatest Upset in Boxing History* (2005), 268.

9 Interview with Truman K. Gibson, Jr.

10 *Omaha World-Herald,* September 24, 1935.

11 Berger, "Portrait of a Strong, Very Silent Man."

12 *Boston Globe,* September 25, 1935.

13 Ibid.

14 *Washington Post,* September 26, 1935.

15 *Los Angeles Times,* September 25, 1935.

16 *Washington Post,* September 26, 1935.

17 Quoted in Richard Bak, *Joe Louis: The Great Black Hope* (1998), 95.

18 For Richard Wright's reaction to the fight, see Richard Wright, "Joe Louis Uncovers Dynamite," *New Masses,* October 8, 1935, in Ellen Wright and Michel Fabre, *Richard Wright Reader* (1997), 31–35.

19 *New York Amsterdam News,* September 28, 1935.

20 *New York American,* September 26, 1935.

21 *New York Amsterdam News,* September 28, 1935.

22 *Binghamton Press,* September 25, 1935; *Washington Post,* September 25, 1935.

23 *New York Daily News,* September 25, 1935.

24 *New York Amsterdam News,* September 7, 1935.

25 Ibid., October 19, 1935.

26 Ibid., September 28, 1935.

27 Ibid., August 24, 1935.

28 Wright, "Joe Louis Uncovers Dynamite," 34.

29 Quoted in Susan J. Douglas, *Listening In: Radio and the American Imagination* (1999), 208.

30 For Maya Angelou's reaction to a Joe Louis fight, see Maya Angelou, *I Know Why the Caged Bird Sings* (1969), 110–115.

31 For Joe Louis in blues songs, see Rena Kosersky, *Joe Louis: An American Hero* (2001), Rounder Records. The CD liner notes contains lyrics of the songs.

32 Martin Luther King, Jr., *Why We Can't Wait* (1964), 100–101.

33 *New York Amsterdam News,* May 30, 1936.

34 Levine, *Black Culture Black Consciousness,* 420–440.

35 Quoted in Bak, *Joe Louis,* 116.

36 Langston Hughes, "Mother to Son," in Arnold Rampersad, ed., *The Collected Works of Langston Hughes,* vol. 1: *The Poems* (2001), 60.

37 *Chicago Defender,* July 13, 1935.

38 *New York Evening Journal,* September 25, 1935.

39 Joe Louis with Edna and Art Rust, Jr., *Joe Louis: My Life* (1978), 73.

40 Ibid.

41 *Variety,* January 5, 1938.

42 Quoted in Frederick V. Romano, *The Boxing Filmography: American Features, 1920–2003* (2004), 187.

43 Louis, *Joe Louis,* 81.

44 *New York American,* September 26, 1935.

45 *Washington Post,* September 26, 1935.

46 *American Experience: The Fight* (PBS, 2004).

47 Adolf Hitler, *Mein Kampf,* trans. Ralph Manheim (1972), 410.

48 For an insightful treatment of boxing in Nazi Germany, see David Margolick, *Beyond Glory: Joe Louis vs. Max Schmeling, and a World on the Brink* (2005), 34–58.

49 Ibid., 30.

50 Max Schmeling as told to Paul Gallico, "This Way I Beat Joe Louis," *Saturday Evening Post,* August 29, 1936, 7.

51 Unless otherwise noted, for Schmeling's story of his strategy for fighting Louis and his first bout with Louis, see Schmeling, "This Way I Beat Joe Louis," *Saturday Evening Post,* August 19, 1936, 5–7, 40–41; September 5, 1936, 10–11, 32, 34.

52 *Chicago Defender,* June 6, 1936.

53 *New York World Telegram,* June 12, 1936.

54 Louis, *Joe Louis,* 83.

55 Ibid.

56 *New York Evening Journal,* June 17, 1936.

57 *New York Sun,* June 18, 1936.

58 Ibid.

59 *New York Herald Tribune,* June 21, 1936.

60 *New York American,* May 18, 1936.

61 Max Schmeling, *Max Schmeling: An Autobiography* (trans. and ed. George von der Lippe, 1998), 117.

62 Paul Gallico's introduction to Schmeling, "This Way I Beat Joe Louis," September 5, 1936, 10.

63 *Pittsburgh Press,* June 20, 1936.

64 Louis, *Joe Louis,* 87.

65 *Pittsburgh Press,* June 20, 1936.

66 *American Experience: The Fight.*

67 *San Francisco Examiner,* June 20, 1936.

68 Lena Horne with Richard Schickel, *Lena* (1965), 75–76.

69 *American Experience: The Fight.*

70 Quoted in Margolick, *Beyond Glory,* 160.

71 *New York Times,* June 20, 1936.

CHAPTER 5 **King Louis I**

Epigraph: Quoted in David Margolick, *Beyond Glory: Joe Louis vs. Max Schmeling, and a World on the Brink* (2005), 11.

1 *Daily Oklahoman,* June 21, 1936.

2 *New York Times,* June 21, 1936.

3 *Dallas Morning News,* June 20, 1936.

4 *New York Sun,* June 20, 1936.

5 Ibid., June 22, 1936.

6 For the southern reaction to the first Louis-Schmeling fight, see Lane Demas, "The Brown Bomber's Dark Day: Louis-Schmeling I and America's Black Hero," *Journal of Sport History* 31 (Fall 2004): 253–271; Jeffry T. Sammons, *Beyond the Ring: The Role of Boxing in American Society* (1988), 105–111.

7 Sammons, *Beyond the Ring,* 108.

8 *Chicago Defender,* June 27, 1936.

9 *Pittsburgh Courier,* July 11, 1936.

10 Ibid.

11 Rena Kosersky, *Joe Louis: An American Hero* (2001), Rounder Records. The CD liner notes contain lyrics of the songs.

12 *New York Amsterdam News,* July 4, 1936.

13 Ibid.

14 *Detroit Free Press,* June 21, 1936.

15 Langston Hughes, *I Wonder as I Wander,* in Arnold Rampersad, ed., *The Collected Works of Langston Hughes,* vol. 14 (2001), 307.

16 *Detroit Free Press,* June 21, 1936.

17 Joe Louis with Edna and Art Rust, Jr., *Joe Louis: My Life* (1978), 90–93.

18 *Washington Post,* July 4, 1936.

19 *New York World Telegram,* June 20, 1936.

20 *Washington Post,* July 4, 1936.

21 Ed Van Every, *Joe Louis, Man and Super-Fighter* (1936), 1–2.

22 Jack Dempsey, "Dempsey Sees Louis Comeback Not Easy," *Ring,* September 1936, 8–9, 43.

23 James J. Braddock, " 'Louis Bubble Has Burst,' Writes Braddock," *Ring,* September 1936, 6–7.

24 *Brooklyn Daily Eagle,* August 19, 1936.

25 *New York Amsterdam News,* September 26, 1936.

26 Ibid.

27 For Schmeling's reception in Germany, see Max Schmeling, *Max Schmeling: An Autobiography,* trans. and ed. George von der Lippe (1998), 129–141; Margolick, *Beyond Glory,* 182–183.

28 *New York Times,* November 20, 1936.

29 Ibid., August 18, 1936.

30 Ibid., December 4, 1936.

31 *New York Mirror,* January 9, 1937.

32 *New York Times,* February 19, 1937.

33 Ibid., April 14, 1937.

34 *Washington Post,* February 10, 1938.

35 *New York Times,* March 8, 1937.

36 *New York Evening Journal,* June 4, 1937.

37 *New York Times,* June 5, 1937.

38 *New York Sun,* June 9, 1937.

39 Ibid., June 12, 1937.

40 *New York Evening Journal,* June 9, 1937.

41 Ibid., June 12, 1937.

42 *Sentinel* (South Norwalk, Conn.), June 12, 1937; *New York Daily News,* June 15, 1937.

43 *Chicago Sunday Times,* June 20, 1937.

44 *Pittsburgh Courier,* May 22, 1937.

45 Quoted in Ronald K. Fried, *Corner Men: Great Boxing Trainers* (1991), 144–145.

46 *New York Amsterdam News,* June 19, 1937.

47 *Boston Sunday Post,* June 13, 1937.

48 *New York Enquirer,* June 13, 1937.

49 *Chicago Daily Tribune,* June 23, 1937,

50 Ibid.

51 Fried, *Corner Men,* 145.

52 *Chicago Daily Tribune,* June 23, 1937.

53 Quoted in Jeremy Schaap, *Cinderella Man: James J. Braddock, Max Baer, and the Greatest Upset in Boxing History* (2005), 273–274.

54 *Chicago Daily Tribune,* June 23, 1937.

55 Quoted in Lewis Erenberg, *The Greatest Fight of Our Generation: Louis vs. Schmeling* (2006), 125.

56 Quoted in Schaap, *Cinderella Man,* 274.

57 *Chicago Daily Tribune,* June 23, 1937.

58 Quoted in Schaap, *Cinderella Man,* 274.

59 F. X. Toole, *Million Dollar Baby: Stories from the Corner* (2000), 8.

60 Quoted in Schaap, *Cinderella Man,* 274.

61 *Chicago Daily Tribune,* June 23, 1937.

62 *Chicago Daily News,* June 23, 1937.

63 Quoted in Margolick, *Beyond Glory,* 229.

64 *Philadelphia Daily News,* June 23, 1937.

65 *New York Amsterdam News,* June 26, 1937.

66 *Pittsburgh Courier,* June 26, 1937.

67 Interview with Truman K. Gibson, Jr.

68 *New York Amsterdam News,* June 26, 1937.

69 *Daily Worker,* June 27, 1937.

70 *St. Louis Star-Times,* June 23, 1937.

71 Malcolm X with Alex Haley, *The Autobiography of Malcolm X* (1964), 23.

72 Alistair Cooke, *Letter from America, 1946–2004* (2004), 19.

73 Louis, *Joe Louis,* 119.

CHAPTER 6 Red, White, Blue, and Black

Epigraphs: Heywood Broun, *New York World Telegram*, June 24, 1938. Bob Considine, "Louis Knocks Out Schmeling," in David Halberstam, ed., *The Best American Sports Writing of the Century* (1999), 138–139.

1 "View from Left Field: Interview with Lester Rodney," in *Political Affairs*, 2004 (politicalaffairs.net).

2 Quoted in Irwin Silber, *Press Box Red: The Story of Lester Rodney, the Communist Who Helped Break the Color Line in American Sports* (2003), 3.

3 *Daily Worker*, June 20, 1938.

4 Ibid., June 18, 1938; June 19, 1938.

5 Ibid., June 22, 1938.

6 Maxwell Bodenheim in ibid., June 18, 1938. Richard Wright in ibid., June 22, 1938.

7 Ibid., June 21, 1938.

8 *New York Times*, June 23, 1937; *Boston Post*, June 23, 1937; *Detroit Evening Times*, June 23, 1937.

9 *New York Times*, June 24, 1937.

10 Ibid., June 23, 1937.

11 Ibid., July 10, 1937.

12 Ibid., July 14, 1937.

13 Ibid., August 31, 1937.

14 Ibid.

15 Quoted in David Margolick, *Beyond Glory: Joe Louis vs. Max Schmeling, and a World on the Brink* (2005), 237.

16 William E. Dodd, Jr., *Ambassador Dodd's Diary, 1933–1938* (1941), 447.

17 Quoted in Franklin L. Ford, "Three Observers in Berlin: Rumbold, Dodd, and François-Poncet," in Gordon Craig, ed., *The Diplomats, 1919–1939* (1953), 450.

18 Quoted in ibid., 451; Dodd, *Ambassador Dodd's Diary*, 126.

19 Ford, "Three Observers in Berlin," 452.

20 Richard D. Mandell, *The Nazi Olympics* (1987), 77.

21 Quoted in Marshall Jon Fisher, *A Terrible Splendor: Three Extraordinary Men, a World Poised for War, and the Greatest Tennis Match Ever Played* (2009), 160.

22 Quoted in Guy Walters, *Berlin Games: How the Nazis Stole the Olympic Dream* (2006), 47.

23 Quoted in Mandell, *Nazi Olympics*, 75; Walters, *Berlin Games*, 47.

24 Ibid., 140.

25 Mandell, *Nazi Olympics*, 75.

26 For discussions of the Berlin Olympics, see Mandell, *Nazi Olympics*, 122–158; Walter, *Berlin Games*, 183–194, 236–262.

27 For Hollywood and the Nazis, see David Welky, *The Moguls and the Dictators: Hollywood and the Coming of World War II* (2008).

28 For comic books on the eve of World War II, see Bradford W. Wright, *Comic Book Nation: The Transformation of Youth Culture in America* (2001), 30–55.

29 For news commentators and the coming of World War II, see David Holbrook Culbert, *News for Everyman: Radio and Foreign Affairs in Thirties America* (1976).

30 Paul Gallico, *Farewell to Sport* (1937), 279.

31 Interview with Nat Fleischer.

32 *New York Times*, November 30, 1937.

33 Ibid., December 14, 1937; December 15, 1937.

34 Ibid., September 26, 1937.

35 *New York Amsterdam News*, October 2, 1937.

36 Review in ibid., January 8, 1938. *New York Times*, August 17, 1937.

37 For Winchellese, see Richard Ben Cramer, *Joe DiMaggio: The Hero's Life* (2000), 192–198.

38 *New York Times*, May 9, 1938.

39 Ibid.

40 Ibid., June 18, 1938.

41 Ibid., May 10, 1938.

42 *Journal Every Evening* (Wilmington, Del.), May 11, 1938.

43 *Baltimore News Post*, June 22, 1938.

44 For discussion of the Louis-Roosevelt encounter, see Margolick, *Beyond Glory*, 98.

45 *Baltimore News Post*, June 22, 1938.

46 *Daily Worker*, June 22, 1938.

47 Quoted in Ronald K. Fried, *Corner Men: Great Boxing Trainers* (1991), 148–149.

48 *New York Daily Mirror*, June 18, 1938.

49 Ibid.

50 Ibid.

51 Max Schmeling, *Max Schmeling: An Autobiography*, trans. and ed. George von der Lippe (1998), 152.

52 *New York World Telegram*, June 22, 1938.

53 *New York Journal American*, June 20, 1938.

54 Margolick, *Beyond Glory*, 261.

55 *New York World Telegram*, May 13, 1938.

56 Ibid.

57 *Toronto Daily Star*, June 22, 1938.

58 *New York World Telegram*, June 22, 1938.

59 *New York Times*, June 23, 1938.

60 Richard Wright, "High Tide in Harlem: Joe Louis as a Symbol of Freedom," *New Masses*, July 15, 1938, 18–20.

61 Roy Wilkins, *Standing Fast: The Autobiography of Roy Wilkins* (1982), 164.

62 Unknown newspaper, June 22, 1938, JLS.

63 Jimmy Carter, *Why Not the Best? The First Fifty Years* (1996), 33.

64 *Joe Louis: America's Hero . . . Betrayed* (HBO, 2008).

65 Joe Louis with Edna and Art Rust, Jr., *Joe Louis: My Life* (1978), 141.

66 Quoted in Fried, *Corner Men*, 123

67 Louis, *Joe Louis*, 141.

68 Schmeling, *Max Schmeling*, 153.

69 *Pittsburgh Courier*, June 25, 1938.

70 *American Experience: The Fight* (PBS, 2004).

71 *Daily Worker*, June 24, 1938.

72 Ibid.

73 Ibid.

74 Count Basie as told to Albert Murray, *Good Morning Blues: The Autobiography of Count Basie* (2002), 216.

75 As quoted in Bak, *Joe Louis*, 165–166.

76 Wilkins, *Standing Fast*, 164.

77 For the calls of the Louis-Schmeling fight see Margolick, *Beyond Glory*, 297–301.

78 Carter, *Why Not the Best?* 33.

79 *American Experience: The Fight*.

80 *Daily Worker*, June 25, 1938.

81 Ibid., June 24, 1938.

82 *New York Times*, June 23, 1938.

83 Wright, "High Tide in Harlem," 18–20.

84 *Daily Worker*, June 24, 1938.

85 Ibid.

86 *New York Daily News*, June 23, 1938.

87 *Chicago Daily News*, June 24, 1938.

88 Ibid.

89 *New York Times*, June 23, 1938.

CHAPTER 7 **The Last Perfect Night**

Epigraph: Peter Heller, *"In This Corner . . . !" Forty World Champions Tell Their Stories* (1973), 225; Joe Louis Barrow, Jr., and Barbara Munder, *Joe Louis: 50 Years an American Hero* (1988), 122.

1 For the details of the Louis-Conn fight, see Billy Conn interview in Peter Heller, *"In This Corner,"* 221–226; Andrew O'Toole, *Sweet William: The Life of Billy Conn* (2008), 206–216; and Frank Deford, "The Boxer and the Blond," *Sports Illustrated*, June 17, 1985, 66–96.

2 For sports in 1941, see Mike Vaccaro, *1941: The Greatest Year in Sports* (2007); and Michael Seidel, *Streak: Joe DiMaggio and the Summer of '41* (1988).

3 Leigh Montville, *Ted Williams: The Biography of an American Hero* (2004), 93.

4 Memphis Minnie, "He's in the Ring (Doing the Same Old Thing)," 1935.

5 For Louis' earnings, see Richard Bak, *Joe Louis: The Great Black Hope* (1996), 297–299.

6 Franklin D. Roosevelt, "We Choose Human Freedom," Radio Address, May 27, 1941.

7 Robert L. Miller, Letter from the Publisher, *Sports Illustrated*, September 16, 1985.

8 Bak, *Joe Louis,* 184.

9 Joe Louis with Edna and Art Rust, Jr., *Joe Louis: My Life* (1978), 159.

10 Bak, *Joe Louis,* 184.

11 Barrow, *Joe Louis,* 201–202.

12 Ibid., 106.

13 Louis, *My Life,* 73.

14 Barrow, *Joe Louis,* 200. Joe Louis Barrow, Jr., interviewed his mother extensively for his book.

15 Ibid., 202–203.

16 Deford, "Boxer and the Blond," 70.

17 Vaccaro, *1941,* 101. For background on the Conn-Jacobs relationship, see O'Toole, *Sweet William,* 85–116.

18 Vaccaro, *1941,* 102.

19 Ibid., 96; *New York Times,* June 4, 1941.

20 Quoted in O'Toole, *Sweet William,* 189.

21 Ibid., 185.

22 Ibid., 191.

23 Ibid., 192.

24 *New York Times,* June 16, 1941.

25 Quoted in Deford, "Boxer and the Blond," 75.

26 Quoted in ibid., 86.

27 Quoted in Vaccaro, *1941,* 128.

28 Ibid., 129.

29 *New York Daily Mirror,* June 19, 1941.

30 *New York Times,* June 17, 1941.

31 Quoted in ibid., June 18, 1941.

32 *New York Times Herald,* June 19, 1941.

33 Heller, *"In This Corner,"* 224–225.

34 Quoted in O'Toole, *Sweet William,* 209.

35 Barrow, *Joe Louis,* 223.

36 *New York Times,* June 19, 1941; *Chicago Herald American,* June 19, 1941.

37 O'Toole, *Sweet William,* 211.

38 Vaccaro, *1941,* 139.

39 "Fight Account Fatal to 3," undated newspaper article in JLS.

40 *New York Times,* June 19, 1941.

41 *New York Herald Tribune,* June 19, 1941.

42 Heller, *"In This Corner,"* 225.

43 *New York Times,* June 19, 1941.

44 Quoted in Vaccaro, *1941,* 142; Heller, *"In This Corner,"* 226.

45 O'Toole, *Sweet William,* 244.

CHAPTER 8 **Uncle Sam Says**

Epigraphs: Josh White, "Uncle Sam Says," 1941. William Hastie quoted in Truman K. Gibson, Jr., with Steve Huntley, *Knocking Down Barriers: My Fight for Black America* (2005), 83.

1 Elijah Wald, *Josh White: Society Blues* (2000), 7.

2 Josh White, "Southern Exposure," 1941.

3 Josh White, "Defense Factory Blues," 1941.

4 Wald, *Josh White*, 89.

5 Quoted in Sherie Mershon and Steven Schlossman, *Foxholes and Color Lines: Desegregating the U.S. Armed Forces* (1998), 38.

6 A. Philip Randolph, "Why Should We March?" *Survey Graphic*, November 1942, 488–489.

7 "Exit the Curmudgeon," *Time*, February 11, 1952.

8 *New York Times*, October 27, 1940.

9 Ibid., October 31, 1940.

10 Ibid., November 1, 1940.

11 Ibid., November 2, 1940.

12 Ibid.

13 Ibid., November 3, 1940; also see Jack Cavanaugh, *Tunney: Boxing's Brainiest Champ and His Upset of the Great Jack Dempsey* (2006), 393.

14 *New York Times*, November 5, 1940.

15 Ibid.

16 "Black Moses," *Time*, September 29, 1941, 60–64.

17 Ibid., 60–64.

18 Ibid., 62.

19 *New York Times*, September 30, 1941.

20 Ibid.

21 Ibid.

22 Ibid.

23 *Atlanta Daily World*, September 10, 1941; *New York Times*, September 10, 1941.

24 *Atlanta Daily World*, October 8, 1941; *Pittsburgh Courier*, September 13, 1941; *New York Amsterdam News*, September 27, 1941.

25 *New York Amsterdam News*, September 27, 1941.

26 Ibid.

27 *Atlanta Daily World*, October 8, 1941.

28 Ibid.

29 *Chicago Defender*, October 18, 1941; *Atlanta Daily World*, October 16, 1941.

30 W. E. B. DuBois, *The Souls of Black Folks* (1903), 3.

31 Joe Louis with Edna and Art Rust, Jr., *Joe Louis: My Life* (1978), 170.

32 White, "Uncle Sam Says."

33 Quoted in Mershon and Schlossman, *Foxholes and Color Lines*, 47.

34 Ibid.

35 Ibid., 48.

36 Quoted in Thomas R. Hietala, *The Fight of the Century: Jack Johnson, Joe Louis, and the Struggle for Racial Equality* (2002), 271.

37 *New York Amsterdam News*, December 6, 1941.

38 *Pittsburgh Courier*, November 22, 1941.

39 Quoted in Hietala, *Fight of the Century*, 271; also see *New York Amsterdam News*, December 6, 1941.

40 Quoted in Hietala, *Fight of the Century*, 271.

41 Ibid., 273; *New York Amsterdam News*, January 17, 1942.

42 *Pittsburgh Courier*, December 13, 1941.

43 Quoted in Richard Bak, *Joe Louis: The Great Black Hope* (1996), 205.

44 *New York Times*, January 10, 1942; Bak, *Joe Louis*, 205.

45 Quoted in Hietala, *Fight of the Century*, 272.

46 *New York Times*, January 10, 1942.

47 Ibid.

48 Ibid., January 13, 1942.

49 Ibid.

50 Ibid., January 15, 1942.

51 Thomas Doherty, *Projections of War: Hollywood, American Culture, and World War II* (1999), 205.

52 Quoted in Gibson, *Knocking Down Barriers*, 5.

53 Ibid., 86.

54 White, "Uncle Sam Says."

55 Doherty, *Projections of War*, 205–206.

56 Gibson, *Knocking Down Barriers*, 143.

57 Quoted in Hietala, *Fight of the Century*, 276.

58 Gibson, *Knocking Down Barriers*, 17.

59 Ibid., 11.

60 Quoted in ibid., 11.

61 *Pittsburgh Courier*, January 31, 1942.

62 *The Crisis*, January 1943, 8.

63 White, "Uncle Sam Says."

64 *New York Times*, April 25, 1942.

65 For propaganda and film, see Clayton R. Koppes and Gregory D. Black, *Hollywood Goes To War: How Politics, Profits, and Propaganda Shaped World War II Movies* (1987), 48–81.

66 Ibid., 86.

67 *Atlanta Daily World*, January 8, 1942.

68 Quoted in Francis Albertanti, "Ring, Neil Awards Memorable for Joe," *Ring*, April 1942, 41; *New York Times*, January 22, 1942.

69 *New York Times*, March 11, 1942.

70 Ibid.

71 Quoted in Chris Mead, *Champion Joe Louis: Black Hero in White America* (1985), 219; *New York Times,* March 28, 1942.

72 Mead, *Champion Joe Louis,* 219.

73 Paul Gallico, "The Private Life of Private Joe Louis," *Liberty,* May 22, 1942, 52–54.

74 Quoted in Lauren Rebecca Sklaroff, "Constructing G.I. Joe Louis: Cultural Solutions to the 'Negro Problem' During World War II," *Journal of American History* 89 (December 2002): 965–966.

75 Quoted in Gibson, *Knocking Down Barriers,* 85.

76 Ibid., 106.

77 Ibid., 69–70.

78 Interview with Truman K. Gibson, Jr.

79 Sklaroff, "Constructing G.I. Joe Louis," 973.

80 On the tour, see Will Haygood, *Sweet Thunder: The Life and Times of Sugar Ray Robinson* (2009), 55–96.

81 Tom Ephrem, "Wounded GI Risks Sight to Get a Glimpse of Joe Louis," *Ring,* October 1944, 7.

82 Gibson, *Knocking Down Barriers,* 12.

83 Arnold Rampersad, *Jackie Robinson: A Biography* (1997), 89–95.

84 Quoted in Gibson, *Knocking Down Barriers,* 13.

85 Quoted in Rampersad, *Jackie Robinson,* 102–109.

86 Ibid., 92.

87 Quoted in Gibson, *Knocking Down Barriers,* 239.

88 *This Is the Army* (1943).

89 *Chicago Defender,* October 2, 1943.

90 *The Negro Soldier* (1944).

91 Ibid.

92 *Chicago Defender,* February 26, 1944.

93 Quoted in Thomas Cripps and David Culbert, "*The Negro Soldier* (1944): Film Propaganda in Black and White," in Peter C. Rollins, ed., *Hollywood as Historian: American Film in a Cultural Context* (1983), 130–131.

94 Quoted in Sklaroff, "Constructing G.I. Joe Louis," 978.

95 *New York Times,* September 24, 1945.

CHAPTER 9 **An Old Man's Dream**

Epigraph: Red Smith in *New York Herald Tribune,* October 28, 1951.

1 For the story of Louis and Rose Morgan, see Gay Talese, "Joe Louis: The King as a Middle-Aged Man," *Esquire,* June 1962, collected in Gay Talese, *Fame and Obscurity* (1993), 317–328.

2 Quoted in ibid., 318–319.

3 Ibid., 321.

4 *New York Times,* June 20, 1946.

5 Ibid.

6 Ibid., April 13, 1981.

7 Quoted in Richard Bak, *Joe Louis: The Great Black Hope* (1998), 236.

8 Joe Louis with Edna and Art Rust, Jr., *Joe Louis: My Life* (1978), 198.

9 Quoted in Barney Nagler, *Brown Bomber: The Pilgrimage of Joe Louis* (1972), 157–158.

10 Louis, *Joe Louis,* 202.

11 Nagler, *Brown Bomber,* 159.

12 Joe Louis as told to Edward Linn, "Oh, Where Did My Money Go?" *Saturday Evening Post,* January 7, 1956, 68.

13 Ibid.

14 *New York Times,* December 6, 1947.

15 Barney Nagler, *James Norris and the Decline of Boxing* (1964), 3–7.

16 *New York Times,* June 26, 1948.

17 Ibid.

18 Ibid.

19 For Louis' tax troubles, see "Boxer Tax Troubles," *U.S. News & World Report,* December 28, 1956; "The Blow That K.O.'d Joe Louis," *U.S. News & World Report,* January 25, 1957, 63–68; Louis, "Oh, Where Did My Money Go?" 22–23, 68–70.

20 For Louis and the IBC, see Nagler, *James Norris and the Decline of Boxing.*

21 Quoted in "Marva Louis Spaulding, Ex-Wife of Heavyweight Boxing Great Joe Louis, Succumbs," *Jet,* December 18, 2000; for Joe and Marva, see Joe Louis Barrow, Jr., and Barbara Munder, *Joe Louis: 50 Years an American Hero* (1988), 195–206.

22 *New York Times,* September 28, 1950.

23 Ibid.

24 Quoted in Richard Bak, *Joe Louis: The Great Black Hope* (1996), 250.

25 Louis, "Oh, Where Did My Money Go?" 69.

26 Quoted in Russell Sullivan, *Rocky Marciano: The Rock of His Times* (2002), 100.

27 Ibid.

28 A. J. Liebling, *The Sweet Science* (1956), 45.

29 Quoted in Sullivan, *Rocky Marciano,* 100.

30 Liebling, *Sweet Science,* 45.

31 Ibid., 46.

32 Sullivan, *Rocky Marciano,* 102.

33 *Boston Globe,* October 27, 1951; Sullivan, *Rocky Marciano,* 102.

34 *New York Times,* October 27, 1951.

35 Liebling, *Sweet Science,* 47.

36 *New York Times,* October 28, 1951.

37 *Boston Globe,* October 27, 1951.

38 F. Scott Fitzgerald, *The Great Gatsby* (1925), 8.

39 Louis, "Oh, Where Did My Money Go?" 22.

40 Interview with Truman K. Gibson, Jr.

41 *New York Times,* April 19, 1981; Louis, *Joe Louis,* 233.

42 Quoted in Talese, *Fame and Obscurity,* 319.

43 Ibid., 322–325.

44 Louis, *Joe Louis,* 253.

45 *New York Times,* April 19, 1981.

46 Peter Heller, *"In This Corner . . . !": Forty World Champions Tell Their Stories* (1973), 226.

47 Nagler, *Brown Bomber,* 171.

48 Ibid., 183.

49 Quoted in Donald McRae, *Heroes Without a Country: America's Betrayal of Joe Louis and Jesse Owens* (2002), 350–353.

50 Nagler, *Brown Bomber,* 213–214.

51 Interview with Vic Ziegel.

52 Dave Kindred, *Sound and Fury: Two Powerful Lives, One Fateful Friendship* (2007), 239.

53 Nagler, *Brown Bomber,* 235.

54 *New York Times,* April 13, 1981.

55 Ibid., April 14, 1981.

56 Ibid., April 17, 1981.

57 Ibid., April 18, 1981.

58 Ibid.; Chris Mead, *Champion Joe Louis: Black Hero in White America* (1985), 296–297.

59 *New York Times,* April 22, 1981.

60 Ibid., April 13, 1981.

61 Ibid., April 19, 1981.

A NOTE ON SOURCES

The starting point for any serious examination of the life and image of Joe Louis is the popular press. Between 1935 and 1945 probably more was written about Louis in newspapers, and particularly African American newspapers, than about any other American. All of Louis' public life, and much of his private life, is fully documented. For a wide selection of newspaper and magazine articles on Louis, see the Julian Black Collection of Joe Louis Scrapbooks at the Archives Center of the National Museum of American History, Smithsonian Institution. The scrapbooks are available on 304 microfiche cards distributed by Chadwyck-Healey under the name "Joe Louis Scrapbooks, 1935–1944." This collection contains thousands of articles about Louis. I systematically followed Louis' life in the mainstream white press and in the black press. Particularly helpful were the *New York Times, New York Daily News, Chicago Tribune, Detroit Free Press, New York Amsterdam News, Pittsburgh Courier, Chicago Defender,* and the *Daily Worker.* I also followed Louis' career closely in the boxing magazine *Ring,* an essential source for the business of boxing. The Records of the Department of State, the Records of the Department of the Army, the Records of the Office of War Information, and the Records of the Civilian Aide to the Secretary of War also contain important material on Louis, particularly during his years in the Army.

For a celebrity so frustratingly reticent with the press and consciously discreet in his personal life, Joe Louis opened up in a surprising number of autobiographical works, though none were written independently. The first, *My Life Story* (1947), was written with Chester L. Washington and Haskell Cohen. The trio reworked the book several years later and published *The Joe Louis Story* (1953). Twenty-five years afterward, with the aid of Edna Rust and Art Rust, Jr., Louis collaborated on a much more revealing memoir, *Joe Louis: My Life* (1978). Finally, seven years after Louis' death, Joe Louis Barrow, Jr., and Barbara Munder published *Joe Louis: 50 Years an American Hero* (1988), which included substantial excerpts of interviews they had conducted on the life of Joe Louis. Also valuable are the collaborative articles of Louis with Meyer Berger and Barney Nagler that were published in *Life* (November 8, 1948, and November 15, 1948).

Since the 1970s a host of scholars, journalists, and historians have addressed issues related to Joe Louis. Some useful works on Louis include A. J. Young's "Joe Louis, Symbol: 1933–1949," Ph.D. diss., University of Maryland, 1968; M. Jill Dupont's " 'The Self in the Ring, the Self in Society': Boxing and American Culture from Jack Johnson to Joe Louis," Ph.D. diss., University of Chicago, 2000; and Barbara Jean Keys' "The Dictatorship of Sport: Nationalism, Internationalism, and Mass Culture in the 1930s," Ph.D. diss., Harvard University, 2001. Published biographies of Louis include Barney Nagler's *Brown Bomber: The Pilgrimage of Joe Louis* (1972), Anthony O. Edmonds' *Joe Louis* (1973), Gerald Astor's " . . . *And a Credit to His Race": The Hard Life and Times of Joseph Louis Barrow, A.K.A. Joe Louis* (1974), Rugio Vitale's *Joe Louis: Biography of a Champion* (1979), and Thomas Hauser's "Joe Louis Revisited," in *The Greatest Sport of All* (2007), 127–141.

Chris Mead's *Champion—Joe Louis, Black Hero in White America* (1985), Richard Bak's *Joe Louis: The Great Black Hope* (1996), Donald McRae's *Heroes Without a Country: America's Betrayal of Joe Louis and Jesse Owens* (2002), and Thomas Hietala's *Fight of the Century: Jack Johnson, Joe Louis, and the Struggle for Racial Equality* (2002) pay greater attention to Louis' particular place in and impact on American race relations, and all are essential reading for different aspects of Louis' life. Similarly, David Margolick's *Beyond Glory: Joe Louis vs. Max Schmeling, and a World on the Brink* (2005) and Lewis A. Erenberg's *Greatest Fight of Our Generation: Louis vs. Schmeling* (2006) consider race in America through the rise of Joe Louis, climaxing with Louis' epic rematch against Max Schmeling. Both authors examined German as well as English sources, and their books are particularly valuable. Erenberg connects Louis to a wide variety of themes of interest to scholars of American history, and Margolick's book is a beautifully written, compelling narrative of the subject. A. J. Liebling's *Neutral Corner: Boxing Essays* (1952) and *The Sweet Science* (1956), as well as Budd Schulberg's *Loser and*

Still Champion: Muhammad Ali (1972), are useful and great reads. Jeffrey Sammons' *Beyond the Ring: The Role of Boxing in American Society* (1990) is the essential study of boxing in the twentieth century, and Kasia Boddy's *Boxing: A Cultural History* (2008) is an insightful cultural study of boxing. Each contains valuable political, social, and cultural material on Louis.

CHAPTER 1

The standard works on racial segregation in the American South remain C. Vann Woodward's *Strange Career of Jim Crow* (1955) and Leon Litwack's *Trouble in Mind: Black Southerners in the Age of Jim Crow* (1998). Other recent studies include James C. Cobb's *Most Southern Place on Earth: The Mississippi Delta and the Roots of Regional Identity* (1992) and *Away Down South: A History of Southern Identity* (2005). For a gendered analysis of the Jim Crow South, see Glenda Gilmore's *Gender and Jim Crow: Women and the Politics of White Supremacy in North Carolina, 1896–1920* (1996). Interesting studies of whiteness and racial segregation include Melton A. McLaurin's *Separate Pasts: Growing Up White in the Segregated South* (1987) and Grace Elizabeth Hale's *Making Whiteness: The Culture of Segregation in the South, 1890–1940* (1998). Two complementary intellectual histories are George M. Fredrickson's *Black Image in the White Mind: The Debate on Afro-American Character and Destiny, 1817–1914* (1971) and Mia Bay's *White Image in the Black Mind: African-American Ideas About White People, 1830–1925* (2000). Richard Wright's experience and insight on race relations in America are chronicled in Hazel Rowley's *Richard Wright: The Life and Times* (2001).

The racism inherent in Jim Crow was not restricted to the rural South. Works on race relations in the urban North include Gilbert Osofsky's *Harlem: The Making of a Ghetto. Negro New York, 1890–1930* (1966) and Allan H. Spear's *Black Chicago: The Making of a Negro Ghetto, 1890–1920* (1967). For information specifically on Detroit during Joe Louis' early years, see Olivier Zunz's *Changing Face of Inequality: Urbanization, Industrial Development, and Immigrants in Detroit, 1880–1920* (1982), Kevin Boyle's *Arc of Justice: A Saga of Race, Civil Rights, and Murder in the Jazz Age* (2004), and former mayor of Detroit Coleman Young's memoir *Hard Stuff: The Autobiography of Coleman Young* (1994). For further reading on the second incarnation of the Ku Klux Klan, see David M. Chalmers' *Hooded Americanism: The History of the Ku Klux Klan* (1987) and Nancy MacLean's *Behind the Mask of Chivalry: The Making of the Second Ku Klux Klan* (1994).

The Great Migration from the rural South to the urban North during the first half of the twentieth century has received a wealth of historical attention. Two books that are particularly useful include James R. Grossman's *Land of Hope: Chicago, Black Southerners, and the Great Migration* (1989) and James M. Gregory's *Southern Diaspora: How the Great Migrations of Black and White Southerners Transformed America* (2005).

Popular culture and Jim Crow is a broad topic unto itself. Four signal and useful works in the area are Lawrence Levine's *Black Culture and Black Consciousness: Afro-American Folk Thought from Slavery to Freedom* (1977), Jack T. Kirby's *Media Made Dixie: The South in the American Imagination* (1978), Melvin Patrick Ely's *Adventures of Amos 'n' Andy: A Social History of an American Phenomenon* (1991), and Melvyn Stokes' *D. W. Griffith's Birth of a Nation: A History of "The Most Controversial Motion Picture of All Time"* (2007).

Background on John Roxborough, Julian Black, and Jack Blackburn can be found in Roxborough's "How I Discovered Joe Louis," *Ebony,* October 1945, 64–76, Dave Anderson's *In the Corner: Great Boxing Trainers Talk About Their Art* (1991), Ronald K. Fried's *Corner Men: The Great Boxing Trainers* (1991), and John Jarrett's *Champ in the Corner: The Ray Arcel Story* (2007).

CHAPTER 2

As the two most iconic boxing figures in the late nineteenth and early twentieth centuries, John L. Sullivan and Jack Johnson have each engendered several biographies. On Sullivan, see Donald Barr Chidsey's *John the Great: The Times and Life of a Remarkable American, John L. Sullivan* (1942), Nat Fleischer's *John L. Sullivan: Champion of Champions* (1951), Adam Pollack's *John L. Sullivan: The Career of the First Gloved Heavyweight Champion* (2006), and Thomas Hauser's "John L. Sullivan Revisited" in *An Unforgiving Sport: An Inside Look at Another Year of Boxing* (2009), 3–32. All provide colorful narratives of the "Boston Strong Boy." Michael T. Isenberg's *John L. Sullivan and His America* (1988) remains the most scholarly work on the boxer. Dale A. Somers adds biographical information on Sullivan in *The Rise of Sports in New Orleans, 1850–1900* (1972), while John Higham's "Reorientation of American Culture in the 1890s," in *Writing American History: Essays on Modern Scholarship* (1970), 73–102, discusses the cultural context in which Sullivan thrived.

For Johnson, Al-Tony Gilmore's *Bad Nigger! The National Impact of*

Jack Johnson (1975), Randy Roberts' *Papa Jack: Jack Johnson and the Era of White Hopes* (1983), Thomas Hietala's *Fight of the Century: Jack Johnson, Joe Louis, and the Struggle for Racial Equality* (2002), and Geoffrey C. Ward's *Unforgivable Blackness: The Rise and Fall of Jack Johnson* (2004) all contain valuable information on the early life, professional career, and equally intriguing years in exile and retirement. Johnson's prosecution under the Mann Act is discussed in David J. Langum's *Crossing the Line: Legislating Morality and the Mann Act* (1994).

Films of early championship prizefights, as well as the Hollywood renditions of boxing matches and boxers' lives, are equally important to understanding the significance of boxing in turn-of-the-century America. Information on Hollywood's boxing movies can be found in Frederick V. Romano's *Boxing Filmography: American Features, 1920–2003* (2004) while Dan Streible's *Fight Pictures: A History of Boxing and Early Cinema* (2008) includes detailed information on fight films from the 1890s through to the end of Johnson's reign as champion. Not to be overlooked is Ken Burns' documentary film *Unforgivable Blackness: The Rise and Fall of Jack Johnson* (2005).

Both the sport and its fictional representations were inextricably linked to ideas of masculinity as a new sense of manhood emerged in the United States. The finest work on American masculinities is Michael Kimmel's *Manhood in America: A Cultural History* (1996). Other contributions to the study of American masculinity include Robert Ernst's *Weakness Is a Crime: The Life of Bernarr Mcfadden* (1990), Gail Bederman's *Manliness and Civilization: A Cultural History of Gender and Race in the United States, 1890–1917* (1995), and Sarah Watts' *Rough Rider in the White House: Theodore Roosevelt and the Politics of Desire* (2003). Jane P. Tompkins adds to the understanding of fin de siècle masculinity and popular culture in *West of Everything: The Inner Life of Westerns* (1992), and Neal Gabler's *Life: The Movie. How Entertainment Conquered Reality* (1998) extends the discussion deeper into the twentieth century. Black masculinities are explored in bell hooks' *We Real Cool: Black Men and Masculinity* (2004), Ronald L. Jackson's *Scripting the Black Masculine Body: Identity, Discourse, and Racial Politics in Popular Media* (2006), and Riché Richardson's *Black Masculinity and the U.S. South: From Uncle Tom to Gangsta* (2007), while the class tensions of black masculinity are evident in E. Franklin Frazier's *Black Bourgeoisie: The Rise of a New Middle Class in the United States* (1957).

For the specific relationship between boxing and masculinity in the early era of American prizefighting, see Elliot J. Gorn's masterful *The Manly Art: Bare-Knuckle Prize Fighting in America* (1986). Hietala's *Fight of the Century* discusses how race complicated that relationship in America. Eldridge Cleaver's quotation, taken from his *Soul on Ice* (1968), suggests that the conflict between boxing, masculinity, and race lasted well into the twentieth century.

CHAPTER 3

Langston Hughes' poetic observations of Harlem specifically, and black America broadly, are available in *The Collected Works of Langston Hughes* (2001), ed. Arnold Rampersad. Further information on Harlem and New York City during the 1930s can be found in Osofsky's *Harlem* and Cheryl Lynn Greenberg's *Or Does It Explode? Black Harlem in the Great Depression* (1991). Two particularly good overviews of the Great Depression are Robert S. McElvaine's *Great Depression: America, 1929–1941* (1984) and David M. Kennedy's *Freedom from Fear: The American People in Depression and War, 1929–1945* (1999). John Hope Franklin's discussion of the link between race and internationalism in the 1930s can be found in his *From Slavery to Freedom: A History of Negro Americans* (1974).

Several biographies illuminate the state of boxing in the 1920s and 1930s, including Daniel M. Daniel's *The Jacobs Story* (1949), Frederic Mullally's *Primo: The Story of "Mountain Man" Carnera* (1991), Jeremy Schaap's *Cinderella Man: James J. Braddock, Max Baer, and the Greatest Upset in Boxing History* (2005), Jim Hague's *Braddock: The Rise of the Cinderella Man* (2005), M. C. DeLisa's *Cinderella Man: The James J. Braddock Story* (2005), and Randy Roberts' *Jack Dempsey: The Manassa Mauler* (1979). Nat Fleischer's *50 Years at Ringside* (1940) provides a more comprehensive view of the sport. The poem "Dempsey, Dempsey" can be found in Horace Gregory's *Poems, 1930–1940* (1941), and the importance of American sports generally in the 1920s and 1930s is discussed in Paul Gallico's *Farewell to Sport* (1937).

CHAPTER 4

Richard Wright's comments about Joe Louis are located in his *Richard Wright Reader* (1978), as well as Rowley's *Richard Wright*. Wright's affiliation with Communists is emblematic of the larger relationship between Communism and African Americans, a topic that is detailed in Mark Naison's *Communists in Harlem During the Depression* (1983) and Dan T. Carter's *Scottsboro: A Tragedy of the American South* (1969). The com-

parison between Louis and black folk legend John Henry was drawn by
Levine in *Black Culture and Black Consciousness.* A historical investigation
of the John Henry legend can be found in Scott Reynolds Nelson's *Steel
Drivin' Man: John Henry, the Untold Story of an American Legend* (2006).

A broad spectrum of real American legends and celebrities included
vivid recollections of Joe Louis' fights in their own memoirs. Some examples include Miles Davis and Quincy Troupe's *Miles, the Autobiography*
(1989), Maya Angelou's *I Know Why the Caged Bird Sings* (1969), Martin
Luther King, Jr.'s *Why We Can't Wait* (1964), Malcolm X, *The Autobiogra-
phy of Malcolm X* (1973), Count Basie and Arthur Murray's *Good Morning
Blues: The Autobiography of Count* Basie (2002), Ossie Davis and Ruby
Dee's *With Ossie and Ruby: In This Life Together* (1998), Lena Horne and
Richard Schickel's *Lena* (1965), and Jimmy Carter's *Why Not the Best? The
First Fifty Years* (1996). The views of Adolf Hitler on boxing are from *Mein
Kampf,* trans. Ralph Manheim (1972).

Millions of people felt a connection with Joe Louis in part because of
the burgeoning mass media of the 1930s. A glut of popular songs were
written about Louis during and after his career, many of which have been
collected on one album, arranged by Rena Kosersky and produced by
Rounder Records, entitled *Joe Louis: An American Hero* (2001). Some other
popular songs that referenced Joe Louis are included in Guido Van Rijn's
Roosevelt's Blues: African-American Blues and Gospel Songs on FDR (1997).

Radio play of songs about Louis, as well as broadcasts of his fights, were
crucial to creating and spreading his popularity. Two scholarly works on
the historical significance of radio in America include Ray Barfield's *Listening to Radio, 1920–1950* (1996) and Susan J. Douglas' *Listening In: Radio and
the American Imagination, from Amos 'n' Andy and Edward R. Murrow to
Wolfman Jack and Howard Stern* (1999). Motion pictures were similarly
important to disseminating images of Joe Louis across the country. For
information regarding American film in the 1930s, see Andrew Bergman's
We're in the Money: Depression America and Its Films (1971), Robert Sklar's
Movie Made America: A Social History of American Movies (1975), and Tino
Balio's *Grand Design: Hollywood as a Modern Business Enterprise, 1930–1939*
(1993).

Further details about Louis' early professional boxing career can be
found in Hietala's *Fight of the Century,* Erenberg's *Greatest Fight of Our
Generation,* and Margolick's *Beyond Glory.* The views of legendary boxing
trainer Ray Arcel are recorded in Elli Wohlgelernter's "Interview with Ray

Arcel, October 11, November 8, 1983" in *American Jews in Sports*, Oral History Collection. The social significance of the first Louis-Schmeling fight is discussed in Lane Demas' "The Brown Bomber's Dark Day: Louis-Schmeling I and America's Black Hero," *Journal of Sport History* (2004): 253–271.

CHAPTER 5

The stark changes in public perceptions of Joe Louis between his loss to Schmeling in 1936 and his victory over Braddock in 1937 are analyzed in Jeffrey Sammons' "Boxing as a Reflection of Society: The Southern Reaction to Joe Louis," *Journal of Popular Culture* (1983), 23–33, and Lane Demas' "The Brown Bomber's Dark Day," while the burden of being an African American icon is explained in Wilson J. Moses' *Black Messiahs and Uncle Toms: Social and Literary Manipulations of a Religious Myth* (1982).

Some personal reactions of contemporaries can be found in Langston Hughes' *I Wonder as I Wander: An Autobiographical Journey* (1956), F. X. Toole's *Million Dollar Baby: Stories from the Corner* (2005), Alistair Cooke's *Letter from America, 1946–2004* (2004), Truman Gibson's *Knocking Down Barriers: My Fight for Black America* (2005), and Roy Wilkins and Tom Mathews' *Standing Fast: The Autobiography of Roy Wilkins* (1982), as well as Malcolm X's *Autobiography of Malcolm X*.

For information about Chicago, particularly its African American sections, both before and after the Louis-Braddock championship fight, see St. Clair Drake and Horace Cayton's *Black Metropolis: A Study of Negro Life in a Northern City* (1962). Other reactions to Louis' first match against Schmeling and descriptions of his fight with Braddock are contained in Erenberg's *Greatest Fight of Our Generation*, Margolick's *Beyond Glory*, Schaap's *Cinderella Man*, Hague's *Braddock*, DeLisa's *Cinderella Man*, and Patrick Myler's *Ring of Hate: Joe Louis vs. Max Schmeling: The Fight of the Century* (2005), as well as Max Schmeling and George B. von der Lippe's *Max Schmeling: An Autobiography* (1998).

CHAPTER 6

Boxing in particular and sports in general were not immune to the political extremism of the mid-1930s. For Lester Rodney's negotiations with Communism and American sports, see Irwin Silber's *Press Box Red: The Story of Lester Rodney, the Communist Who Helped Break the Color Line in American Sports* (2003), and for Communism and sports in the United States generally, see Mark Naison's "Lefties and Righties: The Communist Party and Sports During the Great Depression," *Radical America* (1979), 47–59. For a collection of interviews with mainstream sportswriters, see Jerome Holtzman's *No Cheering in the Press Box* (1974).

The 1936 Summer Olympics in Berlin is a fitting subject through which to consider sport and fascism. Three particularly useful studies of the Eleventh Olympiad are Richard D. Mandell's *Nazi Olympics* (1971), Guy Walters' *Berlin Games: How Hitler Stole the Olympic Dream* (2006), and *The Nazi Olympics: Sport, Politics, and Appeasement in the 1930s* (2003), ed. Arnd Kruger and W. J. Murray. William E. Dodd's perceptions of Nazi Germany are drawn from *Ambassador Dodd's Diary, 1933–1938* (1941) ed. William E. Dodd, Jr., and Franklin L. Ford's "Three Observers in Berlin: Rumbold, Dodd, and François-Poncet," in Gordon Craig's *Diplomats, 1919–1939* (1953), 437–476.

For examples of American popular culture's response to the tenuous political climate of the interwar period, see Clayton R. Koppes and Gregory D. Black's *Hollywood Goes to War: How Politics, Profits, and Propaganda Shaped World War II Movies* (1987) and Bradford Wright's *Comic Book Nation: The Transformation of Youth Culture in America* (2001). Woody Guthrie's observations can be found in his memoirs *Bound for Glory* (1968) and *Seeds of a Man: An Experience Lived and Dreamed* (1976), as well as in Ed Cray's *Ramblin' Man: The Life and Times of Woody Guthrie* (2004).

There are several accounts of the Joe Louis–Max Schmeling saga, many of which have already been listed. The two finest works, however, remain Margolick's *Beyond Glory* and Erenberg's *Greatest Fight of Our Generation*. For more details about the Jewish response to the Louis-Schmeling bouts, see Allen Bodner's *When Boxing was a Jewish Sport* (1997). The political significance of the second Louis-Schmeling fight is also discussed in Anthony O. Edmonds' "Second Louis-Schmeling Fight—Sport, Symbol, and Culture," *Journal of Popular Culture* (1973), 42–50. Louis' symbolic role in world affairs is addressed in Dominic J. Capeci, Jr., and Martha Wilkerson's "Multifarious Hero: Joe Louis, American Society and Race Relations During World Crisis, 1935–1945," *Journal of Sport History* (1983), 5–25. Two documentary films provide a fine overview of the fight and Louis' impact on America and the world: *American Experience: The Fight* (PBS, 2003) and *Joe Louis: American Hero . . . Betrayed* (HBO, 2008).

CHAPTER 7

Mike Vaccaro gives vivid descriptions of 1941's significant sporting feats in *1941: The Greatest Year in Sports* (2007), as does Richard Ben Cramer in *Joe DiMaggio: The Hero's Life* (2000), Michael Seidel in *Streak: Joe DiMaggio and the Summer of '41* (1988), Leigh Montville in *Ted Williams: The Biography of an American Hero* (2004), and Bert Clark Thayer in *Whirlaway: The Life and Times of a Great Racer* (1946).

Narratives of the Louis-Conn fight and background information on Billy Conn can be found in Paul F. Kennedy's *Billy Conn: The Pittsburgh Kid* (2007) and Andrew O'Toole's *Sweet William: The Life of Billy Conn* (2008), as well as Mead's *Champion—Joe Louis. "In This Corner . . . !" Forty World Champions Tell Their Stories* (1973), edited by Peter Heller, contains an interview with Conn. For stories of Joe Louis' extramarital affairs, see Dan Burley's "Love Life of Joe Louis," *Ebony,* October 1951, 22–26, "Loves of Joe Louis," *Ebony,* November 1978, 43–46, and Louis, *Joe Louis: My Life.*

CHAPTER 8

Further information on Josh White is available in Elijah Wald's *Josh White: Society Blues* (2000), and many of his works can be found in *The Josh White Song Book* (1963), ed. Walter Raim. A. Philip Randolph's quotation comes from "Why Should We March?" *Survey Graphic* (1942), and Benjamin O. Davis' observations come from his *Benjamin O. Davis, Jr., American: An Autobiography* (1991). The reflections of Truman Gibson come from his autobiography *Knocking Down Barriers,* while Lena Horne's are recounted in her autobiography, *Lena.* Winchell's experiences are retold by Neal Gabler in *Walter Winchell: Gossip, Power, and the Culture of Celebrity* (1994). Further information on the 1940 general election can be found in Charles Peters' *Five Days in Philadelphia: The Amazing 'We Want Willkie!' Convention of 1940 and How It Freed FDR to Save the Western World* (2005) and Steve Neal's *Dark Horse: A Biography of Wendell Willkie* (1984).

For discussions of racial tensions in the American military up to and during World War II, see Ulysses Lee, *United States Army in World War II, Special Studies: The Employment of Negro Troops* (1966), Bernard C. Nalty's *Strength for the Fight: A History of Black Americans in the Military* (1986), Sherie Mershon and Steven Schlossman's *Foxholes and Color Lines: Desegregating the U.S. Armed Forces* (1998), and Maggi M. Morehouse's compilation of letters and oral histories, *Fighting in the Jim Crow Army: Black Men and Women Remember World War II* (2000). Joe Louis' impact on those tensions is insightfully discussed in Lauren Rebecca Sklaroff's "Construct-ing G.I. Joe Louis: Cultural Solutions to the 'Negro Problem' During World War II," *Journal of American History* (2002), 958–983. The similar experi-ences of Jackie Robinson can be found in Jules Tygiel's *Baseball's Great Experiment: Jackie Robinson and His Legacy* (1983), Arnold Rampersad's *Jackie Robinson: A Biography* (1997), and Robinson's *I Never Had It Made: An Autobiography of Jackie Robinson* (1972).

The messages and influence of World War II films are best covered by Koppes and Black's *Hollywood Goes to War* and Thomas Doherty's *Projec-tions of War: Hollywood, American Culture, and World War II* (1993), as well as Thomas Cripps and David Culbert's "*The Negro Soldier* (1944): Film Propaganda in Black and White," in *Hollywood as Historian: American Film in a Cultural Context* (1983), ed. Peter C. Rollins, 109–133.

CHAPTER 9

Joe Louis discussed his tax problems openly in *Joe Louis: My Life*, but Louis had admitted his financial woes twenty years earlier to Edward Linn for an article entitled "Oh, Where Did My Money Go?" *Saturday Evening Post*, January 7, 1956. The extent of his travails with the IRS was reported later that year in "Boxer Tax Troubles," *U.S. News and World Report*, Decem-ber 28, 1956.

Louis' battle against encroaching mental illness is chronicled in Barney Nagler's *Brown Bomber*. Nagler wrote as well on Louis' "sale" of the heavy-weight title and the rise of the IBC in his *James Norris and the Decline of Boxing* (1964). Louis' bout with Marciano is discussed in Everett M. Skehan's *Rocky Marciano: Biography of a First Son* (1977) and his updated revision, *Undefeated: Rocky Marciano, the Fighter Who Refused to Lose* (2005), as well as Liebling's *Sweet Science* and Russell Sullivan's *Rocky Mar-ciano: The Rock of His Times* (2002), which contains an extended considera-tion of the fight.

Rose Morgan's anecdote was retold by Gay Talese in "Joe Louis: The King as Middle-Aged Man," *Esquire*, June 1962, and Howard Cosell's recol-lection has been recounted in two slightly different variations in Edwin Shrake's "The Defection of Dandy Don," *Sports Illustrated*, April 22, 1974, and Ferdie Pacheco's *Blood in My Coffee: The Life of a Fight Doctor* (2005). Dave Kindred also discussed the state of Louis in his later years in *Sound and Fury: Two Powerful Lives, One Fateful Friendship* (2006).

ACKNOWLEDGMENTS

Maybe it doesn't take a village, but it seems so when you are writing a book. Help comes from everywhere—from strangers who ask you what you do and then listen, from family and friends who listen when they don't really want to, from experts who read and critique drafts, from publishers who do their jobs expertly and tolerate authors who tell them how to do it better. Not me, mind you. But I've heard stories. All this is to say there are too many people to acknowledge and thank, but I want to single out a few.

For almost forty years I have discussed boxing and boxers with the leading journalists and participants of the sport. I still value a few letters from the late Nat Fleischer and the late Dan Daniel, as well as conversations with them at the old *Ring* offices near Madison Square Garden. Not long after that I interviewed Jack Dempsey. The first talk was in his legendary restaurant—but that's another story. Truman K. Gibson, Jr., was also willing to share his thoughts on boxing and Joe Louis. I want to thank them, and the others who are no longer around. They knew what they were talking about. I would also like to thank Tom Hauser, one of the most generous, decent, intelligent men I know, and a fount of information on all things boxing. Conversations with Robert Lipsyte, Jerry Izenberg, Vic Ziegel, and Budd Schulberg added to my fund of Louis stories. Thanks, guys.

Over the years I have worked with many gifted graduate students, and several have contributed to this book. Larry Jewell, Eric Hall, and Andrew Smith each helped me in the research stage. John Matthew Smith read and offered a valuable critique of the entire manuscript. David Welky gave the manuscript a close reading—and close for David means in-your-face close.

Bruce Schulman and Aram Goudsouzian also improved the manuscript with their critiques.

The staff at Yale University Press could not have been more professional and helpful. I don't think William Frucht, my editor, blanched when I turned in a manuscript indecently over the contracted word length. I say "think" because I told him in a telephone conversation; if he did, it didn't sound like it. From that first conversation he has been great to work with. Jaya Chatterjee, Bill's assistant, has been patient and helpful in more ways than I can count. Heidi Downey performed her manuscript editor duties wonderfully, with humor and warm support.

My agents Donald Lamm and Christy Fletcher of Fletcher and Company have been supportive and encouraging from the start. I could always count on Don to check up on my progress without ever once seeming to push too hard. Both Don and Christy love their work, and their authors are better for it.

I've saved the ones I love the most for last. They are the women in my life. My mother has been unconditionally supportive and loving all my life, regardless of what I am working on or doing. I've tried to follow her example with my twin daughters, Alison and Kelly. They have given me more joy than I can express, and not one disappointment. When it comes to love, decency, and patience, my wife, Marjie, is the gold standard. I have dedicated this book to her, though it does not seem even close to enough.

INDEX

Abney, James, 96

Abyssinian crisis, as backdrop to Louis-Carnera fight, 74–75, 84

Acunto, Steve, 119

African Americans: in army (*See* Army, U.S.); attendance at JL's fights, 77, 78, 88, 136, 163–164; celebration of JL's victories, 81–82, 95–97, 140–141, 169, 170–171; civil rights for, 199–200, 201; film portrayal of, 217–218, 227–229; in Great Migration, 11–13; importance of JL to, 97–106, 134, 137, 204, 246–247; and JL's loss to Schmeling, 119–124; radio broadcasts of JL's bouts, 101–102, 165; symbolism of Louis-Schmeling rematch, 144–145, 157, 160, 163; "two-ness" of culture, 206–207, 215; and war effort, 209–210, 221–222. *See also* Civil rights; Race

Alabama, birthplace of JL in, 3–4

Alger, Horatio, 93

Ali, Muhammad (Cassius Clay), x, xi, 258

Ambers, Lou, 58

American Speech, 72

"Amos 'n' Andy" radio show, 135

Angelou, Maya, 101–102

Angriff, 145, 149

Anti-Nazi boycotts, of Schmeling's matches, 131, 153, 156, 161–162

Apostoli, Fred, 185

Arcel, Ray, 20, 91

Arlington National Cemetery, 258

Armstrong, Henry, 58, 121, 141, 158, 163

Armstrong, Louis, 163

Army Emergency Relief Fund, 218, 219, 221

Army, U.S.: African American soldiers helped by JL, 224–226; boxing exhibition tours of, 223–224, 234; committee on black soldiers, 222–223; Jim Crow conditions on bases of, 213, 224; JL's appearances supervised by, 230; JL's induction into, 211; Legion of Merit award to JL, 230–231; portrayed in films, 226–229; promotion of black war effort, 221–222; racial incidents in, 214–215, 225–226; segregated structure of, 212–214, 216

Australia, Johnson-Burns fight in, 39–41

Australian Star, 39

Bacon, Augustus, 48

Baer, Buddy, 177, 178, 210–211

Baer, Max, 64, 85, 145, 204, 210; -Brad-
dock title match, 58, 133, 136; -Carnera
title match, 57, 69; characterized, 87,
93; death of Ernie Schaaf, 68, 90–91;
death of Frankie Campbell, 90; -Louis
match, 86–95; -Miler match, 2;
-Schmeling match, 109, 115
Bak, Richard, 17
Balogh, Harry, 78
Baltimore Afro-American, 201
Baltimore Times, 46
Bare-knuckle boxing, 25–26, 27, 28,
30–31
Barrow, Cora (aunt), 4
Barrow, Joe Louis. *See* Louis, Joe
Barrow, Joe Louis, Jr. (son), 240, 254
Barrow, Lonnie (brother), 121, 251
Barrow, Munroe "Mun" (father), 4, 10
Barry, Jim, 38
Barry, Reds, 53, 70
Baseball, xii, 143, 175–176
Basie, Count, 168
Bennett, James Gordon, 26
Bennett, Robert C., 236–237
Berbick, Trevor, 256
Berger, Meyer, 87
Berkow, Ira, 256
Berlin, Irving, 226
Berlin Olympic Games, 148–150
Bethune, Mary McLeod, 209, 223–224
Bettina, Melio, 184
Bimstein, Whitey, 138, 139
Birkie, Hans, 53
Birth of a Nation, The, 8–9
Black, Julian, 18, 19, 52, 83, 92, 123, 177,
194, 223, 236
Black Americans. *See* African Ameri-
cans; Civil rights; Race
Black Bottom neighborhood, Detroit, 13
Blackburn, Jack: boxing career of, 19–
20; death of, 216; and Jack Johnson,
70; at JL's wedding, 92; on legacy of

Jack Johnson, 51; on loss to Schmeling, 123, 124; and social conduct code
for JL, 83; trainer to JL, 21–23, 79, 114,
118, 134, 137, 158, 159, 165, 173–174, 210–
211; violence of, 20–21, 114
Blake, Arthur, 12
Blockade, 150–151
Bodenheim, Maxwell, 144
Boll weevil, 5
Boxing: army exhibition tours, 223–224,
234; bare-knuckle, 25–26, 27, 28, 30–
31; "Brewster style" of, 15; brutality of
sport, 2, 25–26; color line in, 37–38,
39; *Daily Worker* coverage of, 143–
144; decline in 1930s, 58–59; fear of
fighters, 91; films about, 107–108; during Great Depression, 56–59; Hitler's
promotion of, 111; hustlers in world
of, 16–17; irrelevance in contempo-
rary sports, xi; London Prize Ring
Rules, 25, 28; and masculine ideal, 34–
36; New York promoters, 61–65; nonheavyweight divisions of, 58; opposed
by progressive reformers, 38–39;
penny press coverage of, 26–27; prefight atmosphere, 88; Queensberry
Rules, 28, 33, 38; racial integration of,
xii, 9; radio broadcasts of, 100–103;
revival of, JL's role in, 59, 89–90; on
television, 243–244; in west, 39. *See
also* Heavyweight championship; *and
specific names*
Boxing Writers Association, 218
Braddock, James J.: -Baer title match, 58,
133, 136; boxing record of, 136; characterized, 58, 136–137; at Louis-Baer
match, 89, 91; on Louis-Carnera
match, 70; on Louis-Schmeling
match, 126; -Louis title match, 132,
133–141; -Schmeling title match plan,
130–133
Brann, Louis J., 89